Hitler's
Rise to Power

*the text of this book is printed
on 100% recycled paper*

Hitler's
Rise to Power

*The Nazi Movement
in Bavaria, 1923–1933*

Geoffrey Pridham

HARPER TORCHBOOKS
HARPER & ROW, PUBLISHERS
NEW YORK, EVANSTON, SAN FRANCISCO, LONDON

A hardcover edition of this book is published by
Harper & Row, Publishers, Inc.

HITLER'S RISE TO POWER:
THE NAZI MOVEMENT IN BAVARIA, 1923–1933

Copyright © 1973 by Geoffrey Pridham

First HARPER TORCHBOOK edition published 1974.

LIBRARY OF CONGRESS CATALOG CARD NUMBER: 73–511

STANDARD BOOK NUMBER: 06–131814–0 (PAPERBACK)

STANDARD BOOK NUMBER: 06–136116–X (HARDCOVER)

To my mother

Contents

List of Tables

Abbreviations

1. Regional and local authorities

BA   Bezirksamt (district office)
LA   Landratsamt
P.D.   Polizeidirektion (Police headquarters)
Mfr.   Mittelfranken (Middle Franconia), e.g. Reg. v. Mfr. = Government of Middle Franconia
Niedb.   Niederbayern (Lower Bavaria)
Obb.   Oberbayern (Upper Bavaria)
Ofr.   Oberfranken (Upper Franconia)
Opf.   Oberpfalz (Upper Palatinate)
Schw.   Schwaben (Swabia)
Ufr.   Unterfranken (Lower Franconia)
HMB   Halbmonatsbericht (fortnightly report), e.g. HMB/Mfr.

2. Political parties and organizations

Apa   Agrarpolitischer Apparat
BBMB   Bayerischer Bauern- und Mittelstandsbund
BVP   Bayerische Volkspartei
CNBL   Christlich-Nationale Bauern- und Landvolkspartei
DAP   Deutsche Arbeiterpartei
DDP   Deutsche Demokratische Partei
DNVP   Deutschnationale Volkspartei
DSP   Deutsche Sozialistische Partei
DVFP   Deutschvölkische Freiheitspartei
DVP   Deutsche Volkspartei
GVG   Grossdeutsche Volksgemeinschaft
HJ   Hitlerjugend
KPD   Kommunistische Partei Deutschlands
NSBO   Nationalsozialistische Betriebszellenorganisation
NSDAP   Nationalsozialistische Deutsche Arbeiterpartei (Nazi Party)
NSDStB   Nationalsozialistischer Deutscher Studentenbund
NSFB   Nationalsozialistische Freiheitsbewegung

NSVB	Nationalsozialistischer Volksbund
SA	Sturmabteilung
SPD	Sozialdemokratische Partei Deutschlands
SS	Schutzstaffel
Uschla	Untersuchungs- und Schlichtungsausschuss
VB	*Völkischer Beobachter*

3. *Archives*

AR	Alte Reichskanzlei
ASA	Allgemeines Staatsarchiv, Munich
BSA	Bayerisches Staatsarchiv
GSA	Geheimes Staatsarchiv, Munich
HA	Hauptarchiv der NSDAP, e.g. HA 2/25 = Hauptarchiv Reel 2, Folder 25

Preface

This book originated in my wish to examine the Nazi rise to power in depth and to provide new insight into this unique phenomenon. My choice of a regional study settled on Bavaria because this offered important new aspects of the problem, and because the party's development here has been neglected, although Munich remained the seat of party headquarters and in spite of the vast amount of material on the subject. The origins of the NSDAP in Bavaria have been the subject of several studies, but not its development there from a small party into a mass movement. This book is based largely on unpublished material. Details of archival sources used are supplied at the end of the book together with a list of secondary works which have helped me.

Although the acknowledgments in the text are to recorded evidence, I owe a great debt to many persons in both England and Germany during the course of my work. Professor F. L. Carsten supervised my thesis and gave me the benefit of his invaluable advice and sympathetic understanding. Dr Jeremy Noakes originally encouraged me to do a study on Bavaria, and our common interest in the subject has since extended to cooperation in another work on the Nazi period. I am particularly grateful to the staffs of the various departments of the Bavarian State Archives in Munich, Nuremberg, Bamberg, Landshut, Amberg, Neuburg a.d. Donau and Würzburg. I would like to thank especially Dr Hermann-Joseph Busley of the Hauptstaatsarchiv, Munich, for his assistance and advice with my work over many years, as well as Freiherr Fritz von Rehlingen, Dr Sebastian Hiereth, Dr Reinhard Seitz, Dr Hildebrand Troll, Dr Otto Puchner, Dr Eberhard Weis, Dr Scherzer, Dr Scherl, Dr Berndl, Herr Kreuzer, Herr Wunschel and Fräulein A. H. Bayer for their patience in answering my numerous requests.

I owe a further debt to Dr Anton Hoch and the staff of the Institut für Zeitgeschichte for their expertise and help during my many visits to Munich, and would also like to thank Fräulein Kinder and the staff of the Bundesarchiv Koblenz for their assistance, Mr K. Hiscock of the Foreign Office Library, London, for providing me with additional material and Herr Günther Buttman for permission to read the *Nachlass* Buttmann. I visited several town archives in Bavaria and would like to mention in particular Dr

Gustav Wulz (Nördlingen), Dr Hirschmann (Nuremberg), Dr S. Hofmann (Ingolstadt) and Herr Weikmann (Kaufbeuren) with whom I discussed my work. I would like to give my warm thanks to the entire staff of the Institute of Contemporary History and Wiener Library, London, with whom I had the pleasure of working for two years, and to Professor Walter Laqueur especially for his invaluable help. The Central Research Fund of London University provided me with two generous grants to visit Germany during the summers of 1968 and 1970, while the Colston Research Fund of Bristol University also gave me financial assistance.

Several friends and colleagues have given me help at various stages in my work. I am very indebted to Mr Martin Crouch, who read through the final manuscript and provided me with useful and often incisive comments, and Mr Charles Gray, Mr P. G. James, Herr Klaus Sieveking and Mr Anup Ray, who read an earlier version of the manuscript. I also benefited from discussions with Herr Rainer Hambrecht and Mr T. L. Jarman, and would like to thank Miss Suzanne Sproston for assisting with the progress of the manuscript at different stages. My greatest personal debt is to my mother, who gave me much encouragement over the years and first inspired me with the urge to learn.

I wish also to thank Mr Michael Sissons, my literary agent, for his advice during the production of this book. I am also grateful to Mrs Tina Shell, Mrs Anne Merriman and Mrs Jan Nicholas for typing the final manuscript.

Geoffrey Pridham

Bavaria 1923

Urban areas

1. Alzenau i. Mainfr
2. Aschaffenburg
3. Obernburg
4. Miltenberg
5. Marktheidenfeld
6. Lohr
7. Gemünden
8. Brückenau
9. Hammelburg
10. Karlstadt
11. Würzburg
12. Ochsenfurt
13. Kitzingen
14. Gerolzhofen
15. Schweinfurt
16. Bad Kissingen
17. Bad Neustadt a.d. Saal
18. Melbidistadt
19. Königshofen i. Grabfeld
20. Hofheim i. Mainfr
21. Haßfurt
22. Ebern
23. Bamberg
24. Scheinfeld
25. Uffenheim
26. Rothenburg ob d. Tauber
27. Ansbach
28. Neustadt a.d. Aisch
29. Höchstadt a.d. Aisch
30. Forchheim
31. Ebermannstadt
32. Lichtenfels
33. Staffelstein
34. Coburg
35. Kronach
36. Naila
37. Hof
38. Münchberg
39. Stadtsteinach
40. Kulmbach
41. Rehau
42. Wunsiedel
43. Bayreuth
44. Tirschenreuth
45. Kemnath
46. Neustadt a.d. Waldnaab
47. Eschenbach i.d. OPf.
48. Sulzbach
49. Pegnitz
50. Hersbruck
51. Lauf (Pegnitz)
52. Erlangen
53. Fürth
54. Nuremberg
55. Schwabach
56. Gunzenhausen
57. Feuchtwangen
58. Dinkelsbühl
59. Nördlingen
60. Donauwörth
61. Weissenburg i. Bay
62. Hilpoltstein
63. Neumarkt i.d. OPf.
64. Amberg
65. Nabburg
66. Vohenstrauss
67. Oberviechtach
68. Waldmünchen
69. Neunburg vorm Wald
70. Burglengenfeld
71. Parsberg
72. Beilngries
73. Cham
74. Roding
75. Kötzting
76. Regen
77. Viechtach
78. Bogen
79. Regensburg
80. Kelheim
81. Riedenburg
82. Eichstätt
83. Inglostadt
84. Neuberg a.d. Donau
85. Wertingen
86. Dillingen a.d. Donau
87. Günzburg
88. Neu Ulm
89. Krumbach (Schwaben)
90. Augsburg
91. Aichach
92. Schrobenhausen
93. Pfaffenhofen a.d. Ilm
94. Mainberg
95. Rottenburg
96. Mallersdorf
97. Straubing
98. Deggendorf
99. Grafenau
100. Wolfstein
101. Wegscheid
102. Passau
103. Vilshofen
104. Landau a.d. Isar
105. Dingolfing
106. Landshut
107. Freising
108. Dachau
109. Fürstenfeldbruck
110. Friedberg
111. Schwabmünchen
112. Mindelheim
113. Illertissen
114. Memmingen
115. Kempten (Allgäu)
116. Landau (Bodensee)
117. Sonthofen
118. Füssen
119. Markt Oberdorf
120. Kaufburen
121. Landsberg
122. Starnberg
123. Munich
124. Erding
125. Vilsbiburg
126. Eggenfelden
127. Griesbach
128. Pfarrkirchen
129. Altötting
130. Mühldorf
131. Wasserburg a-Inn
132. Ebersberg
133. Laufen
134. Traunstein
135. Berchtesgaden
136. Rosenheim
137. Bad Aibling
138. Wolfratshausen
139. Weilheim
140. Schongau
141. Garmisch-Partenkirchen
142. Bad Tölz
143. Miesbach

Hitler's
Rise to Power

One

Bavaria and the Weimar Republic

This is a case study of the organization, propaganda and popular appeal of the Nazi movement (NSDAP) in Bavaria from the Munich Putsch in 1923 to Hitler's appointment as German Chancellor in 1933.

There is always a certain unique quality about any case study, but its relevance depends on the reasons for which it is selected and how far it is representative of the general problem with which it is dealing. The merit of a case study is that it should provide new insight into this general problem through the medium of detailed illustration and analysis.

The NSDAP was a mass movement without precedent in German history. One can only fully understand its rise to power, which has so far been examined mainly at the level of national politics, if a sufficient number of regional and local studies are made available. As the NSDAP developed unique methods of popular agitation, it is essential to examine how it operated at the 'grass-roots' level. General histories inevitably focus on the more dramatic events of national politics, but a case study pays more attention to particular examples and different situations. While throwing new light on the general problem, it should guarantee against too superficial an interpretation of it by providing a more 'realistic' picture.

Bavaria has become known as the birthplace of the Nazi Party. The party was founded early in 1919 in Munich, which remained the centre of its activities during its early years and became the scene of Hitler's abortive attempt at a coup d'état in the autumn of 1923. When the party reappeared in 1925 after a period of prohibition, Munich continued as the seat of its headquarters and later earned the Nazi title of 'capital of the movement' (*Hauptstadt der Bewegung*). Hitler, who had moved to Munich from his native Austria shortly before the First World War, showed a strong affinity with Bavaria which remained with him through the years of the Third Reich, when he often preferred to spend weekends at his mountain retreat near Berchtesgaden rather than in the more stringent atmosphere of Berlin. Nuremberg, the other major city in Bavaria, became the traditional site of the party rallies.

While Bavaria has strong associations with the Nazi Party, detailed studies of its development there have concentrated on its early history before the Putsch of 1923.[1] There are valid reasons for this. The NSDAP was essentially a Bavarian party in the early 1920s, although branches were founded in cities of Northern Germany from 1921. Conditions in postwar Munich fostered the growth of organizations of the extreme Right, and provided Hitler with opportunities to assert his dominance over these organizations and to gain public attention. These years of its Bavarian provenance also saw the establishment of the party's structure of leadership with Hitler's assumption of dictatorial control over its activities.

The development of the NSDAP from a small party into a mass movement during the decade from the Munich Putsch to the Nazi 'seizure of power' in 1933 has been examined in the form of biographies of its main leaders, general histories of the party and regional or local studies of its rise in popular support in areas of Northern Germany.[2] While these works continue to tell us much about the character and activities of the NSDAP, a study of the party's development in Bavaria during the later 1920s and early 1930s is important for several reasons.

Regional differences in Germany, which derive much from the country's late unification in the nineteenth century, have accounted for many of the varieties in its political development. Individual states and cities in Germany have shown diverse political traditions, such as Württemberg with its liberalism, the Rhineland's Catholic sympathies and its tendency to look westwards to France as well as the Social Democratic strongholds of Hamburg and Berlin. These regional differences, which have had an important influence on voting patterns in German elections, are related in part to economic and social structure but also to confession for Germany has been a country of

1. For example, Werner Maser, *Die Frühgeschichte der NSDAP, Hitlers Weg bis 1924* (Frankfurt, 1965) and George Franz-Willing, *Die Hitlerbewegung, Der Ursprung 1919–22* (Hamburg, 1962). For the Munich Putsch of 1923 see H. H. Hofmann, *Der Hitlerputsch* (Munich, 1961); Ernst Deuerlein (ed.), *Der Hitler-Putsch, Bayerische Dokumente zum 9. November 1923* (Stuttgart, 1962); Harold J. Gordon jr., *Hitlerputsch 1923, Machtkampf in Bayern 1923–24* (Frankfurt, 1971).
2. For example, Alan Bullock, *Hitler, a Study in Tyranny* (London, revised edition 1964). General histories include Dietrich Orlow, *The History of the Nazi Party, Vol. 1 1919–22* (University of Pittsburgh, 1969, and Newton Abbot, 1971); Joseph Nyomarkay, *Charisma and Factionalism in the Nazi Party* (Minneapolis, 1967); F. L. Carstein, *The Rise of Fascism* (London, 1967); Ernst Nolte, *Three Faces of Fascism* (London, 1965). The best regional and local studies of the NSDAP are: Jeremy Noakes, *The Nazi Party in Lower Saxony 1921–1933* (Oxford, 1971); Rudolf Heberle, *Landbevölkerung und Nationalsozialismus, eine soziologische Untersuchung der politischen Willensbildung in Schleswig-Holstein 1918 bis 1932* (Stuttgart, 1963); Gerhard Stoltenberg, *Politische Strömungen im schleswig-holsteinischen Landvolk 1918–1933* (Düsseldorf, 1962); Ernst-August Roloff, *Bürgertum und Nationalsozialismus 1930–33, Braunschweigs Weg ins Dritter Reich* (Hanover, 1961); W. S. Allen, *The Nazi Seizure of Power, the Experience of a single German Town 1930–35* (London, 1966).

mixed religion since the Reformation. These factors likewise influenced the degree of popular support for the NSDAP, especially during the last elections of the Weimar Republic in 1930–32. The most striking difference in the size of the Nazi vote is between the strongly Catholic areas of Southern and Western Germany and the strongly Protestant areas of the Northern and Eastern part of the country.

Bavaria offers an unusually relevant case study of this problem. It was the largest, most compact and most Catholic state in Germany. The Rhineland and Upper Silesia were the other main Catholic areas, but they were smaller and were not individual states like Bavaria, being part of the state of Prussia. Bavaria's population was 70 per cent Catholic, but the most useful feature of its confessional structure was that its minority Protestant population was concentrated in certain areas of Franconia (northern Bavaria). The reason for this relatively clear-cut confessional division of the state was historical. Until she became a kingdom in 1806, Bavaria had consisted only of the areas of Upper and Lower Bavaria and the Upper Palatinate later known as 'Old Bavaria' (*Altbayern*). These areas were almost totally Catholic. As a result of her alliance with Napoleon, Bavaria acquired much new territory including Franconia and Eastern Swabia. Middle and Upper Franconia were predominantly Protestant, while Lower Franconia and (Bavarian) Swabia were largely Catholic. Bavaria later received additional territory on the left bank of the Rhine (the Bavarian Palatinate), which remained part of the state until the Third Reich, but for the purposes of this study 'Bavaria' refers to the state of Bavaria proper.

This study of the NSDAP's organization and propaganda in Bavaria is therefore concerned, among other things, with the confessional factor in politics in so far as this related to support for the Nazis. It examines the problems of Nazi propaganda among a largely Catholic population, including the strong opposition provided by the confessional party—the Bavarian People's Party (BVP). No major study of the NSDAP in the Weimar period has so far paid special attention to this problem, for works on the relationship between the Nazi leaders and the Catholic Church have concentrated on the period from Hitler's appointment as Chancellor in 1933.[3] The general

---

3. For example, J. S. Conway, *The Nazi Persecution of the Churches* (London, 1968); Guenter Lewy, *The Catholic Church and Nazi Germany* (London, 1964). F. J. Heyen, *Nationalsozialismus im Alltag, Quellen zur Geschichte des Nationalsozialismus vornehmlich im Raum Mainz-Koblenz-Trier* (Boppard am Rhein, 1967) is a collection of documents on the NSDAP in a Catholic region, covering part of the Weimar period, but it provides no analysis of party activities there. Ludwig Volk, *Der Bayerische Episkopat und der Nationalsozialismus* (Mainz, 1966) deals more with attitudes of the Church towards the NSDAP than with activities of the party.

assumption has usually been made that support for the NSDAP was stronger among Protestants than Catholics without sufficient discussion of the reasons for this. As a result the Catholic support for the NSDAP has sometimes been underestimated.

There is a second reason for this study of the NSDAP in Bavaria after the Putsch. While the party originated in the cities and towns, its major breakthrough in electoral support during the Depression years of the early 1930s occurred in the rural areas. The Nazis had by this time changed the emphasis of their propaganda from the cities to the countryside, and concentrated on winning the support of the rural as well as the town middle classes. Bavaria is again an important example of this development, because it was a thoroughly agricultural region. Bavaria had been much less affected by industrialization in Germany in the nineteenth century than many other regions of the country. The special feature of her industrial economy was the preponderance of small businesses, for as many as 63·4 per cent of the workers in Bavaria in 1907 were employed in firms with less than fifty people (1). Although the inevitable economic pressures against home industry operated in Bavaria as elsewhere, the relatively high proportion of craft industries was evident from such concentrations as basket-making in the mountainous areas of Upper Franconia, the production of straw hats in the Allgäu and wood-cutting around Berchtesgaden. In Franconia, whole villages often devoted themselves to particular crafts. Heavy industry was less conspicuous, although the electrical industry in Nuremberg, the machine industry in Augsburg, Munich and Nuremberg, not to mention the widespread brewing industry, are worth noting. Although some changes resulted from the location of munitions factories during the First World War especially in Munich, Bavaria remained essentially an agricultural state during the Weimar period. Munich had the disadvantage of being in an isolated position, for the lack of large sources of raw materials in the vicinity made the city an unsuitable location for big industry.

Bavaria's agriculture, which accounted for more than 40 per cent of her economic activity compared with 30 per cent for Germany as a whole, was marked by the predominance of small- and medium-sized holdings. The absence of large landed estates was striking compared with other parts of the country, especially Prussia where farms of more than 200 hectares constituted as much as 22·6 per cent of (unforested) agricultural land in contrast to only 0·8 per cent in Bavaria in 1907 (2). The size of holdings varied somewhat from area to area within the state, as did the speciality of agricultural activity. The Allgäu, like the rest of the sub-Alpine region, was noted for its pastoral farming and cattle-raising, just as parts of Middle

4

Franconia were known for hops and Lower Franconia for wine. This strong agricultural bias of the Bavarian economy had a political importance, for variations in the economic and social character of different areas within Germany influenced the degree of support for the NSDAP, although this was secondary to the confessional factor in Bavaria. Peasants like craftsmen became a major source of support for the NSDAP, but more so in Protestant than in Catholic areas.

Thirdly, the political complexion of Bavaria must be taken into account when assessing the nature of popular support for the NSDAP there. The profoundly conservative character of Bavarian politics, which owed much to the prominence of Catholic and agricultural interests, provided a different milieu in which the party operated from areas where the Social Democrats controlled the government. Bavaria has earned a name for right-wing attitudes in German politics, an impression reinforced by the dominant position of the CSU in the state since the Second World War. These right-wing tendencies have generally been of a more conservative than radical kind, although the impulsive element in Bavarian society has led in certain circumstances to a greater interest in right-wing radicalism. This happened in the first years of the Weimar Republic, when Bavaria became known as the 'cell of order' in Germany (*Ordnungszelle Bayern*) and the chief haven for right-wing extremist opponents of the new political system. The Munich Putsch of 1923 was a turning-point, for it brought a distinct change in the atmosphere of Bavarian politics. Not only did it discredit right-wing extremist violence, but it also left a deep imprint on the attitude of the Catholic political establishment in Bavaria towards the NSDAP. The Bavarian leaders who had been associated with Hitler in his plan to overthrow the Republic were pushed out of office. They were replaced by Dr Heinrich Held, leader of the conservative BVP, who remained Prime Minister throughout the period under review. The policy of his Government towards the NSDAP is a continual theme of this book, for it is maintained that the role of the party in the Weimar period must be examined with reference not only to its organization and propaganda but also to its relationship with the state. While the character of the Nazi movement is the main subject of this study, its full significance cannot be appreciated without viewing it in the context of the political system within which it was operating.

The Munich Putsch of 1923 was therefore an important stage in both Bavarian politics and in the history of the NSDAP, but the party's later development cannot be fully understood without reference to its formative years. While the unrest and instability in Bavaria at the beginning of the Weimar Republic were by no means unique in Germany at this time, the combination of certain factors in Bavaria's case created a situation unusually favourable to the growth of the extreme Right. They included the effects of the First World War, the left-wing revolutionary upheavals in Munich during 1918–19 with the resulting polarization of Bavarian politics, and the policies of the Bavarian authorities.

The German collapse in 1918 came as a sudden shock, although feeling against the War had grown strong in Bavaria during its last years. Discontent had increased among the peasantry over food regulations, the important tourist industry suffered considerable harm because of the restrictions imposed by war conditions, while people in general complained about the rise in food prices. There was little compensation as in the industrialized regions of the country in the form of war profits and food allowances for war work. The inevitable impingement of war measures on the administrative rights of individual states provided a source of resentment in Bavaria, which helped to sour her relationship with the Reich.[4] As early as July 1916, Reich Chancellor Bethmann-Hollweg had written in anguish to Count von Hertling, the Bavarian Prime Minister: 'I hear that the long duration of the War and the scarcity of foodstuffs, which is naturally attributed more to human mistakes than to actual shortcomings, has given rise to a critical mood among Upper and Lower Bavarian peasants, whose sons have so distinguished themselves on the field, expressing itself ultimately in opposition to the North' (3).

This atmosphere of disquiet formed the background to the revolutionary ferment which hit Munich immediately after the War ended. The Wittelsbach monarchy, which had reigned in Bavaria since the twelfth century, fell and was replaced by a Marxist régime under Kurt Eisner, a leader of the Independent Social Democrats. Eisner attempted to institute a new system of government based on soldiers' and peasants' councils, but this experiment failed to achieve sufficient support outside Munich because the provinces were far less extreme in their political attitudes than the Bavarian capital. Initial enthusiasm for Eisner was based more on expectation of better conditions than on a desire to effect a revolution as such. The success in founding these councils depended on the proximity of towns to Munich as well as their individual economic and social character (4). The failure of

4. The term 'Reich' (literally 'Empire') is used with reference to Germany as a political entity after unification in 1871. In spite of the collapse of the Empire in 1918, the term continued to be applied during the Weimar period to the central institutions of the Republic; for example, Reich Government, Reich Chancellor and Reich President. The heads of government in the federal states (*Länder*) were generally called 'minister presidents' or prime ministers. The Bavarian Government is referred to as the 'state government' and the parliament in Munich as the 'state parliament' (*Landtag*).

Eisner's régime was already evident by the time of his assassination in February 1919 by a young aristocrat called Count Arco. There followed a short-lived Soviet republic in Bavaria, which was suppressed in May by troops from Northern Germany and Bavarian paramilitary units.

The most lasting effect of these events was the reaction they produced among political circles in Munich and to a lesser extent in Bavaria as a whole. While the middle classes in the city became possessed with an irrational fear of Communism—the Russian Revolution had occurred only a short time before—the working-class supporters of the left-wing régimes felt betrayed. It was inevitable with the conservative bias of Bavarian politics that the swing towards extremism should have moved more to the Right. This tendency was reinforced by a revival of antagonism in Bavaria towards the Reich as a result of the more centralized form of government introduced by the Weimar Constitution. During the next few years, there developed in Bavaria an uneasy marriage of convenience between the nationalist Right and Bavarian particularism, which sought its final outlet in the Munich Putsch of 1923.

Under the Bismarckian Constitution of 1871, which formalized the new unified Germany, Bavaria had retained certain special rights including control over the postal and railway system and a share in the administration of taxation. Bavaria had also preserved her own monarchy with the constitution of 1818 which had helped to buttress her sense of individuality within the Reich. These rights disappeared with the Constitution of 1919, but what made this change even more unpalatable to Bavarian leaders was that it appeared to tie them more closely to the new political system, which appeared in their eyes to have an unwelcome left-wing complexion. The Social Democrats formed the largest party in the country, and were the principal sponsors of the Republic. They dominated the government of the large state of Prussia, while the extreme Left had shown alarming tendencies in Berlin just after the War.

Faced with these developments, Bavarian leaders began to conceive a new role for their state as a counterbalance to the 'Marxist North'. This idea of Bavaria as the 'cell of order', which would restore the whole of Germany to her 'true' national self and erase the 'shameful' November Revolution of 1918, was held by such differing personalities as Georg Heim, the Bavarian peasants' leader, and Georg Escherich, head of the paramilitary Citizens' Defence Forces (*Einwohnerwehren*), but its most notable spokesman was Gustav von Kahr (5). Kahr was Bavarian Prime Minister during 1920–21, and assumed the role of Bavaria's 'strong man'. He was a monarchist with noted anti-Republican sympathies whose lack of political tact and finesse only exacerbated the state of disharmony between Bavaria and the Reich.

Kahr's attitude became clear with his encouragement of paramilitary organizations in defiance of the Reich authorities during his short time as Bavarian Prime Minister. The national government was engaged in difficult negotiations over war reparations with the Allied Powers, who applied pressure for the dissolution of the Citizens' Defence Forces on the grounds that they violated the disarmament clauses of the Treaty of Versailles. Kahr refused to comply and claimed that he was a better defender of German interests than the Reich Government: 'It is, I am sorry to say, possible that the federal government will not wholly identify itself with our own position; in this case Bavaria will continue on her way, even at the price of a temporary separation of Bavaria from the Reich' (6). The prevailing ideological hostility to the Left in Bavaria was again evident from actions of Ernst Pöhner, head of the Munich police, who showed extraordinary partiality in his suppression of left-wing groups and tolerance of political murders by right-wing extremists. Consistent with this outlook was the decision of the Knilling Government in Bavaria not to follow other German states with a ban on the NSDAP in 1922.

Hitler had by this time established himself in Bavaria as the most prominent party leader on the extreme Right. Although not the original founder of the German Workers' Party as it was first called, Hitler early proved his indispensability to its leaders through his organization of public meetings in the city of Munich. In February 1920 he was responsible for presenting the party programme at a meeting in the Hofbräuhaus. This programme, which comprised a list of conventional nationalist, anti-semitic and anti-capitalist demands, remained official policy of the NSDAP throughout its varied history in the Weimar period. Opposition from the party's original leaders to Hitler's dominant attitude finally came to a head in the summer of 1921 over the issue of cooperation with other parties of the extreme Right, but Hitler used this opportunity to resign in protest and then force the NSDAP to accept him as its leader with dictatorial powers.

Hitler's action had also been motivated by the belief that the NSDAP should be different in character from other parties on the extreme Right. The NSDAP owed much of its ideology to nationalist and anti-semitic groups which had existed in Germany, Austria and Bohemia before the First World War, and to the rise of nationalist feeling in postwar Munich. Anti-semitism, which had formerly been promoted by the Pan-German League and racialist groups like the Thule Society, now found a wider popular appeal through the association of Eisner and other Jews with left-wing extremism. According to Hitler, the NSDAP should nevertheless distinguish itself from the other parties in its political methods. He explained his ideas in a memorandum of 7 January 1922 (7). Hitler began by saying that the traditional nationalist movement had suffered from too much attention to theories instead of concentrating on 'the chief task of winning the broad masses for the national cause'. The NSDAP was by contrast a party of action and of the people:

> The new movement aims to provide what the others have not: a nationalist movement with a firm social base, a hold over the broad masses, welded together in an iron-hard organization, filled with blind obedience and inspired by a brutal will, a party of struggle and action . . . If this new kind of movement should become great and important, its aims should be propagated with fanatical ardour and the total force of its few supporters should be placed at the service of its propaganda as there is nothing available to organize (8).

Although Hitler did not enjoy the prestige of nationalist figures like General Ludendorff—the war hero turned active opponent of the Weimar Republic— he distinguished himself in his ability to appeal to the common man. His superiority as a mass orator over other leaders on the extreme Right led some of them to declare their allegiance to him. Support came in the autumn of 1922 from Julius Streicher, the notorious anti-semite from Nuremberg who controlled the German Socialist Party in Franconia. Early in 1923, Hitler held in Munich the first of the NSDAP rallies. He was now showing increasing signs of self-confidence and, encouraged by the example of Mussolini's 'march on Rome' the previous autumn, was looking for an opportunity to stage an action against the Republic.

The political and economic condition of the country became more and more critical as the year progressed. Germany was already hit by heavy inflation, but the value of the Reichsmark spiralled even faster downwards after the occupation of the Ruhr by French and Belgian troops in January 1923. The occasion for this drastic measure was the declaration by the German Government of her inability to continue paying reparations, although it also reflected French unease over internal developments in Germany. The conservative government of Reich Chancellor Cuno ordered passive resistance to the occupation, but the financial loss caused by these events had a catastrophic effect on the state of the mark. The result was harrowing, especially for the middle classes, who with their savings reduced to nil felt their sympathies for the Republic wearing thin.

It seemed as if 1923 was going to be a decisive year for the future of the Weimar Republic. In August the Cuno Government resigned and was succeeded by Gustav Stresemann, leader of the right-wing liberal German People's Party. His inclusion of Social Democrats in the Cabinet and his decision to accept the inevitable by calling off the passive resistance in the Ruhr proved highly provocative to the Bavarian Government, which declared a state of emergency on the same day and appointed Gustav von Kahr State Commissioner with dictatorial powers, although the office of Bavarian Prime Minister remained formally in existence. Stresemann's action revived Bavarian feelings of contempt for the 'weak' Reich Government in the defence of German interests. Political talk in Munich centred on the need to establish a national dictatorship, and Gustav von Kahr made little effort to disguise his involvement in plans to further this cause. The issue which lit the fuse of revolt was the demand by the Stresemann Government for the prohibition of the NSDAP organ, the *Völkischer Beobachter*, following an abusive article attacking the Chancellor for his decision over the Ruhr. Kahr refused once more to bend to the Reich Government's wishes, and asked the Bavarian divisions of the Army to swear an oath of loyalty to the Bavarian Government. The Army, which had fostered connections with nationalist groups in Munich since the end of the War and had even given financial assistance to the NSDAP for the purchase of the *Völkischer Beobachter*, complied readily with Kahr's request.

The final crisis came on 8 November. Kahr had arranged to make a speech that evening in the Bürgerbräukeller in Munich. Hitler had now strengthened his position by becoming head of the Fighting League (*Kampfbund*), an organization which coordinated the activities of the NSDAP and other nationalist and paramilitary groups in Bavaria. Hitler had been concerned that Kahr would overshadow him as leader of the plot against the Republic, but Kahr's last-minute indecisiveness prompted Hitler to take the initiative. Hitler staged a dramatic entry into the Bürgerbräukeller after Kahr had begun his speech, and forced Kahr and his fellow conspirators to adopt his own plans for a national government. The whole affair had something of the atmosphere of a South American coup d'état, but it was too improvised to follow a carefully planned course of action. Hitler's apparent triumph was short-lived, for the situation changed completely overnight. Kahr and his colleagues had resented Hitler's strong-arm tactics, and their expressed willingness to cooperate with him evaporated by the following day. Arrangements for a march into the city centre of Hitler's supporters still went ahead, but it ended in a violent clash with the police. This scene on the Odeonsplatz marked the final collapse of the Munich Putsch.

Two

After the Munich Putsch: Ban on the Nazi Party in Bavaria (1923–25)

Repercussions of the Putsch

The Munich Putsch of 1923 was a failure in the immediate sense that its aim of establishing a counter-revolutionary 'national government' in Berlin to replace the parliamentary system of Weimar, introduced after the Revolution of 1918, came nowhere to success. Its ringleaders were either arrested, scattered abroad or in some cases shot down, and the Nazi Party and the other nationalist groups which had cooperated in the affair were prohibited.

The Putsch was nevertheless a landmark in the history of the Weimar Republic. It brought to the surface many of the antagonisms which had been present in German politics since the end of the First World War, notably the emotional antipathy of the conservative Right towards the new parliamentary system, as well as the traditional conflict between Bavaria and the central government over the former's constitutional and political rights within the Reich. The Putsch coloured political attitudes in Bavaria especially among the authorities, who took a long time to recover from the shock of November 1923 and were quick to respond to any indication that Hitler's former followers might resort once more to direct political action.

Although the Nazis appeared as disturbers of the peace and dangerous radicals in the eyes of the Bavarian political establishment, an attitude supported by the feeling that the Nazis were hostile to the Catholic Church, the Bavarian authorities were not themselves free of the suspicion of disloyalty towards the Weimar state. As was clearly demonstrated at Hitler's trial in the spring of 1924, the behaviour of the authorities towards the Nazis was complicated by the embarrassing fact that Gustav von Kahr, the Bavarian State Commissioner, and his associates had also been involved in the Putsch. The Munich Putsch was not easily forgotten, and Hitler's expected political demise did not in fact occur. Hitler was prevented from any further political activity and even resigned from the leadership of his banned party in the summer of 1924, but he continued to dominate the behaviour of his former followers from his prison in Landsberg. Hitler used the occasion of this trial in Munich to establish one of the great myths of the Nazi movement, that he was the primary figure behind the Putsch and that he alone could save Germany from the disastrous consequences of her defeat in the War and the Revolution which had followed.

The Putsch aroused considerable excitement, especially in Munich where public disappointment at its collapse vented itself on the green-uniformed state police, who were insulted on the streets and referred to as a 'green disgrace' (1). Some sympathy for the Putsch was shown too among sections of the Army stationed in Munich, particularly among younger officers, and demonstrations by university students in favour of Hitler and against von Kahr, because he had withdrawn his support for Hitler at the last moment, were reported in different parts of the city. Disturbances occurred in other cities in the country, including Berlin where some six or seven hundred Hitler supporters demonstrated on the Alexanderplatz and the Wilhelms-platz (2). The events of 8–9 November had received much attention in both the national and the international press but after a few days the Putsch ceased to make news (3). The *Mannheimer General-Anzeiger*, for instance, covered the event on its front page on 9 and 10 November but the following day the headlines had nothing more to do with the Putsch (4).

The Putsch had a strong sensationalist appeal, so public enthusiasm was bound to wane, but this did not remove the concern of the authorities that disorder might break out once again in spite of the arrest of Hitler and the prohibition of his party. In various localities of Bavaria the police, who were keeping a watch on the activities of members of the banned party, reported on the tension which still remained several weeks after the Putsch. In the middle of December the police headquarters in Nuremberg-Fürth wrote to Munich that the situation had changed little since the month before. The continuation of the excitement caused by the events of November was 'unmistakable', encouraged by the agitation of Nazi groups which carried on distributing propaganda leaflets in defiance of the authorities. The police then confiscated the printing press used to produce these leaflets but the author responsible for them managed to escape arrest. The police had also been forewarned about a street demonstration held a few days before and had taken precautionary measures to prevent any outbreak of violence, but they did not reckon with any easing of the tense atmosphere in radical right-wing circles there: 'The upheaval will not come to an end so quickly—it is to be feared that many supporters of the National Socialist movement will more than before leave the ranks of the patriotic movement because of the dissolution and prohibition of their groups and move over to the national Bolshevists or the Communists' (5). Country areas were generally quieter, although police action in confiscating caches of firearms sometimes aroused resentment, which threatened to disturb the peace.

The impact made by the Putsch particularly in Bavaria was explained by the rumours which continued to circulate involving wider issues than merely the events of 8–9 November. This was evident in areas of Franconia, where the feeling of distrust among the Protestant population towards the ruling Bavarian People's Party and the Catholic Bavarian Government in Munich was revived by further talk of separatism. Rumours fed on old complexes and phobias and for this reason were difficult to erase. In the provinces the call for a 'national' government at the meeting in the Bürgerbräukeller had been welcomed in the hope that this would bring better times. According to the Munich police, 'it must be kept in mind that at that time the economic situation had reached the most desperate proportions and the rejoicing in the national dictatorship involved generally less political aims than economic ones'. Disappointment soon set in when it became known that the Putsch had misfired and opinion hardened in opposition to Gustav von Kahr. In some places Nazi groups exploited this feeling of disenchantment so that the police had to issue proclamations in some towns for the maintenance of law and order. Generally, there was little difficulty in dissolving the different patriotic associations—in Rosenheim the police faced no opposition when they disarmed the Nazis and members of the *Bund Oberland*[1] who had returned from Munich—but it was still clear that 'the National Socialists enjoyed strong backing from a large section of the population and that severe measures against them would not be approved of'. The peasant population seemed little affected by the events of November 1923 and their consequences (6).

Undoubtedly, the theatrical nature of the Putsch had a certain attraction among those conservative political circles which tended to favour direct action and view politics from the standpoint of romantic nationalism. Although the political atmosphere in Upper Franconia had calmed down by the end of the year and attacks on von Kahr had become less blatant, the female members of the Wagner family in Bayreuth were carrying on an outspoken Hitler cult while in Bamberg 'true German' women were holding

---

1. The *Bund Oberland* was one of the patriotic associations in Bavaria associated with the Nazi Party. Others included the *Reichskriegsflagge*, the *Frankenland* and the *Jungdeutscher Orden*.

tea evenings to whip up adoration for Hitler and his supporters and promote opposition to the present state order (7). In time, the measures taken by the authorities to stamp out political violence had their desired effect. The organization of the Nazi Party was broken up and its property seized by the police. The Munich police swooped on the headquarters in the Cornelius-strasse and drew up long inventories of confiscated articles including membership cards, propaganda material, address books, chairs and other pieces of furniture, not to mention a whole string of more trivial items such as typewriters, petrol cans and portraits of Bismarck and Hitler (8).

The membership of the NSDAP had stood at well over 55,000 on the eve of the Putsch but there was now no longer any organizational machine to hold them together and control their activities. A common feeling of loyalty towards Hitler as leader remained but over a period of time proved insufficient to maintain morale among members and prevent serious differences between party leaders over the tactics to be followed. Some Nazis joined other parties and groups, while others formed cover organizations to try to carry on the activities of the NSDAP. Obstacles in the way of this were often considerable. These new organizations had to take particular care not to provide the authorities with an excuse to take action against them. The police were perfectly aware of what was going on. In the middle of December the local branch in Ingolstadt of the so-called 'Working Association' held a meeting at which large numbers of former members of the NSDAP were present. It was quite obvious that the 'Working Association' was merely 'the camouflaged NSDAP' (9). Similar organizations grew up in other towns often with eccentric names like the 'Patriotic Alpine Club' and the 'Savings Association of South Munich'. The latter issued a memorandum in January 1924 to its members about the misfortunes of the past years which had deprived them of 'the German sense of saving' and that the only answer to the disastrous effects on the German economy was 'the yearning for a redeemer' (10). Some of these groups proved harmless, but the authorities thought otherwise about 'Command North', founded in Nuremberg shortly after the Putsch for the purpose of holding together all SA groups in Northern Bavaria. Officially, this organization paraded as the 'Shooting and Hiking League' but in December the Nuremberg police rounded up its leaders and the organization was banned (11).

Spring Elections and the Trial of Hitler

Within a few months of the Putsch the movement appeared to be recovering from its setback, although it still suffered from official prohibition and the absence of an effective leader. One reason was the forthcoming state elections in Bavaria, which crystallized the efforts of the various substitute organizations which had appeared since November 1923.

Early in 1924 the *Völkischer Block* was founded with the aim of coordinating the efforts of these organizations in Bavaria to fight the election. Not surprisingly, the Putsch overshadowed the campaign. Rudolf Buttmann, a prominent *völkisch*[2] leader in Bavaria, declared defiantly at a meeting of the *Block* on 24 January that 'as the shots on 9 November died away after Germans had shot at Germans, it gradually became clear to me that the *völkisch* movement in Bavaria and the Reich was not finished but that the moral success was on our side'. Buttmann went on to warn that in this election campaign, which would be fought bitterly, 'we will carry the nationalist idea into the last mountain village' and the Jews and its other mortal enemies would no longer rejoice as they had done on 9 November (*12*) The *Völkischer Block* conducted a very lively campaign and many incidents were reported involving attacks by its speakers on the authorities. In Ingolstadt, which had been a stronghold of the NSDAP in Bavaria, the organization of the *Block* enrolled over 800 members including many Nazis and attracted the support of other patriotic associations like the *Bund Bayern und Reich* and even members of the liberal Democratic Party there, which dissolved itself and joined the *Block*. A certain bitterness towards the authorities was evident in the tone of election meetings held by the *Block*. Tempers rose in Traunstein when an article appeared in a local newspaper casting aspersions on the constabulary in the town and claiming it was the wish of the inhabitants that the command should be withdrawn as soon as possible. The mayor, concerned in case the withdrawal of the constabulary led to radical elements gaining the upper hand, rejected this assertion in a public meeting and exposed the author of the article as a Nazi (*13*).

It was a reflection on the legalistic attitude of the authorities that the *Block* was allowed to function as the electoral organization of members of the

---

2. The German word *völkisch* (from *Volk* meaning 'people' or 'race') is used as there is no satisfactory translation in English. It could mean both 'nationalist' and 'anti-semitic', but the term implied a certain mystical quality and had been frequently employed by German Romantic thinkers. During the period 1923–25, when the NSDAP was officially banned, the term was used in place of 'Nazi', for example, *völkisch* movement, although this in fact referred to all groups on the extreme right, of which the NSDAP was one. The word is sometimes translated later in this book as 'nationalist', depending on the context.

former NSDAP and other right-wing groups in spite of the official ban on the NSDAP. Several reasons suggest themselves—the nervous reluctance of the police to carry through an absolute suppression of all activities by these groups because of the continuing popularity of Hitler's supporters, a sympathy in some official quarters for the ideas expressed by these groups and a certain naïve belief that the very participation of these groups in the election indicated a readiness to adopt constitutional methods—but the prohibition on the NSDAP was more than just a formality. It did provide the Bavarian Government with the necessary means to act against political excesses if the situation should get out of hand. Not surprisingly, the Bavarian Government reacted unfavourably to Berlin's proposal to lift the state of emergency. In a communication to the Reich Chancellor on 23 February the Ministry of External Affairs in Munich expressed its opposition on the grounds of the forthcoming trial of Hitler and his associates in the Putsch and the effect this might have on public order. But the matter also touched on the sensitive question of Bavaria's constitutional rights *vis-à-vis* the national government, particularly with reference to the President's emergency powers granted by article 48 of the Weimar Constitution, which in the view of the Bavarian Government were used by certain parties to further the interests of a unitary state.[3] 'The inviolable retention of her sovereign rights involving questions of the police and justice is for Bavaria a matter of life and death'. Any trespassing on these rights would arouse the 'utmost opposition' from the Bavarian Government (*14*).

The Hitler trial, which lasted for almost one month from the end of February to the end of March, posed a new problem for the authorities. They were aware of the danger that the publicity surrounding the trial would revive public interest in Hitler and draw attention to the involvement of von Kahr in the Putsch, but Hitler and Ludendorff and the other eight accused had to be put on trial for treason for the sake of upholding the authority of the state. The failure to do so would automatically have opened the Bavarian authorities to charges of connivance in the attempt to overthrow the political system. The government certainly wanted to avoid any such suspicion and had quietly forced Gustav von Kahr out of office as

3. Article 48 of the Weimar Constitution of 1919 allowed the Reich President to use armed forces to compel a state government to 'fulfil the obligations laid upon it by the Reich Constitution or by the Reich laws' as well as to restore public security and order if that were 'seriously disturbed or threatened'. These emergency powers had already been used to intervene against Communist plans to take over power in Saxony and Thuringia in 1923. The presidential emergency powers became the most controversial aspect of the Weimar Constitution when from 1930 the Reich Government under Brüning chose to use them to pass measures for lack of a stable majority in the Reichstag.

State Commissioner a week or two before. The mistake was in the timing of the trial. It took place in the middle of the election campaign, when political tempers were already aroused, and gave Hitler a unique opportunity to build up his political image as the spokesman of all those who were in some way dissatisfied with the political order. Hitler was assisted by the presentation of the prosecution's case, which concentrated on attacking Hitler rather than Ludendorff, who still enjoyed considerable prestige as a war hero.[4] Hitler therefore enjoyed the limelight of the proceedings and, acting on the principle that the best means of defence is attack, turned them into a blatantly political occasion. He accused the Bavarian authorities of failing to back him up fully the previous November and raised the level of debate to that of patriotism. 'I do not feel like a traitor but a German who wanted the best for his people.' How could one commit treason against the Revolution of 1918, Hitler asked, when that Revolution was itself treason? Hitler's arguments about his 'national act' against the Republic and his sharp attacks on 'Marxism' were designed to appeal to certain prevalent attitudes in Bavaria then. Hitler enjoyed a wide public audience during these weeks. The trial was front-page news in the German press for the whole of this time, and many foreign journalists were also present. Hitler clearly saw himself as a man of destiny whose merit would be judged by history, not by the court. 'You may declare us guilty a thousand times, but the goddess who presides over the eternal court of history will with a smile tear in pieces the charge of the public prosecutor and the judgement of the court—for she declares us guiltless,' Hitler proclaimed as he ended his closing speech at the trial.

None of the other defendants made a mark at the trial, except Ludendorff who conducted his defence in a great booming voice and caused a sensation with his bitter attacks on the Roman Catholic Church. For hours he ranted about the pernicious influence of 'ultramontane' circles and the protection given to Jews by Catholic clergy. The outcome of the trial was hardly a surprise to those who had been following its sham proceedings. Hitler, together with Weber, Kriebel and Pöhner, was given five years on the understanding that he would be released on probation after a short spell in prison. The others were given a year and three months each for aiding and abetting, while Ludendorff was acquitted on the grounds that he had 'not comprehended' the importance of the events on 8 November. Significantly, the pronouncement of the sentences included a reference to the 'pure patriotic

4. General Ludendorff had emerged from the First World War as one of the military heroes with Hindenburg for his share in the German victory at Tannenberg in 1914. During the Weimar period he became associated with the extreme right in opposition to the new republic and was one of the conspirators in the Munich Putsch of 1923.

outlook and the most noble and unselfish purpose' of the accused. The sentences caused much excitement in the public gallery so that the president of the court ordered the building to be cleared. Ludendorff was greeted as a hero as he left the scene of the trial (*15*).

The fears of the authorities, who had little to relieve their moral defeat suffered through the trial of the Putsch conspirators, were confirmed five days later when the results of the Bavarian state elections showed a massive vote for the *Völkischer Block*. It won 512,300 votes or 17·1 per cent of the total vote in Bavaria, making it the third strongest party in the state after the Social Democratic Party (17·3 per cent) and the ruling Bavarian People's Party (32·9 per cent). One month later elections took place for the Reichstag, showing a slight drop in the vote for the *Block*. The view in official quarters was that the *Block* had benefited considerably from the public interest aroused by the trial of Hitler. The press almost unanimously ascribed the results of the election to the trial, a view confirmed by Dr Held, the leader of the BVP parliamentary group in the Bavarian diet, in a conversation he had with the Reich representative in Munich on 11 April (*16*). A police report on the voting later commented that 'the popularity of Hitler and the other leaders was only increased by their conviction and their quasi-martyrdom' and that the agitation and organization of its campaign had allowed the *Block* to gain a footing in several places where it had never previously been active (*17*). The decrease in its vote in the Reichstag elections in May was attributed to the fact that the Hitler trial was no longer fresh in the minds of the voters.

The spring elections of 1924 had a sensationalist value which was not necessarily supported by the voting patterns for the *Völkischer Block*. Support for the extreme right was in fact concentrated largely in certain towns, where the NSDAP and its successor organizations had been particularly active. One-fifth of the vote for the *Block* in the Bavarian election was accounted for by Munich, the scene of the Hitler trial.[5] Nuremberg, the headquarters of Streicher's organization, also registered a high vote. In smaller towns like Ingolstadt, Bayreuth, Coburg and Ansbach the *Block* emerged as the strongest party with sometimes more than 40 per cent of the vote (*18*). Bayreuth with its Wagnerian associations and Coburg, normally a stronghold of the German National People's Party (DNVP), were both towns with a strong Protestant and politically conservative tradition. The high vote for the *Völkischer Block* in Ingolstadt was attributed by the local authorities to its continuous election meetings held during the last week of the campaign. All of these meetings had attracted large crowds, especially

5. The *Völkischer Block* won 105,000 votes in Munich in the Bavarian election, making it the largest party in the city.

18

the one at which Streicher had spoken on the racial question (*19*). But the *Block* had made far less impact in the rural areas of Bavaria where the Catholic Bavarian People's Party (BVP) and the Bavarian Peasants' and Middle-Class League (BBMB) largely controlled the electorate between them.[6]

As far as the public was concerned, it was the impression made by the election which counted. In Catholic circles Ludendorff's uncomplimentary remarks about the Church were remembered particularly after he followed them up with further attacks on the influence of the Church in politics by accusing the BVP of being not a party of the Right but 'a Roman party'. Soon after the election a demonstration of Catholics took place in the Löwenbräukeller. The chief speaker of the evening was Hans Rauch, chairman of the Central Committee of Munich Catholics and a Reichstag deputy of the BVP, who concerned himself almost exclusively with recent statements made by Ludendorff. Ludendorff earned all the abuse for his 'hatred of Rome' while Hitler curiously emerged virtually unscathed from the meeting. The view was expressed several times that the nationalist movement had originally been a healthy reaction against the Revolution of 1918 until Hitler had been seduced by 'powers hostile to Christianity'. Other speakers at this rally included Karl Scharnagl, a prominent local politician and BVP town councillor, and Cardinal Faulhaber, Archbishop of Munich-Freising, a figure held in wide respect in the city. Ludendorff had become a divisive figure in Bavarian politics—worshipped by patriotic groups, his very name was sufficient to arouse strong hostility in circles close to the Church and to the government in Munich (*20*).

The Bavarian Government felt sufficiently concerned about the possible effects of electoral success on the further development of the *völkisch* movement to write to local authorities on how to deal with the problem. On 6 May the State Ministry of the Interior warned the regional government of Upper Franconia of the dangers emanating from the activities of this movement (*21*). The Ministry was very critical of the attitude of the authorities there, who had frequently behaved in a 'feeble, timid, uncertain and indecisive' way towards these groups and had not followed the in-structions of the state government. The events of 8 and 9 November had shown what was to be expected from the *völkisch* movement and officials should not be deceived when its activities were disguised as patriotic

6. This was particularly true of Catholic Southern Bavaria and the Catholic areas in Franconia (Northern Bavaria), but in the Protestant rural areas of Middle and Upper Franconia the Nationalist Party (DNVP) was strong. Generally, the vote for the *Block* was much lower in the countryside, for example, in the Reichstag Election in May it won 28·2 per cent in the larger towns and 10·4 per cent in the rural districts of Upper Bavaria.

occasions. Its leaders were plausible with their promises and assurances of good conduct which had made the authorities reluctant to take necessary action. Legal action after the event was not good enough, immediate steps had to be taken to suppress such excesses. A case in point had been the recent visit of Ludendorff to Upper Franconia, which had been 'purely a nationalist propaganda journey'. In spite of this, civil servants had taken part in meetings even in the presence of 'members of the *Völkischer Block* wearing uniforms and carrying flags'. Torchlight processions had taken place in spite of their prohibition and had been justified as preserving order at meetings and providing protection for Ludendorff. 'The participation of General Ludendorff in nationalist propaganda should with all due respect to his services in the World War not lead to his party being treated in any exceptional way by the authorities.' The Ministry, alarmed at the sympathy shown in certain official quarters for the followers of Hitler, remarked that these events had cast 'an exceptionally unfavourable light on the handling of the police' and warned that 'the authority of the state should not be put at stake any more by gullibility in the face of assurances' given by members of the *völkisch* movement.

Formation of the Held Government

In Munich the government of Dr Eugen von Knilling handed in its resignation, which was in accordance with the requirements of the Bavarian constitution following the election of a new state parliament.[7] It was inevitable that the Bavarian People's Party would lead the new government, but the question remained of the choice of a new Prime Minister and of coalition partners. Dr von Knilling had lost much favour with his own party because of his handling of events since the Putsch, so that the BVP had to look for a new leader. The choice soon settled on Dr Heinrich Held, leader of the BVP faction in the Landtag, who became Prime Minister of Bavaria for the remaining nine years of the Weimar Republic.

Dr Held was a prominent Catholic politician, one of the founders of the Bavarian People's Party and a former president of the German Catholic Assembly. One of his closest political colleagues was that noted clerical politician, Dr Georg Wohlmuth, provost of Eichstätt cathedral, who succeeded to Held's former position as parliamentary leader of the BVP. Held

7. Von Knilling, the BVP leader, had been Prime Minister of Bavaria since November 1922, but his had been a weak government especially during the time of Gustav von Kahr's office as Bavarian State Commissioner.

was by inclination a conservative and a monarchist and had opposed Social Democratic proposals for parliamentary reform in 1917 as they intended 'a fundamental restriction of the royal prerogatives and will lead ultimately to the actual elimination of the constitutional monarchy, to the introduction of a parliamentary form of government and finally to the republicanization of our state' (22). Held believed that reform should be granted from above by the grace of the monarchy, but he became no monarchical activist during the Weimar period.[8] His attitude was typically that of a constitutionalist who followed the rules of the game more out of a sense of rightness than out of any sympathy for the parliamentary system as such. At the same time, he was as a spokesman of the Bavarian federalists an ardent advocate of constitutional reform in the Reich, in spite of his not being a Bavarian by birth, a fact sometimes held against him by Bavarian patriots.[9] His austere attitude to politics was above all determined by his sense of 'Christian public ethics'—in the words of Karl Schwend, the BVP publicist, 'as a Catholic politician he was a fanatic of legality, to the point of weakness in the eyes of the world' (23). Held's Catholic conservatism and his strict sense of what was constitutionally proper helped to explain his abhorrence of left-wing parties including the SPD (they were all 'Marxists') and of the mass politics practised by the Nazis.

The matter of coalition partners proved more difficult to solve. The BVP had lost much support in the spring elections and held only 46 seats out of a total of 129 in the Bavarian parliament, far less than the absolute majority. Eventually, agreement was reached between the BVP and the DNVP and the Bavarian Peasants' and Middle-Class League to form a government but not without many differences arising between these parties. The DNVP leader, Hans Hilpert, demanded negotiations first with the leaders of the *Völkischer Block*. Held was forced against his will to go through the motions of these talks, which as expected came to nothing. Held then had to sacrifice Hans Schweyer as Minister of the Interior, who had earned the lasting hatred of nationalist conservative circles for his readiness to take action against political extremists. The other controversial figure was Dr Franz Gürtner, who as DNVP representative in the government had been Minister of Justice

8. Held remained basically a monarchist at heart. He continued to have the title *Königlicher Geheimer Hofrat* (Royal Privy Councillor) on his visiting card, although the Bavarian monarchy had been abolished at the end of the First World War.
9. He was born in Hesse-Nassau in 1868, studied law, history and political science at the universities of Strassburg, Marburg and Heidelberg and moved to Bavaria to become a journalist, editing a newspaper in Regensburg from 1899 to 1914. In 1907 Held was elected a Centre Party deputy to the Bavarian state parliament and became leader of the party's parliamentary group in 1914.

since 1922. BVP circles were already incensed at the dropping of Dr Schweyer from the government and demanded the head of Gürtner, who it was felt had been instrumental in procuring light sentences for Hitler and his associates in the trial in the spring. The DNVP refused to give in to pressure to withdraw his name, and Held had no choice but to include him in his government. The widespread dislike for Gürtner in the ranks of the ruling party became evident when the *Bayerischer Kurier*, which supported the BVP, created a furore over Gürtner's reappointment and claimed it would prevent any chance of a purification of Bavarian justice (24).

Divisions Widen Within the Movement

The banned Nazi Party had in the context of extreme right-wing organization as a whole continued to enjoy impressive public support in the months following the Putsch because of the impact of the Putsch itself on political attitudes in Bavaria, the tolerant attitude of the authorities towards its activities and a lucky combination of circumstances, but the success of the *Völkischer Block* in the spring elections of 1924 raised new problems concerning the tactics and nature of the movement, the divisive effect of which was magnified by the lack of a uniform and structured organization based on the supreme authority of the party leader and the absence of the crystallizing force of Hitler. During the spring, the election campaign and the trial had provided a common centre of activity for Hitler's followers but now little held the rival factions in the movement together except a general sense of loyalty towards Hitler.

The divisions within the *völkisch* movement, which grew wider and became more public during the summer and autumn of 1924, revolved around questions of policy and personalities, but inevitably the two factors were strongly linked. The issue of electoral participation by the successor groups to the NSDAP became the subject of an internal conflict of views over the attitude to be taken towards parliamentary democracy and whether participation was inconsistent with the assumed aim of changing the political system; but this very issue was also used by one faction against another in an attempt to displace the other's influence within the *völkisch* movement.

In Bavaria opposition to participation in parliamentary elections was voiced most strongly by Julius Streicher, Hermann Esser[10] and other leaders who

---

10. Hermann Esser had been one of Hitler's early associates in the Nazi Party in Munich, and had been in charge of party propaganda before the Putsch. He was a young man in his mid-twenties and radical by temperament, having formerly been a Social Democrat.

formed the Greater German People's Community (*Grossdeutsche Volks-gemeinschaft*—GVG), an organization of former Nazis based primarily on the two major cities of Bavaria—Nuremberg and Munich—in February 1924. At the time of the spring elections the split between the GVG and the *Völkischer Block*, as the electoral alliance of the extreme right in Bavaria, had not yet developed and did not become final until the autumn. Streicher in fact spoke at election meetings and was himself elected a member of the Bavarian parliament, but increasingly the different class attitudes of the GVG leaders, their more radical tendencies and the fact that in any common front to fight an election the GVG would be at a disadvantage *vis-à-vis* the *Block* as a whole, because of its shortage of funds and its more limited organization, produced rifts between the two main groups in Bavaria ostensibly over the principle of electoral participation.

The origins of this rupture in the *völkisch* movement lay to some degree in Streicher's own temperament and his career as a party activist in Nuremberg. Streicher came from Swabia in Southern Bavaria—he was born in 1885 in the village of Fleinhausen near Augsburg as the ninth child of a strictly Catholic family—although he was throughout his political career associated with the city of Nuremberg, where he took up residence as an elementary school-teacher in 1909. After Streicher's demobilization at the end of the First World War, in which he had risen to the rank of lieutenant and served with some distinction, he soon took an active part in local politics and became associated with various anti-semitic groups in Nuremberg, including initially a 'cultural association' consisting of former Army officers. Streicher joined the German Racialist Defence and Offence League, a protégé organization of the Pan-German League, and became prominent in the German Socialist Party (DSP), which he left in 1921 after differences with its moderate leaders who could not stomach Streicher's violently anti-semitic propaganda. Eventually, Streicher decided to make common cause with Hitler in October 1922 and brought his followers into the ranks of the NSDAP. The first branch of the NSDAP was founded in Nuremberg with Streicher as its chairman. Financial motives seem to have influenced Streicher strongly in his decision for his journalistic activities as editor of the *Deutscher Volkswille*, his tendency to become involved in expensive lawsuits with political opponents and his sheer inability to administer his affairs in any orderly manner led to mounting costs, which he was unable to meet (25). The NSDAP soon provided an outlet for his irrepressible energies. In the first few months after he joined the Party, he took the initiative of organizing thirteen new branches in towns mainly in the Franconian region (26).

As far as the Nazi Party was concerned, Streicher proved indispensable because of his unquestionable loyalty to Hitler and his work in establishing the Party in Northern Bavaria, although his inability to cooperate with other Party leaders and his partiality for political and personal scandals caused considerable embarrassment to the Party on more than one occasion. Streicher was typical of a certain authoritarian type, willing to submit himself totally to his *Führer* while intolerant to the point of obsession of his subordinates and any political opponents who crossed his path. His personal and political conflict with Dr Hermann Luppe, the mayor of Nuremberg, became the subject of many court cases and frequently heightened the political tension in the city. Streicher became a prima-donna figure in Nuremberg politics. He was the sort of person who aroused either blind devotion from his admirers or intense dislike from his opponents. He had made his political reputation as a rabid anti-semite, his paper *Der Stürmer* becoming the mouthpiece for his views on the Jews, while he was already notorious for his obsession with pornography and his curious habit of carrying a dog-whip.

Streicher's strength was as a rabble-rouser while his very notoriety could not help but give the Nazi movement publicity, even if not always favourable. The Catholic Church was another frequent object of attack by Streicher. The origins of his anti-Catholicism—interesting in view of the Catholic background of his family—are not clear. Streicher later gave as one of the reasons for his move to Nuremberg from Southern Bavaria a quarrel he had had as a young teacher with a priest, but all Streicher's stories about himself were extremely tendentious and often coloured by his persecution complex (27). The likeliest explanation is that Streicher's views on the Church formed part of his general political outlook, influenced as it was by *völkisch* ideology, which with its element of paganism and racialism saw Christianity, and Catholicism in particular, as an outgrowth of Jewish tradition and therefore alien to the German character. In any case, Streicher's opposition to Catholicism was certainly no disadvantage in the predominantly Protestant city of Nuremberg and Protestant region of Middle Franconia.

The differences between the more moderate and radical groups among Hitler's followers in Nuremberg came to the fore after the Putsch and the ban on the Nazi Party. Streicher was free to pursue his political activities, not being one of those leaders of the Putsch who were imprisoned and sent for trial, although he had been briefly arrested and suspended from his job as a school-teacher by the city of Nuremberg. In December 1923 Dr Stöcker, a doctor for nervous diseases, founded the German Workers' Party (DAP) in Nuremberg which favoured electoral participation and became the local organization in Nuremberg and Middle Franconia of the *Völkischer Block*. Streicher resented this challenge to his domain and refused to cooperate. On 8 February 1924 he founded the GVG in Munich in cooperation with Hermann Esser and several other prominent NSDAP leaders, including Arthur Dinter from Thuringia and Franz Xaver Schwarz, later treasurer of the NSDAP. The GVG was more radical than the other Nazi groups in Bavaria, opposed participation in parliamentary elections, was more aggressively anti-semitic, despised the 'theoretical racialists' of the bourgeoisie and appealed to the working-class. Streicher had been appointed by Hitler as his representative in Northern Bavaria (*28*), and regarded his group as the only rightful heir to the NSDAP in that area.

The conflict between Streicher and the DAP in Nuremberg broke out after the spring elections of 1924. The two parties developed entirely separate organizations and held rival public meetings, sometimes on the same day. Meetings organized by the GVG were usually better attended because of Streicher's superior qualities as a mass orator, while those of the DAP suffered from disturbances by followers of Streicher. In July Streicher and Esser formally opened the local branch of the GVG in Nuremberg with the aim of 're-establishing the old National Socialist movement, creating a National Socialist power, which can successfully exert pressure on the new *völkisch* men who are sitting in parliament' (*29*). Streicher further organized a group of former SA men as the *Völkischer Bund Reichsadler* (Nationalist League of Imperial Eagles), whose members wore 'a storm-suit, black armbands with a red swastika on a white background'. The DAP replied to these moves with the threat to expose Streicher's ways of living and opened a campaign for the 'purification action of the *völkisch* movement from vermin' to get rid of Streicher. Streicher answered with a special number of *Der Stürmer*, which in turn provoked the *Völkisches Echo*, the organ of the DAP, to publish a virulent article about 'the enfeebled fallen dictator' on 26 July, attacking the 'action inspired by him [Streicher] against those with different views and displeasing competitors inside the *völkisch* movement'. Such was the state of relations between the two rival groups in Nuremberg that Streicher saw it in his interest to form his own bodyguard with the pompous title of 'the twelve apostles' (later renamed 'the death's head group', then the 'criminal department Streicher') and set up a 'news service' for spreading sensational rumours about his opponents (*30*).

As far as Nuremberg was concerned, Streicher had little difficulty in asserting his authority, but the GVG was in a weak position seen in the context of the national *völkisch* movement. Efforts were made by the North German leaders to prevent further splits and unite the different groups in the movement at a congress held in Weimar in the middle of August 1924 when Ludendorff was proclaimed national leader in Hitler's absence, but the leaders of the GVG declined the invitation to join. Their attitude was the subject of sharp criticism at the Weimar meeting as it was felt that their offensive behaviour, in particular Streicher's 'terroristic methods of influence', would jeopardize Hitler's chances of release later in the year. The delegates at Weimar included leaders of the Berlin-based German Nationalist Freedom Party (DVFP), a splinter group under Albert von Graefe and Count Reventlow of the conservative German National People's Party (DNVP), as well as former NSDAP leaders such as Gregor Strasser, so it was not surprising that the more radical GVG was regarded with disfavour. Esser in particular aroused the utmost dislike among the North German leaders. Adalbert Volck, writing from Lüneburg to Hermann Fobke, who was acting as Hitler's secretary in Landsberg prison, described Esser as 'a destructive and disintegrative influence whose sense of duty does not keep pace with his abnormal ambitions—such men will not be tolerated as fighters here in the North'. Volck went on to express the wish that Hitler should come to the North, where he would not be surrounded by people like Esser and where 'men of Nordic blood live . . . not speakers and mercenaries, but men who know, want and are able to do something' (*31*). In a further letter to Fobke a fortnight before the Weimar meeting, Volck criticized Hitler's intention of using Bavaria again as his base, 'The South is much easier to inflame but it does not last; that was seen in the war, when the Bavarian was brilliant in the attacking movement but weak in holding on to a position; down there "Rome" inhibits their striking force; only in the North can a real *völkisch* assault be let loose' (*32*).

Anti-Bavarian feelings, coupled with a dislike of Catholic dominance in the South, influenced the North German leaders against the idea that Munich should remain the centre of the movement, although this hardly affected their feeling of loyalty towards Hitler as the real leader of the movement. It was typical of the various rival *völkisch* groups that each one claimed to represent Hitler's real intentions. The Weimar meeting discussed the question of a more tightly organized national movement, and formed the National Socialist Freedom Movement (NSFB) as an alliance which broadly accepted the idea of parliamentary participation. The GVG appeared in danger of isolation within the movement as a whole, but nevertheless chose to remain a separate organization for various reasons. The principle of electoral participation was an important reason but not the only one.

Firstly, the radical bent of the leaders of the Greater German People's Community predisposed them to reject electoral participation as a betrayal of National Socialist principles. The Nazi Party was opposed to the political system of the Weimar Republic and should therefore not take part in any of its institutions as this implied recognition of them. Had Adolf Hitler himself not condemned parliamentary government as the ruin of the German people on many occasions before the Putsch of 1923?[11] Hitler refused in prison to become involved in intra-party quarrels and declare his views publicly on this question. Kurt Ludecke, a regular visitor to Hitler in Landsberg, recorded that the Nazi leader was at first definitely against participation because 'he feared for his own position as the supreme leader of the party' (33), but visiting Hitler again shortly after the spring elections Ludecke was surprised to find him changing his mind. Hitler reportedly said to Ludecke:

When I resume active work it will be necessary to pursue a new policy. Instead of working to achieve power by an armed coup, we shall have to hold our noses and enter the Reichstag against the Catholic and Marxist deputies. If out-voting them takes longer than out-shooting them, at least the results will be guaranteed by their own constitution! Any lawful process is slow. But already, as you know, we have thirty-two Reichstag deputies under this new programme, and are the second largest party in the Bavarian state parliament. Sooner or later, we shall have a majority—and after that, Germany. I am convinced this is our best line of action, now that conditions in the country have changed so radically (34).

Hitler's statement has sometimes been used as evidence of his conversion to the policy of 'legality', that is of working within the political system and coming to power constitutionally. Ludecke was of the view that 'the unexpected success in the elections had undoubtedly swayed him' (35). It is possible that Hitler in his impulsive way had been impressed by the *völkisch* vote. Furthermore, the failure of the Putsch had been a traumatic shock to Hitler. Ludecke noticed his reluctance to talk about it, that it was an 'unprofitable subject except insofar as it provided a lesson in party procedure for the future' (36). The implication was that he could not afford another open clash with the powers of the state. All the same, it is unlikely that

11. At a meeting of GVG leaders in Munich in August, it was resolved that Hitler was the 'only authoritative leader for us in the last analysis' and that: 'We recognize neither the Reichstag parliamentary group nor the parliamentary groups in the state parliaments as having the right to exercise a decisive influence over the movement ... We demand recognition from our representatives in parliament of the principle that the emphasis of the old Hitler movement as before lies outside the parliaments; more essential than parliamentary successes is constant contact with the broad masses of working people through a skilful and popular propaganda to liberate them from the clutches of the Marxists and lead them into the nationalist camp, as was the main purpose of the old Hitler movement.' (Summary of meeting, HA 42/857.)

27

Hitler made any hard and fast decision about electoral participation at this time. There was nothing he could do about the problem since he was confined to prison, and in any case the issue might split the movement right open, all the more if Hitler himself took sides. The quarrel was moreover not restricted to leadership circles for it affected opinion at the grass-roots level of the movement, especially as more traditionalist Nazi circles in Bavaria still firmly believed that Hitler was opposed to 'parliamentarism'. Supporters of the GVG in the town of Pfarrkirchen in Lower Bavaria wrote to the GVG's headquarters in Munich in November 1924, when new Reichstag elections were less than a month away, that 'it would not be understood especially in the provinces if the GVG should be drawn into the election campaign and contribute to the success of those, who until now have pursued selfish aims in parliament'. Members of the *Völkischer Block* were little more than 'ambitious careerists' who were prepared to sacrifice National Socialist principles for the sake of positions of power:

> The place-hunting of the people of the *Völkischer Block* has even taken strong roots here in Pfarrkirchen in that the chairman of the local group has for some time played with the idea of advancing by means of the town council to regional or district councillor in order to improve his position as much as possible. Such action accords in no way with the programme of Hitler. Even if it came to an open breach with the local branch of the *Völkischer Block* through me and my brother-in-law, Herr Greiner (member of the West End section of the GVG [in Munich]), I still think that those who 'still want to become something' will not shrink from achieving their selfish aims (37).

This antipathy towards the *Völkischer Block* was also explained by the different social background of GVG supporters.[12] A report from Munich at the beginning of November commented on the differences between the audiences at meetings of the two *völkisch* groups:

> Whereas members of the officer and civil servant class, tradesmen and young people from these circles as well as the upper middle class and some workers turned up for the *Völkischer Block*, one came across at the

12. These class differences appeared in a speech which Rudolf Buttmann, the *Völkischer Block* leader, made in May 1924 attacking Streicher and Esser. Buttmann referred to the GVG leaders as 'Bolshevists' and that 'Bolshevist-nihilistic elements' were at work in the movement. He urged that people from 'the so-called bourgeois circles' should be brought into the movement to provide a counter-force. (Albert Krebs, *Tendenzen und Gestalten der NSDAP*, p. 200.)

protest meeting of the GVG predominantly members of the small trading middle class and workers, including a surprising number of women . . . while the officer and the highly educated were conspicuous in the *Völkischer Block*, the worker was most prominent in the other camp (*38*).

In Nuremberg Streicher's followers concentrated on winning support among the working class and even for a time attempted to make common cause with the Communists. Karl Holz, Streicher's number two in the party there, invited Communists to a mass meeting of the GVG on 21 August: 'Come in masses, bring your leaders with you for a free exchange of views' (*39*). Cooperation failed to develop because of differences over the Jewish question and the disapproval of large numbers of GVG supporters of the whole idea of working with the Communists.

The other main reason for the opposition of the GVG to electoral participation was tactical. The GVG simply did not have the organization or the money to compete with the *Völkischer Block* in the event of an election, in which the *Block* would easily dominate the activities of the *völkisch* campaign. If Streicher was able to maintain his position as *völkisch* leader in Nuremberg and receive frequent invitations to speak at meetings in Franconia, he had little success in making the GVG into a competitive organization to the DAP outside Nuremberg (*40*). The local branch of the GVG in Erkersreuth-Selb wrote to Esser on 19 August pleading with him to come and address a meeting there, especially as Ludendorff, Brückner and Roehm would be appearing at a mass rally in the neighbouring town of Hof at the beginning of September. The quarrels within the *völkisch* camp in Selb revolved around the person of Esser and it was necessary that he should appear himself as this would strengthen the position of the GVG branch. Perhaps he would come before the meeting held by the *Block* and combine his visit to Selb with a speech in Hof as well (*41*). It was easy for the *Völkischer Block*, as the stronger organization in the provinces, to claim that the GVG was undermining the unity of the *völkisch* movement. The branch of the *Block* in Straubing wrote on behalf of other branches in Lower Bavaria to GVG headquarters on 1 August attacking bitterly the refusal of the GVG to cooperate and deploring the divisions produced among supporters of the *völkisch* movement in the provinces by the quarrels in Munich and Nuremberg. The GVG could not boast of important personalities like Ludendorff, who 'on 9 November 1923 walked into the fire at the head of the *völkisch* ranks, which one cannot say of anyone who today talks big in the GVG'. 'We old National Socialists in the provinces have welcomed strongly the merger of all *völkisch* groups in the *Völkischer Block* for the period of its duration, as we see in this a way of

29

removing the conceit of leaders of certain groups for the sake of the greater cause.' Only by joining this electoral alliance could they become a 'power factor'. The leaders of the GVG would do well to remember that 'Munich and Nuremberg is not Bavaria and Germany' and concentrate on building up the movement in the two cities 'as there is no solid base for your divisive efforts in the provinces' (*42*). Although the GVG was in fact stronger in the rural areas than granted by its opponents in Straubing, the GVG was not in the position to finance its political activities on any lavish scale because it did not have the necessary funds at its disposal. In a letter to a Munich party member on 16 September, the business manager of the GVG apologized for their inability to underwrite an extensive propaganda campaign:

> We refer to the fact that the GVG, since its leadership was taken over by Messrs. Esser and Streicher, has again developed a big programme of meetings—unfortunately, it is not possible to organize as much propaganda work as we would like, as alas we have to observe the greatest economy in producing propaganda material so that we can at least gradually reduce the enormous debts met during the election (*43*).

The split between the two groups of the *völkisch* movement in Bavaria became final and public during the autumn of 1924 following further attempts by the national organization (NSFB) under Ludendorff and Strasser to create some order in the movement. The *Völkischer Block* finally gave up its position as a semi-independent Bavarian organization inside the *völkisch* movement and was formally incorporated into the *Reichsführerschaft* (the national organization) with the new name of '*Völkischer Block*, National Socialist Freedom Movement of Greater Germany (Bavarian Branch)'. The GVG then called a conference of branch leaders in Munich on 19 October, at which Esser outlined the 'terms' on which the GVG would consider co-operating, in a speech lasting four hours: the GVG must have an important say in the running of the NSFB since 'the oldest National Socialists are to be found in it and it is the only *völkisch* organization which fosters the true spirit of Hitler'; that a directory of five, including two representatives of the GVG, should replace the *Reichsführerschaft*: the NSFB should assume responsibility for the debts of the GVG; the GVG should maintain its district organizations in Munich, Nuremberg, Augsberg, Bamberg and Memmingen; and finally Streicher should become a member of the *Reichsführerschaft*. Esser made it quite clear that the GVG would not dissolve itself as an organization if it joined the *Völkischer Block*.

Esser's uncompromising manner only provoked the leaders of the national organization into expelling him and Streicher formally from the *Völkischer Block* at a meeting in Munich a week later. The vindictive mood of the meeting, at which Strasser emphasized the need to close ranks to fight the forthcoming Reichstag Election, was evident from the personal accusations against the GVG leaders, including the charge that Esser had acted cowardly during the Putsch by leaving Hitler's supporters in the lurch and fleeing to Austria, there 'to lead a fast life at party costs'. The expulsion of the GVG leaders had repercussions the following day when the branch of the GVG in central Munich decided to ally with the *Block*. Esser and Streicher walked out of the meeting in the Hofbräuhaus with some eighty supporters under a storm of protest and held a rival meeting in a nearby pub, where Esser exploded in a tumult of abuse against Ludendorff. Certain other leaders of the NSFB were described as ' scamps and scoundrels'. Relations between the two rival organizations had taken such a violent turn that the Munich police made a special point of confiscating weapons from those who attended their meetings as opponents were always likely to be present to cause a disturbance. A large number of rubber truncheons were taken off visitors at a public meeting of the *Block* on 30 October as they entered the meeting hall (*44*).

The open rupture between the Greater German People's Community and the *Völkischer Block* did nothing but harm to the prospects of the movement in the Reichstag Election in December. Already there was a noticeable drop in attendance at their public meetings, which was attributed mainly to the public airing of their differences by Hitler's supporters, tarnishing the attractive image the movement had enjoyed at the time of the spring elections. The parliamentary activities of the *Block* deputies had alienated many of its radical supporters, who, disillusioned with the fact that the *Block* had ' grown from a movement into a party' because of its entry into parliament, turned their backs on it and joined the Communists out of protest (*45*). The GVG refused to cooperate in the Reichstag Election, although it decided to put up a few separate lists of candidates for the Bavarian municipal elections, which were taking place on the same day. The *Block* suffered from the lack of issues to exploit, for the economic situation was no longer so acute following the success of the policy of Dr Schacht, the special currency commissioner, in restoring the currency, which had brought the worst effects of the inflation to an end by the summer of 1924. The new reparations agreement, the Dawes Plan, also brought an end to the occupation of the Ruhr by French forces.

The Reichstag Election on 7 December 1924 was a great disappointment to the forces of the extreme right, which won only 907,000 votes compared with the impressive figure of 1,918,000 in May. In Bavaria the drop in support for the *Völkischer Block* was even sharper from 16 per cent of the vote to little

31

more than 5 per cent. It looked like a defeat for Ludendorff and Strasser, who had hoped to keep supporters of the Nazi Party and other banned nationalist groups united in an electoral alliance. Clearly, circumstances were no longer favourable to the extreme right, but the controversial issue of electoral participation had itself driven away a sufficient number of supporters to affect its vote. In the municipal elections Streicher won a minor triumph when the GVG received as many as 25,000 votes in Nuremberg, giving it six seats on the city council. Streicher himself was elected a town councillor, which now gave him the opportunity to harass the mayor inside the council chamber as well as on the public rostrum. Streicher's success seemed to justify his tactical decision to participate in elections only where his chances appeared good.

Hitler's Release

Hitler's release from prison on probation on 20 December, only two weeks after the Reichstag election, was not in fact influenced by the sharp drop in support for the *Völkischer Block*. The loss of votes by the extreme right may have calmed some fears concerning Hitler's reappearance in public life, but his release followed the failure of persistent efforts by the Bavarian Government to have him deported to Austria, ostensibly on the grounds that Hitler was not a German citizen.[13] The real reason for these efforts was political, the fear that Hitler's impending release would lead to political unrest. The Bavarian Government reckoned with the probability that the Munich People's Court would set Hitler free later in the year, as had been indicated at the trial in the spring. When it became clear that the Austrian Government refused to recognize Hitler's Austrian citizenship, the Bavarian Government had to accept the situation but regarded Hitler's release with considerable foreboding. They had not forgotten the Putsch, nor did they think that Hitler had learnt any lessons from it.

The Bavarian police had made a first approach to the Austrian authorities as early as January 1924, when they enquired of the police in Linz, where Hitler had spent some of his early life, whether Hitler's Austrian citizenship

13. Hitler was born in Austria in 1889, but he had lived in Germany (Munich) since 1913 and had fought for the German Army in the First World War. His Austrian citizenship was now in doubt, although he could at any time try and claim German citizenship. In fact, he did not succeed in acquiring this until 1932, when the Nazis took advantage of their participation in the state government of Brunswick to appoint Hitler to an official post, which entitled him to German citizenship. (See Rudolf Morsey, *Hitler als Braunschweiger Regierungsrat*, in *Vierteljahreshefte für Zeitgeschichte*, 1960.)

would be recognized. Following a further enquiry in March, the regional government in Linz replied to Munich police headquarters on 20 April that the Austrian authorities would recognize Hitler's citizenship and would be willing to accept his deportation to Austria (*46*). With this positive answer the Munich police took no further action until the autumn, when the time for Hitler's release was approaching. On 22 September, the Bavarian police formally recommended Hitler's deportation in the event of his unavoidable release on the grounds that 'the moment he is set free, Hitler will, because of his energy, again become a driving force of new and serious public riots and a menace to the security of the state' (*47*). Three days later the State Court in Munich announced its decision to set Hitler free.

The matter was now in the hands of the Bavarian Government. On the same day as the Court's decision, Haniel, the Reich envoy in Munich who had many close contacts with the Bavarian authorities, reported differences in the Bavarian cabinet over Hitler's deportation to Austria. Three ministers then went off to visit the Prime Minister, who was away on holiday, to put the views of the Cabinet to him. Those who advocated Hitler's banishment were of the opinion that 'now is the most suitable moment for a measure of this kind, whereas perhaps later the implementation of such a deportation would involve a much more serious trial of strength for the Government, should Hitler succeed in reuniting the *völkisch* movement, which is for the moment broken up' (*48*).

Quite apart from their concern about the likely effect of Hitler's release on the political atmosphere, the Bavarian Government could not ignore frequent complaints about the continuing repercussions of the Putsch of the previous year on the tourist industry in Bavaria. Bavaria had earned a name for political extremism and violence so that, in the words of the Munich Tourist Association in a letter to the State Ministry of the Interior on 2 August, 'business circles in Southern Bavaria have been complaining for a long time that businessmen of the Jewish religion no longer come to Southern Bavaria to make their purchases' (*49*). This feeling was not confined to Jews, for Bavaria was being boycotted by tourists from abroad as well as from other parts of Germany. The reason was, according to the Tourist Association, not so much the accommodation charges as 'the political attitude of certain sections of the population here and the rowdy manner in which political attitudes are displayed in public'. In the same month, the Hotelkeepers' Association in Garmisch-Partenkirchen attributed the decline in the number of tourists visiting Bavarian spas and other holiday resorts that summer chiefly to 'the swastika movement'. The Association criticized the government for not taking action earlier as the campaign against the Jews was leading to an economic fiasco. 'We have no doubt that judicious Bavarians will see the absence of upright Jewish Germans as a consequence of the events of the previous year. If all circles in Bavaria had proceeded against the encroachments of the Hitler movement like, for example Garmisch-Partenkirchen, then it would not have become such a danger for the common good' (50). Similar complaints were heard from Munich and Nuremberg, which had been empty of tourists, as well as other towns which depended on the tourist industry.

The question of Hitler's deportation took a new turn at the end of September, when the Austrian Government, with Hitler's immediate release in mind, suddenly announced its refusal to permit Hitler entry to their country. It was clear from an interview the Austrian Chancellor, Dr Ignaz Seipel, gave to Dr Kohlendorfer, a senior official in the Bavarian Ministry of the Interior, that the authorities in Vienna were also afraid of the effects of Hitler's presence in Austria. Dr Seipel said that 'Hitler's presence in Austria would bring serious dangers for the Government of this country as regards both domestic and foreign politics, so that every effort must be made here to keep these elements of unrest away from Austrian territory' (51). To support their view, the Austrian authorities argued the case that Hitler was no longer eligible for Austrian citizenship since he had fought for the German Army in the First World War.

The Bavarian Government disputed this case, arguing that it was contrary to an agreement between Germany and Austria concerning ex-servicemen injured in the War, but there was nothing further they could do in the face of Austrian determination to refuse Hitler entry. A meeting between Dr Held and the Austrian Chancellor in Lindau in the autumn had no effect in changing the mind of the government in Vienna. The Bavarian State Prosecutor had succeeded in procuring a delay in Hitler's release, which should have been at the beginning of October, because of the suspicious activities of the *Frontbann*, a paramilitary organization under Ernst Roehm which included members of the former SA.

The view that Dr Gürtner, the Bavarian Minister of Justice, was really responsible for preventing Hitler's deportation, supposedly because of his sympathies with the *völkisch* movement (52) is further contradicted by the general alarm felt by the Bavarian Cabinet at the prospect of Hitler's release. At a Cabinet meeting two days before Hitler's release, Dr Held warned that strict police measures would have to be taken to prevent the occasion being used to stage ovations for the Nazi leader. Dr Stützel, who as Minister of the Interior was responsible for public security, agreed that in view of the impossibility of expelling Hitler everything should be done to prevent the

Nazi movement from taking on a new impetus especially in Munich (*53*). The Prime Minister repeated his fears to Haniel, who reported that 'the Government is certainly afraid that Hitler has in no way taken possession of himself as a result of his confinement and that he will pursue his aims with the same old energy—in case of emergency, should Hitler show signs of relapsing, then the period of probation must be suspended' (*54*). Dr Held thought for legal as well as political reasons that one could not extradite a person without nationality from one state to another inside Germany.

The Bavarian Government therefore decided to make the best of the unwelcome situation. Hitler could not be prevented from enjoying his freedom, but he would be watched closely. The slightest indication that he had not mended his ways would lead to immediate action by the police. The state of emergency, involving the ban on the Nazi Party, still remained in Bavaria. This had been lifted in other parts of the country some months before, following a resolution passed by the Reichstag in July for an end to the prohibition on political parties. The Reich Government had decided then to respect Bavaria's claim that it was a matter of its own security, but clearly the state of emergency could not last for ever.

On 4 January 1925 Dr Held granted an interview requested by Hitler and agreed with reluctance to lift the ban on the NSDAP as from 16 February. Hitler played the tame man, promising that his party would assist in the fight against 'Marxism' and insisting that he had no use for the attacks of Ludendorff and the North German *völkisch* leaders on the Catholic Church. Held was apparently not very impressed and the meeting took place in a frosty atmosphere. In order to make his attitude clear Held issued a statement immediately after the meeting that he had warned Hitler he would not tolerate circumstances 'as they had been before and after the ninth of November' (*55*). It was significant how much importance the Bavarian authorities attached to Hitler's role as a political leader in spite of the collapse of his movement and its considerable loss of popular support.

Three

The Years of Stagnation (1925–27)

Hitler Returns to Political Life: the Party Refounded, 1925

Hitler's release from prison and the end of the prohibition on the NSDAP gave his followers a new lease of life. Developments in the *völkisch* movement during 1924 had underlined its dependence on Hitler's unifying qualities as party leader and his appeal as a public orator. Party morale and organization had deteriorated with the growth of internal divisions and personal rivalries and had suffered a further setback in the Reichstag elections. Yet no other leader had appeared as a serious challenger to Hitler's dominant position in the movement. Ludendorff, a figure-head who enjoyed considerable prestige among conservative *völkisch* circles, was no politician and too divisive a character to bring the rival factions together. Like Gregor Strasser, he had remained basically loyal to Hitler in spite of the latter's refusal to commit himself on the question of electoral participation, which both he and Strasser as leaders of the NSFB had supported. If there was any common denominator between the feuding groups which represented the former NSDAP, it was their persistent allegiance to the absent Hitler. This was just as true of the leaders of the *Völkischer Block* as it was of the GVG in Bavaria. Both groups in the Nuremberg area were competing to win Hitler over to their side at the beginning of 1925 but the bitterness of their squabbles was now lessened by the fact that 'the will of Hitler was more than ever the sole determinant among supporters of the National Socialist idea' (*1*). It was not surprising that the police regarded Hitler's discharge as 'of special importance for the Nazi movement' since 'the large mass of its supporters have set the greatest hopes on Hitler, who is regarded in *völkisch* circles as the only man with a sure political instinct' (*2*).

The same degree of unquestioning acceptance of Hitler as the *Führer* was not always evident in some other areas of Germany, where party organizers often owed little or nothing to Hitler (*3*), but Bavaria had been the centre of his activities before the Putsch, and it was here that he enjoyed his strongest support. It was with this in mind that Hitler decided as early as August 1924 that he would 'create order in Bavaria first of all' after his release (he was then expecting to leave prison in October) (4).

Ludecke had suggested moving the party headquarters to Thuringia, which was more centrally placed in Germany and boasted of a strong organization under Artur Dinter who was loyal to Hitler, but Hitler did not hesitate to reply that he could not leave Munich because he was well known there and 'there are many here are who are devoted to me, to me alone and to nobody else' (5). Prestige was also involved.[1] Hitler later confessed that leaving Munich would have meant losing face and 'the end of the movement'. It would be a mistake to leave because his supporters were being 'threatened', for martyrs always strengthened a movement. 'The most sacred place is that where one has suffered the most' (6). Munich was the city associated with the powerful Hitler myths, the site of his greatest mass rallies and above all of the Putsch of 1923. Hitler needed a centre from which he could control his party. In the first part of *Mein Kampf*, written during his confinement in 1924, Hitler outlined the principles for the re-establishment of the party:

a. That at the beginning all activity should be concentrated in one town: namely, Munich. That a band of absolutely reliable followers should be trained and a school founded which would subsequently help to propagate the idea of the movement. That the prestige of the movement, for the sake of its subsequent extension, should first be established here through gaining as many successful and visible results as possible in this one place. To secure name and fame for the movement and its leader it was necessary, not only to give in this one town a striking example to shatter the belief that the Marxist doctrine was invincible but also to show that a counter-doctrine was possible.

b. That local groups should not be established before the supremacy of the central authority in Munich was definitely established and acknowledged ... (7).

Consequently, it was with conditions in Bavaria particularly in mind that Hitler set about recreating order in the movement, which meant re-establishing

1. Hitler had in mind objections by North German *völkisch* leaders to the party headquarters remaining in the south in Munich. Earlier, in 1921, he had opposed the suggestion from other party leaders to move the headquarters to another German city, possibly Berlin or Augsburg, and had in fact resigned from the party on this issue and plans to merge the NSDAP with other National Socialist parties in Germany and Austria. The real issue behind these differences had been Hitler's determination to seize dictatorial control over the party, and he won because of his indispensability as a public speaker and because opposition to him within the party was divided. This explains Hitler's sensitivity on the question of party headquarters remaining in Munich. Any proposal to make a change was seen as a challenge to his leadership.

his undisputed position as leader and taking a firm line with the disputes which had torn the movement apart during his period of confinement. In spite of the expectations which had greeted his release from prison, Hitler held himself in reserve for the first two months of his freedom. The reason was his indecisiveness in the face of a major quandary, for even in Bavaria he was presented with a serious tactical problem. Hitler was required to meet conflicting demands. On the one hand, he could not disappoint the hopes of his more radical followers who had little but contempt for constitutional niceties and impatience with the compromises he was required to make with the authorities in order to get the ban on the party lifted. He needed their support to reassert his leadership, for in Bavaria this radical element with its strong anti-semitic, anti-urban and anti-clerical leanings was not insignificant. At the same time, Hitler was under pressure to fulfil his promises to the Bavarian Government, on which he was dependent for his chance to resume his political activities, to forego violent methods. Hitler attempted to solve this dilemma, partly by pretending simply that it did not exist and adopting his former radical style of speaking to emphasize the continuity of his method of leadership; while in practice he ruled out a further Putsch as party policy, at least for the time being, and introduced certain changes in organization which took into account the different circumstances of 1925. It was not surprising that the Bavarian authorities, who were very sceptical of Hitler's motives and little prepared to give him credit, took his public statements at face value.

Hitler broke his silence on 26 February, when the *Völkischer Beobachter* published his guidelines for future party policy under the heading *Fundamental Regulations for the Re-formation of the NSDAP*. He began by emphasizing that there would be no radical change in party policy or structure, which implied that he intended to assert his former dictatorial control:

> The new party recognizes as its guiding principles and programme the rules of the old NSDAP which was disbanded on November 9, 1923. The struggle will be fought according to the same tactical rules. The organization will be carried out following the conditions and principles laid down by the law of our association on the basis of the old statutes.

Dissensions and splits within the movement would have to be eliminated because they only weakened it. By way of emphasizing that all past differences should be forgotten, he ordered that membership should start from scratch again: 'Membership of the new party can only come from re-enrolment; enrolment forms are obtained from party headquarters and so are membership books.' Hitler would have full control over the incorporation of other groups into the NSDAP, negotiations on such matters being conducted by him personally. The statement underlined the priorities which should be given to party organization:

> He who is not prepared to submit himself to the properly elected leadership is not fit to be in the ranks of the NSDAP and may therefore keep away from it. Membership books are issued uniformly for the whole movement. Every member is first of all under the control of party headquarters, which then calls for the formation of individual local groups so long as firm organizational bodies are not already available through the inclusion of closed groups. The merger into regional or further subgroups is to be carried out organically. The criterion here is not the division into Reichstag electoral districts but the question of suitability for propaganda as well as available leadership material.
>
> The precondition for the formation of larger sub-groups is always: first the *Führer* and then the organization, and not vice versa.
>
> The following has to be observed as a matter of principle: the organization is not an end in itself but the means to an end. It should only make possible the political agitation struggle of the movement and create those organizational prerequisites for the action of enlightenment which are absolutely necessary.
>
> The best organization is not that which provides the largest intermediate apparatus between the leadership and the individual members but establishes this link in the shortest way. Ultimately, the organization must develop organically and not be artificially inflated.

Hitler made it clear in his guidelines concerning the SA that its function was primarily political and it was subordinate to the political leadership. It should be rebuilt according to the principles which had been applicable until February 1923.[2] The SA's role was to conduct propaganda, protect party meetings and fulfil its duties of 'steeling the physique of our youth, education in discipline and devotion to the common ideal', and it should forego

2. That is, before the formation of the alliance between the Nazis and various military patriotic associations in Bavaria in February 1923 to 'destroy' the Weimar Republic. This alliance, later called the Fighting League (*Kampfbund*), gave a more military emphasis to the activities of the NSDAP and allowed the SA under Roehm to gain a more influential position in the party.

any idea of staging a further Putsch. The organization of the SA must comply with the laws of the party and could not admit armed groups. Those who carried weapons against the orders of the party leadership would be dismissed from the SA and the party. Any provocative behaviour, which might provide the authorities with grounds for a 'further persecution of the movement', would be suppressed.

In his editorial on the same day, Hitler repeated many of the same arguments but there was one further consideration in his mind. He singled out for attack those who wanted to launch the movement into religious disputes for this would mean its end. 'Religious reformations cannot be made by political children.' Hitler declared that his chief task would be to see that 'members of both confessions live peacefully side by side in the newly founded NSDAP to lead the common fight against the power which is the deadly enemy of real Christianity'. He based his opposition to the Centre Party and its 'supporting groups' on political grounds only. 'Therefore the fight against the Centre Party will be carried on, not as it is allegedly "Christian" or even "Catholic", but exclusively because a party which allies with atheistic Marxism for the suppression of its own people is neither Christian nor Catholic.'[3] Hitler had two problems in mind when he made this statement. The North German *völkisch* leaders had been more outspoken in their criticism of the Catholic Church (voicing the traditional Protestant attitude which viewed ultramontanism as the enemy of national unity) than those in the South, and he wished to prevent confessional conflicts from dividing the movement any further. Secondly, he did not wish to offend the (Catholic) government in Munich on religious grounds, while at the same time he wanted to avoid the impression of so having compromised with the authorities in Bavaria that he alienated *völkisch* support elsewhere. Count Reventlow, one of the *völkisch* leaders in Berlin, had referred to Hitler as a 'lackey of Rome'. Hence, the emphasis on a place for both Catholics and Protestants in the movement and the justification for the attack on the Catholic parties on political grounds alone.

The National Socialist Party was formally refounded at a public meeting on 27 February 1925 in the Bürgerbräukeller in Munich. It was attended largely by Bavarian leaders of the party and members of the Munich branch as well as a public audience. Some 3,000 people turned up. Such was the curiosity of the local population that the hall was packed hours before the meeting began,

3. A reference to the coalitions between the Catholic Centre Party and the Social Democrats in Prussia and in the Reich governments in Berlin. This was not the case in Bavaria, where the Prime Minister, Dr Held, was absolutely opposed to any cooperation with left-wing parties on ideological grounds.

so that the police had to cordon off a large crowd which was gathering outside. The leaders of the GVG—Streicher, Esser and Dinter—took their place at tables near the speaker's desk, and were joined by Frick, Feder, Kriebel and Buttmann. Strasser, Roehm and Rosenberg were not present, nor was Drexler, whom Hitler had initially invited to take the chair.

At eight o'clock the meeting was opened by Max Amann, the party's business manager, who spoke briefly before handing over to Hitler amid wild applause. Hitler spoke for two hours on 'Germany's future and our movement'. He began with a customary historical survey which led up to the collapse of Germany in 1918, the only rescue from which lay in bringing the masses together in one 'People's Community'. He blamed the lack of spirit of the bourgeoisie for the events of 1918. The Nazi Party was distinguished from the 'bourgeois' parties because it alone concentrated on attacking 'Marxism' and was concerned with the masses:

> As assailant against Marxism only we National Socialists come into question. Either the enemy goes over our dead bodies, or we go over his. Just as in the War the English allegedly conducted the fight against the German Kaiser and militarism, so we will in future certainly conduct our fight against person and object, namely against the Jew as person and Marxism as the object.

Hitler had the usual few words of contempt for parliament, which he compared to a beer tavern where people talked. The party needed as before 'fighters and not parliamentarians'. He ended on a note of warning to those who sought to perpetuate factious disputes. These must now cease in the new movement for only the party leader represented its interests. All previous differences should be forgotten and those who wanted to make conditions for their entry to the party would have no success. He alone held absolute responsibility (8).

Hitler's caution failed to satisfy the authorities, whose reaction to his speech was immediate. The police banned a further five public meetings in Munich where he would be the main speaker. The reason they gave was that the Nazi leader had tried unmistakably to provoke political violence, that his speech had led to disturbances among the city's population and elsewhere in Bavaria and that their fears 'seem only too justified in view of the development of the NSDAP under Hitler's leadership especially in the year 1923' (9). On many occasions they quoted as an example of incitement Hitler's remark about the corpses of the enemy. The Bavarian Cabinet met on 9 March, when the Minister of the Interior, Dr Stützel, said he had taken this action to maintain the security of the state and because the 'revival of the Hitler movement would especially endanger the tourist traffic'. Dr Held commented that the whole of Bavaria's credit was at stake and the tourist industry would be destroyed. Exhibitions were currently being held and these were threatened (10).

This measure became in effect a ban on Hitler's public speeches in Bavaria for the next two years, causing considerable hardship to the Nazis at a time when they sought to attract wider support through mass rallies, at which Hitler was always a big draw. By acting in this way, the government appeared significantly more concerned with the threat coming from Hitler as a person than from his movement which was regarded as hopelessly split. This became clear from a report of 15 March on the state of the Nazi movement compiled by the State Ministry of the Interior. In spite of the division of the movement into several groups and opposition to his leadership from North Germany, Hitler was seen in the Bavarian context as a dangerous radical bent on repeating the history of the Putsch. 'Those who have expected a fundamental change from Hitler's recent political appearance are likely to have been disappointed; from what has become known of his speech, it can only be said that he has learned nothing and forgotten nothing from the long period of his removal; the Hitler of 1924 [sic] entertains the same demagogic phraseology with which he aroused himself in the year 1923.' Hitler had made clear at the meeting in Munich that he preferred violent methods to parliamentary means. 'With his excessive self-confidence and an astonishing over-estimation of his personal importance and personal influence Hitler has resumed the open fight against the power of the state' (11).

Rebuilding the Party Organization in Bavaria, 1925–27

The ban on Hitler's public meetings in Bavaria, which was followed by similar bans in most other states of Germany including Prussia, Saxony, Baden, Hesse, Oldenburg, Anhalt, Hamburg and Lübeck, seriously inhibited the activities of the Nazis during the first years after the party was refounded, but there were further reasons for the difficulties which faced the NSDAP.

Hitler's resumption of political life did not produce the expected outbreak of violence (admittedly, partly because of the speaking ban) and the initial excitement aroused by his release soon disappeared, but there was in any case little general interest in extremist solutions in Bavaria outside the limited circle of Munich politics which reflected the much quieter political atmosphere. Conditions were different, as the authorities kept reminding the

Nazis. The NSDAP was a party associated with an abortive attempt to seize power by force, and was not likely to appeal to a population whose main concern was the enjoyment of a quiet life. The Reichstag Election in December, in which the parties most associated with support for the Republic (especially the Social Democrats) had gained votes, had a stabilizing effect.

The meeting in the Bürgerbräukeller had attracted the crowds in Munich, but it apparently made little impact on people in the provinces. A week later, the authorities of Upper Bavaria reported that 'in the rural areas the National Socialists will hardly succeed in reaching their former position again and winning back all their former supporters; the longing for a quiet period and the strict rejection of all putsches is strong in the rural population and will provide a fairly solid defence against certain endeavours of Hitler' (*12*). In Lower Bavaria there was no fear of political disturbances in the near future for the mass of the population was more interested in carnivals and strong beer (*13*). The NSDAP was making no better progress in Swabia a few months later. It held public meetings in Memmingen and Augsburg but they were badly attended (*14*). Even in Nuremberg, the centre of Streicher's activities, the police noted later in the year that 'the driving forces of the NSDAP in Bavaria are becoming increasingly aware of their decline into political insignificance' (*15*). The situation was aptly summed up by the Catholic paper, the *Augsburger Postzeitung*, which commented that 'one has had enough of the uproar caused by Hitler in Bavaria—he is either superfluous or he is a lot of hullabaloo, neither of which we need' (*16*).

Another problem facing the newly founded NSDAP was the weak state of its organization, a result of the disintegrating effects of personal disputes and of the prohibition on the party for more than a year, which had forced its members to operate through a variety of cover groups rather than act as a cohesive body. In its memorandum to its local branches on the results of the December election, the Bavarian headquarters of the *Völkischer Block* had commented that 'the outcome of the elections shows us that the loss of votes is to be attributed not only to the common agitation of our opponents but also to our faulty organization' (*17*).

The election of a new President of the Republic shortly after the party was refounded provided a temporary common focus of activities. Friedrich Ebert, the first incumbent of the presidential office, had died suddenly on 28 February. There were as many as seven candidates in the first ballot held on 29 March. In contrast to the other *völkisch* groups, which supported Karl Jarres, the general candidate of the Right, Hitler decided to sponsor Ludendorff as a candidate. This would hardly gain Hitler any credit in Bavaria, where

Ludendorff had made a name for himself as an enemy of the Catholic Church and had publicly quarrelled with Crown Prince Rupprecht, the pretender to the Bavarian throne. Hitler's decision was influenced by internal party reasons. He seems to have intended Ludendorff's candidacy as a test of loyalty to his own leadership. Furthermore, Ludendorff was the one figure in the movement who had sufficient prestige to present a possible challenge to Hitler himself. An alliance with him would help to reunite the NSDAP in Bavaria, where Ludendorff's name was still revered in *völkisch* circles.

The result of the election was as expected. Ludendorff won no more than 1 per cent of the national vote, while his greatest support came from Bavaria. The Nazis had been unprepared for the campaign and were without a propaganda machine. Voter interest in the election was low, and in some places the election was taken for a joke. A very large number of voting papers in the district of Freising were returned inscribed with humorous poems or filled in facetiously with the names of local personalities (*18*). Only in a few places was there a noticeably high vote for Ludendorff, such as in Ingolstadt, a garrison town. In the second ballot, Hitler had no qualms about dropping Ludendorff and aligning his party with the campaign for Field Marshal von Hindenburg, who was elected President by a narrow margin. Ludendorff's candidacy meant the effective end of his career as a *völkisch* politician and as a rival to Hitler. The vote for him also demonstrated the degree of support for Hitler in the movement as a whole. An official report on the result noted: 'the resulting picture shows that in Bavaria Hitler has brought together all available supporters of the *völkisch* idea save a few fractions; in Baden and Württemberg the *völkisch* movement is split, as it is in Thuringia and Saxony; in Prussia and the other North German states the German Nationalist Freedom Movement will probably unite the larger part of the supporters of the *völkisch* idea in its organization' (*19*).

The first sign that Hitler would meet little opposition to his leadership in Bavaria was the self-dissolution of the two main *völkisch* organizations which had operated during 1924—the Greater German People's Community (GVG), and the *Völkischer Block*—and their amalgamation with the NSDAP. On 6 March, the *Block* called a special members' meeting and announced that it would join the NSDAP. Two days later Gregor Strasser, its leader, proclaimed at a further meeting in Munich that the NSDAP was the movement with the most promising future and the greatest chance of success. With Hitler's authority quickly re-established in Munich, most local branches of the *Block* followed suit and joined the NSDAP during March. A general meeting of the GVG took place on 13 March, when it declared its absolute allegiance to Hitler. Its members would join the NSDAP as individuals and not with their branches as Hitler wished to exclude possible opposition groups within his party (20). Neither Esser nor Streicher, the leaders of the GVG, were present at this meeting, but this had no significance. Both had shown constant loyalty to Hitler during his imprisonment. The support of Streicher was essential to Hitler because he controlled the party organization in Northern Bavaria. Hitler had expressed his appreciation of Streicher's work in the first speech he made in Nuremberg at the beginning of March: 'this same man was one of the first who came over to me after my release from the fortress and placed himself unconditionally under my authority—this man was Streicher, whom I will never forget for this; he may have faults, but a man who acts in this way is faithful . . .' (21). By the end of April the Bavarian police could report on the amalgamation of the GVG and the *Block* with Hitler's newly founded NSDAP that 'the main body of supporters of both groups, not only in Bavaria south of the Danube but also in Northern Bavaria, has gone over to him; thus, the regional branch of Lower Franconia decided completely in favour of Hitler, and so did the majority in Upper and Middle Franconia' (22).

Hitler's rapid reassertion of his control over the movement in Bavaria did not pass without some friction between the two former rival organizations, but nothing which involved a serious challenge to Hitler's authority. In Augsburg the refounding of the NSDAP branch was delayed by a personal dispute, in which the leaders of the *Block* objected to Hitler's appointment as branch leader of one Dr Frank, the city magistrate, who had the full backing of the GVG there (23). *Völkisch* groups in Bavaria which refused to submit themselves to Hitler's leadership were small and insignificant. A rival group did exist in the National Socialist People's League (NSVB), led by Drexler and Dörfler, which continued to look to Ludendorff for inspiration. When the NSDAP parliamentary group was formed by Buttmann in the Bavarian state parliament in September 1925, several *völkisch* deputies refused to join and supported the NSVB. The latter remained as a separate organization and campaigned in the 1928 Reichstag Election, winning a derisory vote (24).

Meanwhile, Hitler was busy making personal contact with local branch leaders outside Munich. During the summer of 1925 he held separate conferences with party leaders in almost every *Gau* and successfully reaffirmed his determination that the party's development should proceed on no other basis than the recognition of his absolute leadership.

On 5 July he addressed a conference of local branch leaders from Upper Bavaria at Rosenheim, the place where the first branch had been founded outside Munich in 1920. The meeting was chaired by Streicher. In his three-hour speech Hitler sought to 'educate' the seventy delegates present in the

45

aims of the NSDAP. The first task of the local branch leader, he emphasized, was to win the support of the proletarian masses, for the NSDAP should not be a party of the educated élite—a 'party of men with the doctor's title' (*keine Doktorenpartei*)—which characterized the traditional *völkisch* groups. The formation of new local branches was most important but these would no longer be the only organizational unit in the party, which would in future be divided hierarchically into regions (*Gaue*) and districts as well as local branches. Local branch leaders who showed the most loyalty to himself would be promoted to higher positions in the party—'only he can become local branch leader who has most taken to heart the meaning and aims of the movement, and the ablest *Gau* leaders will come from those local leaders who are true to their convictions'. In repeating that the seat of the movement would remain in Munich—'all the more as it is here we are opposed most fiercely'—Hitler announced the opening of new party headquarters in the Schelling-strasse in Schwabing, the cost being met by contributions from all members of the party, who would be obliged to buy 'bricks'.[4] Hitler revealed the bitterness he felt towards the Bavarian Government, for the measures it had taken to restrict his activities, when he remarked that the party now had more supporters in the former 'red' states of Saxony and Thuringia than in 'nationally-minded' Bavaria; the liberation of Germany by the Nazi movement would come from the North German seaboard (the *Wasserkante*) and no longer from Bavaria. The meeting closed after the branch leaders had, like a body of retainers, sworn an oath of loyalty to Hitler in which they pledged that 'their entire strength and their entire will belong from now on to the National Socialist work of salvation—nothing for ourselves, everything for the Fatherland' (*25*).

Hitler was able to re-establish his authority over the party in Bavaria in 1925 with relative ease because of the proximity of party headquarters in Munich, which allowed more direct supervision of local branches, and because party organization before the Putsch had its strongest roots in Bavaria, especially in the 'traditional Gau' of Munich–Upper Bavaria; while on the ideological level there was little interest in the 'socialist' ideas proposed by North German party leaders, which Hitler saw as a challenge to his authority. The reason for this ideological conservatism was the predominantly conservative bourgeois background of local party leaders and workers, in so far as their background can be ascertained from the local membership lists which survive.

Several lists dating from the end of 1924 and the beginning of 1925 remain

4. The headquarters were first housed after the NSDAP was refounded in the building of the party's publishing firm, the Eher Verlag, in the Thierschstrasse.

for a number of small towns in Upper Bavaria.⁵ The district organization for Northern Upper Bavaria of the *Völkischer Block* late in 1924 consisted of fifteen branches in such towns as Ingolstadt, Erding, Dachau, Neuburg an der Donau and Pfaffenhofen. The occupations of the branch leaders included two doctors, a few civil servants, one ex-Army officer, a publisher, a chemist, a factory owner, an architect and an innkeeper. Not one of them followed an occupation which could in any conceivable way be called working-class. At the same time, the four local branches of Berchtesgaden, Traunstein, Brannenburg and Freilassing in the south-eastern corner of Bavaria, near the Austrian border, consisted in total of 188 members. The largest group (thirty) was government employees (especially of the post office and the railways), then twenty-three tradesmen, followed by a variety of occupations such as engineers and craftsmen (for example clockmakers and shoemakers). The party even attracted a professor and a student in these remoter parts of the country. This reservoir of support for Hitler could hardly be called a group on the fringes of society. Similarly, the thirteen members which refounded the branch at Starnberg early in 1925 consisted of two civil servants (one of them was branch leader), a lawyer, a mason, a commercial pilot, an innkeeper, the owner of a cigar-shop, a school-master, a professor, a gauger, an interior decorator, a master plumber and a master bookbinder.⁶

There is no evidence to suggest that the predominance of the small-town bourgeoisie in these groups was very untypical of the NSDAP in Bavaria at the time of its refounding. Even the strongest party branch in the city of Munich, that of Schwabing, consisted a year later of 494 members with a preponderance of white-collar workers.⁷ Broadly, it may be said that the membership of the NSDAP reflected the non-industrial character of Bavarian urban society then. One important social group, however—the peasantry—was missing in the ranks of the Nazi movement in 1925.

The social background of party members in Bavaria does much to explain their general lack of interest in the 'socialism' embodied in the party programme of 1920, although there had been some evidence of the contrary in the attempts by the GVG in Nuremberg to win the support of the workers

---

5. These are to be found in the NSDAP archives (HA 4/88).
6. Two-and-a-half years later, in June 1927, the membership of the Starnberg branch had increased to thirty-three but was of similar social composition, not surprising in this well-to-do residential town on Lake Starnberg just outside Munich (Franz Buchner, *Kamerad! Halt aus! Aus der Geschichte des Kreises Starnberg der NSDAP*, (1938), pp. 35–6, 159–60).
7. The membership of the Schwabing branch in January 1926 included 158 civil servants and white-collar employees, 73 self-employed tradesmen, 36 industrial workers and craftsmen, 22 from the liberal professions, 17 students, 95 housewives, 25 pensioners, 7 without an occupation and 61 whose occupation was unknown (HA 8/182). Women were apparently not so commonly found as NSDAP members in the provinces.

(see chapter 2, p. 29). Bavarian Nazis seemed content with the staple diet of anti-semitism, anti-Communism and nationalism. There was also no great pressure on the party in the South to compete with the left-wing parties for the allegiance of a strong industrial working class, because it did not exist there.

By contrast, party leaders in Northern Germany, concerned more with the problems of making their appeal in the large cities, had reason to take the 'socialist' element in National Socialism more seriously. In August 1925, many of them formed the Working Association of the North and West *Gaue* to press for greater emphasis on radical social aims within the party. But the conflict which began to develop between the Northern leaders and the national leadership was far from being mainly ideological. It involved a clash of personalities as well as policies, for some Bavarian leaders like Esser and Streicher were very unpopular among Nazi circles in the North; and it also expressed resentment at the efforts of the headquarters in the South to establish a centralized control over the activities of the party throughout the country. What followed was more a crisis about the meaning of National Socialism and an outburst of frustration over differences of opinion with Munich and the 'bureaucratic' methods of party officials there; it was not in fact a challenge to the leadership of Hitler, who remained the common focus of loyalty within the NSDAP. But Hitler chose to see it as a challenge to his principle of absolute leadership. He used the loyalty to himself, which remained among the Northern leaders, to break the back of their revolt and called a conference of *Gau* leaders at Bamberg in February 1926, which fully endorsed the policies of the headquarters in Munich.[8]

Not surprisingly, Hitler had chosen to fill the important posts at the Munich headquarters with Bavarians, who preferably had sided with the GVG during the troubles of 1924. Max Amann, who remained as head of the party publishing firm, was now active in Munich politics as a town councillor and had been a prominent member of the GVG. Another former GVG leader was Franz Xaver Schwarz, appointed party treasurer in March 1925, who had worked for a long time as an accountant in the Munich city hall. The crucial post of party business manager, who supervised the organization of the NSDAP, went to Philipp Bouhler, a young man of twenty-six, Munich-born and a former Army officer. All three could be typified as bureaucrats by nature rather than party leaders with any charismatic appeal of their own, and as such were the ideal subordinates for Hitler. According to Albert Krebs, later *Gau* leader in Hamburg, Bouhler was ' by nature not a fighter but a civil

8. For a full account of the activities of the Working Association of the North and West *Gaue* see Jeremy Noakes, *The Nazi Party in Lower Saxony, 1921–1933*, chapter 4; also, Joseph Nyomarkay, *Charisma and Factionalism in the Nazi Party*, chapter 6.

servant, who adhered to directives, went by the rule-book and had a respect for superior authorities'. With his taciturn manner he revealed no ambitions of his own and declined to become involved in the intrigues of the party cliques. Krebs said ironically that Bouhler was 'a perfect administrator, whose ambition was to become one day a completely secret privy councillor' (26). The other important official at headquarters did not fit into this category. Hermann Esser, who was now propaganda leader of the refounded NSDAP, was also a young man—he was born at Röhrmoos near Munich in 1900—who had made a name for himself as a rabid demagogue and a violent anti-semite. By occupation a journalist, Esser had formerly been a Social Democrat who changed his political colours through the experience of the Munich Soviet Republic of 1919 and soon after joined the NSDAP to become one of Hitler's early associates. According to Ludecke, he 'had a feeling for local politics and a special flair for scandals and corruptions, which he would denounce from the tribune with righteous though happy indignation; for some time he paved the way for Hitler's orations by raising the crowd's pulse to the proper pitch' (27). Clearly, Esser looked up to Hitler as his idol, for even Goebbels described him as 'a smart pocket-size Hitler' aping the mannerisms of his model (28). This suited Hitler except that Esser proved incapable by temperament of being a reliable administrator—he was relieved of his post as propaganda leader in 1926—and marred his chances of promotion in the party hierarchy through his capacity for making numerous enemies. Julius Streicher, the other prominent leader of the GVG, was never given a position at headquarters simply because Hitler needed him for his work as *Gau* leader in Franconia. As the high priest of anti-semitism in the Nazi movement, Streicher operated best in the setting of Nuremberg politics.

Two major tasks faced Bouhler in his work of reorganizing the NSDAP: securing the subordination of local branches to party headquarters in Munich in accordance with the principles outlined by Hitler in *Mein Kampf* and the *Völkischer Beobachter* on 26 February, and rekindling enthusiasm among party workers.

At the end of May 1925 Bouhler wrote to local branch leaders urging them to make haste: 'all local groups must set about their activities in the most lively manner with all their strength and energy; the slack attitude which has prevailed till now must give way to an increasingly new victory-conscious National Socialism'. Each branch should hold at least one public meeting and had until 5 June to submit an exact list of its members, a statement of its accounts and a plan of its activities to headquarters. Any branch which did not comply would be expelled from the party for 'party headquarters expects from each single person the strictest fulfilment of duty, as only in this way can the movement reach that level which will guarantee victory'. Above all, each branch should do its best to advertise the party newspaper by displaying it publicly on a notice-board or in the front-window of a bookshop (29). Propaganda material would be issued by headquarters or at least had to be vetted there. Bouhler supplemented his general memorandum with special instructions to those local leaders who were busy refounding branches and enclosed confidential directions on the method to be employed there (30). Branch leaders were required to send Munich regular reports giving details of all political activities in their localities as well as meetings arranged by the party. All available local newspapers were to be examined carefully for important articles to be cut out and sent to the editorial office of the *Völkischer Beobachter*, which should also be notified of any noteworthy events in the area. Reports on the organization of local NSDAP branches should be counter-signed by the branch leader or *Gau* leader appointed by Munich to prevent 'misunderstandings and attempts to confuse by intriguers and those malic-iously inclined' (31).

Control over the issue of membership cards was one of the more effective ways of ensuring that local groups remained loyal to Munich. At the begin-ning of 1925 all previous membership cards were cancelled, which meant that even the longest-serving members had to re-apply for membership. In this way, headquarters hoped to vet every applicant and exclude those who had a record of insubordination or opposition. This measure brought to the surface much resentment against the bureaucratic attitude of party officials in Munich, especially in Southern Bavaria where many party workers had been in the NSDAP since its early days. Karl Wahl, later *Gau* leader in Swabia and then branch leader in Augsburg, expressed his ill-feeling on the subject:

> Former membership cards have lost their validity. Those who have lived near Munich or had good relations with the party central office received the lowest membership numbers. Later many would boast about their low membership numbers, which I found ridiculous. I had for example a number round about 9,000, not because I joined later but because the Augsburg enrolments were dealt with only later (32).

Wahl had joined the NSDAP in 1921, the year after the branch was founded in Augsburg, and like many early Nazis had felt a curious pride in possessing a membership card with a low number, like a badge of those 'old fighters' who had committed themselves to the movement before it began to attract mass appeal. Applications for membership cards had to follow a strict pro-cedure, so it was not surprising there were frequent bottlenecks in the administration especially in view of the lack of sufficient staff at headquarters to deal with the rush of applications in a speedy manner. The branch at Starnberg received the following communication from Bouhler's staff:

Dear party comrade
Unfortunately the completion of the notification forms has for technical reasons been delayed until today. We are then letting you have immediately forty copies and request that they be filled in legibly and then collected and sent back to the office. When the notification forms have been received, the membership cards will then be issued from here and sent to the local group (*33*).

Bouhler's rigid methods alienated many in the party, who were discouraged from re-applying for membership, so that in June Hitler felt it necessary to repeat his order that all those members or groups who supported the NSDAP should get in touch with headquarters. 'Only he can be a member of the NSDAP who has in his possession a membership card issued in Munich in the year 1925' (*34*).

Active branches were encouraged with the promise of a visit from Hitler, which always provided the greatest occasion any branch could hope for. Rudolf Hess, Hitler's private secretary, made it clear in a circular to branch leaders in September 1925 that 'meetings with Herr Hitler as speaker only come into question for those local groups which can already show a success, especially where the number of members is in a certain proportion to the size of the place; these local groups will if possible be supported by Herr Hitler with an address in the grand style; Herr Hitler is not a wandering propaganda speaker but the *Führer* of the movement' (*35*).

Hitler's appearances were usually restricted because of the speaking ban to meetings of party members and were not therefore made public or even advertised. Admission to a meeting in the Hercules Assembly Rooms in Nuremberg at the beginning of December was allowed only after a rigorous inspection of membership cards. In spite of this as many as 1,500 members were present. The evening began with a march played by the 'Imperial Eagle Band', followed by a procession carrying banners which were placed on both sides of the stage, already sumptuously bedecked with flowers. At a quarter past eight Streicher appeared and mounted the stage amid a chorus of *Heil* greetings. Then half an hour later, Hitler's impending arrival was made known to the impatient audience. The band immediately changed to a fanfare which greeted Hitler as he made his entry. The party members in the hall stood up from their places to shout in acclamation, while women present threw flowers at Hitler's feet. When order had been restored, Streicher opened the proceedings with a speech (*36*).

Hitler's remarks at these meetings were often extremely brief for fear that the police might interpret any long speech as a violation of the ban and use it as an excuse to impose further restrictions. Some meetings were even prohibited in advance. The police of Fürth, which had the strongest Jewish community of any of the larger towns in Bavaria, refused permission for the NSDAP to hold a rally there in September 1925 because it would coincide with the celebration of the Jewish New Year and would almost certainly lead to unpleasant scenes between Jews in festive dress and the thousands of Nazis expected to turn up for the occasion, to which Hitler was invited (*37*).

The work of organization had to keep pace with the gradual increase in membership. At the end of 1925 the Nuremberg police recorded that there were between 1,700 and 1,800 members in the city, including an increase of a hundred during November, with a rise in applications to join the party in other large towns like Bayreuth, Bamberg and Würzburg. The branch in Ansbach had recently acquired 300 new members and new branches were being opened in places like Uffenheim and Neustadt an der Aisch (*38*). Three months later, the same police reported that the increase in recruits to the NSDAP was continuing, except that the total membership in Northern Bavaria was nothing to compare with 1923 (*39*). The growth of membership meant a greater administrative load for the Munich headquarters. At the end of 1925 there were 27,117 enrolled members in the whole of Germany divided among 23 *Gaue* and 607 local branches. Saxony had the largest number of branches (88), followed by the *Gau* of the 'Bavarian *Ostmark*' with 57.[9] By 1928 the total membership of the party had climbed to 108,717 with 1,378 branches. Of these branches, 115 were in the 'Bavarian *Ostmark*', 36 in Franconia and 32 in Upper Bavaria (*40*).

Since it was those *Gaue* further away from Munich rather than in its vicinity—in Bavaria, the areas of Middle and Upper Franconia; in Germany altogether, the North and the North-East—which showed the highest rate of expansion in terms of membership, it was essential for headquarters to establish an effective chain of command, linking it with the branches, which would assure its overall control of party activities. In his circular to local branches of 20 March 1926 on organizing local propaganda cells, which helped to lay the groundwork for the propaganda machine which Goebbels

9. The *Gau* 'Bavarian *Ostmark*' (after 1933) consisted of Lower Bavaria, the Upper Palatinate and Upper Franconia, that is, those regions bordering on Czechoslovakia and Austria. The Nazis revived the Germanic term of *Ostmark* (Eastern Marches meaning Austria), implying that Austria was really part of Germany.

later developed, Bouhler pointed out that the NSDAP lacked the propaganda system of the other parties, which consisted of 'a network of cells spread over the whole Reich supplied from a control centre'. He argued that

> the first flush of enthusiasm among the masses for our idea cannot be maintained without a propaganda network which is constantly in operation, for it cannot otherwise be expected that the leaders of the young groups in our movement in the Reich will either know the viewpoint of the party leadership or be financially in a position to finance the enlightenment of the public, when political situations occur which can be exploited by agitation.

Bouhler outlined his plan as follows: each local branch in the whole country should at once form a propaganda cell as a committee of the branch, consisting of two-thirds male and one-third female party members; the head of this committee had until 25 March to inform the propaganda department at headquarters of the formation of the cell; those members should be preferred for the committee who 'are possessed by a fanatical burning enthusiasm for our movement' and attention should be given to the composition of the committee which should be representative of different occupations; the propaganda cells should not operate through the *Gau* offices but maintain direct contact with the central propaganda department of the *Völkischer Beobachter* in Munich, which would supply pamphlet material on the orders of headquarters; and once the head of the propaganda cell had announced its formation, he would receive guidelines on propaganda activities for the coming weeks (*41*).

In May 1926 a revised set of party statutes (necessary for the registration of the NSDAP as a legal association) were adopted at a meeting of party leaders in Munich, reaffirming Hitler's supreme authority over the party machine. Hitler made a speech laying the blame for the earlier divisions of the party on democratic methods of decision making. The statutes stated that:

> The association consists in first place of local groups, which are subordinate to party headquarters. As the need arises these local groups will be combined in *Gau* units. The *Gau* leaders are appointed by the Reich leadership. Further sub-organizations are created where necessary by the local group leaders or even the *Gau* leaders. These do not have a statutory importance. The Reich leadership work only with local groups and *Gaue*. In order to make possible decisive leadership of the movement,

the chairman of the association, respectively of the party, is above all responsible for the leadership of the association (42).

The headquarters consisted of the chairman, the secretary, the treasurer, the chairmen of the sub-committees and the business manager. The wording of the 1926 statutes, which differed little in substance from the original statutes of 1921 reaffirmed by Hitler in 1925, reinforced Hitler's dominant position in the party hierarchy. His decisions as party chairman were subject only to the approval of a general assembly, which at the most was a theoretical limitation on his powers as he was responsible for calling this meeting, which in practice was a formal gathering of the members of the Munich branch. The statutes, like those of 1925, declared the party programme of 1920 'unalterable' and devoted much space to the question of the expulsion of party members. A person qualified for membership of the NSDAP if he was an 'irreproachable member of the German people, who has completed his eighteenth year and is of pure Aryan descent'. Section four listed grounds for expulsion from the party, including opposition to the endeavours of the party, immoral behaviour and the provocation of disputes within the party.

The formal structure of the Nazi Party was further amplified in 1926 by a series of directives outlining the functions of the SA. The SA had been in broad terms the military branch of the party, which had threatened to become an independent branch of its own within the movement, especially during Roehm's attempt to revive the SA in the form of the *Frontbann* during the period of the party's ban in 1924. Hitler had now found a new SA leader in Captain Franz von Pfeffer, who proved willing to accept Hitler's dictates concerning the role of the SA in the Nazi movement. Hitler presented his conditions for von Pfeffer's appointment in a letter to the latter on 1 November 1926:

The formation of the SA does not follow a military standpoint but what is expedient to the party. In so far as its members are trained physically the emphasis should not be on military exercises but sporting activities. Boxing and ju-jitsu have always seemed more important to me than any bad, semi-training in shooting ... What we need are not one or two hundred daring conspirators but a hundred thousand, indeed a hundred thousand fighters for our ideology. The work should be carried on not in secret conventicles but in mighty mass processions; not through the dagger and poison or the pistol can the way be opened for the movement but through the conquest of the streets. We have to teach Marxism that the future master of the streets is National Socialism just as one day it will be the master of the state (*43*).

The SA statutes of September 1926 (with modifications introduced in the May 1927 version) elaborated many of these points. 'The SA is not a military association, for the military training of the nation is the task of the Army and not the NSDAP . . . the weapon of the National Socialist, and especially of the SA man, is a healthy fist and love for the fatherland in his heart.' The SA should set an example of discipline in public for 'those who indulge in violent excesses do not belong in the SA and bad drinking habits will not be tolerated'. The tasks of the SA were to provide stewards at mass meetings of the party, to protect party members on the streets against the 'Red terror' and to do propaganda work in factories and workplaces as well as selling newspapers in Communist town districts and the distribution of leaflets. The Chief SA Leader was appointed by party headquarters and all his orders had to receive the countersignature of the party chairman. The SA was sub-divided into three departments: the men's department, women's department and the youth section. The proper activity of the SA woman was the traditional conservative one of caring for the needs of the men by making flags, caps and shirts, looking after impoverished party members and distributing presents at Christmas. The SA youth in his training as part of the 'pure free German race' was required to abstain from all 'modern rottenness and decay along with Marxism, Liberalism and all other foreign Jewish filth' (*44*).

Several motives determined Hitler's attitude towards the SA: he wanted to eliminate a possible future threat to his absolute control over the party machine by making the SA fully dependent on the political leadership of the party; the existence of a semi-military organization within the movement, which had been a source of concern to the Bavarian Government at the beginning of 1925 and had influenced the decision to impose the speaking ban on Hitler, could provide the authorities with a valid reason for declaring a general ban on the NSDAP on the grounds that it was unconstitutional; and finally, Hitler needed the services of the SA to provide the impetus for the propaganda efforts of the party.

The second main problem facing the NSDAP in the mid-1920s was the inability of the party to make a wide popular appeal. A police report in April 1926 commented that the NSDAP was getting little return for all its feverish activity. It had held 2,370 mass meetings and 3,500 discussion evenings in the twelve months after it was refounded and produced literally millions of leaflets and other propaganda material, but 'the NSDAP has nowhere discarded its position as a radical right-wing splinter party and it is far from winning back in numbers or influence the position it had reached before the Hitler Putsch of 1923' (45). The prospects for the NSDAP had changed little by the summer of 1927, when a further police report summarized the state of the party as presenting 'itself as a radical revolutionary minority group, not considerable in numbers but strictly organized, very well disciplined and led by a uniform will, which cannot exert any noticeable influence on the masses of the population and on the course of political events' (46). There were several reasons for the NSDAP's failure to attract mass support: the appeal of the party was limited geographically; the scarcity of party finance reduced the scale of propaganda activities; and the effects of the lack of success on the morale of party workers.

The general point might be made that the political situation in the second half of the 1920s did not provide any major opportunities favourable to a radical party, whose professed aim was the destruction of the parliamentary system of the Weimar Republic. This was true in the sense that there was no economic–political crisis of the proportions of the early 1930s, but there were areas of discontent especially among the agricultural population—as the case of Bavaria shows—which the Nazis made little effort to exploit. In April 1926 the authorities had noted with surprise that 'although the past winter with the effects of the strong economic depression and its catastrophic increase in unemployment furnished the National Socialists with a par-ticularly favourable ground for their activities, the rise in supporters has re-mained relatively small' (47).

In general, this had to do with the fact that the NSDAP concentrated its propaganda on the cities, a policy supported firmly by the *Gau* leaders in Northern Germany where their organization was strongest in such places as Berlin, Chemnitz, Plauen, Elberfeld and other cities in the Ruhr as well as the industrial region of Thuringia (48). Party propaganda attempted to win over the working class from the Communists and Social Democrats and, under the influence of leaders like Gregor Strasser and Joseph Goebbels (who became *Gau* leader of Berlin late in 1926), took a strong anti-capitalist line. Urban propaganda retained priority until 1927, when the failure to make impressive inroads into the body of electors supporting the left-wing parties had become evident and confirmed Hitler's original doubts about this plan.[10] In Bavaria the plan for urban propaganda did not apply simply because there were no large urban industrial areas. The party organization was in any case strongest there in the two cities of Munich and Nuremberg but they hardly came into this category. In Munich roughly half of the working class were employed in

10. For a discussion of the NSDAP's plan for urban propaganda see Dietrich Orlow, *The History of the Nazi Party*, *Vol. 1*, *1919–1933*, chapter 4.

firms with less than fifty people. Nuremberg had a higher proportion engaged in heavy industry, especially in engineering and railway construction, but there still remained a large number of craft trades in spite of considerable industrialization since the end of the nineteenth century.[11] Party organizers in Bavaria had as yet shown little interest in winning the support of the rural electorate. The district of Münchberg in Upper Franconia, in north-eastern Bavaria, explained the lack of success of the Nazis there by the fact that 'their supporters send out inexperienced youths with a doubtful past who arouse no respect especially among the rural population' (49).

Some Nazi leaders were aware of the possibilities of propaganda among the predominantly agricultural community of Bavaria. Adolf Wagner, *Gau* leader in the rural area of the Upper Palatinate, said in a speech in Regensburg in April 1926 that 'we will start a campaign among the peasants here and above all in the country outside; we will say to the peasants how deplorably they are treated and how the financial authorities are trying to cut their throats' (50). Streicher more than any other party leader in Bavaria then cultivated peasant audiences and made frequent visits to rural communities in the neighbourhood of Nuremberg. He had made a name for himself through his sensation-seeking articles in *Der Stürmer*, which provoked many legal actions from those he attacked including Catholic priests, local Nuremberg officials and even a minister in the Bavarian state government. Streicher was already famous through his much-publicized clashes with the mayor of Nuremberg, leading in one case to a violent exchange of insults between the two men and an outbreak of disorder in the chamber of the city council. The same evening Streicher had held a public protest meeting which had brought out a crowd of 2,500. Streicher had then related in glossy detail the proceedings of the city council to the excited audience (51). Consequently, Streicher was much in demand as a public speaker in Middle Franconia and even further afield. In April 1926 he received an invitation to speak from the NSDAP branch in Amberg, sixty miles to the east of Nuremberg. The local party was facing difficulties with opposition from trade unionists, who were preventing people from attending Nazi meetings, and because people in the Upper Palatinate were 'stubborn and incapable of enthusiasm'. Amberg was a stronghold of the Catholic Bavarian People's Party. The branch leader pleaded with Streicher to come: 'Only you are in a position to break the ice here in Amberg and spur us on forwards; as we have read in the *Beobachter*

11. In 1925 21 per cent of Nuremberg's working population were still employed in enterprises with less than six people (Robin Lenman, *Julius Streicher and the Origins of the NSDAP in Nuremberg*, in A. Nicholls and E. Matthias, *German Democracy and the Triumph of Hitler*, p. 139).

and the *Stürmer*, you have recently spoken in even smaller towns than Amberg' (52).

Streicher's speeches around the countryside attempted to encourage resentment against the tax-collector as the representative of the state, which did not have the interests of the peasant class at heart. Addressing an audience of some 400 at Ansbach in 1927 Streicher bewailed the fate of the peasants:

> The German peasantry is today forced to send its sons to the town because they do not have the chance of obtaining land, and the property of the parents cannot supply it; in the towns they share the misery of the working masses; the peasantry is without a fatherland; German land is sold and mortgaged to the International Jewish controlling power; today the peasant no longer possesses his own corn for he must pay four-fifths of his income in taxes, and woe betide him who does not pay, for then the bailiff comes (53).

Part of the secret of Streicher's success with his peasant audiences was his simplistic manner of speaking. The following remarks made in a speech in Nuremberg in June 1926 are an example of the Nazi *kitsch* of which Streicher was a past master:

> A swarm of bees which is without a queen perishes if a new queen is not created within three days; this is exactly the case with the state; a state without a king must perish; today, Germany has no longer a king and must perish because the Jew will see to that; the NSDAP and its leaders want to make a clean sweep of this society, so that either a king or a president rises to the summit of the German people . . . (54).

Streicher's brand of anti-semitism also went down well during his speaking trips round the country. Streicher's number two in the Nuremberg party organization, Karl Holz, also toured the surrounding areas.[12] Early in 1926 Holz painted a grim picture of the machinations of the Jewish cattle-traders

12. Karl Holz, born in Nuremberg in 1895, was Streicher's right-hand man. He had organized the Fürth branch of the GVG in 1924, and the same year had been elected a deputy of the Nuremberg city council with Streicher. Holz had a reputation for aggressive public behaviour and 'uncouth ways of expressing himself', and in 1925 was relieved of his post as a local civil servant by the city authorities. He was an extreme anti-semite and shared the job of chief editor of *Der Stürmer* with Streicher. The reason for this arrangement was the frequent legal cases brought against the paper, usually involving one of the two men in court appearances and sometimes prison sentences.

to an audience at Beilngries, drawn from surrounding communities. These 'bloodsuckers', he called them, were offering absurdly low prices for the livestock of the peasants. Holz had ready at hand the story of a Jewish cattle-trader called Einstein from a local village who had become a millionaire and 'not through work'. Holz went on: 'in the Jewish secret laws it is laid down that Jews should deceive non-Jews; Christian maidservants are to be kept in Jew houses so that fornication may be carried on with them' (55). Holz's remarks were designed to appeal to the peasant's religious feelings and sense of uprightness as well as his economic interests.

This kind of propaganda was not at this time typical of the NSDAP in Bavaria; it was left to a few activists like Streicher and Holz. The party in Bavaria during 1926–27 did not have much of a network of local branches outside the two main cities of Munich and Nuremberg, the major provincial towns and a few isolated communities. The first branches to be founded in Franconia in 1925 were in Nuremberg, Erlangen, Fürth, Würzburg, Bamberg, Amberg and Schwandorf—all larger towns by Bavarian standards (56).

Another reason for this restriction on party activities in the remoter parts of the country—in fact, the third principal reason for the difficulties the NSDAP was facing—was the lack of finance. Hitler later admitted this at a meeting of party leaders in Munich in July 1927:

> How difficult it was . . . to lift the movement out of the era of complete disorganization in 1924, and beyond 1925, to that state of absolute discipline, as we all recall . . . I have deliberately related to you how at the beginning, when this movement was newly founded, obligations were everywhere badly honoured and how gradually circumstances improved so that today practically twenty of the twenty-five *Gaue* have a completely tidy and orderly financial administration (57).

Propaganda was costly, involving the production and distribution of vast quantities of printed material and the cost of hiring public halls for the frequent meetings which branches were required to hold. The NSDAP indulged in a degree of propaganda activities quite out of proportion to its size and importance compared with the other parties of the time. There was also the upkeep of the new headquarters in the Schellingstrasse in addition to the cost of maintaining a more elaborate party machine. According to a police source, the party's income during the year 1926 was only 13,000 Reichmarks, an amount totally inadequate to meet the demands on outlay from the vast administrative and propaganda system of the party (58). There were three possible sources of income for the NSDAP: admission fees and collections from public meetings; the profits made by the party newspaper, the *Völkischer Beobachter*; and party membership dues. All three sources proved insufficient.

The income from mass meetings suffered heavily as a direct result of the speaking ban on Hitler. Since Hitler attracted the largest crowds of any of the Nazi speakers, the collections made at his meetings had always been profitable. Many people had come out of curiosity to hear him; they helped to swell the crowds at these meetings to the thousands, even in smaller towns in the provinces. These occasions ceased during the two years which the speaking ban lasted in Bavaria. Hitler discouraged such mass rallies with other Nazi leaders, presumably because he feared the possible emergence of a rival leader as the NSDAP's main public attraction.

The frustration caused by the speaking ban is evident from the attention given to it by the propaganda department in Munich, which frequently urged local branches in Bavaria to attack the ban at their meetings. In March 1926, Bouhler sent out instructions proclaiming that ' we will now turn the tables, and the speaking ban on Adolf Hitler offers us the biggest subject for agitation by our movement' (*59*). Various attempts were made to remedy the situation— by raising the entrance charges at public meetings (which in the end only reduced the size of audiences), by announcing special contributions from party members and even by efforts to evade the speaking ban itself. These attempts were nearly always unsuccessful as the authorities were keeping a wary eye on the activities of the NSDAP, as is clear from the regular police situation reports to the State Ministry of the Interior during these years. On one occasion the Munich branch arranged for two meetings, to which certain wealthy people were invited as their sympathies with the Nazis might lead them to support the party financially. The meetings were really public but were described on the invitation cards as ' meetings of confidants of the NSDAP' and 'closed meetings of friends of the NSDAP'. The cards also indicated in smaller type that Hitler would be present at both functions, but the Munich police were quick to spot the loophole and banned both meetings (*60*). In September 1925 the Ministry of the Interior went further and prohibited collections at public meetings of the party. In reply, party organizers devised the method of selling picture postcards of Hitler at meetings for twenty-five pfennigs apiece. Collection bags would be surreptitiously passed round the audience. Postcards with Hitler's own signature on them went for two marks each (*61*).

The *Völkischer Beobachter* hardly made up for the loss of income from public meetings in spite of the frequent exhortations from party headquarters to boost its sales. In March 1925 the propaganda department sent a circular to all local branches urging them to cooperate in a campaign in favour of the newspaper. The *Führer*, it said, was of the opinion that only he was an 'absolutely reliable National Socialist' who 'awaits his daily combat newspaper with visible tension, devours its spirit and helps its distribution with all means'. The prize for the branch with the highest number of subscribers was a leather-bound 'luxury copy' of *Mein Kampf*, with a dedication from Hitler himself and a public commendation from Hitler in the *Völkischer Beobachter*. The ten next best branches would each receive a free 'people's edition' of the same book with a dedication plus autographed pictures of Hitler for distribution among the local members. Furthermore, Hitler promised to give a preference to these branches in his list of speaking engagements (62).

The ban on the newspaper had been lifted at the same time as the ban on the party in February 1925. Its circulation in May 1925 was only about 14,000, half of which was accounted for by Bavaria. It was becoming clear that the paper was not paying its way and matters reached the point where it could not even meet the demands of the printers (63). Bouhler's memorandum in May warned local leaders that 'in future it should not happen again that local groups with sixty and more members receive barely three copies of the *Beobachter*', but the effort to make the *VB* into a more profitable concern met with no success. The editorial office did its utmost to stamp out competition from other party newspapers; it was decided at the party rally in 1927 that provincial Nazi publications could only appear with the explicit permission of headquarters. Late in 1926 three members of the editorial staff were dismissed for refusing to sign an agreement not to write for other newspapers, not to use material for private purposes and not to communicate information to other party newspapers (64). All the same, the circulation of the *Völkischer Beobachter* hardly increased at a rate to justify this strict control of the Nazi press.

The same general loss of interest among members in the activities of the NSDAP, which had explained their failure to respond to the promptings of headquarters, also accounted for the substantial arrears in the payment of membership fees. This was a major problem for the party treasury, which is obvious from the frequent demands, even from Hitler himself, that party members should pay up. The Munich police noted in May 1925 that 'not much weight is attached to membership fees as it is common knowledge that party members are negligent in their payments' (65). Headquarters demanded regular statements of their accounts from local branches, and now and then warnings like the following would be inserted in the party newspaper: 'A man by the name of Hasenklever has collected money for enrolment subscriptions for the NSDAP in the area of Dachau and has made off with it; everyone should be warned of him! Enrolment subscriptions and

61

membership fees should be given only to headquarters or the local leaders' (66). Franz Xaver Schwarz, the party treasurer, felt it necessary to make an urgent request to all *Gau* and branch leaders in June 1925 for the prompt payment of outstanding fees 'in the interests of regulated auditing and book-keeping and punctual accounting' (67). Schwarz considered the state of party finances so desperate that members behindhand in their payment of fees were threatened in November 1926 with expulsion from the party. This would affect 150 members in Munich alone. The same month Schwarz issued a circular for a special contribution of one mark per member to be raised to pay for the forthcoming state elections in Saxony (68).

A measure of the apathy affecting party workers was the condition of the Schwabing branch, the most active and the largest in Munich. Meetings in the Bürgerbräukeller continued to attract large crowds when speakers like Streicher, Esser and Buttmann were on the bill, but the number of Nazi public meetings in the city generally declined sharply. The authorities noticed that 'among party supporters a considerable weariness has set in, which seems all the easier to understand as party life has become extremely monotonous over some months' (69). By the autumn of 1925, most local branches in the city had ceased to play an active role except the Schwabing branch, which still had a regular attendance of 300 at its meetings (70). The branch owed much to its energetic leader, Ernst Woltereck, whose ambitions brought him so much into conflict with headquarters that Hitler removed him from his post in the summer of 1926 for 'insubordination'. The new branch leader was Karl Fiehler, a Nazi city councillor. Fiehler took considerable pains to put the branch in some financial shape. His report on the Schwabing branch for the year 1927 recorded the admission of forty-five new members and the resignation of seventy-eight old members, an overall loss of thirty-three. Membership at the end of the year stood at 526. Income for the year had been 1,600 marks, expenditure 1,350 marks, making a surplus of 250 marks. Expenditure included 460 marks involving extra building costs for the party headquarters (71).

This state of affairs produced a vicious circle. Apathy in the party ranks led to lack of success in winning public support, which in turn produced a further lack of interest and increasing frustration. Restlessness developed among the Munich SA centring on the restrictions imposed on their activities by the shortage of party funds and the wish of the political leaders not to provoke the authorities. On the evening of 25 October 1927 there was a meeting of all SA leaders in the city. Seidenschwang, the SA leader in Munich, announced that the plan for a general SA rally on 6 November would have to be dropped for financial reasons. The same evening section leaders in the city met Himmler in party headquarters to discuss the programme of activities for November. They complained bitterly about the low attendance at meetings to Himmler, who replied painting the blackest picture of the state of party finances. 'The party is not in the position to provide money for propaganda purposes as other parties do' (72). Feeling was now running high in the SA. A further meeting of Munich SA leaders took place on 8 November, the fourth anniversary of the Putsch of 1923. Major Buch, the commander of the whole SA in Bavaria, felt his presence was necessary. The atmosphere at the meeting was one of commotion. All troop leaders who spoke were sharply critical of party headquarters. They referred to party bureaucrats as 'cowards' who sat in their offices, put a brake on party activities and did not have the courage to organize a march on 6 and 9 November (73).

The crisis in the Munich SA seemed to be coming to a head. Hitler, afraid lest the SA resort to violence out of protest, decided at this juncture to intervene in person and use his magic *Führer* appeal on his intractable followers. He announced that he would himself take the Munich SA in hand and spend a whole evening with them. More funds would not be available for the SA but Hitler assured them through a message delivered at a meeting of their leaders that 'his whole heart is with the SA; he was a soldier, is a soldier and will remain a soldier and should he sooner or later take a prominent position in the Reich, then he will still be a soldier and personally fight the enemy with a weapon in his hand if there is a shortage of manpower'. He asked troop leaders to be patient for the time being and not give the police an excuse for issuing a prohibition (74). Hitler's declaration of solidarity with the most activist element in the Munich party and his appeal for loyalty had the desired effect in bringing an end to the mood of rebelliousness, for this had been aimed not at Hitler in person but at the general situation facing the party and the absence of rewards for the time and energy spent by the SA in the service of party propaganda.

The Nazi Party in Bavaria had reached a state of stagnation for three main reasons: difficulties in party organization, especially the limited scope of its activities; the lack of popular appeal; and the shortage of finance. It was these factors, rather than the absence of favourable circumstances, which explained the position in which the party found itself. In terms of its organization and membership, the NSDAP was still a fringe party on the Right, although one whose membership was steadily rising. But the NSDAP had not yet become a mass movement, although it had enjoyed some degree of mass sympathy during 1923–24. In the eyes of the public, the NSDAP seemed basically a party of protest for it was associated above all with the event of the Putsch. This preference for the *status quo* showed itself in the stability of the major parties in Bavaria.

The State of the Parties in Bavaria

If political and economic circumstances were generally not favourable to the NSDAP in the mid-1920s compared with the time of the Putsch and its aftermath, and if the state of party organization in the years following its refounding further inhibited its function as a potential movement of mass protest, the state of the major parties in Bavaria aligned against the NSDAP, especially those involved in the responsibility of government, must also be considered as a reason for the stagnation of support for the NSDAP. How stable were these parties and how vulnerable were they to loss of support to a movement, which in Bavaria at least, combined an appeal to anti-Communism, nationalism and anti-semitism with the methods of popular agitation? The most important of these parties was the Bavarian People's Party (BVP), the principal party of government during the period under review and the political voice of Catholic interests.

The Bavarian People's Party was founded in the autumn of 1918 as an offshoot of the main Catholic party, the Centre Party, by Georg Heim, the Bavarian peasants' leader, and former leaders of the Bavarian branch of the Centre Party. The formation of a separate Bavarian confessional party arose from a concern in Bavaria at centralist tendencies in the early Weimar Republic associated with the apparently dominant role then played by the Social Democrats in the drafting of the constitution of the new republic.

The BVP had several main advantages as a political force in Bavaria: a largely Catholic electorate (unlike the Centre Party in the rest of Germany), the support of the Roman Catholic Church and the strength of Bavarian regional feeling. Taking into consideration the network of Catholic lay associations and the important part played by the local clergy in provincial and community life, it could be said that the sub-structure of Bavarian politics was clearly weighted in favour of the BVP.

In the Reichstag Election of December 1924 the BVP had, as the strongest party in the state, won one-third of the vote. Its nearest rivals, the SPD and the DNVP, owed much of their support to their high vote in the two regions of Middle and Upper Franconia, where the Catholic population was in a minority and consequently support for the BVP lower. In the five other regions the BVP was by far the strongest party, in two cases winning an absolute majority (the Upper Palatinate and Lower Franconia). The BVP owed its constant vote in both national and state elections, which remained at broadly one-third of the Bavarian electorate during the rest of the Weimar Republic even through the crisis years which preceded its final collapse, to the fact that it was first and foremost a pronouncedly Catholic party in what was the most solid Catholic state in the whole country.

The Bavarian People's Party advocated the application of Christian values in public life and emphasized its support for the traditional virtues of family life, the sanctity and indissolubility of marriage and religious instruction for children. At its inaugural meeting in the autumn of 1918 the leaders of the BVP had resolved to found 'a real people's party, which excluding any class character includes all levels of the Bavarian people on the basis of the Christian view of the state, furthers the idea of the fatherland by bringing in our brotherly comrades from German Austria, revives all sources of strength in the German character by restoring the German Reich according to federalist principles[13] and brings about a moral revival' (75). The BVP also maintained close links with the Christian Social Party in Austria and showed strong sympathy for a 'reunion' with Austria, which would of course strengthen the Catholic element in such an enlarged German Reich. In this way, the party could appeal aggressively both to Catholic interests and to German patriotism.

The support of the Church in Bavaria was undoubtedly the main reason for the consistent hold of the BVP over its voters (roughly one-half of the eligible Catholic voters in the state). The party had developed a more independent organization of its own since the inception of the Weimar Republic with structural units for the seven Bavarian administrative regions and the cities of Munich, Augsburg and Nuremberg, each of which was subdivided into district and local associations. The BVP also boasted a network of newspapers such as the *Bayerischer Kurier*, the principal organ of the BVP published in Munich, as well as the *Regensburger Anzeiger*, at one time edited by no less a person than Heinrich Held before he became Prime Minister, the *Augsburger Postzeitung* and the *Fränkisches Volksblatt* in Würzburg. All the same, it was the active as well as moral backing from the Church which really counted in elections, which traditionally in Germany took place on a Sunday. Local priests were usually the principal figures in Bavarian rural life and their influence on the community was certainly great, in view of the regular practice among village inhabitants of attending church. How far this influence affected political behaviour is difficult to measure directly, for it

---

13. The term 'federalist' was used in Weimar times in reference to the movement in Bavaria in particular for more independence in internal affairs for the federal states within the Reich. It opposed centralism in government but was not the same as the secessionist movement, which also existed in Bavaria as well as in the Rhineland.

depended partly on the readiness of local priests to advocate openly support for the Catholic party. Sometimes such influence could often work more effectively and subtly through pressures to conform in community life. It is a reasonable assumption that the solid support for the Bavarian People's Party at election time came above all from those Catholics who had strong and regular links with the Church as an institution and were therefore the most integrated members of the community. They were consequently less susceptible than other sections of the Bavarian electorate to emotional appeals from a radical mass movement. The other half of the Catholic electorate, which did not support the BVP, either gave its vote to the Bavarian Peasants' and Middle-Class League (BBMB), which was supported largely by Catholic peasants in Southern Bavaria, or consisted of more nominal than practising Catholics, who expressed their dissidence through non-voting or a preference for rival parties.

Some idea of the extent to which the Bavarian People's Party depended on the Church is provided by voting behaviour among Catholics in certain areas during the Presidential Election of 1925. Officially, the BVP refused to cooperate with the Centre Party in proposing Wilhelm Marx, the Centralist leader, and instead announced its support for Hindenburg, who as a Prussian field-marshal and landowner as well as a Protestant appeared the most unlikely candidate of a party which was both consciously Bavarian and Catholic. The BVP's unusual choice, which is generally credited with settling the election in Hindenburg's favour, had its origins in disagreements between the two Catholic parties, especially the BVP's antagonism towards the Centre Party's coalition with the Social Democrats. In the words of one *eminence grise* of the BVP, Dr von Pichler, the provost of Passau cathedral:

If I were to follow the dictates of my heart, I would give my vote to Marx; the decision must however be determined by a cool examination of judgement—what is this election all about? It is a question not of the personality of Dr Marx but of the Marx candidature linked to the coalition with the Social Democrats and Democrats, burdened with the moral obligations arising from the election of the Social Democratic Prime Minister of Prussia by the Centre Party of the Prussian state parliament (76).

Possibly, Hindenburg's conservative and monarchist image had some appeal in Bavaria, for Crown Prince Rupprecht, the head of the House of Wittelsbach and pretender to the Bavarian throne, made a public statement in his support.

The decision to ally with the Hindenburg forces was taken by an over-whelming majority of the BVP's executive committee, but it did not go without strong reservations among BVP supporters, who did not understand the failure to support Dr Marx who was known as a pious Catholic. In many instances in Upper Franconia, BVP supporters openly disobeyed the party directive and were encouraged by the local clergy to vote for Marx instead. A noteworthy case in point was the propaganda conducted on Marx's behalf by local priests in the district of Höchstadt an der Aisch contrary to in-structions from BVP headquarters. BVP supporters were ready to vote for Hindenburg as he appealed to their right-wing tendencies until the Catholic clergy came out in favour of Marx shortly before the election. On the eve of polling leaflets were distributed bearing the signature of 'the Clergy of Höchstadt an A.' and warning against voting for Hindenburg instead of Marx. Although Hindenburg won a majority of the votes in this district, support for Marx was high and could only be attributed to the influence of the Church (77). Similarly, the influence of the archbishopric of Bamberg was discernible in communities around neighbouring Lichtenfels, where acolytes were sent on errands to distribute election material in favour of Marx; while the vote in his favour varied from village to village in the district of Kronach, according to the efforts made on his behalf by the local clergy (78).

Generally, BVP supporters voted for Hindenburg in the 1925 Presidential Election, although there was a high abstention rate, presumably because many were confused by the contrary pressures of clergy and party; there was also a sufficiently high vote among the BVP electorate in favour of Marx to suggest that the influence of the Church on voting behaviour could be stronger than that of the Catholic party. The basic dependence of the Bavarian People's Party on the support of the Church could also make the party vulnerable in the event of the Church taking a different standpoint on a major political issue, as the ambiguous attitude of the Church to the NSDAP in the early 1930s and its acquiescent policy towards the new Nazi Government in the spring of 1933 was to show. Yet, the Church realized the importance of lending its full support to the BVP for Bavaria was the strongest Catholic state in Germany and, apart from Baden, the only one with a Catholic majority population. The Church therefore encouraged Bavarian regionalism as part of its policy of protecting Catholic interests in Germany. The Bav-arian envoy to the Holy See wrote in 1927 that 'the centralistic movement in Germany is making visible progress . . . the support which Catholic interests in the Reich have in Bavaria and its government is due exclusively to Bavaria's state independence' (79). A year later the envoy reported from Rome the view of the Pope that the maintenance of Bavaria's own statehood was of the

67

greatest importance to the Church and that the creation of a centralized German state would only be to its detriment (*80*).

Bavarian regional feeling was the third main pillar of support for the BVP. It was the federalist leanings of so many BVP politicians, which sometimes bordered on anti-Prussian hysteria, that marked them off from the leaders of the Centre Party. The BVP programme of November 1918 expressed a concern about the centralism of the Prussian Socialists by demanding that 'the far-reaching dependence of Bavaria hitherto on the too powerful North in political, economic and taxation matters must in all cases cease' (*81*). Although the BVP basically accepted the Weimar Constitution, it advocated constitutional reform along more federalist lines and in its Bamberg Programme of 1920 demanded the re-establishment of a Federal Council, the protection of the competences of the federal states and the execution of Reich laws by the state authorities. Federal states should also have the right to send representatives to foreign countries (*82*). Bavarian patriotism was exploited by the BVP at election time with such slogans as 'Bavaria for the Bavarians', and remained strong through the Weimar period. The question of Bavaria's position in the Reich was a sensitive issue for the Weimar Constitution had abolished certain powers and privileges previously enjoyed by the states.[14] The BVP's role as spokesman of Bavarian interests helped to solidify its popular support, for antagonism towards Berlin and Prussia was most evident in the Catholic regions which had formed the old pre-Napoleonic state of Bavaria, while federalism had less appeal in Franconia where loyalty to Bavaria had weaker roots.[15]

Regional feeling in Bavaria theoretically placed the Nazi Party in a quandary as it clearly preferred a strong central state. The party programme of 1920 demanded 'the creation of a strong central power of the state and unquestioned authority of the politically centralized parliament over the entire Reich and its organization'. It had of course suited Hitler's purpose to exploit Bavarian resentment against the national government in 1923, but at the same time he had expressed irritation in *Mein Kampf* with the BVP for

14. During the period of the Empire from German unification in 1871 to 1918, Bavaria had retained certain special privileges including control of her own finances, posts, railways and currency. The Bavarian Army, although part of the German armed forces, was still divided into the old Bavarian regiments with their distinctive Bavarian uniforms and with the Bavarian king as its peacetime Commander-in-Chief. The abolition of these privileges under the Weimar Republic, although of no great constitutional importance, was seen as a blow to Bavarian pride and patriotism.

15. Before the addition of the Franconian areas to the enlarged Kingdom of Bavaria early in the nineteenth century as a result of her alliance with the French in the Napoleonic Wars, Bavaria consisted of the regions of Upper Bavaria, Lower Bavaria and the Upper Palatinate, known as 'old Bavaria' (*Altbayern*), which were almost exclusively Catholic.

'its own narrow and particularist standpoint' and for using the federalist doctrine 'just as they use the name of religion, merely as a means of promoting their own base party interests' *(83)*. The Nazis chose for reasons of convenience not to antagonize regional susceptibilities in Bavaria, so Hitler's statements on the matter were usually ambiguous and sometimes contradictory. In March 1927 he went so far as declaring in an article in the *Völkischer Beobachter* that his solution of the question would have no place for either states or provinces but only for a 'Greater German national state', but later in the same year an editorial in the same newspaper said it did not matter if the 'November Republic' was federalistic or centralistic for it would still serve the interests of high finance and lead to the enslavement of Germany *(84)*.

The issue of Bavarian federalism came to a head late in 1928 over new measures introduced by the national government to standardize taxation. One proposal was to raise a tax on beer, a measure guaranteed to arouse Bavarian tempers. One deputy in the state parliament commented that 'the beer tax has exhausted the farmers' patience entirely and their wrath is being richly exploited by those who have an interest in revolt', while it was reported from Lower Bavaria that 'the proposed increase in the beer tax with the resulting increase in the price of beer is a lively topic of conversation everywhere and causes a fairly strong bitterness especially in rural circles, which see in it a new burden' *(85)*. The resulting public outcry in Bavaria could not be ignored by the Nazis, who joined the government parties in the state parliament in upholding the rights of the state and decided to participate in a large demonstration planned by the Bavarian Citizens' Council in Munich. The main Nazi speaker at the rally was the Bavarian patriotic figure of Ritter von Epp, who had recently joined the party. Goering also made a speech claiming that National Socialists fully supported Bavarian independence, but the impression left by the Nazi attempt at solidarity with the cause of federalism was weak. It was seen for what it was by the BVP and Social Democratic press, as an effort to ride the crest of the federalist wave in the hope of gathering popular support. Bavarian regional feeling in so far as this affected political behaviour was monopolized primarily by the Bavarian People's Party.

If the BVP was the most stable political force in Bavaria and as such was not very vulnerable to competition for popular support from the NSDAP, the Bavarian Peasants' and Middle-Class League (BBMB) presented the picture of an economic interest rather than 'ideological' party whose position was thereby more subject to shifts of support in time of crisis. It was not then threatened by the NSDAP, which had not yet developed a propaganda machine in the rural areas. The BBMB was the main spokesman of farming interests in the Catholic regions of the state, and was especially strong in Lower Bavaria and Swabia. Founded during the agricultural crisis of the 1890s, the BBMB offered a curious mixture of left-wing radicalism, Bavarian particularism and an emphasis on traditional values. Although the BBMB had a Catholic and Bavarian background—it stressed the virtues of the 'Christian family' as the 'foundation of human society' and supported a less centralist structure for the Reich—it was not a confessional party as such and did not enjoy the active backing of the Church, nor could it compete with the BVP as the spokesman of Bavarian regionalism. The BBMB's main concern was the defence of agricultural interests in Southern Bavaria. The party programme claimed that 'the roots of our national strength and revival lie in the middle class'[16] and urged that 'recognition of the value of the peasants' work' should be made in the form of better prices for agricultural produce and a more favourable taxation policy (86).

The BBMB remained true to its origins as basically a party of protest, although it was represented in the Bavarian Government from 1924 by one of its leaders, Dr Anton Fehr, who was Minister of Agriculture. Participation in the government led to greater friction between the moderate and radical wings of the party. The radical wing was led by Karl Gandorfer and Konrad Kübler, both of whom had played a prominent part in the left-wing revolutions in Bavaria of 1918–19. Gandorfer's brother Ludwig had as leader of the Peasants' League been an active supporter of Eisner but was killed in a car accident late in 1918. Karl Gandorfer took over the leadership of the Peasants' League, promoted the idea of peasant councils and became a member of the Central Council of the Soviet Republic. He was now mayor of Pfaffenberg and was largely responsible for making the BBMB the most active and best organized party in Lower Bavaria. Konrad Kübler had been People's Delegate for Justice in the Soviet Republic in Bavaria. He maintained close contacts with Moscow, participated in the World Congress of Peasants in Moscow in 1923 and was usually referred to as 'the Moscow pilgrim' in the BVP press. Kübler also concentrated his activities on Lower Bavaria and had an important influence on agricultural circles there through his newspaper, the *Landauer Volksblatt* (87).

Lower Bavaria was a stronghold of the BBMB because agrarian discontent

16. The term 'middle class' is a literal translation of the word *Mittelstand*, which usually referred to the lower middle class of shopkeepers, craftsmen, self-employed businessmen and sometimes civil servants. Some contemporary sociologists preferred to call these groups the 'old middle class' (*alter Mittelstand*) to distinguish them from the 'new middle class' of industrial and commercial white-collar workers. The use of the term in the present context is restricted, meaning the peasant class of the *Mittelstand*, as in the title of the party Bavarian Peasants' and Middle-Class League (BBMB).

was more marked there than elsewhere in Bavaria in the mid-1920s and the feeling of loyalty towards the Weimar Republic was not particularly strong. The end of inflation in 1924 did not benefit all sections of the population, least of all the peasants, who suffered from a structural depression in the industrialized German economy which had been aggravated by deficiencies imposed during the First World War. The return of financial stability brought an end to a brief agricultural boom, for the inflation of 1923–24 had made industrial goods cheaper in relation to agricultural prices. Increasing bitterness was noticeable, and complaints that peasants could not dispose of their produce became more common. There were frequent stories of younger peasants migrating to the towns and even abroad because of the diminishing prospects on the land.

This discontent provided fruitful ground for radical propaganda by the BBMB. The authorities regarded its leaders as dangerous revolutionaries and feared that the moderates in the party were capitulating to the extremists so that the BBMB was becoming a stalking-horse for the Communists. The extremists made the most noise and held frequent meetings which attracted large crowds. It is clear from the situation reports of 1925–26 that the authorities in Lower Bavaria were far more alarmed by the agitation of the Peasants' League than that of any other party including the NSDAP. They reported on Gandorfer and Kübler that

> their meetings usually bring out the masses and they are winning more and more support even among previously moderate circles . . . radicalization is proceeding in a way which threatens danger . . . this movement demands the most serious attention of all authorities, as it seems far more dangerous to the public order than the Free Peasants' Association, which has faded away, or even than the National Socialists, who, following the desertion of the large part of their supporters and the divisions among the remainder, are badly weakened for the foreseeable future (*88*).

Gandorfer's demagogic skill, the tone of the BBMB's radical propaganda and the threats of violence and terror strongly resembled the methods employed by the Nazis themselves, and inevitably the latter came to see the BBMB as their main rival for the support of the peasants in the Catholic rural areas of Bavaria. At this time, the BBMB was safe because there was little competition from the NSDAP, whose organization and propaganda was still concentrated in the towns and cities. The BBMB had won as much as 30 per cent of the vote in the rural districts of Swabia and Lower Bavaria in the Reichstag Election of December 1924, but it was potentially vulnerable to a mass movement, which had a more extensive organization and a superior propaganda machine at its disposal. The BBMB was less cohesive as a party than the BVP, and its own supporters compared with the latter's were less bound by party loyalty through a common ideology. The main determinant among BBMB voters was their interest in the land, and consequently they were more prone to vote for another more dynamic party, which promised greater satisfaction of their needs, in a time of economic crisis.

The situation of the parties in the Protestant regions of Franconia was somewhat different. Except in such Catholic enclaves as Eichstätt in Middle Franconia and Bamberg in Upper Franconia, the BVP was not nearly so strong as elsewhere in Bavaria while the vote for the BBMB was negligible in both regions. The two foremost parties here were the SPD and the conservative Nationalist Party (DNVP). The former as elsewhere in Germany proved generally resistant to the NSDAP and it lost support instead to the Communists. The NSDAP made little effort to attract working-class voters in Bavaria, except in a few towns like Nuremberg, a major stronghold of the Social Democrats in the state. Even here the working-class districts of the town showed little inclination to support the Nazi movement. The Nazis encountered extreme difficulties in establishing a branch in St Johannis, 'the reddest quarter of Nuremberg', with the hostility of the left-wing parties and 'dangers which individual party comrades had to suffer' (89).

The DNVP was potentially more vulnerable because it was more similar ideologically to the Bavarian NSDAP than any other major party in the state with its conservative, nationalist and anti-semitic sentiments; and because even the relatively independent Bavarian regional organization of the DNVP was affected by divisions within the party at the national level. The Bavarian DNVP had originally been founded in November 1918 as a separate organization known as the Bavarian Middle Party on the initiative of Franconian Protestant circles, including the Middle Franconian Peasants' Union, the Middle Class Association of Nuremberg and a number of agrarian and conservative groups. Its chairman was Hans Hilpert, a former supporter of the German Conservative Party and various anti-semitic organizations. The Bavarian Middle Party, which became the Bavarian branch of the DNVP in February 1920, was distinguished from the party on the national level by a greater emphasis on agrarian interests and its attention to Bavarian particularist views. In fact, the merger with the national party was delayed because of apprehension about possible reactions to this among particularist circles (90). The stronghold of the DNVP in Bavaria was the Protestant rural areas of Middle and Upper Franconia. It had won an absolute majority of the votes in seven of the seventeen rural districts of Middle Franconia in the Reichstag Election of December 1924, many of its voters coming from the *Völkischer Block*, which lost considerable support in this election mainly to the DNVP.

There was therefore a bloc of voters in Protestant Franconia, who would vote for either the DNVP or the NSDAP according to political and economic circumstances. They were quite capable of returning to the Nazi fold should these circumstances change. It was indicative of the position of the two rival parties then that while the DNVP represented the anti-Catholic element in Bavarian politics, the NSDAP still felt obliged to take into account Bavarian particularist feelings and to try and exploit Bavarian resentment against the Reich, although without its success in doing so in the autumn of 1923. The NSDAP still pretended to be on the side of Bavaria in her conflicts with the Reich authorities because the party's strongest electoral support still came from Bavaria, as shown in the Reichstag Election of 1928. But there was clearly no future for the Nazis in this role, for Bavarian particularism was the monopoly of the Bavarian People's Party. The position of the BVP seemed impregnable for it had the whole of the Bavarian Establishment on its side. The NSDAP had a better chance of success by concentrating on winning support from the non-confessional parties, for the BBMB and the DNVP did not possess the propaganda machine which the Nazis later developed.

The End of the Ban on Hitler's Public Speeches, 1927

The speaking ban on Hitler had remained a considerable source of resentment to the NSDAP. The Nazis had made numerous attempts to have the ban lifted since it was introduced in March 1925. Bouhler sent a memorandum to Munich party leaders in 1925 asking them to collect eye-witness reports from those members who had attended the meeting in the Bürgerbräukeller, at which the party had been refounded. Efforts to have the ban revoked through court action were unsuccessful.

Nazi propaganda had continued to attack the ban in the hope of winning sympathy supporters, but this could not alter the fact that the Nazis were deprived of their principal public speaker and an important source of income. Rudolf Buttmann, the leader of the NSDAP group in the Bavarian state parliament, had insisted that the Nazis had no intention of staging another putsch. The party press was more blatant and bitter. The *Völkischer Beobachter* called the ban a 'disgrace to Bavaria' and the result of 'Bavarian party dictatorship'. In April 1926 a special edition appeared outlining the 'people's protest against the speaking ban on Adolf Hitler' and asking 'why may the front-soldier Adolf Hitler not speak?' Hitler, the newspaper reminded its readers, had fought in forty-eight battles on the Western Front in the First World War and it even listed every one of these battles. This attempt to make Hitler into a patriotic martyr went so far as devising a poster showing Hitler's face with his mouth covered by a piece of sticking plaster marked 'speaking ban' with the caption 'he alone of 2,000 million people on earth may not speak in Germany'. The ban had continued to inhibit the party's propaganda activities for as late as February 1927 the authorities reported that the NSDAP was still suffering badly from the lack of money which had come from the well-attended Hitler meetings (91).

Early in 1927 negotiations were opened between government representatives and Buttmann for the NSDAP. The government agreed to raise the ban provided certain conditions were met. These included a guarantee by Buttmann that the NSDAP would not pursue illegal aims and would 'not employ illegal means for achieving its aims'; that the SA, SS or similar auxiliary organizations of the party would not transgress the law and would not concern themselves with military matters; that Hitler's first public meeting would take place outside Munich; that the Nazis recognized that the government would at all times take the necessary measures to maintain public order and security; and finally, that the government if need be could make use of Buttmann's declarations on these matters in public (92).

Hitler made his first public appearance at Vilsbiburg in Lower Bavaria on 6 March. The meeting was well attended. The authorities had supposedly thought that the excitement caused by Hitler's first public speech would be less if he made it in a provincial town, but as many as 4,500 turned up to hear Hitler at the Zirkus Krone in Munich three days later. He spoke on the 'wretched state of Germany'. For a long time, he said, there had been two main political groups in the country, the national bourgeoisie and the international proletariat. Centuries had passed without either achieving its aims. Both the 'workers of the mind' and the 'workers of the hand' were fighting each other. The country suffered most from this struggle, and the only solution was cooperation between both sides in National Socialism (93). Hitler studiously avoided any remarks which might provoke the police in this appeal for an end to class warfare. He made further speeches in Augsburg, Coburg and Nuremberg later in the month, where attendance was again large.

Having learnt his lesson with the authorities, Hitler took precautions to avoid repeating the same mistake. On the day of his meeting in Munich, he issued instructions to all party members and supporters warning them not to give the police any pretext for taking action on the grounds that they were causing a public disturbance. 'Those who harass police officials or try to stir up the masses are serving the enemies of our movement' and 'resistance to the forces of the state and their lawful regulations is forbidden in all circumstances'. Special care should be taken not to make any noise in the streets after the meeting as 'we will not win any sympathy through shouting and singing at a time when others are sleeping'. Members of the SA and SS should provide an example of discipline and order (94).

Hitler's emergence from his enforced silence at once gave him the opportunity to put new life into the sluggish state of party activities. He announced that he would fulfil most of his speaking engagements in the coming months in Bavaria, which he had neglected the previous two years, and that 90 per cent of the income from his public meetings would flow directly into party funds (95).

What motivated the Bavarian Government's decision to lift the ban on Hitler's public speeches after two years? The same ministers originally responsible for imposing the ban in the first place, on the assumption that Hitler's political aims and methods had not fundamentally changed since the Putsch of 1923, were still in office. It can be assumed that they now thought otherwise. The reasons for their change of mind are worth some comment as they throw interesting light on the attitude of the authorities towards Hitler and the Nazi movement, all the more as the Bavarian Government was not well disposed towards the Nazi leader and did not find it easy to come to the decision allowing Hitler the freedom to resume his full political activities.

The Bavarian Government had not been absolutely wholehearted about the speaking ban, and one detects a subtle change of view from the official records of ministerial meetings during 1925–26. In April 1925, Dr Gürtner, the DNVP Minister of Justice, had used the Presidential Election to repeat his opposition to the ban using the argument that the Communists were able to present the most dangerous speakers during the election while Hitler had to remain silent. Most other ministers then took the view that the lifting of the ban would be a mistake as Hitler would only misuse his freedom. 'Since Hitler has ceased appearing, there has been a sharp decline in interest in the movement' was the comment of Dr Matt, the Minister of Education (96). Generally, the security officials in the provinces were conscientious in seeing that the ban was observed. The Nazi leader in Rosenheim, for instance, was warned in July 1925 not to go ahead with plans for a reception of Hitler at the railway station, to be followed by a procession through the town, as this involved a 'public demonstration' although Hitler apparently did not intend to speak (97).

Later that year Stützel, the Minister of the Interior, felt it necessary to define the scope of the ban after some recent meetings, including one in Nuremberg, at which Hitler had spoken. Stützel maintained that the ban applied not only to public meetings but also those closed meetings which resembled public meetings because of the size of the audience or the nature of the proceedings (such as indirect methods of attracting new members). But there was no absolute ban on Hitler's appearances, which could be interpreted as an indirect prohibition on the NSDAP, for he could appear at party sections in Munich and Nuremberg and closed meetings of small branches in the other towns (*98*).

During 1926 Stützel, the minister most directly concerned with the matter, showed signs of harbouring doubts about the ban. At a session of a ministerial sub-committee in March, he remarked that the ban was a 'bitter duty' for him and wondered if there were grounds for lifting it. The Nazi leader had only to adopt a different attitude towards the state to show that he was 'no longer the Hitler of November 1923'. Nobody was interested in maintaining the speaking ban for ever, and there was no reason to suppose it would be kept any longer than was necessary for the good of the state. Hitler could open the way to restoring his freedom to address meetings 'if he does that which is expected of a good citizen who acts on the basis of law and justice' (*99*). Stützel's remarks indicated a certain defensiveness on the part of the government. Dr Held had taken a similar line in a statement to the parliament the previous December when he said, in answer to a question about the continuation of the speaking ban, that all that was needed was a clear confession from Hitler that he was 'no longer the Herr Hitler of 8 November 1923' (*100*). It was a curious legalistic attitude which appeared to give priority to constitutional behaviour without questioning the motives which might induce Hitler to act in a constitutional way.

No doubt Hitler's cautious behaviour towards the authorities helped, but the main reason for the lifting of the speaking ban in 1927 was the unpromising future for the NSDAP. An officially inspired editorial appeared in the *Bayerischer Kurier*, the organ of the BVP, in March 1927 claiming that 'the Hitler of March 1927 who is loyal to the state is different from the Hitler of November 1923 . . . a new period, the era of legality, is beginning for Herr Hitler and perhaps Herr Hitler will carry legality so far that he will let himself be elected to the Bavarian state parliament' (*101*). This pious hope was of course not fulfilled, but in fact Hitler's supposed conversion to 'legality' was not the principal factor behind the government's decision. By 1927 fears of Hitler seem to have worn thin if only because his movement was failing to win any sizeable following among the public. The view that Hitler's prospects were gloomy was reinforced by the poor showing of the

NSDAP in state elections in Saxony in October 1926 and Thuringia in January 1927, and confirmed by reassuring reports from provincial authorities. The regional government of Swabia, for instance, wrote to the State Ministry of the Interior at the beginning of February 1927 that although Hitler's reappearance would attract public curiosity 'he will no longer be dangerous as he was in 1923 for the state and the economy are too secure and the population too shrewd' (*102*).

Dr Stützel confirmed that this optimistic forecast concerning the outlook for the NSDAP had determined his decision to lift the speaking ban in an interview later in the year with the envoy of the Reich Government in Munich. Stützel was confident there was no question of an expansion of the Nazi movement for 'in Upper Bavaria and especially in Munich National Socialism is almost completely ruined and even Hitler has lost his old attraction for the Bavarian population', and the position was similar in other areas of the state. Stützel pointed out that right-wing organizations were generally split and numerically much weaker than people thought. The Berlin envoy concluded his report on the conversation with the comment that the government in Munich had the Nazi movement completely in hand (*103*).

Gürtner, the object of much criticism concerning the leniency of the Bavarian authorities towards Hitler after the 1923 Putsch, does not seem to have played a decisive part in the affair. The main reason for the end to the ban on Hitler's public speeches was the view of the Bavarian Government as a whole, and of the Minister of the Interior in particular, that circumstances had changed greatly and that the NSDAP with a Hitler free to speak in public would cause no further concern to the authorities. This view was accompanied by a certain feeling of embarrassment about the whole question, presumably because the government never envisaged the ban as a permanent measure and had, it seems, certain qualms about the legal grounds on which the ban rested.

It is easy with the knowledge of later events to talk about lack of foresight, but the policy of the Bavarian Government in this matter did in a sense confuse cause and effect. Political circumstances were not favourable to the NSDAP, but the party's weak position was not least a result of the limitation on Hitler's public activities. Once these limitations were removed, the possibilities for party propaganda were automatically enhanced should there be a change in the political situation to the benefit of the Nazis. If popular support for the Nazis should increase, the Bavarian Government would find it increasingly difficult to restrict their activities.

Four

The Expansion of
the Movement
(1927–30)

The Reichstag Election, May 1928

The Reichstag Election of 1928 has generally been regarded as a confirmation of the relatively stable years of the middle and later 1920s. The SPD, the party most sympathetic towards the Republic, emerged from the election as the principal winner with an increase in its popular support by well over a million votes while its representation in the Reichstag rose from 131 to 152 seats. For the first time in eight years a Social Democratic leader became Reich Chancellor. Hermann Müller's government turned out to be the longest-lasting in the short history of the Republic. Public confidence seemed restored with the return of prosperity, so that the appeal of the right-wing parties hostile to the Republic accordingly waned. The German Nationalist Party lost votes heavily, while the NSDAP was returned with no more than twelve seats in the Reichstag.

The Nazi Party now appeared to have adopted constitutional methods, having overcome its doubts about electoral participation. The question had arisen during the period of prohibition in 1924, but Hitler had effectively decided in favour of participation through his promotion of Ludendorff's candidacy in the Presidential Election of 1925, shortly after his own release from prison. The issue had ceased to be a subject of contention within the Party once Hitler had successfully reasserted his control during 1925–26. There still remained those who objected to the acceptance of parliamentary methods for ideological reasons, but the matter was no longer the occasion for challenging the authority of the party leadership in Munich. Hitler's policy of 'legality' was expressed most clearly in an editorial written by Goebbels in his Berlin newspaper a few weeks before the 1928 Election:

We enter Parliament in order to supply ourselves, in the arsenal of democracy, with its own weapons. We become members of the Reichstag in order to paralyse the Weimar sentiment with its own help. If democracy is so stupid as to give us free tickets and salaries for this bear's work, that is its own affair ... We do not come as friends, nor even as neutrals. We come as enemies. As the wolf bursts into the flock, so we come (*1*).

Hitler's reasons for accepting participation by the NSDAP in elections were mixed. Generally, his change of mind on the subject was based not on conviction but on the assumption that a direct challenge to the state in the form of a coup d'état would in the different circumstances since his return to political life be a mistake (see chapter 2, p. 27). Any repetition of the fiasco of the Munich Putsch of 1923 would at least have provided the Bavarian Government with the perfect excuse for placing a ban on the NSDAP again, and may well have brought about its swift end. On the positive side, elections whether for the Reichstag in Berlin, the various state parliaments or even the town councils provided the Nazis with an opportunity for propaganda. There were also certain practical advantages accruing from having representatives in the parliamentary bodies. According to Karl Wahl, a candidate for the Bavarian parliament (which was up for re-election at the same time as the Reichstag) and later *Gau* leader of Swabia, 'the chronic lack of money in the party probably helped to determine the matter for there was the prospect of a few cheap propagandists after the election; it made a difference whether a speaker with a small income met all his own expenses or whether he could pay them with his deputy's allowance' (*2*). The salary of the parliamentary deputy and his free railway pass were very welcome when the Party was short of funds. Because of their freedom to travel around the country at no extra cost to the party, Nazi Reichstag members were usually the NSDAP's most active public speakers. Hitler acknowledged his dependence on these speakers at a general party meeting in Munich in 1926:[1]

For us the deputy's ticket is the main thing. This makes it possible for us to send round agitators thereby serving the interests of the Party. The men who represent us in the parliaments do not travel to Berlin to cast their votes but travel around uninterrupted with their tickets in the service of our movement. It was largely through this that we were able to hold over 2,370 mass meetings in the past year (*3*).

1. Hitler did not stand as a parliamentary candidate himself because of his ineligibility as an alien. Only in 1932 did he acquire German citizenship so that he could run as candidate for President. He became a member of the Reichstag in 1933 after his appointment as Chancellor.

By way of emphasizing that the post of parliamentary deputy was entirely at its disposal, the Nazi Party made its candidates sign a declaration that in the event of their leaving the party they would represent no other party as deputy but hand over their seats to the party leadership; they would have no ties or relations whatsoever with Jews; they would hold no bank directorships or other similar posts during their time in parliament; and they would always represent the interests of the party, observe the twenty-five points of the party programme and remain 'subordinate to Adolf Hitler and his orders'. Finally, the post of deputy was not without its legal benefits. Nazi deputies like those of other parties were free from arrest and by virtue of their parliamentary status could if necessary use their influence to prevent legal action being taken against the party.[2] Goebbels commented tersely after his election to the Reichstag in 1928: 'I am not a member of the Reichstag [MdR]—I am a PI and a PRP: a Possessor of Immunity and a Possessor of a Railway Pass.'

In February 1928 the Reichstag was dissolved following the breakdown of the coalition government of Wilhelm Marx, the Centre Party leader, and new elections were called for 20 May. The Nazis organized their campaign with considerable thoroughness, especially in Bavaria where elections were taking place simultaneously for the Reichstag, the Bavarian state parliament in Munich and the district councils. On 15 February Gregor Strasser issued instructions from the organization department at party headquarters concerning the division of Bavaria into 'working districts' for the purposes of electoral propaganda. The leaders of these districts were responsible for organizing all campaign activities in their areas and should have direct contact with the election manager—for the Bavarian state election Dr Buttmann, and for the Reichstag election Dr Frick. There were forty-four of these 'working districts' and each of them was allotted a number of local branches, of which there were 165 in Bavaria at this time.

Generally, the Nazi campaign failed to excite the voters because it was restricted mainly to the towns, while in the rural areas especially of Southern Bavaria it was overshadowed by the Peasants' League (BBMB). The whole campaign in Lower Bavaria centred on the rivalry between the Bavarian People's Party and the BBMB, while the Nazis attracted little attention here. The election disclosed a widespread public apathy towards politics. Some districts ascribed this to the system of proportional representation, where

2. For example, in 1924 the Thuringian Government, depending on the support of the *völkisch* deputies in the state parliament, had been forced to raise the ban on the NSDAP. Thuringia was one of the few states where Hitler was allowed to continue speaking in public after the party was refounded, and for this reason the party rally was held at Weimar in 1926.

80

the method of presenting a list of party candidates in place of individual party candidates in each constituency removed the personal element. More generally, it was a result of the quiet political situation. Apathy affected the turnout at the meetings of all parties, including those of the BVP and the BBMB, but the party which suffered most from this was the NSDAP. Except with Hitler meetings, where attendance was usually high, the Nazis found no major issues which they could exploit to arouse public interest.

Some excitement was caused in Bavaria by the candidature of Dr Gustav Stresemann, the Foreign Minister. He wanted to strengthen his position in the government through an improvement in support for his German People's Party (DVP) in Bavaria, where it had never previously won a Reichstag seat. He placed his name at the top of the DVP's list of candidates for the electoral district of Upper Bavaria–Swabia and opened a campaign to overcome traditional Bavarian hostility towards the 'Prussian' DVP. His campaign was marked by the one major disturbance of the election in Bavaria, when a DVP rally in the Bürgerbräukeller in Munich at the end of April was broken up by a gang of Nazi gatecrashers. They caused rowdy scenes and forced Stresemann to discontinue his speech.

Stresemann had long been one of the Nazis' main objects of vilification because of his identification with the Weimar Republic and his foreign policy of reconciliation with the former Allied Powers. As their 'answer to Stresemann' the Nazis presented Franz Ritter von Epp at the head of their list of candidates for the same district. Epp was a well-known figure in Bavaria as a former commander of the royal Bavarian *Leibregiment*, the most esteemed military unit in the state. His candidature was designed to make an impression in Munich, where he had earned the reputation of the man who (as leader of the Free Corps Epp[3]) had saved the city from the Soviet Republic in 1919. Although Epp had little political influence, he was a most welcome catch for the Nazis, who hoped to benefit from his prestige and his anti-Communist image. The party newspaper introduced him as 'one of the most outstanding German front-soldiers' and a 'man of action' who had intervened in 'the fate of Bavaria at a time when professional politicians were at their wit's end and were helpless in the face of chaos' (4). Epp was an excellent example of the popular figure who joined the NSDAP and helped to give it an appearance of respectability.

Epp's change of political allegiance caused a public uproar especially

3. The Free Corps were para-military units organized after the First World War and composed of ex-Army officers and soldiers, mostly young men from the middle and lower middle classes. They were recruited by the Socialist Reich Government to suppress left-wing revolutionary activity and were extremely right-wing. One of these units in Bavaria was named after its leader, Ritter von Epp.

among leaders of the BVP, who accused him of betraying Bavarian interests by supporting a movement that was 'centralist' and only concerned with the future of 'Greater Prussia' (5). In answer to repeated criticisms in the BVP press, Epp published a political confession in the *Völkischer Beobachter* on 10 May, in which he made clear the attraction for him of the Nazi conception of the 'People's Community' (*Volksgemeinschaft*), which would restore the national unity destroyed by 'class hatred and class struggle'. Epp mentioned his earlier contacts with the BVP but he had become disillusioned with its failure to promote 'the national will for freedom'.[4] He felt strongly about the reduction of the German Army to 100,000 men by the Treaty of Versailles, which had produced a similar 'disarmament of national morale'. Epp gave his reasons for joining the National Socialists:

> I noticed in them the firmest will, a greater awareness of danger, the greatest certainty about the German strength to resist and the strongest cohesion. Above all I see in it [the NSDAP] the spirit of the German front transferred to the struggle for political power, which I certainly missed in all the other nationalist groups. Rough elements are always found together with youthfulness and rebelliousness but strength and the future lie with youthfulness, both physically and spiritually . . .

The Nazis made full use of their new standard-bearer. Epp began his campaign with a meeting in the Bürgerbräukeller with Hitler on 2 May, followed by speeches in Ingolstadt and Augsburg, both garrison towns, and other cities in Bavaria. On 14 May there was the greatest propaganda event of the entire campaign. The Nazis staged twelve mass meetings in the main beer halls of Munich. Hitler and Epp were the principal speakers at each meeting. They also brought in several of their major national speakers including Goebbels, Gregor Strasser, Frick and Kube as well as Bavarian leaders like Adolf Wagner, Rudolf Buttmann and Hermann Esser. On election eve Hitler and Epp addressed a rally at the Zirkus Krone.[5] Epp's candidature proved attractive especially in military circles, where his name was revered. The Nuremberg police noted that Army officers and members of military associations were taking the view: 'We are not National Socialists but we are going to elect Epp' (6). Equally, the association of former members of the *Leibregiment* announced its decision to join the NSDAP (7).

4. Although he did not mention it, Epp had earlier had contacts with the NSDAP in 1920, when he had been persuaded by Roehm, whose commanding officer he then was in the Army, to help raise money so that the NSDAP could purchase the *Völkischer Beobachter*.
5. The Zirkus Krone was a large circular assembly place in Munich, where the Nazis held many of their big mass meetings.

In spite of their prodigious energies, the Nazis failed to win any sizeable block of votes compared with their support in the previous national election in December 1924. As elsewhere in Germany there was a swing to the moderate Left in Bavaria with the Social Democrats gaining support from the Communists. Although Bavaria still remained the stronghold of the NSDAP in terms of voting support,[6] the NSDAP had failed even here to make much impact on the country areas, which in the predominantly rural state of Bavaria was crucial. Writing shortly before election day, the Reich envoy in Munich, an informed observer of the Bavarian scene, had predicted that the election result for the National Socialists would 'hardly stand in relation to the amount of money and effort they have spent, because the decision in Bavaria depends on the country where the National Socialists have little influence' (8). The average vote for the NSDAP was much higher in the urban areas in Bavaria, and only really in larger towns like Ingolstadt, Munich, Landshut, Bayreuth, Coburg and Neustadt bei Coburg did the Nazi vote rise above 10 per cent.[7] There were a few exceptions, all rural districts in Protestant Franconia. Radical or protest voters in the Catholic areas—peasants who blamed their plight on the government and complained about rising taxes—tended to support the Bavarian Peasants' and Middle-Class League (BBMB), which increased its vote remarkably (rising to 40·3 per cent in the rural districts of Lower Bavaria and 35.9 per cent in Swabia). In some country towns the small Economic Party, which appealed to the petty bourgeoisie (especially craftsmen and smaller business-men), won a surprisingly high vote—all towns where the NSDAP later scored impressive electoral successes.

The election result caused disappointment in the leadership circles of the NSDAP, but there was sufficient awareness of the weaknesses of their campaign. The party newspaper commented just over a week after the election:

The election results in the country show that with less expenditure of effort, money and time greater successes can be achieved there than in the large towns. National Socialist mass meetings in small towns and market communities are important events and form the topic of daily

6. The average vote for the NSDAP in Bavaria was 6·8 per cent compared with 2·6 per cent in the whole of Germany, and the only two districts in which the party won the 60,000 votes required for the direct election of a Reichstag deputy were in Bavaria.

7. 'Urban areas' in the case of Bavaria meant *kreisunmittelbare Städte* or towns unattached to a rural county, e.g. the vote for the NSDAP was: Upper Bavaria (urban areas 10·6 per cent, rural areas 3·9 per cent), Lower Bavaria (9·9 per cent, 2·5 per cent) and Upper Franconia (17·8 per cent, 7·9 per cent).

conversation for weeks afterwards, while in the large towns meetings even with 3,000 and 4,000 people sink into insignificance and pass away (9).

A party report on the Bavarian district elections submitted in July to Buttmann as election manager complained that in the case of Upper Bavaria the NSDAP was 'little known outside the city of Munich'. The reasons given for the lack of impact made by Nazi propaganda in the provinces were the indifference of the press, the disruption of Nazi meetings by political opponents but above all the lack of organization in country areas. According to the report 'the bourgeois press has deliberately ignored us in the provincial towns, and where that was not possible all kinds of things were attributed to us'. It accused the BVP newspapers of defaming the party. The 'Marxists' were blamed for breaking up party meetings especially in towns which attracted tourist traffic, and in the case of Garmisch members of the Geneva Association of Hotel Employees were singled out as the guilty party. The report's most relevant comments were on the state of party organization. Propaganda had been non-existent in some areas 'which has partly to be attributed to the fact that a series of local branches were founded only shortly before the election and organizationally were not yet absorbed into the party apparatus'. Tasks like the placing of posters and distribution of leaflets demanded a minimum of organized party workers on the spot. Attendance at Nazi meetings during the election had varied greatly, depending on the efforts of the local branches or even on their existence (10).

The Reichstag Election of 1928, which seemed on the surface a vote for stability and the *status quo*, had an important effect for the anti-Weimar forces because it made the Nazis aware of the limitations of their propaganda. This lesson was not lost on the Nazis for within a few months they took major steps to provide a more elaborate organization and propaganda machine.

Young Plan Referendum and the Bavarian Municipal Elections, 1929

In the 1928 Election the Nazis had lacked a popular issue to exploit; by the autumn of 1929 they had found one on which they could beat the nationalist drum. In the summer of 1929 the German Government agreed to a final arrangement on reparations for German war damages known as the Young Plan, which fixed German payments for the next fifty-nine years but lowered the amount of the annual instalments originally demanded, abolished the international controls over German's economy established by the Dawes Plan of 1924[8] and secured the promise of the withdrawal of Allied troops from the Rhineland in 1930, five years earlier than previously arranged. In spite of these concessions the new plan opened old popular sores in Germany, especially the feeling, not by any means confined to nationalist circles, that the postwar settlement (above all, the Treaty of Versailles with its 'war-guilt clause') was totally unjust.

Together with the Nationalist Party, the Stahlhelm (the ex-servicemen's organization associated with it) and a number of patriotic groups, the Nazis organized a referendum campaign against the Young Plan.[9] The plebiscite took place on 22 December, but the campaign in effect lasted through the autumn months and coincided with a number of state elections in Germany, including one in Bavaria on 8 December, which for the first time since 1924 indicated a modest vote increase for the NSDAP. The Nazis owed this rise in support primarily to the fact that in the referendum campaign they benefited from their association with the traditional conservative Right and from the financial sources provided by the Nationalist Party. Unemployment was not an important issue in the town council elections in Bavaria.[10]

The Nazi Party had already shown an interest in local politics by setting up a small department at Munich headquarters under Karl Fiehler, the party's expert on municipal politics, who was at this time leader of the NSDAP group on the Munich city council and branch leader in Schwabing. This department became known as the Central Office for Municipal Politics (*Hauptamt für Kommunalpolitik*) in 1930, and was responsible for issuing instructions to Nazi town councillors about party policy on local matters. But the work of Fiehler's office in controlling the activities of Nazi councillors was limited so long as there was only a small number of them around. The Munich council, for instance, had only three Nazi members.

In June 1929, the Nazis had scored their first local success by winning an absolute majority of thirteen out of twenty-five seats in Coburg. An election had been called there prematurely because of a successful protest referendum in favour of dissolution of the city council organized by the local Nazis, following the dismissal of their leader, Franz Schwede, from local government

8. The Dawes Plan was the previous agreement on Germany's payments of war reparations.
9. The other groups in Bavaria which signed the appeal for a referendum were the *Vereinigte Vaterländische Verbände Bayerns*, the *Alldeutscher Verband in Bayern*, the *Heimat-und Königsbund* (which later declined to participate in the campaign), the *Bayerischer Landbund* and various officers' and naval associations.
10. The Depression of the early 1930s was sparked off by the fall of the Wall Street stock market in October 1929, but even before then unemployment had been increasing in Germany and had reached 1½ millions in 1929.

service for making violent anti-semitic speeches. Schwede, a mechanical engineer, was not a local man. He came from East Prussia, served in the Navy during the First World War and moved to Coburg in 1922 after his appointment as inspector by the City Electricity Works. The following year he joined the NSDAP and became local branch leader after the NSDAP was refounded early in 1925. Schwede was by then one of the three Nazi councillors and soon made a name for himself because of his obstructionist tactics on the city council. The Nazis typically selected the 1929 election in Coburg as a test-case, concentrating all their energies on it and bringing in some of their most popular speakers like Ritter von Epp, Hermann Esser and Hermann Goering. The latter, who introduced himself with his service rank as 'Flight Captain Goering', performed the ceremony of laying a wreath at the war memorial and made a speech designed to touch patriotic feelings in this city which had a strong nationalist voting record.[11] On election eve, Hitler himself appeared for a meeting at the local Hofbräuhaus and stayed overnight to wait for the results.

The Coburg result encouraged the Nazis to take a more active interest in local politics. German municipal politics were in any case almost as partisan as national politics. Local issues did feature in town council elections. Sometimes local parties or associations ran candidates, but they often acted as covers for national parties. In Memmingen seven parties contested the election in December 1929—apart from the SPD, the NSDAP and the KPD there were the Catholic Interest Association (*Katholische Interessengemeinschaft*), the 'Free Citizens' (*Freie Bürger*), the 'Middle-Class' (*Mittelstand*) and the *Treuhand*. The Catholic group was the Bavarian People's Party in disguise, the *Mittelstand* a combined ticket of the DNVP and the Economic Party while the *Treuhand* represented the interests of the Bavarian Peasants' League and the local Evangelical Association. Only the *Freie Bürger* was a local party and this merely won a couple of hundred votes.

Municipal affairs had become more politicized in the Weimar period than before 1919 with the introduction of universal suffrage in place of the restricted franchise, while the extension of Reich jurisdiction particularly in

11. Coburg was formerly part of the Duchy of Saxe-Coburg-Gotha (and its alternate capital with Gotha) until it joined Bavaria (Upper Franconia) in 1920 after a plebiscite. The city was 90 per cent Protestant. Half the electorate voted for the two main right-wing parties, for the NSDAP usually won supporters from the Nationalists (DNVP). In May 1924 the *Völkischer Block* had won the exceptionally high vote of 41·9 per cent. In the Reichstag Election of 1928 the NSDAP won 24·8 per cent and the DNVP 26·8 per cent. In the June 1929 election the NSDAP again drew support from the DNVP to win its 5,146 votes (out of a registered electorate of about 13,000).

financial matters after the War had blurred the line between national and local issues leading to greater participation by the national parties in municipal affairs. Voter participation in municipal elections was as high as in national elections. The easy system of voter registration partly accounted for this, but so did the general view prevalent among German voters that it was a citizen's duty rather than his right to vote.[12] On the day of the elections in Bavaria, the *Münchener Katholische Kirchenzeitung*, organ of the Catholic Press Association for Bavaria and one of the diocesan Sunday papers with the widest circulation, exploited this feeling by urging all Catholic voters to remember that 'the right to vote is a duty to vote'. It was even 'a matter of conscience and a great burden is laid on those who do not exercise their right to vote'. The paper quoted the example of the Bishop of Trier who insisted on going to the ballot-box on crutches in 1921 in spite of a serious illness, so that he could support the party 'which alone can save us and with which the affairs of our Church are in safe hands'. Although it did not specify the BVP, the paper said that Catholics had a duty to vote for that party which best looked after 'their interests of conscience and their religious life' (*11*). The Church viewed local elections in the same light as a national election—as a challenge to the Catholic confession.

A measure of the importance the NSDAP attached to the Bavarian local elections was the fact that initial preparations were already in hand three months before. On 18 September Himmler sent a memorandum from the Propaganda Department to all party speakers asking them to be ready for the campaign in Bavaria in the last three weeks before polling day. Although state elections were being held in Thuringia on the same day as the Bavarian elections, other local elections in the autumn would be over and the party could concentrate its best speakers on Bavaria. During these weeks, each speaker was required to address eight meetings and submit beforehand a list of his fixtures. Headquarters would then compile a programme for the election, which 'considering its importance must be carried out with the greatest vigour' (*12*).

The Nazis made an early start with their electioneering and held far more meetings than any other party. As early as the middle of October the authorities in Swabia reported that 'meeting functions are scanty, but the National Socialists were again very busy and according to reports from the districts seem to have held more meetings than all other parties together' (*13*). Such intensive campaigning was necessary because the NSDAP did not have at its disposal that network of semi-political associations which held together

12. In some states compulsory voting had been introduced, e.g. in Mecklenburg-Strelitz and Lippe.

87

voters for the other parties, as the Catholic associations did for the Bavarian People's Party.

Inevitably, the issue of the Young Plan dominated the election campaign, while matters of more local concern like the burden of taxation or the insufficient assistance received by towns from the state government were secondary. The Nazis carried the burden of propaganda in the referendum against the Plan. In Upper Bavaria alone, the NSDAP held twenty-three meetings in the last weeks before the plebiscite while the Nationalists held only one. The Nazis were freer to conduct radical propaganda as they were not involved in government, unlike their main allies. Since the referendum campaign was directed not merely against the new agreement on reparations but also against the political system of Weimar (the *Völkischer Beobachter* called it 'a struggle for control of the state'), the Nazis tried to make a virtue of the fact they were, so they claimed, the only party not tainted with responsibility for any of the mistakes committed by the governments of the Republic. An official report on the campaign in Upper Bavaria commented: 'one notices from their behaviour that the National Socialists have nowhere shared responsibility in public life; they have no inhibitions about exploiting the advantages which this offers'. The same report explained the reluctance of the DNVP to take such an active part in the campaign by the 'false position in which it finds itself through its participation in the coalition in Bavaria and its opposition at the national level which may have contributed to a certain reserve it was obliged to adopt' (*14*). With an eye to winning votes from the Economic Party, which had recently done well in the state elections in Saxony, Fiehler published an article in the summer attacking that party because it was just as 'guilty' as the other parties in being an 'accomplice' of the Dawes Plan (*15*). Fiehler was fully aware of the opportunity presented by the Young Plan for party propaganda. Replying to a request from the branch leader in Bruckmühl near Rosenheim for advice on organizing the town council campaign there, Fiehler wrote: 'I am convinced that through the propaganda, which is itself necessary for the campaign against the Young Plan and on which in the last analysis the fate of the communities depends, you will gain quite an important increase in votes which will give us a seat or two on the local council' (*16*).

For the referendum campaign in Bavaria the Nazis brought in one of their most sensationalist and inflammatory speakers from North Germany—Ludwig Münchmeyer, a former Lutheran priest expelled from the Church in 1926 for slander, who joined the NSDAP in 1928. Münchmeyer already had a reputation as a violent anti-semite and rabid nationalist so he was quickly adopted as a party candidate in the Reichstag Election of that

88

year.[13] He had already spoken at several meetings in Bavaria in July 1929, and reappeared in the autumn to continue his agitation against the Young Plan.

Münchmeyer always attracted large crowds if only because of his entertainment value, especially his habit of making outrageous statements. At Ingolstadt a crowd of some 600, consisting largely of young people, turned up to hear him in spite of midsummer storms (*17*). The branch leader at Traunstein recorded in his diary that Münchmeyer spoke there about 'Christian Cross and Swastika': 'He attacked the BVP bitterly, which earned him exuberant applause; the hall was packed to the last seat' (*18*).

Local authorities in Bavaria banned several of his meetings for 'inciting the public', but this only made Münchmeyer even more boastful of his single-handed skirmishes with the authorities. He invariably began his speeches—the ones he was allowed to make—with a list of the latest prohibitions on his public appearances, which would produce in Pavlovian fashion a chorus of catcalls and whistles from the audience. Münchmeyer would then titillate his listeners with some of his 'conspiracy' stories, like the one about the negotiators of the Young agreement assenting to a secret protocol for sending young Germans abroad to do forced labour, or that contrary to accepted opinion Friedrich Schiller, the famous poet and dramatist of the eighteenth century, had in fact been poisoned. In spite of his unfrocking by the Church, Münchmeyer used the title *Pfarrer a.D.* (retired priest), which was more than just a touch of vanity since he went out of his way to exploit religious feeling during his speaking tours in Catholic Bavaria. Few people in his audiences apparently guessed that Münchmeyer was in fact not a Catholic, judging by the tantrums of the BVP press. Catholic politicians found his behaviour simply too much to bear. The *Bayerischer Kurier* referred to him as a 'wandering preacher and prophet of that swastika-religion, which takes its essential characteristics from National Socialist and vulgar anti-semitic ideas' (*19*).

The climax of the Nazi campaign was a massive demonstration in Munich. As many as twenty rallies were staged on the same day, 3 December, in all the beer-halls of the city. Hitler spoke at every one of them and was accompanied by several of the party's national speakers including Goebbels, Goering, Strasser and Frick as well as some of the *Gau* leaders in Bavaria. The Nazis clearly intended to make an impression in their home city, for two days earlier an SA propaganda procession had marched through the main

13. Münchmeyer furnished the public with his views in publications with such titles as *Marxists as Murderers Among the German People in the Pay of the Enemy*, *Struggle for Germany's Awakening* and *Germany Stay Awake*.

streets of Munich lasting four hours. On election eve, Hitler and Esser addressed 4,000 people at the Zirkus Krone in a last effort to get the voters out to vote for the NSDAP.

Voter participation in the Bavarian municipal elections was as high as 80 per cent. Polling took place in more than 8,000 Bavarian communities, but the gains made by the NSDAP were chiefly in the cities, where its organization was more established and where its propaganda had concentrated, rather than in the rural towns and villages. In Munich the Nazis more than doubled their number of seats on the city council, winning 14,000 more votes in the city than in the Reichstag Election the previous year. Successes were also recorded in Ingolstadt (six out of thirty seats) and a number of cities in Upper and Middle Franconia such as Nuremberg, Selb, Fürth and Bayreuth (nine seats where previously the NSDAP had none). In Coburg the Nazis retained their absolute majority and even increased it by more than a thousand votes. In all these cases the Nazis won votes mainly at the expense of the Nationalist Party, which had been overshadowed by the NSDAP in the referendum campaign and which seemed the less attractive choice to that section of the electorate primarily motivated by nationalist feeling. There was little change in the vote for the Bavarian People's Party and the Social Democrats. Results in the country areas were by no means dramatic. In the vast majority of cases local mayors were re-elected, while the NSDAP made little impact except in isolated instances like Obermenzing near Munich, where the Nazis formed the largest group in the town council. Generally, the Nazi vote was lowest in those communities where local interest groups were well-entrenched. The NSDAP won seats in only six of the twenty-seven communities in Southern Bavaria, where local parties formed the largest groups (20).

The plebiscite on the Young Plan a fortnight later was a failure for the 'National Opposition', which won little more than a quarter of the 21 million votes needed for acceptance of the 'Freedom Bill' it sponsored. But voting patterns further explained the increase in support for the Nazis in the local elections, especially among conservative Protestant voters. Through their alliance with the DNVP the Nazis were able to create a more 'respectable' image for themselves in traditional conservative circles. The latter broadly sympathized with the anti-Weimar, anti-semitic and nationalist propaganda of the NSDAP and had voted for it in large numbers in the spring election of 1924 (in many of the same cities as they did in the Bavarian municipal elections of 1929); but had returned to supporting their traditional party, as the NSDAP appeared to have little future in the years after its refounding. Now in 1929 the Nationalists were bedevilled with internal feuds, while the Nazis had meanwhile developed a more efficient propaganda machine.

The referendum bill received considerably less than the national average of 13·8 per cent in Catholic Bavaria (Upper Bavaria–Swabia 8 per cent, Lower Bavaria 4·3 per cent), while in Franconia it won 20·7 per cent). The front against the Young Plan generally did much better in Protestant areas in Germany. The strong influence of the confessional factor—associated with the fact that the DNVP, although not a confessional party, was supported almost exclusively by Protestants—was evident in the sharp local differences in both turnout and support for the referendum. Voter participation was extremely high, to the advantage of the 'National Opposition', in Protestant rural districts in Middle Franconia like Uffenheim, Dinkelsbühl and Gunzenhausen, while in Catholic districts like Eichstätt, where the BVP predominated, the turnout was very low. Where large numbers of Catholics did vote, as in the city of Dinkelsbühl, this was ascribed by the local authorities to dissatisfaction with economic circumstances (21).

The increase in the Nazi vote in the municipal elections in Bavaria was confirmed by the result in the state election in Thuringia on the same day, when the NSDAP won 11 per cent, following which a Nazi—Wilhelm Frick —became Minister of the Interior in the Thuringian Government, the first Nazi minister in a state government. Gregor Strasser, as head of the party's organization department, felt compelled to take account of the new situation now there were several hundred Nazi deputies in town councils throughout the country. He issued instructions in January 1930 to Nazi local councillors reminding them that they were elected primarily to act as 'representatives of the National Socialist point of view and of its organization, the NSDAP'. Deputies were required to act in close cooperation with local branch leaders, and when differences arose the branch leader had the final say (22). Already the same month the authorities in Ingolstadt were complaining that the newly elected Nazi councillors were showing little interest in positive work and were introducing their election campaign manners into the sessions of the town council (23). This kind of behaviour seemed to confirm the view of leading Nazis that participation in parliamentary bodies merely provided another forum for party propaganda.

Organizational Developments, 1928–29

Disappointment with the results of the Reichstag Election of 1928 did not produce a leadership crisis in the NSDAP, as it might have done with 'democratic' parties, because of the totalitarian nature of the party and Hitler's charismatic role as party leader. The NSDAP rose or fell with Hitler for he was not appointed party leader on approval. Nor did electoral failure or disappointment lead to policy changes, for the official party programme of 1920 had been declared 'unalterable' by Hitler and was therefore part and parcel of the *Führer* myth.[14] But the reassessment of the position of the NSDAP after this election did bring about important changes in organization based on the criterion that the party's activities should be geared to winning voters.

Party propaganda had been limited in the 1928 Election for it had concentrated firstly on the urban areas and secondly on those states like Bavaria, Saxony and Thuringia where the NSDAP was likely to be most successful. The Nazis did not possess in 1928 a nationwide electoral machine covering all areas of the country in the way they had in the early 1930s. Electoral disappointment reinforced the other main reason for these changes, the realization by party leaders of the insufficiently methodical character of party organization and propaganda. If the NSDAP was to become more than just a movement based on *Führer* appeal, it had to create a more elaborate organization to take account of increasing members and voters—all the more so as the decision to participate in elections was strategic and therefore involved a degree of organization hitherto missing. The NSDAP had to become institutionalized.

The annual party rally was not held in Nuremberg in 1928 because the election campaign in the spring was hardly a cause for celebration and had been a drain on party funds.[15] Also, a mass gathering of party members was not the most suitable occasion on which to announce major changes in the internal organization of the party. Instead, a meeting of party leaders—officials from headquarters, *Gau* leaders and Nazi deputies in the Reichstag and the state parliaments—was held in Munich from 31 August to 2 September 1928. The agenda covered the role of the SA in the party, relations with the Communists, party finance and the case of Arthur Dinter, *Gau* leader in Thuringia, who contrary to Hitler's wishes had turned into a religious fanatic, but in a sense all these questions had to do with the main issue at

14. Only Hitler could make official changes in the party programme, e.g. in April 1928 Hitler, conscious of the need to avoid offending the conservative-minded agricultural population, 're-interpreted' point 17 of the programme relating to land reform. For the NSDAP's change of emphasis to rural propaganda see chapter 4, p. 83.

15. According to the *VB* of 30 June, the NSDAP admitted to having held 10,000 meetings in the three months before the election of 1928. The sources of Nazi electoral funds had been a matter of public dispute. Various sources were suggested in the opposition press, including the Italian Fascists. The party rally would have been an extra expense, having cost 16,000 Reichmarks in 1927.

the meeting, the nature of party organization and with it the authority and supremacy of the *Führer*. Hitler's opening speech made it absolutely clear that he had no intention whatsoever of relinquishing his dictatorial control over the party. He emphasized:

> Order and discipline are the foundations of organizations. A meeting of leaders like this one has however not been called to debate broad principles or even discuss basic problems. Discussion of these matters is within the framework of a political party just as impossible as discussion of ideology and religion. Just as the National Socialist knows no distinction between monarchy or republic, bourgeois or proletarian, Prussian or Bavarian, so the question of Catholic or Protestant does not exist for him (*24*).

This was a clear reference to Dinter's obstinate efforts to make an issue of his religious views at the conference by proposing a motion that the party chairman should set up an advisory council on the subject. Nothing could have more offended Hitler's sense of his own position as leader, that any one of his subordinates should have been so presumptuous as to challenge official party policy, for this implied in Hitler's eyes a challenge to his own authority. Hitler regarded religious disputes within the NSDAP as divisive, as he had warned in his editorial in the *Völkischer Beobachter* when the party was refounded in 1925. Dinter was one of those Nazi leaders who took his ideology extremely seriously, which made him suspect for Hitler who demanded loyalty to himself as the first qualification of a *Gau* leader. The previous year Dinter had gone so far as establishing his own religious reform association known as the 'Religious Community of the Christian Spirit' (*Geistchristliche Religionsgemeinschaft*). Based in Nuremberg, it saved most of its abuse for the Roman Catholic Church ('this Jewish–Roman devil's pestilence') and claimed to revive the original spirit of the German Reformation. Hitler declared at the conference in Munich that 'religious founders do not have under any conditions a place in our movement', and Dinter was expelled from the NSDAP.[16]

16. The Dinter question proved something of a minor embarrassment for the NSDAP, which is shown by Gregor Strasser's circular to party leaders of 8 October, asking them to play down the importance of the issue in public and not to give political opponents any opportunity to exploit it. Each party leader was required to sign a declaration refusing to become involved in religious quarrels and rejecting Dinter's claim that he had support within the party (Bundesarchiv Koblenz, Schumacher Sammlung, FA 48/373). The Catholic press had not surprisingly taken up the matter, e.g. the *Augsburger Postzeitung* of 19 October 1928 asked whether in fact Dinter was more representative of a certain element in the party than Hitler was prepared to admit.

The party's decision to work within the political system by participating in elections created a potential source of discontent in the SA, which had little sympathy and patience with parliamentary methods. Hitler, aware of this danger, made a further speech at the conference in which he praised the role of the SA and played down the constitutional aspects of his policy of 'legality':

> The highest aim of the SA, which is much more important than protecting a meeting, is to maintain and carry out the internal organization itself against the dangers coming from our law as a democratic association, which provides the opportunity for the destruction of every organization.[17] It is necessary to have something as an antithesis to the law of association, which must have a subversive effect—namely, within the organization of the law of association a further organization which carries through the *Führer* idea to the full degree in order to preserve the instrument of the unity of the movement against all attempts to destroy it (25).

Hitler also felt compelled to take a firm stand on the question of relations between party members and Communists. In spite of Hitler's success in asserting his control over the more 'socialist' minded party leaders in Northern Germany at the Bamberg meeting in 1926 (see chapter 3, p. 48), there had been recent signs in some party circles in the North of a friendly attitude towards the Communists. Hitler emphasized 'there is no going along with the Communists—either we or they will be destroyed'. Hitler presumably chose to make this point as the NSDAP was starting to change the emphasis of its propaganda, from concentration on the cities to winning support from the rural and small-town middle classes, who would look askance at any cooperation between the Nazis and the Communists.

In his speech on 2 September, Hitler gave his attention to the central theme of the Munich conference, party organization. He reiterated his old view that it was not the number of people who became members that mattered so much as the character of the movement they joined. He saw the NSDAP as a strongly organized 'historical minority', which would at the right moment impose its will on the German people: 'The National Socialist movement must become the strongest and most powerful organization; it will only be able to retain this on the basis of the idea of *Führer* authority and ruthless opposition to any appearance of democratic ideas, and through

17. Being a political party the NSDAP was required to register as a legal association.

rose fast—from branch leader in Herrsching the same year, district leader of Upper Bavaria-South in 1927 to *Gau* leader of Upper Bavaria from 1928 to 1930.[24]

Reinhardt showed a remarkable talent for detailed organization, and seemed to owe his promotion to the name he had made for himself as an effective propagandist while branch leader in Herrsching. Within a week or two of his appointment he was issuing countless directives to his local leaders. These concerned the collection of funds, the holding of public meetings, the setting-up of an 'auxiliary fund' and the training of party speakers.

Reinhardt's order number 7 of 21 June introduced an extra source of income making it possible for Nazi sympathizers, who were reluctant for professional reasons to demonstrate their allegiance to the NSDAP by becoming members, to further the party's cause by supporting it financially (*32*). Each member of the 'auxiliary fund' paid a monthly sum directly to the *Gau* office in Herrsching. Reinhardt explained his idea as an attempt to overcome 'the serious financial crisis' in the party. The money collected would be used for founding new local branches and financing campaigns to win new members (*Werbefeldzüge*). Although the fund bypassed the branches, the directive emphasized that 'this institution will benefit each single local branch as pamphlets, posters and similar things will be placed at its disposal by the *Gau* leadership without cost, and propaganda marches of the SA, for example, could be financed'.

Reinhardt's directives were always imperative in tone and studded with bureaucratic turns of phrase, which did not make him popular with his subordinates. Complaints were made against the flood of directives, 'which because of their scope are not complied with by most leaders and because of their dictatorial character are felt to be disagreeable' (*33*). Party finance was always a sensitive issue. Reinhardt had instructed in his order number 2 of 8 June that subscriptions should be sent to the *Gau* office instead of directly to the party treasurer's office in Munich. Fifty pfennigs per member had to be submitted to the *Gau*, while the branches retained only thirty pfennigs a head. The *Gau* would not tolerate delays in the payment of subscriptions and the settlement of accounts could only be made with the *Gau* (*34*). Order number 12 of 28 July demanded that each branch hold one public meeting

24. In 1929 Reinhardt founded and became editor of the party newspaper on economic questions, the *Wirtschaftlicher Beobachter*. The following year he was elected to the Reichstag and became chief NSDAP representative on the Reichstag budgetary committee. In 1933 he finally earned his place in the Third Reich as State Secretary in the Reich Ministry of Finance. (Details on Reinhardt's career from *Der Grossdeutsche Reichstag 1938* (Berlin, 1938), pp. 355-56.)

a month. Arrangements could only be announced when each branch had obtained the written permission of the *Gau* leader and the announcement of each meeting was made only by the *Gau* office (*35*).

Reinhardt's most important contribution to party organization was the training of party speakers. The plans for more intensive propaganda in country areas could only be carried out with a large regular supply of speakers. In a memorandum from the Reich Propaganda Department to *Gau* leaders and party deputies in May 1929, Himmler commented:

> With the enormous growth of the movement there is the danger that a necessary institution does not grow at the same rate, namely that of speakers. The result of this is often the extremely unwelcome fact that we are not in the position to exploit the most abundant opportunities of winning people and the favourable mood in the population, because we have no or not sufficient speakers. This shortcoming makes itself particularly felt at election time (*36*).

Reinhardt had first introduced the idea of training speakers in his own *Gau* in July 1928 with a school in Herrsching, which became officially the National Socialist Speakers' School in June 1929. The aim of the School according to Himmler's memorandum was to 'impregnate each speaker with lasting and incontestable material so that with the certainty of his knowledge he does not from the outset suffer from stage-fright, as he knows that his material is irrefutable even for his sharpest opponent'. Reinhardt had originally organized his course with the Bavarian municipal elections of 1929 in mind, for successful participants would be given preference in the selection of election candidates (*37*).

Now the School took over responsibility for training Nazi speakers throughout Germany. The course was conducted by correspondence. Each *Gau* leader was asked to nominate two candidates from every district in his area. The course lasted a full year, costing each participant two marks a month in return for which he received monthly instructions detailing the programme of work, giving advice on the composition of speeches and providing samples of completed speeches for study. The pupil speaker was required to post his comments on the content of these speeches, which contained deliberate mistakes, to the School, which would then criticize his report and furnish him with the 'model version' of the speeches. After four months were up the trainee had to prove his worth by making his first speech in the presence of the *Gau* leader, who had to send a report on the candidate's performance to the School. The candidate if considered suitable would then have to show his ability in the field, by making as many as thirty public speeches in the remaining eight months of the course before qualifying as an official party speaker. By May 1930 as many as 2,300 party members had taken part in the course and by the 'seizure of power' in 1933 the School claimed to have trained 6,000 party speakers (*38*).

Official lists of party speakers were compiled for use by local branches when planning their programmes of meetings. 'Reich speakers', who could speak at any meeting in the country, included the most famous names in the party; '*Gau* speakers' were the ablest speakers in each *Gau* and restricted their speaking engagements to their areas; while there were even 'district speakers' who versed themselves in the politics of their particular districts. Each speaker was issued with a permit. 'Reich speakers' were allowed to speak on any subject, but those of a lower grade usually specialized in particular topics. By 1931 the 'Reich speakers' in the *Gau* of Munich–Upper Bavaria included Adolf Wagner (the *Gau* leader), Reinhardt, Rudolf Buttmann and Heinrich Himmler (now a Reichstag member for Upper Bavaria–Swabia), while '*Gau* speakers' consisted of specialists in economic questions, cultural questions, youth and foreign policy. There were also seven 'district speakers' who covered such questions as Jewry, Marxism, race, the peasantry, history, the press, SA problems and one whose speciality was making speeches attacking the Bavarian People's Party (*39*).

An important consequence of the party reorganization of 1928 was the stronger position of the *Gau* leaders through their key role in effecting these organization measures, their direct supervision of all propaganda activities in their areas and their appointment of branch leaders and promotion of party speakers. The reforms in the party machine were particularly crucial in Franconia, where the organization was not so well established as in Southern Bavaria, for the Protestant rural electorate was more vulnerable to nationalist appeals, judging from their voting preferences in the past, than the Catholic peasants of Upper and Lower Bavaria.

With the rural voters in mind the new *Gau* leader of Upper Franconia, Hans Schemm, took advantage of the provision in Hitler's directive of September 1928 to initiate a system of district leaders. Schemm was a more colourful character than the arid and humourless Reinhardt. Born in Bayreuth in 1891 of staunch Protestant parents he received Protestant religious instruction and held a post as school-teacher in the city until 1928, when his increasing preoccupation with politics had become a source of friction with the authorities. In spite of his background Schemm was anything but sombre and introduced unconventional and sometimes eccentric ways of winning new supporters for the NSDAP. From the time of his promotion to *Gau* leader in October 1928, Schemm devoted more attention in his speeches to the conditions of the agricultural population and embarked on frequent tours of the country areas around Bayreuth, Coburg and Bamberg, which soon became known as the 'Upper Franconia Wandering Circus'. He would usually be accompanied by several lorry-loads of bandsmen, who would announce his arrival at each town with a clamour of drums, pipes and horns—a version of the whistle-stop tour. These tours invariably succeeded in attracting audiences at each place of a hundred or so small-town people, who were used to a more 'serious' style of political meeting and came along mainly out of curiosity (*40*). According to the Bayreuth police, Schemm's countryside tours accounted for 'the influx among younger people which gave the party a clear advantage over other parties' (*41*).

Schemm's favourite slogan was 'organization is power' for 'a way of thinking only becomes a force when it is followed by organization; if that does not happen, then it peters out without any effect' (*42*). Early in 1929 he held conferences with branch leaders in Münchberg and Lichtenfels and with district leaders in Bayreuth to discuss forthcoming rallies, including the *Gau* congress in Bamberg in June, and organizational questions. At the meetings of branch leaders Schemm selected as the main adversaries of the party the Bavarian Peasants' Union (*Landbund*) and the middle-class economic organizations. The latter in his view were a divisive force for 'the united Marxist block of the left can only be opposed by a union of all members of the middle classes with the clear slogans of deadly enmity to Marxism and Jewry' (*43*).

The meeting of district leaders in Bayreuth was followed by a detailed directive from Schemm outlining the duties of each district leader. A district leader had to maintain regular contact with the *Gau* office in Bayreuth by submitting monthly situation reports on the following matters: the state of the branches which already existed; the possibility of founding new branches and the availability of suitable branch leaders; and which villages were most likely to respond to an 'enlistment drive'. One of the essential tasks of the district leader was the 'nursing' of new branches (for 'a new branch just like a child which enters life does not know the rough and hard sides of our struggle'), by instructing new branch leaders in the techniques of staging discussion evenings and branch treasurers in managing their funds. Above all he was responsible for organizing public meetings in his area and had to remain in constant contact with the *Gau* office which supplied him with speakers (*44*).

The neighbouring *Gau* of Middle Franconia, based on Nuremberg, went one stage further by requiring district leaders to nominate 'contact men'

(*Vertrauensleute*) in every community who would be attached to the nearest local branch and would be kept informed of party policy through copies of directives and circulars sent to branch leaders. In July 1929, Karl Holz issued his first memorandum as *Gau* propaganda leader describing the method of organizing a public meeting. Each community had to hold at least two meetings a year. They had to solve the problem in the past when only meetings with well-known speakers had been any success, and the only way was by more efficient propaganda:

It is the absolute duty of every convener to make the most abundant use of propaganda for all meetings. This is carried out in the most effective way as follows: a week before the meeting each house receives a sample copy of the *Stürmer*. Distribution is carried out by uniformed SA men. (Issues can be obtained free of cost from Wilhelm Hardel, publisher, Nuremberg, Meuschelstr. 70.)

A few days later the locality will be 'cultivated' by free copies of the *Völkischer Beobachter* and the *Illustrierter Beobachter*. (Obtainable from the Franz Eher Publishers, Munich, Thierschstr. 15.)

Three days before the meeting hand-notices are distributed (perhaps together with leaflets) announcing the meeting. At the same time posters (colour red, black wording in heavy type) are pasted up. (Posters can be obtained from the *Gau* manager's office, Nuremberg, Hirschelgasse 28) . . .

Those who want to do something extra can put a cleverly worded advertisement in the local paper (*45*).

The emphasis of Nazi propaganda was still on frequent public meetings, but how were all these detailed blueprints for the reorganization of propaganda actually put into practice? This depended on a number of 'bureaucratic', environmental and personal factors. The nature of the Nazi Party's organization with its elaborate system of graded commands provided headquarters with a framework for controlling activities at the grass roots level. This was reinforced by the fact that a large number of party leaders owed their initial appointments or their promotion to the reorganization changes of 1928–29, which involved an increased demand for leadership personnel, and their continuation in office to their success in carrying these changes out. A new *Gau* leader's worth was judged by the rise in party membership in his area, the number of new branches founded and the attendance at public meetings. In view of the importance of the latter, the control over party speakers was a very relevant aspect of this question. After each meeting he addressed, a party speaker had to fill in a detailed questionnaire, of which the following is a typical example:

How was the meeting prepared?
How were people invited—by posters—by handbills?
                                        (where possible send copies)
How was the local branch represented?
Was protection provided by the SA (SS)?
                                        (give name and number of troop)
Was music available?
How was the meeting chaired? Who chaired it?
Was there an admittance fee? How much for party members?
                                        How much for unemployed party members?[25]
How would the speaker judge the success of the meeting?
Did the speaker come across any annoyance and trouble? (46)

These regular sources of information, together with the reports of district leaders and their 'contact men', enabled the central Propaganda Department to form an overall picture of politics at the grass roots level and to plan propaganda to suit local conditions. The flexibility of Nazi propaganda was an important factor in explaining its appeal in the early 1930s, for propaganda leaders were able to concentrate on those areas which seemed the most promising. They developed the technique of 'saturation campaigns' (*Grosskämpfe*), selecting certain areas for an intensive programme of meetings, in the months leading up to the Reichstag Election of 1930. The four rural districts of Wasserburg, Mühldorf, Ötting and Laufen in the eastern corner of Upper Bavaria were chosen for such a campaign for the period of 21 May–6 July, when some 150 meetings were arranged making an average of three a day (47). The *Gau* had already organized one campaign in western Upper Bavaria during February, resulting in the admission of 170 new members and the formation of two new local branches. The party brought in some of their best speakers. One of the new branches was set up in Hausham, a coal-mining village near the Schliersee, after Gregor Strasser had spoken there.

Public meetings served the Nazis not only as a propaganda weapon, but also as a means of spreading the party organization. A branch was started in Mindelheim in January 1930 after the SA and SS from the neighbouring

25. The admission charge at NSDAP meetings was usually lowered for the unemployed and the war-wounded.

town of Memmingen had staged a propaganda march through the streets, and the *Gau* leader of Swabia had made a speech there *(48)*. From October 1928 to May 1930 the number of branches in Swabia rose from twelve to fifty-eight with forty-four additional 'strong points' *(49)*.[26] Many of these were in places of only a few thousand inhabitants each, especially in the mountainous Alpine region of the Allgäu populated chiefly by small pastoral and dairy farmers. This backward area of the Allgäu, where a severe climate and poor soil allowed for little more than cattle raising and the production of butter and cheese, became a stronghold of the NSDAP. The district authorities in Füssen commented: 'Because of the feeling of desperation among Allgäu peasants—a consequence of the catastrophic milk price—radical propaganda falls on fruitful ground and we have to reckon with a further spreading of National Socialist ideas in the open country' *(50)*. During the spring the Nazis had been very active in the districts of Kempten, Kaufbeuren and Markt Oberdorf. At a conference of branch and district leaders held in the Café Schachameyer in Augsburg in May 1930 Karl Wahl, the *Gau* leader, boasted that the membership of the *Gau* had increased fourfold in the past year and was particularly strong in the Allgäu: 'Strong branches have come into being especially in the Allgäu, which can be considered a National Socialist stronghold; their leadership is almost entirely in the hands of mayors and local councillors, teachers or veterinary surgeons, workers, peasants or civil servants, who with their untiring work lead their enthusiastic followers from success to success' *(51)*.

Energetic propaganda and economic discontent could not alone account for the Nazis' ability to win new supporters; it was the nature of their appeal. A typical local police report of the time noted the frequency of Nazi meetings compared with the slack attitude of the other parties but remarked: 'When the party does not send out a speaker with a well-known name— perhaps more correctly, one with a suitably sharp tongue—who promises some entertainment, then their meetings are just as badly or generally worse attended than those of the other parties' *(52)*. The NSDAP helped to create for itself a different image from the other parties through such 'non-political' events as the ceremony by the local SA in memory of the fallen at the town war memorial, the provision of military bands to introduce party meetings[27] and the emphasis on outdoor activities for young people. In July 1928 the

26. A 'strong point' (*Stützpunkt*) was a local group of Nazis (usually in a village community) which had not yet qualified to become an official branch of the NSDAP because of its small membership.
27. In 1927 an official called Wilhelm Hillebrand had been appointed head of the new music section of the SA department in the Munich headquarters to supervise the activities of the stormtrooper march-bands.

Gau of Upper Bavaria held a 'German Summer Festival' at Herrsching with the following programme:

7.30   Reception of guests at the station.

9.30   Procession of the SA to the church with music.

10.30   Propaganda march of the SA with music.

11.30   Concert in the garden of the Seehof Hotel.

        Lunch

2.30   Swimming relay of the SA at the open-air bath.

3.30   Garden concert at the station hotel with sporting events at the nearby sports ground.

7.00   'German Dance' in the banqueting hall of the station hotel (*53*).

The SA units were required to be on parade early in the morning and to set an example in public: 'Iron discipline! Exemplary appearance in public! The population of Upper Bavaria and Swabia must see in our SA a model of German breeding and orderliness when our SA appears at different party events' (*54*).

The sensationalist behaviour of Hans Schemm was a principal reason for the high attendance at party meetings in Bayreuth and surrounding towns. The *Gau* leader of Upper Franconia had once made an appearance as discussion-speaker at several meetings of Hermann Müller, the SPD Chancellor. On one occasion he suddenly jumped on a chair to urge those present to sing the national anthem, the *Deutschlandlied*.[28] Schemm was accompanied by supporters but fervent socialists in the audience replied to this provocation with the *Internationale*, and the two sides indulged in a riotous 'singing war' (*55*). Several incidents involving Schemm, some of them leading to violence, caused the Social Democrats to place a ban on his appearances at their meetings as a discussion speaker.[29] Schemm turned this to his own advantage by a number of devices. Whenever the SPD arranged a meeting anywhere in Upper Franconia, Schemm would phone the local branch leader who would turn up at the meeting to announce Schemm as the Nazi discussion speaker.

28. The *Deutschlandlied* (*Deutschland, Deutschland über alles*) was composed by von Fallersleben in 1841 and set to Haydn's music. In 1922 it became the official anthem of the German Reich.

29. At party meetings in the Weimar period, political opponents were sometimes invited to take part in the 'discussion' which followed the main speech. More often than not the 'discussion speaker' was used as a foil by the main speaker, who tried to make his opponent look small in the face of a hostile audience. This practice became less popular with the police in the early 1930s as it often contributed to the increase in political violence, because the mere presence of a political opponent was enough to start unrest among those present.

This happened simultaneously one evening at no less than fifteen different meetings. Refusal of permission to speak was usually expected, but Schemm would meanwhile be waiting by the telephone in the *Gau* office at Bayreuth ready to jump into his car in case one SPD meeting took him at his word. Otherwise, the Nazi branch leader would make a statement to the audience to the effect that: 'Everybody is frightened of one man—Schemm is coming all alone, but even that is not permitted—how strong this man must be and how much fear is occasioned by his speaking!' (*56*). The Social Democrats tried to turn the tables on Schemm by their own tricks. Schemm was due to speak at a party meeting in Höchstadt an der Aisch near Bamberg. The SPD invited him as discussion speaker to a meeting of theirs in Klingenthal (Saxony) the same evening with the comment that it was 'a great honour' for the ban on him to be lifted this once. They expected Schemm to turn down the invitation because of his other commitment and hoped to make propaganda out of his 'cowardly' refusal. Instead, Schemm sent someone else to speak in Höchstadt and turned up secretly at the SPD meeting dressed like the Scarlet Pimpernel, 'in a coat and with a hat pulled well down over his face, he stood on the evening of the meeting at the back against the wall of the hall'. After the SPD speaker had begun to attack him for not putting in an appearance, Schemm threw off his disguise and made a speech answering the first speaker point by point (*57*).

On a more serious level, Schemm's emphasis on nationalism and German tradition went down well in conservative Upper Franconia. Schemm was also one of those Nazi leaders who aimed to establish a 'new society' in Germany. In his memorandum to district leaders he had claimed that 'our movement will create new people and has above all to accomplish a great task of education' (*58*). In his early days as branch leader in Bayreuth around 1925–26, Schemm had begun to collect together a group of school-teachers he had got to know locally through his work. Ludwig Ruckdeschel, Schemm's deputy, had kept a file of correspondence with them, and there was an initial meeting of school-teachers sympathetic towards the Nazis in Hof in January 1927. Further meetings took place there during the year which followed (*59*). Finally in April 1929 Schemm founded and became head of the National Socialist School-teachers' League (*NS Lehrerbund*). Some sixty teachers took part in this meeting in Hof. Shortly after, a special newspaper—the *NS Lehrerzeitung*—began publication, but it soon ran into financial straits. Schemm often discussed 'cultural' questions in his speeches and was a strong purist with his opposition to all 'un-German' elements in the national literature. Opening the new Nazi bookshop at Bayreuth in April 1930 Schemm remarked: 'In view of the dominance of the Jew in our literature it is the duty of each party comrade to participate in the fight, which will bring us the long-desired freedom, by fostering a truly German literature' (60). Schemm also used the city's associations with Wagner to establish a link between National Socialism and traditional nationalism, and often gave the address at 'Wagner evenings' there and in other cities in Germany.

By late 1929, the NSDAP had developed the organizational framework, which facilitated its transformation from a small party into a mass movement in the early 1930s. This institutionalization of the NSDAP, which was an essential precondition for its expansion in popular support, was motivated less by the prospect of economic disaster and political crisis in Germany than by more immediate circumstances. Already, some sections of German society were experiencing economic difficulties, especially peasants, who were feeling the pinch with the world slump in agricultural prices since the start of 1928, as well as craftsmen and small businessmen, who were suffering from heavy taxes and high interest rates on their loans. Undoubtedly, the Nazis wished to exploit such feeling of discontent, but the crucial organizational changes of 1928–29 were inspired primarily by other considerations: the lessons of the 1928 Election, which underlined the limited character of party organization and propaganda and the need for it to be coordinated with the electoral system; the realization that organization had in any case to be brought up to date and made more efficient in view of the gradual increase in party membership and the new emphasis on propaganda activities outside the cities (for example the formalization of the position of *Gau* leader and the administration of party finance); and the concern that disappointment after the exhausting election campaign of 1928 might turn the energies of the party inwards and result in recriminations. Hitler had warded off divisive issues at the Munich conference of party leaders in September of that year and redirected these energies by keeping party activists busy with new positions of authority and new forms of propaganda activity. These organizational changes were successful because Hitler gave them the full backing of his authority as *Führer* and because so many party leaders who were appointed or promoted were committed to their success.

A Nazi Local Notable: the Case of Ingolstadt

If the headquarters of the NSDAP in Munich issued directives providing for the framework of organization and propaganda and if the *Gau* leaders provided the energy and drive to carry these directives into effect, the local branch leader was also important for he was the concrete representative of the NSDAP for the local inhabitants, and his popularity or unpopularity in the town, as the case might be, influenced local attitudes towards the party. The fortunes of the NSDAP varied from area to area, which could be explained partly by local economic and social conditions and partly by the strength of the other parties there, but undoubtedly the personal factor counted for it could not be dissociated from the state of local party organization.[30]

At the Nuremberg party rally in August 1927, one local party leader from Dresden had argued the need for greater centralization of party activities through the 'schooling' of branch leaders rather than enforcing 'rigid patterns': 'One ought not to forget that the movement possesses many hundreds of local branches whose leaders are simple manual labourers or peasants whom we cannot burden with a confusion of written orders; the party central office would be pleased if the few orders so far had been fulfilled unremittingly but, so far as this proposal has any practical reason, these are nevertheless discarded' (61). The NSDAP had relied all the more on branch leaders with initiative, before the organizational reforms of 1928–29 institutionalized the selection and training of local leaders and provided a more effective chain of command from the central office in Munich down to the party's 'contact man' at the community level. Hitler ultimately depended on the ability of local leaders to carry out his orders.

Ingolstadt had been one of the early strongholds of the NSDAP in Bavaria. In the Reichstag Election of May 1924 Ingolstadt had been one of the few towns in Bavaria where the *Völkischer Block* had won a higher vote than any other single party.[31] With a population of 27,000 (1926) it was the largest city in Upper Bavaria after Munich and had a predominantly Roman Catholic population (87 per cent). Situated on the Danube, Ingolstadt was also an important road and railway junction. It was one of the largest garrison

30. In his analysis of local voting patterns of the NSDAP 1928–32, K. D. Bracher places individual factors third after confession and economic and social structure in his list of factors determining the ability of opposing parties to resist the NSDAP at the local level (see *Du Auflösung der Weimarer Republik* (1964), pp. 648–56). W. S. Allen in his local study of the party from 1930, *The Nazi Seizure of Power* (London, 1966), p. 274, overstates, however, the role of the local branch in the rise to power: 'It is clear that an essential arena in the Nazi electoral surge and the seizure of power was on the local level; Thalburg's Nazis created their own image by their own initiative, vigour and propaganda', but comments: 'exactly how much was initiated locally and how much was promoted by the example of other Nazi groups in other towns or by the district and national Nazi leadership remains to be determined.'

31. The *Völkischer Block* won 34·5 per cent of the vote in this election, the BVP 31·5 per cent, the Communists 14·6 per cent and the Social Democrats 10·4 per cent. See chapter 2, p. 18.

towns in Bavaria and had been a centre for military production until this ceased with the Treaty of Versailles, a change which adversely affected the economy of the town for this had depended very much on the presence of the garrison.

The military associations of the town seem to have contributed to its nationalist sympathies, for many demobbed soldiers remained there after the closure of the garrison and removal of the war-production factories and joined the Free Corps and later the SA. The most notable case was Hans Georg Hofmann, the commandant of the city fortress, who retired from the Army as colonel in 1926. Hofmann was a close associate of Franz Ritter von Epp, had been a leader of the Free Corps Epp and was known for his pronounced anti-Communist views. Because of his official position—active soldiers were not allowed to take part in politics or even vote—Hofmann at first maintained only informal links with the Nazis in the town. In 1927 he became head of the United Patriotic Associations in Ingolstadt and finally joined the NSDAP in 1931, soon becoming SA group leader for Northern Bavaria. He was known among the locals as the 'Trotsky of Ingolstadt' because of his bearded appearance.

Other local Nazis included Johann Bergler, an official working for German Railways, who became branch leader of the NSDAP in 1929. In the same year Bergler, whose sole political attribute seemed to be his gift for the gab and his name for making inflammatory public speeches, was elected one of the seven NSDAP town councillors (out of a total of thirty-two). The leaders of the party were solidly middle class—they also included a local civil servant and a baker—but the real leading light in the NSDAP in Ingolstadt was no less than *Sanitätsrat* Dr Ludwig Liebl, an eminent local doctor and patron of various cultural associations in the town.

Dr Liebl was born of a Catholic family in Waldkirchen (Lower Bavaria) in 1874. His father was a county-court judge there. Liebl had studied medicine in Munich and had held a number of probationary posts before setting up his practice in Ingolstadt in 1909. Three years later, he opened a clinical hospital in the Kreuzstrasse and served during the First World War as an Army doctor. Since 1911, Liebl had been a town councillor for the liberal bourgeois Democratic Party, and became prominent in the social life of Ingolstadt. He was popular in military and artistic circles—among his close friends he numbered Hans Hofmann—and was often seen at evenings at his *Stammtisch*[32] conversing with his drinking friends. Liebl's desire for local recognition was not satisfied with this, for his amateur interest in the arts

32. A *Stammtisch* was a table reserved in a beer-cellar or inn for a regular circle of drinking cronies.

led him to found and lead the Concert and Art Societies after the War and even compose a volume of songs (62).

Liebl was a classic example of the much-respected local personality who lent his prestige to the Nazi movement. He became a member of the *Völkischer Block* in 1924 and was said to have been very impressed by Hitler, whom he visited in Landsberg prison during the latter's confinement after the Putsch. Liebl became local branch leader for four years when the NSDAP was refounded in 1925 but did not often make public speeches, preferring to work behind the scenes and finance the party's activities, including the local NSDAP newspaper the *Donaubote* which began publication in 1927 (63). The *Donaubote* had a small circulation compared with the other two papers in the town—the *Ingolstädter Zeitung* (BVP) and the *Ingolstädter Anzeiger* (SPD)[33]—but it was unusual as it was a daily and the NSDAP had few daily newspapers at this time (in fact only six before 1930). Because of its wealthy patron, the *Donaubote* faced no money difficulties and felt free to indulge in some of the worst excesses of the gutter press, including sensational gossip about political opponents and stories defaming the Jews. The paper probably did the NSDAP little credit at first for in 1928 it moderated its tone and changed its editor. There were as many as five editors during the first three years of the *Donaubote*'s existence, each reflecting a different line in propaganda. Liebl's standing in the NSDAP was sufficient to make him the first leader of the National Socialist front organization for doctors, the *NS Ärztebund*, which he founded at the Nuremberg party rally in 1929.

Liebl's role was more that of the figure-head and patron of the NSDAP in Ingolstadt rather than its efficient organizer. He had little in common with the 'bureaucratic' type of branch leader and tended to leave administrative chores to others in the local party, if only because he had no intention of sacrificing his medical practice and cultural activities for the sake of politics. Politics was not the be-all and end-all of his life as with most other branch leaders, who owed their local prominence solely to their position in the party. All the same, one asks what led a man of Liebl's local distinction to support a party which at the time he joined it (1924) had a very uncertain future—the NSDAP had been banned and Hitler was in prison.

The *Völkischer Block* had achieved a remarkable success in Ingolstadt in the Bavarian spring elections of that year, but it appeared increasingly to be

33. The readership of the *Donaubote* increased steadily from 900 in 1928 to 2,000 in 1932. It was read in the rural district of Ingolstadt as well as in the town and became the only paper in the area after the 'seizure of power' in 1933, when the other two papers ceased publication.

a lost cause, in spite of which Liebl remained a dedicated supporter of Hitler. He was hardly jumping on a bandwagon. The personal impression made by Hitler on Liebl no doubt influenced the latter, but the real reason seemed to be Liebl's personality and the role he conceived for himself in local society. Liebl wanted to be very prominent in community life in Ingolstadt, which meant he had to enter municipal politics, and this he did very soon after settling down in the town. Looking at his amateur involvement in the arts—he made friends with a number of lesser-known musicians, including Max Reger, the composer—one senses a certain disappointment at not having achieved something himself, and again his strong desire for esteem.

At the time Liebl went into active politics the Liberals were a strong force in Ingolstadt. The newly-founded Democratic Party, which he joined after the War, won the second largest vote (15 per cent) in the town in the Bavarian state elections in 1920. Thereafter, support for the DDP, the main non-confessional bourgeois party there, declined until it won little more than one per cent of the vote in the second Reichstag Election in 1924. Its voters largely transferred their support to the *Völkischer Block*. Ingolstadt had a large nominal Catholic population, but although Liebl was himself a Catholic it was unlikely that he seriously considered joining the BVP with his national liberal background. The fact that he had represented the Liberals on the town council for more than a decade would hardly have endeared him to the fervent Catholics, conscious as they were of the anti-clerical element in the liberal tradition. It was furthermore out of the question for professional and class reasons that Liebl should have allied himself with the other main political party in the town, the Social Democrats.

But Liebl did not join the NSDAP simply for want of anything better, for it did provide him with a further opportunity to make a splash. He was usually on hand to chair public meetings and share the limelight with such famous speakers in the party as Gregor Strasser, Heinrich Himmler and even Hitler. Hitler visited Ingolstadt several times and was usually entertained at the Liebl home (*64*). Because of Liebl's generosity, the local NSDAP was in a position to finance regular public meetings with important speakers which usually succeeded in attracting a broad cross-section of the population, judging by police reports on the kind of people who attended. Hitler's speech in the Schaffbräukeller in March 1928 brought out a crowd of about 1,400: 'All classes of occupations were represented; particularly noticeable was the very large number of peasants, who up to now have kept away from meetings of this party; a few leading figures from the left-wing parties were there, and the fair sex was also well represented' (*65*).

A few months before, a meeting with Adolf Wagner, then *Gau* leader in the Upper Palatinate, had attracted a smaller crowd consisting of 'civil servants, white-collar employees and workers' while tradesmen, who had been strong supporters of the NSDAP in 1922–23, were hardly present (66). The NSDAP did as elsewhere suffer a slump in support around 1926–28, and the *Donaubote* was in fact initiated as one answer to this problem. Ingolstadt never fully recovered the prominent position it had enjoyed in the earlier years of the NSDAP, although it won just under one-third of the town's vote in the elections of 1930–32. It was still one of the party's urban strongholds with a share of the vote higher than that in Munich in these elections, but by this time the NSDAP was concentrating on the rural areas.

Illness had by then forced Liebl to withdraw more and more from active politics, and he resigned as branch leader in favour of Johann Bergler in 1929. Bergler had in any case been managing the affairs of the branch, including the business side of the *Donaubote*, and under his guidance the local party took a more radical bent. Bergler, a Streicher sympathizer and former Social Democrat, had been instrumental in founding a Nazi trade union in the town in 1928. A more temperamental character than Liebl, he emphasized more the social revolutionary aspects of National Socialism, no doubt influenced by the rising unemployment and the fact that Ingolstadt had in the context of Southern Bavaria a large working-class population. Early in 1930 the local Nazis cooperated with the Communists in organizing a demonstration of the unemployed (67). There was a relatively strong vote for the KPD during the Depression years but the local Communists were not as well-organized as the Nazis, who also won support among the unemployed. Although the Bavarian People's Party remained the largest party in terms of popular support, its local branch was divided by personal feuds resulting in many BVP people transferring their support to the *Katholisches Kasino*, a Catholic association which became more political from 1930. These divisions within the BVP were exploited by the Nazis.

In May 1930 Ingolstadt was chosen by the *Gau* of Upper Bavaria as the site for its party rally. The event began on a Saturday evening with a torch-light procession through the streets. The following morning participants in the rally attended church service and then gathered to hear a long political speech from *Gau* leader Reinhardt at the war memorial. In the afternoon, some 1,700 SA men marched through the streets of the town carrying banners and accompanied by four bands playing patriotic music. The local police, possibly sympathetic to the Nazis, reported that 'the population participated in the event in a favourable and lively manner for not only were numerous private buildings decorated with flags but also the municipal buildings' (*68*). The rally closed with two well-attended public meetings later in the afternoon.

By the early 1930s, Ingolstadt's importance as a centre of the NSDAP had declined, although in terms of voting strength it remained one of the party's strongholds in the towns. The main reasons for the strong support the Nazis enjoyed in Ingolstadt during the Weimar period were the feeling of nationalism encouraged by the town's circumstances after the First World War, the weakness of the other political parties in the town and the fact that the NSDAP became 'respectable' through its association with such prestige figures as Ludwig Liebl, Hans Hofmann and Franz Ritter von Epp. Provided that circumstances in a town were favourable to the Nazis and could be exploited by them, an effective local branch leader could make an important difference to the success of the NSDAP there. Some branch leaders owed their success to their energy as propagandists; others like Dr Liebl contributed to the party's success because they were influential local figures.[34]

The NSDAP Agrarian Programme

There were two reasons for the change in emphasis from urban-based to rural propaganda by the NSDAP. Firstly, the Nazis found there were structural limits to the expansion of their vote in the cities, and secondly, they had reason to believe that the agricultural electorate would prove more vulnerable to their appeal than the industrial working class or the capitalist middle classes. In some areas of Germany both factors determined this change,[35] but in the case of Bavaria the second factor was the more important because of her predominantly agricultural economy.

The NSDAP did not face a strong challenge from the left-wing parties in Bavaria. In the 1928 Reichstag Election, when the Left (especially the Social Democrats) had increased their popular following in the country, the SPD and the KPD won a vote in Bavaria well below the national average.[36] The SPD vote of 24·2 per cent was by no means uniform throughout the state for it owed much to its high vote in urban areas like Munich and Augsburg in the South and Nuremberg, Erlangen and Fürth as well as Bayreuth, Hof

34. I am indebted in this chapter to Dr Josef Listl, *Oberbürgermeister* of Ingolstadt 1930–45 and 1956–66, who granted me an interview in August 1968, and to the Stadtarchiv Ingolstadt for giving me access to their archives and newspaper files. See also reports on NSDAP meetings and other activities in Ingolstadt in HA 8/169.

35. For example, see Jeremy Noakes, *The Nazi Party in Lower Saxony, 1921–1933*, chapter 5 (iii).

36. Bavaria: SPD 24·2 per cent, KPD 3·8 per cent; Germany: SPD 29·8 per cent, KPD 10·6 per cent.

and Kulmbach in Franconia. Support for this party was low in the rural areas, except for a few isolated districts like Regen in Lower Bavaria (35·7 per cent) and several districts in Upper and Middle Franconia. Many of these districts were in any case in the neighbourhood of large urban concentrations like Nuremberg–Erlangen.

The basic reason for this relatively low vote for the Social Democrats was the economic structure of the state. Bavaria had very little heavy industry outside the three cities of Munich, Nuremberg and Augsburg. The exceptionally high vote for the SPD in the district of Regen could broadly be attributed to the location of new industry there, especially the glass factories in the Ludwigstal. There was another disadvantage for the Left in Bavaria in the prevailing attitude of anti-Communism, which derived from the influence of the Catholic Church and the reaction against the left-wing régimes in Munich during 1918–19. The vote for the KPD was extremely low throughout the state—except for a few cities like Munich, Rosenheim and Selb—and was minimal in most rural areas, where the conservative-minded peasants saw the Communists as a threat to both their religion and their property.

The principal reason for the change in their propaganda so far as Bavaria was concerned, was not therefore the failure by the Nazis to break the hold of the left-wing parties over the industrial working class, because this did not exist there to any large extent; rather it was the fact that the rural voters, who accounted for more than 60 per cent of the Bavarian electorate, offered a more promising field for party propaganda. The small-town bourgeoisie and the peasants[37] seemed more vulnerable than the urban voters because their electoral support was divided between a number of parties, all of which were less well-organized than the left-wing parties. If they felt sufficiently desperate to vote for an extremist party, they were unlikely to express their protest by supporting the KPD.

The Bavarian Peasants' and Middle-Class League (BBMB) had absorbed much of the agricultural discontent in the middle 1920s, but the strongest obstacle to any new party monopolizing the rural electorate was the Bavarian People's Party. The strong position of the BVP would not have been possible without the support it received from the peasants of Catholic Bavaria, through its control of such auxiliary organizations as the Bavarian Christian

37. The term 'peasant' (*Bauer*) is used in preference to 'farmer' (*Landwirt*) because the agricultural economy in Bavaria consisted mainly of small- and medium-sized farms, and because the word *Bauer* is used in the titles of the agricultural-interest organizations. The term 'peasantry' (*Bauerntum*) also had a special 'romantic' connotation derived from nineteenth-century *völkisch* literature, which is relevant to this discussion of the Nazi appeal to this class.

Peasants' Association (*Bayerischer Christlicher Bauernverein*). The dependence of the BVP on the votes of the peasants was a major reason for its split in 1918 with the Centre Party, which had to take more account of the Catholic working-class from the industrial areas, especially the Ruhr. Support for BVP was generally stronger in the rural areas, as shown by Table 1.

Table 1   *BVP votes in the Reichstag Election, 1928*

	Towns* %	Rural counties %
Upper Bavaria	24·2	39·6
Swabia	28·8	35·2
Lower Bavaria	44·6	36·2
Upper Palatinate	43·9	52·8
Upper Franconia	14·6	28·5
Middle Franconia	8·8	15·7
Lower Franconia	31·5	54·5

Source: Statistisches Jahrbuch für den Freistaat Bayern (1928), pp. 592–605.
* See chapter 4, p. 83, footnote.

Only in Lower Bavaria was the vote for the BVP higher in the towns, but this was because of the small number of urban districts in this overwhelmingly rural area and the stronger position here of the Bavarian Peasants' League. Even in the two Protestant regions of Middle and Upper Franconia, where the vote for the BVP was low, the more favourable poll in the rural districts was still apparent.

The chief weakness of the NSDAP in the 1928 Election had been that its vote in the rural areas was much lower than its vote in the towns. This was not surprising in view of the development of its organization. The movement had originated in the city of Munich, then spread to larger towns like Rosenheim, Landshut and Ingolstadt. Even the more complex organization introduced in 1928–29 continued to be centred on the larger towns. Branches in small communities acted as satellites of the branches in the towns, which provided them with speakers and propaganda material.

Already before the 1928 Election the NSDAP had showed an awareness of the advantages to be gained from rural propaganda. On 13 April of that year Hitler, with the property-conscious peasants in mind, 'reinterpreted' point 17 of the party programme of 1920, which had demanded land reform 'suitable to our national requirements', confiscation without compensation of land for communal purposes, the abolition of interest on land loans and the prevention of all speculation in land. Point 17 was a reminder of the early 'anti-capitalist' days of the NSDAP. Hitler now officially announced that the party recognized the principle of private property and that the expression 'confiscation without compensation' referred in particular to Jews, who speculated in land and did not administer it 'in accordance with the national welfare'.

Hitler's immediate consideration was tactical for the election was only five weeks away, but the official change in party policy also heralded the new strategy of propaganda, which became apparent during the following two years. The Nazis had not so far made their presence felt among the farming population, and their first efforts met with little success. They organized a number of 'peasant meetings' in Swabia early in 1928. One of these was arranged to coincide with market day in Kempten. Heinrich Himmler, then deputy *Gau* leader in Lower Bavaria and a party speaker specializing in agricultural questions, made a speech on 'The Capitalist system and the peasantry', but the attendance was moderate and would have been worse if members of the party had not gone along beforehand to the corn-house and the market-square to persuade groups of peasants standing around to come along to the meeting (69). Peasants were by nature suspicious of newcomers and outsiders—as the German saying goes, 'what the peasant doesn't know, he doesn't eat' (*was der Bauer nicht kennt, frisst er nicht*)—and tended at first to react to Nazi propaganda in an aloof manner. Even the *Gau* leader of Swabia, who had a special interest in rural propaganda, admitted the problems he encountered in making contact with the Swabian peasants, who were 'hard to get on with (*mit ihnen ist es nicht so leicht Kirschen zu essen*)— especially those from the Ries[38] and the Allgäu are difficult to win over' (70).

The Nazis had so far failed to arouse the interest of the peasants because of the latter's innate conservatism and the lack of a strong NSDAP organization in the rural areas. The issue which eventually turned the Bavarian peasants towards the party was the Depression of the early 1930s, for economic considerations more than anything else governed their voting habits.

Early in 1928 the peasants' council for the district of Nördlingen–Oettingen, later one of the rural strongholds of the NSDAP, held a general meeting of its members. The meeting was very well-attended and aired many of the rural grievances. The mood was one of desperation. The chairman of the council, a local mayor, opened with a speech on the 'Origins of the Distress of Agriculture', in which he complained: 'Taxes and mortgage interest rates

38. The Ries was a fertile tract, probably once the bed of a lake, in the district of Nördlingen.

are devouring it; large numbers of the peasant population see the moment at hand, when they will not be able to hold out any more and will have to leave their soil; the prices of agricultural products no longer stand in relation to the production costs; it has already gone so far that real estate announced for sale finds no more buyers because everyone is aware of the unprofitability of agriculture' (*71*). The speaker went on to express himself in terms which revealed a bitterness at the fate of peasants in the state, and suggested a certain affinity with Nazi ideology. It was too easily forgotten that 'the distress of the peasantry is the distress of the country' (*Bauernot ist Landesnot*), because 'pernicious differences' were tearing the German people apart. 'We all form one people's community (*Volksgemeinschaft*) for which there is only one watchword: we are saved together or we perish together.' He voiced the conventional lamentation about the replacement of manual workers by machines and continued: 'Land settlement is not only necessary economically, but is also of the greatest national importance; we will only attract a patriotic generation when the country has something to offer it.' The blame for this calamitous state of affairs lay fairly and squarely with the policy of the Reichstag.[39] A glance at the future gave even less hope for comfort: 'one looks for remedies but finds none' (*72*).

The peasants were becoming more aggressive and political, which reflected similar and often more violent tendencies in North Germany, involving rebelliousness towards the authorities.[40] It was not long before this antagonism took the form of a hostile attitude towards the Weimar state. The *Günz- und Mindelbote*, a right-wing paper in Swabia, commented on the mood of a peasants' demonstration at Kempten, the capital of the Allgäu, early in 1929:

> The position is really serious. It is not only economically but also politically serious. Our peasant, democratically predisposed, is on the point of giving up democracy and hoping for salvation from a downfall. If democracy is further misused against the most important class in society, then the peasant cannot be blamed for seeking his salvation in a dictatorship. It is a warning sign for our parliaments that the name of Mussolini was taken up with enormous enthusiasm in Kempten (*73*).

39. The speaker made special reference to conditions in the cattle-trade. The unsatisfactory proceeds may well have increased anti-semitic feeling, for there were many Jewish cattle-traders in the district of Nördlingen.
40. For the *Landvolk* movement in North Germany see Gerhard Stoltenberg, *Politische Strömungen in schleswig-holsteinischen Landvolk, 1918–1933*, pp. 121 *ff*, and Jeremy Noakes, op. cit., pp. 118–20.

This growing alienation from the state arose from a feeling among peasants of neglect by successive governments. It owed much to economic circumstances, which were soon to become even more desperate, but Erwein von Aretin, the Bavarian aristocrat, went further in providing a psychological reason. He distinguished between the peasant's deference towards the ruling class in the form of the monarchy[41] and his hatred towards the state. The King had even been seen as a protector against 'the wicked government'. Von Aretin quoted the story about the peasant from Lower Bavaria who had commented after the German collapse in 1918: 'Now it will be fine: the state is lying in agony! he said with the clear after-thought: when the brute dies off, then we no longer need to pay any taxes!' (74). Refusal to pay taxes was a common form of political protest among peasants then.[42]

But there was a big step from a general negative feeling among peasants towards the Weimar state to their open support for the NSDAP. Much depended on how far they were willing to carry their hostility to the state in political terms, and in particular on their allegiance to their own traditional organizations. There were several reasons for calling this allegiance into question.

Firstly, the Nationalist Party (DNVP) had undergone a leadership change in the autumn of 1928. Electoral disappointment had aggravated the divisions within its ranks leading to the election of Alfred Hugenberg, the leader of the extremist, violently anti-Weimar wing, as party chairman in October of that year. The election of Hugenberg, the press magnate and former Krupps director, brought a new emphasis of policy with more concern for the interests of business, industry and the landowners over those of the peasants. This change had important consequences in Bavaria, where the vast majority of peasants earned their living on small and medium-sized holdings, in contrast to the preponderance of landed estates in areas of Northern and Eastern Germany.

Secondly, the Bavarian Peasants' and Middle-Class League (BBMB) was also experiencing an internal crisis. It too was divided into extremist and moderate factions, and the former appeared to be gaining the upper hand. The coalition with the Bavarian People's Party had never in any case been an easy partnership. The radical leaders of the BBMB had been the object of sharp criticism at the BVP congress at the end of 1927, and relations had

41. The Wittelsbachs (the Bavarian royal family) had abdicated in 1918, but monarchist feeling remained strong in governing circles and also among the peasants.
42. Dr Held, the Prime Minister, once confessed to the Prussian Prime Minister that in many Bavarian villages the school-teacher and the postman were the only taxpayers. (Otto Braun, *Von Weimar zu Hitler*, p. 261.)

not improved much since.[43] Economic distress and bitterness against the authorities in the rural areas further exacerbated feelings among the leaders of the BBMB.

The matter came to a head in the spring of 1930, when the Held Government felt compelled by economic circumstances to introduce a new tax, the slaughter tax. Nothing could have been designed to provoke the BBMB more, and the proposal precipitated the final collapse of the coalition between the BVP and the BBMB. At a meeting of the Bavarian Cabinet in April Dr Hans Schmelzle, the BVP Finance Minister, justified the new measure with the need to balance the budget. In his view the tax on real estate and commercial transactions could not be raised any more because of 'the small power of taxation in Bavaria'. The strong limitations placed by national legislation on the states forced the government to seek new forms of taxation. Schmelzle was not unaware of the political difficulties this would create but there was no question but that the finances had to be restored for 'political and economic reasons'. Anton Fehr, the BBMB Minister of Agriculture, replied that the slaughter tax was unacceptable and would spell 'a great danger for agriculture and consumers in the population', for it would result in the rise of meat prices and so affect the standard of living (75). In July the BBMB resigned from the Held Government, which had to continue as a minority administration.

These changes had a depressing effect on morale in the parties concerned. Electoral considerations had undoubtedly influenced the decision of the BBMB, for there remained no advantage in being spokesman within the government at a time when unpopular measures had to be taken to deal with the economic crisis. The BBMB failed though to make political capital out of its withdrawal from the government, as it was already beginning to lose its attraction for rural voters. Ironically, it lost prestige as a result of its move and was unable to adjust fully to the role of outright opposition, having been compromised by its participation in the government.

The BBMB suffered all the more now from the fact that it was not the sole spokesman of farming interests in Southern Bavaria for peasants' support was divided between the BBMB and the Christian Peasants' Association (the BVP associate organization). Cooperation between these two organizations

43. At the BVP congress in 1927 Georg Heim, one of the party's founders, had attacked the BBMB for spreading 'Bolshevist' propaganda. Schlittenbauer, a BVP deputy in the state parliament, had attacked the BBMB almost daily in the *Bayerischer Kurier* during the previous weeks and proclaimed at the congress that 'this coalition brother has for years behaved in a more Bolshevist way among the people than the whole Bavarian Social Democracy, including the Communists'. The Reich envoy in Munich commented that the BVP had 'come close to a rejection of the BBMB for a future coalition government'. (Reichsvertretung Munich, 20 December 1927, AR K 2138/593682–4, Foreign Office Library. London.)

was made impossible by the antagonism between the BBMB and the BVP. In the district of Traunstein (Upper Bavaria), an attempt had been made in 1928 to unite the two organizations in one 'Peasants' Party' but failed because the leaders 'with their lack of political experience only succeed in further splitting those forces which uphold the state' (76).

More disturbing to the authorities was the drop in support for peasant associations. The district office in Neuburg an der Donau reported late in 1929 a decline in membership and interest in the activities of the Agricultural Association, the Horsebreeders' Association and even the Riding and Travel Club. The same lack of enthusiasm caused the failure of peasants there to support the voluntary fire brigade, and their inadequate response to collections for communal purposes such as the Red Cross, the sale of welfare stamps and relief for those whose crops had been damaged by hailstorms (77). Agricultural distress was having a dampening effect on community spirit.

These conditions made it easier for the NSDAP to move in and present itself as the main opposition force in the rural areas, untainted with government responsibility and in a position to offer more with its national organization than the BBMB. The Nazis now concentrated in Southern Bavaria on attacking the BBMB. During the year 1929–30 they held more meetings in the rural areas there than ever before. In the first fortnight of April 1930, meetings on the topic 'National Socialism and agriculture' were arranged in Landshut, Passau, Straubing and Vilsbiburg, districts in Lower Bavaria where the situation was particularly acute (78). A few months earlier, the district office in Straubing had reported on repeated complaints in farming circles about the worsening circumstances: 'Again and again it is emphasized that the agricultural business is not paying; sharp criticism is reserved especially for the import of foreign corn; the peasant must hand over his corn for a ridiculous price and still cannot often find a purchaser; in this way agriculture must perish' (79). One of the Nazis' most successful speakers here was Hermann Grassl, a teacher from Rottenburg near Landshut, who 'is well versed in the conditions of the peasant and trading middle class, and knows how to secure the agreement of his audience by moderate and objective statements; even Gandorfer[44] has a hard time as speaker in opposition to him' (80). The party Speakers' School was now beginning to pay dividends for many of its trainees were sent out to address NSDAP 'peasant meetings', having been well briefed and indoctrinated in agricultural problems.

The Nazis made special efforts to win support in those areas where the BBMB was well-entrenched. In June 1930 they systematically covered all communities in the district of Illertissen, a stronghold of the BBMB in West

44. The radical BBMB leader in Lower Bavaria, see chapter 3, pp. 70-1.

Swabia, although without much success for the local BBMB held meetings to counter these incursions (*81*). In the neighbouring district of Neu-Ulm, political life was dominated at this time by the BBMB and the Bavarian People's Party. Attempts by local Nazis to attract public attention were frustrated by the refusal of the BVP authorities to allow them the use of assembly rooms until finally a meeting was held in the village of Weissenhorn. *Gau* leader Wahl came along to speak and a local branch was founded there consisting of nine members. Up to the beginning of 1930, the district had remained untouched by the NSDAP. Now a forester called Reiser was appointed district leader in Weissenhorn, but he made little progress at first due to the opposition of Dr Lenz, the local BVP leader, who did not cease taking measures to harass the Nazis (*82*). If the NSDAP encountered local difficulties, these were usually presented by the BVP rather than the BBMB, which suffered from loss of morale and had lost much of its radical fire. District reports from early 1930 frequently drew attention to the fact that its members were joining the NSDAP. In February numbers of *Bauern-bündler* in the district of Griesbach (Lower Bavaria) had left their party to form local branches of the NSDAP in several villages (*83*). At Weissensee, a village near Füssen by the Austrian border, thirty-two people, mainly young peasants, declared after attending a Nazi meeting that they would join the NSDAP (*84*).

In Franconia, the NSDAP was benefiting from disillusionment with the *Landbund*, the associate organization of the Nationalist Party. The BBMB was not at all well represented in Franconia, save in a few Catholic districts, for the *Landbund* was the main spokesman there for agricultural interests. It was not itself a political party like the BBMB, but it supported the Nationalists in elections. The *Landbund* was inevitably affected by the crisis within the DNVP, for a group of party rebels opposed to the Hugenberg line formed their own party, the Christian National Peasants' and Country Folk Party (*Christlich-Nationale Bauern- und Landvolkpartei* or CNBL), in Southern Germany to represent the views of the peasant smallholders. The formation of the new party caused defections from the *Landbund*, and the Nazis, seeing their chance, attempted to drive a wedge between the *Landbund* and the peasants in Middle and Upper Franconia. The NSDAP branch in Kulmbach distributed in the spring of 1930 a handbill in the surrounding area with the following message:

The gentlemen of the *Landbund*—we don't mean here the peasants who work honestly but the leaders of the *Landbund* who for the most part are not peasants—have not believed for a long time the rubbish which they themselves write; but the peasants are supposed to believe it so that they do not stray away and these gentlemen will not lose their profits. Hence their agitation whenever the Hitlers come into the countryside and reveal the true faces of their leaders. They know very well that when the peasant realizes that he is being taken for a ride, this spells the end of their splendour . . . Come to our meetings and hear the truth (*85*)!

Violent incidents involving Nazis and supporters of the *Landbund* were reported from several districts in Middle Franconia early in the year (*86*). At a meeting in Kitzingen Wilhelm Stegmann, a fanatical thirty-year-old Nazi who was supervisor of the estates of Prince Hohenlohe at Schillingsfürst, presented his listeners with arguments typical of party propaganda in rural areas: 'The activities of the Peasants' League, the Green Front and other organizations are insufficient; a united course must be decided and supported by all those who wish for a real improvement in conditions; the time is fast approaching when two forces will face each other in Germany, namely National Socialism and Communism; those who want to prevent civil war must join the National Socialist Fighting Front' (*87*). Although the Nazis made an impression in some areas, it took some time for their propaganda to sink in and create potential voters for the NSDAP. So far they had not won many deserters from the *Landbund*. An early recruit was one Johann Dorner from Dessmannsdorf, a twenty-eight-year-old member of the *Junglandbund* (the youth branch of the organization), who often appeared as a speaker at Nazi meetings. His opponents accused him of joining the NSDAP for materialistic reasons, for it was said he was ambitious and had been disappointed in not being made leader of the *Junglandbund* in Ansbach a few years before (*88*).

In March 1930 the NSDAP put up its own candidates for the first time in the elections to the district peasant councils in Middle and Upper Franconia. The only other organization to contest the elections was the Green Front, a united front formed the month before consisting of various peasant groups and controlled by the *Landbund*. The results for the NSDAP were not spectacular, but the elections provided it with an opportunity to challenge the monopoly of the *Landbund*. Nazi 'discussion speakers' often presented their party's case at meetings of the *Landbund* and aroused much interest. In Middle Franconia the NSDAP won 2,840 votes against 24,422 of the Green Front, and did as well in Upper Franconia with two seats out of a total of thirty (*89*).[45]

45. Although the overall vote for the NSDAP was relatively small, some local results drew the attention of the authorities. The district of Kulmbach commented: 'it is all the same a

The climax of these efforts to win support among the agricultural population was the publication on 7 March 1930 of the NSDAP Agrarian Programme.[46] This drew on many ideas gained from the experience of the rural campaign so far. Early in 1930 Hitler had acquired the services of R. Walther Darré, an agricultural expert who had published a book in 1928 praising the peasantry—*The Peasantry as the Life Source of the Nordic Race*. Based on anthropological investigations concerning the relationship between race and soil cultivation, Darré's work claimed that the peasant was the guardian of morality and tradition. 'In the peasant lies Germany's future,' he had quoted from Wilhelm Riehl, the nineteenth-century romantic nationalist who had deplored the advance of urban society. Darré seemed the ideal person to appeal to the underlying uncertainty among the peasants about their position in society. Until 1930 the NSDAP's appeal to agriculture had been largely restricted to nationalist propaganda against the Versailles Treaty and the attack in the party programme of 1920 on 'interest slavery', 'effortless income' from loan capital or 'land interest' and on land speculation. Now, many of Darré's ideas were incorporated in the new special party programme for agriculture.

The Agrarian Programme was first and foremost an ideological manifesto, promising the peasantry an elevated position in the future Nazi state, although it also included specific proposals for relieving the agricultural population—such as state credits, reduction and remission of taxes, higher tariffs, cheaper artificial manures, cheaper electricity and the revision of the inheritance laws.

It opened with a statement on the importance of the peasantry for Germany's future existence. The peasantry would be restored to its 'real' position in society not only because of its 'surpassing importance' as the provider of sustenance for the German people (by freeing them from their 'slavish' dependence on 'international high finance') but also because the peasantry was 'the chief bearer of a healthy national stock, the fountain of youth of the people and the backbone of military strength'.

Postwar conditions had brought the question of Germany's livelihood to

sign that the party is gradually winning support among the rural population'. In nearby Redwitz, twenty-two of the thirty-two members of the *Landbund* there voted for the NSDAP, while in the village of Rugendorf the Nazis won 33 per cent of the vote. (Reports in Staatsarchiv Bamberg, Reg. v. Ofr., K3/1880.) According to the Social Democratic *Münchner Post* (21 March 1930), many NSDAP candidates in these elections were members of the *Landbund*.

46. The programme was in fact dated 6 March with Hitler's signature, although it appeared in the *Völkischer Beobachter* on 7 March under the title, 'National Socialism and agriculture, an official party proclamation on the position of the NSDAP towards the agricultural population and agriculture'.

a crisis point, because the country was no longer in a position to pay for its food imports with industrial goods. Government policy had done nothing to alleviate the crisis in agriculture through neglect and disregard of the peasantry. No solution could be found so long as 'the German Reich with the help of the parliamentary-democratic governmental system is ruled by international money barons, for they want the destruction of indigenous German power'.

The answer lay in National Socialist policy, which would work for the maintenance of a strong peasantry as a mainstay of the 'real German people's state'. The task of foreign policy would be the acquisition of food supply and colonization areas for the growing German people. The programme announced that 'a large number of viable small- and medium-sized peasant holdings is above all important from the point of view of population policy', although large farms were also necessary if they maintained a 'healthy relationship' with the smaller ones. Nazi policy would look after the cultural as well as the economic interests of the peasantry. The programme proposed raising the level of 'peasant culture' by building peasant colleges and special youth homes in the country.

Finally, the programme emphasized that only the 'freedom movement of the NSDAP' could change the political system, which was the precondition for the solution to the problem of agriculture. The crisis of agriculture was part of the crisis of the whole German people, and the peasants could only be freed from enslavement by a movement which aimed to free the people as a whole. 'Professional organizations' (that is peasant organizations) could only bring partial relief within the present system.

The political opponents of the Nazis, including rival peasant associations, soon recognized the Agrarian Programme for what it was—it promised the earth with a series of unfulfillable policies. Seen from the ideological viewpoint, the programme contained nothing strikingly new for many of the clichés about the downtrodden peasantry had already appeared in the propaganda of other parties, including the Nationalists, the CNBL and even the *Landbund*. The important difference was that the Agrarian Programme had the Nazi propaganda machine behind it. Already, the party central office in Munich was urging local branches to distribute copies of the programme, which had been reproduced as a four-page pamphlet, among the agricultural population (*90*). The Social Democratic daily, the *Münchner Post*, commented ominously:

What is the situation now? The breakthrough of the National Socialists among the Bavarian peasant masses is surely based on the fact that the peasantry is the largest and most populous element in the state; the fact that the Bavarian peasant has in many areas changed his allegiance from the Liberals to the German Nationalists, and from the former Centre Party to the Peasants' League shows that he is not at all immovable in political matters (91).

The Nazis therefore started to make their impact on the peasant population by introducing their propaganda into rural areas and by basing their appeal not only on the economic interests of the peasants but also on their self-esteem, drawing on the 'romantic' view of the peasant class presented by traditional *völkisch* ideology. This propaganda brought some surprisingly quick results, although it was still at this stage only an extension of urban-based propaganda. The reason for this success lay firstly in the weaknesses of the two main peasant parties and secondly in the economic crisis, which in time allowed the Nazis to break the hold of these parties on the peasant voters. The only firm barrier to the expansion of Nazi support in the rural areas was the Bavarian People's Party, which did not suffer from the problems of the other parties because it was an 'ideological' rather than economic-interest party, but its importance was limited. Although it enjoyed strong support in the countryside, its voting strength was confined to the Catholic areas and even here the BBMB shared much of the peasant vote. The other main barrier was the conservatism of the peasants, but this became increasingly weaker once the course of the Depression accelerated. An essential precondition to their exploitation of the economic distress was that the Nazis should make contact with the rural electorate, and this they had already begun.

The Ban on Party Uniforms and the Growth of Political Violence

On 5 June 1930 the Bavarian Government imposed a ban on the wearing of party uniforms at public meetings and processions. Bavaria was the first state to introduce such a measure, which was soon followed by prohibitions on the wearing of the brownshirt in Prussia on 11 June and in Baden on 13 June. On 25 June, the Prussian Government also prohibited civil servants from becoming members of the NSDAP.

The new regulation of the Bavarian Government did not cover all meetings, processions and demonstrations held in the open air, but only those where participants wore uniforms. It also applied to cases where only some of the participants at a public meeting were in uniform, to the transportation by lorry of uniformed party members but not to individual persons who wore uniform in public nor to meetings which took place in closed rooms not open to the public. The ban referred in particular to the activities of the SA and SS of the NSDAP, the Social Democratic Reichsbanner, the ex-servicemen's Stahlhelm and other semi-military organizations like the Bayernwacht, the associate organization of the Bavarian People's Party. In his order of 5 June Dr Stützel, the Minister of the Interior, pointed out that the measure carried no penal sanctions but relied on the police to ensure that it was observed. The police had powers to dissolve meetings which were prohibited and they could be reinforced when they met resistance (92).

Although the ban applied officially to all party military organizations,[47] it was understood by the Nazis at least as being aimed in particular at the NSDAP. This would not have been surprising in view of the fact that Nazis, in particular members of the SA, had more than anybody else been involved in political brawls recently—with the possible exception of members of the Reichsbanner, with whom they frequently clashed.[48] Stützel justified the measure on the grounds of 'the numerous conflicts between members of different political tendencies, which occurred in the course of the last months and to a considerable degree derive from the fact that members of political organizations appeared at public demonstrations in uniform or the dress of associations and societies' (93).

There were other possible reasons for the ban. The Munich correspondent of *The Times*, London, commented that 'there is little doubt that this step taken by the Government is the result of the numerous affrays which have recently taken place in Bavaria between the different political factions, and especially of the increasingly provocative attitude of the Bavarian National Socialists' but went on: 'In well-informed circles it is considered that the Government's action is due not to its apprehension of any serious disorder, but rather to a resolve to minimize the possibility of the occurrence of minor disturbances which, although of no great significance in themselves, would be liable to make a bad impression on the abnormally large number of foreigners who are visiting Bavaria this summer' (94). Disturbances were not usually of much

47. The Communist Rotfrontkämpferbund was not specifically mentioned.
48. Because of the increasing involvement of party members in such incidents, the NSDAP instituted an SA insurance scheme early in 1929 to cover personal injury 'in the service of the party' and the cost of damages (for example, the destruction of property in meeting halls). All party members were required to join. During the last half of 1929 the scheme dealt with 621 cases involving a total cost in compensation of 34,404 Reichmarks. (Memorandum of the SA supreme command, 1 February 1930, Streicher Nachlass/81, Bundesarchiv Koblenz.)

significance in themselves, but the publicity given to them could be harmful to tourism, as had been the case after the Putsch of 1923. The associations of innkeepers had been complaining about the adverse effect of Nazi disturbances on their trade, and the government had to take note of these complaints. The government was also concerned about the possible subversive effects of Nazi propaganda. A few days after the publication of the uniform ban, the Munich police prohibited a mass rally in the Zirkus Krone arranged by the NSDAP for 14 June because 'the extravagant, offensive language of the placards, disgusting to every decent man, together with the inflammatory content of the National Socialist press over the last few days, reveal that the sole aim of the meeting is to pour scorn on the state government and to incite disobedience to its orders' (95).

Political violence had clearly been on the increase since the autumn of 1929. This owed much to the prominence given to emotional and controversial issues, economic distress, the increased activity of the Nazis and the consequent heightened tension between the political parties. During the referendum campaign against the Young Plan, the Ministry of the Interior in Munich warned police stations and district authorities that 'recently in Bavaria political meetings have already given rise at times to brawls between political opponents, the results of which were to some extent not inconsiderable—weapons were also found in places' (96). Several threats of violence had contributed to this strained atmosphere. *Gau* leader Wahl, normally one of the more placid of party leaders, said in a forceful speech at Memmingen that when the stormtroopers numbered 600,000, they would seize the government. There were also ugly incidents at Augsburg near the end of the referendum campaign between SA men, Communists and members of the Reichsbanner (97).

Wahl's threat about the overwhelming numbers of the SA was no idle one. The most serious incident that autumn had taken place at the village of Schney, outside Lichtenfels in Upper Franconia. The incident became famous for the violence which occurred, but it was also important as it reflected on the state of security forces and undoubtedly caused concern to the government. Schney was a community of some 2,000 inhabitants, many of whom were employed in the manufacture of baskets, and had a record of strong support for the SPD. The Lichtenfels branch of the NSDAP arranged a meeting there on 30 September 1929, with *Gau* leader Schemm as speaker on the subject, 'Sixty years of Social Democracy and still no salvation'. The district authorities had not in fact been notified of the meeting, but they later commented that no special precautionary measures would probably have been taken 'because so far not the smallest incident had occurred at political meetings in the whole district, and a similar meeting in Schney four weeks ago passed without friction' (*98*).

An audience of as many as 500, largely workers and Social Democrats, turned up for the meeting. Klingler, an SPD parliamentary deputy from Coburg, was also present. Schemm soon appeared and was accompanied by more than eighty uniformed Nazis, who took their seats on the rostrum surrounding the speaker. Provocations began at once. The audience insisted that the speaker should only be allowed one-and-a-half hours for his address, but Schemm refused to comply saying that his party had organized the meeting and he was free to take as much time as he wanted.

Schemm had been speaking for only half an hour during constant interruptions, when he remarked that 'Jewish capitalism has supported Social Democracy with money for election preparations' and all hell broke loose. Klingler is supposed to have started the trouble by demanding: 'The schoolmaster is not allowed to continue speaking and must come down.' Klingler then went up to Schemm on the stage and told him to shut up. Schemm stuck out his hand at Klingler repeating that his party had called the meeting and the Social Democrats would be allowed free discussion. He was then seized round the legs, thrown to the ground and manhandled. Nazis sprang to his protection and there followed 'an ugly scuffle'. According to an eye-witness 'beer glasses, litre-mugs, chair-legs, bricks and other stones, stove doors and all kinds of seizable objects were thrown from the audience crowd' (*99*). The Nazis threw the Social Democrats out of the hall, but the latter gathered outside with a crowd of inquisitive passers-by and started to threaten the Nazis in the building.

The local police officer, fearing worse violence, decided he could not master the situation by himself and at 10.30 p.m., two hours after the meeting had begun, notified the district office in Lichtenfels, which sent along relief. There were now seven policemen present, who managed to quieten the crowd outside but could not have dealt with a further outbreak of violence. The police officer then contacted the state police in Coburg, 15 kilometres away, but the commissioner there could not send any reinforcements for two hours because many of his men had gone off on a clearing-up job and had taken all the service cars with them. It was 11.45, so the desperate police officer rang the police station in Bamberg, over 30 kilometres away, which sent along twenty-five policemen who eventually arrived at three o'clock. No more violence had in fact occurred, and by this time the Nazis were in no mood for further trouble and returned home. They were searched for weapons but were found to be carrying only a few steel rods and rubber truncheons. Altogether, twenty-nine people had been injured, two of them seriously, and the hall was in ruins (*100*). The Schney incident apparently made a deep impression on the authorities.

The spring of 1930 saw no abatement in the number of street clashes between political opponents and meetings broken up. The authorities in Upper Bavaria reported that the Nazis were 'apparently going out of their way to organize clashes with other parties'. They had recently gatecrashed meetings of the Reichsbanner in Fürstenfeldbruck and the BBMB in Wasserburg, where a group of SA men had prevented the speaker from making himself heard by singing loudly (*101*). Some of the street incidents happened spontaneously. Early in May fighting broke out between some Nazis and a procession of trade unionists in Neustadt an der Aisch. The trade unionists had just returned from a day's outing and were marching back from the railway station, when they approached an inn on the road into town. A group of Nazis were sitting outside drinking. The leader of the trade unionists told his men to stop singing, but provocations from the Nazis were too much for some of the trade unionists who were drunk. Insults were hurled from both sides, and each group attempted to seize and trample on the flags and banners of the other side (*102*).

During March rumours had been spread in public of plans by the Nazis to stage a putsch in the coming weeks. Evidence of the existence of such plans was never produced, but the rumours were encouraged by their opponents to blacken the name of the Nazis. The Social Democratic *Münchner Post* was the first paper to refer openly to these rumours in a report on 28 March, in which it suggested that the rumours had been started by the Nazis themselves in order to measure the likely reaction from the public (*103*).

The nervous attitude of the authorities was illustrated by events in Oberammergau a few weeks later. The Passion Play was being produced that summer, and the village elders wanted to call a halt to political meetings during the months of the play's production for fear that disturbances might affect tourism, on which the community depended heavily for the only industry there was wood-carving. On Sunday, 6 April, the local Nazis held a meeting in the Rose Inn, which ended in a brawl with a few SPD supporters. The Oberammergau police wrote to the district office in Garmisch the following day that 'the order-loving population, especially the bourgeoisie, have been scandalized by this meeting and don't want to hear any more about political matters' (*104*). The Garmisch office compiled a dossier on the disturbances of 6 April, and the following month the head of the office informed the government of Upper Bavaria: 'On the same day as the scuffle became known, I advised the community to do everything to see that meetings of all kinds are prevented during the duration of the Passion Play (for example, the effect on the owners of the performance hall), as the "Passion" must take place without question against a peaceful background' (*105*).[49]

The general public reaction in Bavaria to the uniform ban of 5 June was therefore one of relief. The Catholic and liberal press wholeheartedly welcomed it. The bourgeois *Nördlinger Zeitung* reflected the law-and-order attitude of citizens of provincial towns when it commented: 'It is a disgrace for a great people when a system grows up which replaces conflict of the mind by rubber truncheons and cudgels, knives and revolvers, and introduces brutal force in place of political tolerance and respect for the honest convictions of those who think differently' (*106*). From Weilheim it was reported that the uniform ban was welcomed by the peasants, who were irritated by propaganda excursions of the Nazis who had the habit of appearing in uniform on workdays when the peasants were busy in the fields (*107*).

The Nazis were of course extremely bitter about the whole matter. The ban on the wearing of uniforms, which applied officially to all party organizations, affected the NSDAP most because much of its propaganda was carried out by the SA, which arranged torchlight processions, marches to church services and ceremonies commemorating the war dead. For many SA toughs the brownshirt had become a sort of virility symbol. The party press kept up a vitriolic attack on the Bavarian Government, and there were a number of unpleasant episodes. Dr Stützel received anonymous letters containing threats and insults. One of these warned that as a reprisal for the ban, the religious procession on the feast of Corpus Christi would be broken up (*108*). Nazi deputies appeared in the state parliament in Munich wearing their brown shirts. One of them spoke so violently that he was suspended. The president of the parliament warned that in future he would have deputies appearing there in political uniforms thrown out (*109*).

The ban caused ill feeling among nationalist circles in general and the Nazis attempted to exploit this. In Coburg the NSDAP group on the city council issued a protest 'in the name of the patriotic population of the German town of Coburg', which won the acclaim of the Stahlhelm (*110*). The Nazis also took advantage of loopholes in the ban. Several districts in Middle Franconia admitted the difficulties of applying the ban in rural areas,

49. The authorities in Oberammergau were not entirely successful. The Passion Play naturally attracted many journalists from abroad, especially England. A minor international incident occurred when a correspondent of the *Daily Express* reported having seen military exercises by Nazis in Ettal, a few miles from Oberammergau. His report coincided with one from Geneva in the same paper that the rise of the Nazis was leading to a rapprochement between Britain and France. The matter caused sufficient concern in London for the German Government to take pains to calm fears there. (Report of the mayor of Oberammergau, November 1930, HA 20A/1749.)

as political marches were easily recognizable even without uniforms when participants wore the same clothing. The local press in Gunzenhausen drew attention to the problems of interpretation. Did the wearing of the same armbands constitute a violation of the regulation, or what should be done when some participants in a procession wore the same alternative clothing and the rest wore something else (*111*)? The Nazis went out of their way to defy the authorities by wearing white shirts. Von Pfeffer, the SA leader, even issued a special order on 10 July introducing what became known in Nazi circles as 'the white prohibition shirt', but by and large the Nazis were careful not to go too far and the uniform ban was generally respected. Late in June, the NSDAP organized a 'midsummer festival' just over the Austrian border in Kufstein. Party members travelling from Munich wore civilian clothes until they crossed the frontier, where they changed into their brown shirts and marched the rest of the way (*112*).

As Stützel had himself admitted in his memorandum to local authorities on 5 June, much depended on the behaviour of the leaders of the parties concerned, whether they chose to comply with the regulation or to resist it. The leaders of the NSDAP decided in spite of its dampening effect on their propaganda to observe the ban, because they feared that provocative defiance would give the Bavarian Government the excuse it needed for imposing a complete ban on the SA. No doubt the fact that public opinion was generally on the side of the government helped to persuade the Nazis not to push the matter too far.

Hitler, who was putting in few appearances at party headquarters in Munich for fear of extradition, issued special instructions completely forbidding the wearing of uniforms. There was the possibility that the SA might get out of hand. SA leaders were asked to destroy all orders they received in case the police decided to find something compromising in them. Party leaders chose not to sleep overnight in their own flats in Munich should the police decide to make arrests. Official sources commented on the atmosphere of nervousness and depression at party headquarters (*113*).

Meanwhile, the political situation had become more uncertain with the dissolution of the Reichstag on 18 July. New elections were called for September, and it remained to be seen what effect the change in political circumstances would have on voting behaviour. The rise in political violence was a symptom of these new circumstances. Although the uniform ban restricted Nazi propaganda, the ultimate loser from the outbreaks of political disorder was not the NSDAP but the state.

The Reichstag Election, September 1930

The premature dissolution of the Reichstag in 1930—two years earlier than was constitutionally necessary—was a sign of the increasing seriousness of Germany's economic problems and the inability of governments to deal with them. The longest serving cabinet in Weimar history under the Social Democratic Chancellor Herman Müller had fallen in March after twenty-one months in office, following disagreement among the coalition parties over the Chancellor's financial policy and the refusal by his own party to support him. His successor as Chancellor, Heinrich Brüning of the Catholic Centre Party, suffered a setback when the Reichstag rejected his programme of financial retrenchment. Brüning reacted by calling new elections.

There were several reasons for regarding this election with foreboding. During the campaign, the Bavarian Government felt it necessary to take more stringent measures to ensure public security because 'experiences up till now compel us to strengthen police protection for election meetings and other legal preparations of the parties for the Reichstag Election' (*114*). Following further incidents, the Ministry of the Interior extended the prohibition on the wearing of uniforms to all political meetings in larger towns rather than only those held in the open air. Any kind of political uniform was banned from the streets between six o'clock at night and six o'clock in the morning as well as on election day. The police in larger towns were also ordered to prohibit the supply of food and drink at Communist and Nazi meetings. Political meetings in Bavaria were often held in beer-halls, and speeches were usually accompanied by much eating and drinking, which was understandable when one speech alone could last as long as two or three hours. The beer only helped to quicken tempers and a disturbance by political opponents easily led to violent scenes. There was always a store of missiles at hand in the form of beer-mugs, plates and cutlery. In some places, the police had even forbidden the provision of ashtrays at political meetings 'as experience has proved that these can be used as missiles of an offensive and even dangerous character'. The Ministry now made this ban general and further ordered the police to confiscate weapons from visitors to meetings and to draw attention to the new measures in the press (*115*).

One wonders what impression the public had of the Nazi Party at this time. The general feeling of relief at the uniform ban would suggest that it was viewed as a threat to peace and order, which certainly it was in government circles in Munich. Yet the circumstances surrounding the calling of the elections could only favour the Nazis. The national government was hardly going to the country at an opportune moment, for it was not in a position to demonstrate its effectiveness to the electorate since deadlock in the Reichstag had been the immediate reason for calling the elections. How much the greater stability of the Bavarian Government (now a minority government since the withdrawal of the BBMB) would influence voters in Bavaria was doubtful, except in so far as this might help the chances of the Bavarian People's Party. The worse economic and political situation of the country was bound to reflect adversely on the Weimar political system, and dim the electoral prospects of the parties in power. The regional government of Lower Franconia expressed alarm at the wide support for the NSDAP:

> In wide circles, especially among the better classes, open and hidden sympathies prevail. Every preventive measure of the police authorities is met with sharp criticism. Altogether, the movement nowadays seems to enjoy considerable attention. Sympathies for it come less from an affirmation of the aims of the movement, than from the widely held conviction that the ruling parties and the consequent inability of legislative bodies to master their problems have undermined healthy democratic ideas to the point of ruin. What is exceedingly critical is the important role that younger university-educated people play to an increasing extent in the movement (*116*).

The Nazis had reason to be optimistic about their chances in the election. Local elections in 1930 had confirmed the trend of popular opinion in their favour, especially after they won a vote of 14·4 per cent in the state election in Saxony in June. They expected results from their reorganization of 1928–29 based on an electoral strategy and the extension of their mass appeal to include rural voters, both of which had occurred since the last national election just over two years before. An election in the autumn had not been unexpected in leadership circles of the party. As early as the beginning of May Gregor Strasser, the head of party organization, had warned a closed meeting of leaders in the *Gau* of Württemberg: 'We must definitely reckon with new elections in the autumn and therefore we must start at once with the organizational preparations for an election . . . the really useful work is to try out everything imaginable to win over to the party those forces which have so far been hostile to it—new enrolments must be more strictly controlled and party organization must become more rigorous and bureaucratic' (*117*).

Within days of the announcement of the Reichstag Election, the party's propaganda machine was set in motion. On 20 July, the *Gau* of Upper Bavaria held a conference of district leaders at Herrsching to discuss plans for the election campaign. Three days later, *Gau* leader Reinhardt issued detailed instructions for the forthcoming campaign (*118*). The *Gau* would be redivided into seventeen districts, each one headed by a district leader who was responsible for most of the detailed organization of the campaign—the collection of funds to finance it, the distribution of propaganda sent from the *Gau* office and the arrangements for public meetings. By 31 July, each district leader had to provide the *Gau* office with a complete programme of all meetings in his district right up to election eve on 13 September. Within a week, each district leader had to hold a meeting of local branch leaders under his authority to inform them of the plans agreed at the conference on 20 July. Although the district leaders in effect took over the organization of propaganda, Reinhardt made it clear that the authority of the *Gau* leader was not diminished. His control over the organization of public meetings was essential as these were the nucleus of Nazi propaganda:

> We find ourselves in an election campaign. Each day counts. The district leader must include in his survey the exact date and place for meetings which are to take place. Particular wishes for certain speakers cannot be taken into consideration. In view of the conditions of the election campaign it is not possible to request particular speakers, only the date and place of the meeting. The selection of speakers is a matter for the *Gau* leadership. Only it assigns the speakers. Rearrangements can under no circumstances be made afterwards, if the plan of deployment is not to be seriously upset (*119*).

The Nazis were clearly determined not to waste their efforts and talent. Propaganda was to be carried out uniformly under the supervision of Goebbels' Propaganda Department at party headquarters in Munich. On 23 July Goebbels circulated a special memorandum for the conduct of the campaign (*120*). While 'the party which begins the election campaign first has the most chances', he warned *Gau* leaders not to exhaust themselves during the first weeks but to build up the momentum of propaganda week by week. Until 18 August each *Gau* had to make the best use of its own propaganda activities, but from that date the party's biggest speakers would be put into action 'evening after evening' and 'in giant mass demonstrations the strength and uniform resolution of the movement will be displayed in a practical way before the electoral masses all over the Reich'.

Goebbels provided guidelines for propaganda, including the following themes: rejection of the 'policy of fulfilment';[50] opposition to the treaties of

---

50. The term used in reference to Stresemann's policy of winning the confidence of the Western Powers by attempting to carry out the Treaty of Versailles. It was used as a term of abuse by the nationalist Right.

Versailles, Locarno and The Hague;[51] demand for a change of direction in foreign policy and for a transformation in the domestic political situation. The slogans which Goebbels fashioned for the campaign were all negative (against the Young Plan, against war-guilt lies, etc.) except for his advocacy of 'a strong foreign policy combined with a responsible socialist-inclined German domestic policy'.

Goebbels devoted considerable attention in his memorandum to the attitude party speakers should take towards the other parties. It was quite clear that he aimed at presenting the NSDAP as the only real opposition force in the election, for even the Communists were classed with the other parties. Although the latter had rejected the 'fulfilment policy', there was in the last analysis 'no distinction' between them and the Social Democrats as both professed the Marxist point of view. They were 'a Russian fifth column' and should be opposed for ideological reasons. The SPD was the party of treason for its betrayal of German interests abroad and its responsibility in government for the disastrous state of the economy, repressive taxation and the 'throttling' of social expenditure. Similarly, the Centre Party was attacked for its share of blame and its participation in governments since 1918.

The election was about 'the future of the German people' and stood 'in the sign of Young', which was the main criterion for judging the parties. Goebbels hoped to revive the emotions aroused during the Young Plan referendum, which had assisted the Nazi electoral successes the previous autumn, because this issue had a wide appeal which cut across parties. In this way the NSDAP should attract new supporters from the other parties, in particular from the smaller bourgeois parties. The latter were also to be attacked because of their internal weaknesses—the Nationalists were now divided into four factions, the Democrats were to be shown up as a 'splinter party', the Economic Party was hardly in a position to save the middle classes because it was not firm enough in the defence of their interests, while the German People's Party was not a convincing opponent of Marxism after its alliance with the Social Democrats (*121*).

All posters and leaflets were designed by the Propaganda Department, and then posted to the *Gau* offices for printing and distribution. But the emphasis of propaganda did vary from area to area. A sample of leaflets distributed by Streicher's organization in Franconia illustrates the conservative appeal of the NSDAP in that region. Female voters, peasants, the petty bourgeoisie and Catholics were chosen as special targets. Leaflets addressed to female voters began with an exhortation:

51. The negotiations on the Young Plan took place at The Hague.

German Woman! German Girl! You also have a decided Influence on the Fate of Your People! One Day your Child will ask you if You shared in the National Guilt ... We say to you: the German Family goes to Ruin if Husband, Son and Fiancé must work off Young Tributes abroad ... as Wife and Mother fight with us for the Future of your Child (*122*)!

The leaflet to peasants followed the lines of the party's Agrarian Programme, reminding them of their betrayal by the state, the rise in prices and taxation and the incompetence of their own leaders; while the petty bourgeoisie were also made aware of the advantages of voting for the NSDAP rather than supporting their own economic-interest organizations. The Catholics were a different problem because the Nazis were on the defensive here, and their propaganda usually consisted of a number of specious arguments: an anti-Jewish attitude was compatible with Christianity (one leaflet quoted at length a speech made by a Hungarian bishop attacking the Jews and Bolshevism); the two Catholic parties had lost credibility because of their cooperation with the Social Democrats[52] (look at what has happened to the Catholic Church in Russia!); the NSDAP was acceptable by the Church because of the agreement of the Papacy with Mussolini's régime in Italy (the National Socialists under Hitler were doing the same as Mussolini by fighting the 'red pest hostile to God') (*123*).

Nazi propaganda therefore concentrated on the issues of the Young Plan (nationalism), the Weimar political system (anti-parliamentary democracy), the economic crisis (the incompetence of parliamentary democracy) and the fear of Communism. It was easy to be impressed by the euphoric tone of this propaganda, which was designed as much to encourage party workers as overwhelm their opponents. Goebbels had urged that 'by 14 September there will be no town, no village, no spot, where we National Socialists have not made our appearance through a large meeting' (*124*); and four weeks before polling day the *Völkischer Beobachter* boasted that from 18 August there would be '34,000 National Socialist meetings' (*125*). In comparison with the other parties, the NSDAP organized the most intensive campaign of all, but the success of its propaganda did vary, depending on a number of factors.

The NSDAP continued to hold an impressive number of meetings

52. The Centre Party had formed coalition governments with the Social Democrats at the national level. This was not true in the case of the Bavarian People's Party, which was not in a coalition with the SPD in Bavaria, although BVP ministers had participated in the cabinet of the socialist Johannes Hoffmann (1919–20). The BVP was in fact a pronouncedly anti-Marxist party.

throughout the campaign, but attendance varied in size from place to place. While in some areas rural voters appeared indifferent to Nazi propaganda, a Hitler meeting in Grafing, a village to the east of Munich, drew a crowd of 4,000 consisting mainly of peasants from the neighbourhood (*126*). A big name always made a great difference. Several Nazi meetings in Günzburg had to be called off in August because so few people turned up. In Memmingen, on the other hand, Ritter von Epp attracted an audience of two or three thousand. Before the meeting began a stunt pilot from Munich dropped Nazi leaflets from the air (*127*).

Epp was such a popular visitor in Holzkirchen that a parallel meeting was organized there and addressed by Reinhardt. The latter made the wild promise that after the Nazis came to power the peasants would no longer have to pay taxes for at least two years until they recovered their position (*128*).

The continuous agitation of the NSDAP was necessary in view of the kind of electorate to which it was primarily appealing—especially to non-voters and those whose attachment to other parties could be shaken. A series of public meetings was the surest way of making contact with voters who were either politically indifferent or had no strong political commitment. The Bavarian People's Party, by contrast, appealed broadly to a different section of the electorate, in particular, strong Catholics—a more stable body of voters, who could be easily mobilized by the Catholic associations and were reminded of their duty to vote by the local priest. The BVP therefore did not need to organize such an intensive campaign of public meetings. All the same, the crucial nature of this election affected even the propaganda of the BVP. The Catholic papers were full of warnings to non-voters in the last week before the ballot. On 9 September the *Augsburger Postzeitung* warned about 'the guilt of non-voters', three days later told non-voters to 'wake up' and on election day added the final touches to the picture of the non-voter as a political pariah. The non-voter was like a man who confronted a heavily armed opponent with his hands in his trouser pockets; he was without self-confidence, without love for his country and 'an ungrateful and wretched figure' (*129*).

As the party of the established order, the BVP emphasized the revolutionary character of the other parties. Now that the BBMB had succumbed to its radical wing and withdrawn from the Bavarian Government, that too was classed along with the left-wing parties and the National Socialists as subversive. BVP propaganda accused the NSDAP of being a stalking-horse for the Communists, a sort of Bolshevist wolf in nationalist sheep's clothing. Attacks on the Nazis became more frequent as election day approached. In the last week of the campaign the *Augsburger Postzeitung* published the following warning:

> German wife—German mother—can you vote National Socialist?
> Oh yes, you can vote National Socialist—
> If you want to sacrifice your husband or your sons to a new war.
> If you do not shrink from a new revolution and a new inflation.
> If you are of the same opinion as the Hitler people that chaos, ruin and civil war are the cheapest foundations for the revival of the German people.
> But if you shudder at such a catastrophic policy and want to protect your loved ones from the certain consequences of Communist and National Socialist all-or-nothing policy.
> Then you will elect on Sunday, 14 September the parties of peace and order, those with a sense of duty and not those which rely on irresponsible slogans.
> Elect the party of the Christian people's community, the BVP (*130*).

As women voted more than men for the confessional and conservative parties, it was not at all surprising that the Bavarian People's Party should in the situation be calling on its staunchest supporters in such strident terms.

The vote on 14 September brought the expected increase in support for the Nazi Party, although its vote in Bavaria was slightly below the national average of 18·3 per cent. The rise in support for the NSDAP was less impressive in the Catholic regions of the state, for while the vote for the party in Germany as a whole increased almost eightfold over that of the 1928 Election it no more than trebled in Southern Bavaria. This was partly because the vote for the Nazis had initially been stronger here than in most other areas of Germany. During 1928–30, there was a definite geographical shift in support for the NSDAP. The Bavarian electoral districts had recorded the highest percentages of the party in 1928, but in 1930 the districts with above-average support for the NSDAP were nearly all in Northern and Eastern Germany.[53]

The vote for the NSDAP in Bavaria nevertheless constituted a political upheaval as elsewhere (*131*). While the rise in Nazi support was general throughout the state, there were considerable regional variations in the degree of that support. By far the highest votes were in the two predomi-

---

53. The electoral districts with the three highest votes for the NSDAP in 1930 were Schleswig-Holstein (27 per cent), South-Hanover-Brunswick (24·3 per cent) and Pomerania (24·3 per cent).

nantly Protestant regions of Middle and Upper Franconia—23·8 per cent and 23·9 per cent respectively—while the vote in the two predominantly Catholic regions of Lower Bavaria and the Upper Palatinate was as low as 11·6 per cent and 12·4 per cent. Only in the Protestant towns of Coburg and neighbouring Neustadt did the NSDAP vote reach above 40 per cent. But the confessional pattern of the results was not always straightforward. The NSDAP was strongly favoured by Protestants in areas of mixed confession, especially in such towns as Memmingen, Neu-Ulm and Nördlingen in Catholic Southern Bavaria, where there was a strong Protestant minority population. But the NSDAP also did well in strong Catholic towns, of which Passau was a striking example.[54]

There was a marked increase in support for the Nazis among rural voters, although quite clearly the NSDAP's rural propaganda had not yet made a full impact. The vote for the NSDAP was still higher in the towns than in the rural districts,[55] but the rise in Nazi support was all the same alarming in some places. In certain districts of Swabia the vote for the NSDAP went up by seven, eight and even ten times that of 1928, such as in the district of Sonthofen from 510 to 4,559. In Middle Franconia the authorities noted the successful exploitation by the Nazis of economic discontent in the rural districts but commented that their increase in support was 'chiefly in the larger localities which did not have a purely farming population, while in the smaller places with an exclusively agricultural population the vote remained for the most part unimportant' (*132*).

In general, the liberal *Münchener Neueste Nachrichten* (a paper by no means hostile to the Weimar Republic) commented on the results and the rise in support for the Nazis in its editorial the day after the election:

> The conviction is universal that the German Reich is badly governed— the endless disputes of the parties, the bargaining over laws, the dreary indecisiveness of the Reichstag, its failure at decisive moments, its narrow-minded passion for small things, its preference for everything which is by half measure and dull, the deterioration of politics to tactical manipulations—all this has damaged the feeling for the state especially among German youth (*133*).

54. Passau was the seat of a bishopric with a Catholic population of 95 per cent. The NSDAP won a vote here of 31 per cent. The city's position on the Austrian border may well have encouraged the trend towards nationalism.

55. For example the NSDAP vote in Upper Franconia was 32·7 per cent (towns) and 20 per cent (rural districts); and in Upper Bavaria 21·6 per cent (towns) and 13·1 per cent (rural districts).

The results in Bavaria to some extent confirmed this disillusionment with the political system and with the parties most associated with it, as the main factor determining changes in voting loyalties in the 1930 Election. The Communists made small gains while the Social Democrats, the BBMB and the smaller parties lost votes. The Nationalist Party lost heavily, especially in its former strongholds of Middle and Upper Franconia, but its position had been ambiguous. Ideologically opposed to the Weimar state, it had nevertheless participated in various governments at both the national and state level. As with the BBMB, its disgruntled supporters found that its fluctuation between involvement in government and its radicalism (not to mention its internal divisions) was unsatisfactory, and they preferred the NSDAP.

The serious loss of support by the BBMB was ominous, for this peasants' party had taken an even more radical turn in the months before the election and might have been expected to benefit from the economic crisis. But its hopes of winning more popular support after its resignation from the government over the slaughter tax were cruelly dashed. A post-mortem report in the official journal of the BBMB, the *Bauernbunds-Korrespondenz*, blamed its losses on the radicalization of the peasant masses by the Nazis, but the Catholic *Augsburger Postzeitung* commented with some glee: 'One can only laugh about it for no party has radicalized the voters to such an extent as the Peasants' League, in fact since its existence the Peasants' League only rose and grew through the radicalization of the peasants' (*134*). The BBMB had directed some of its fire during the campaign at the BVP (thereby further increasing the alienation between the two parties) instead of concentrating its attack on the NSDAP, but it was really fighting between the deep blue sea and the devil.

In the Protestant regions of Franconia, where the BBMB did not operate, the story was somewhat different. There the discontented agricultural voters did not all vote directly for the NSDAP as in the Catholic areas, but changed their allegiance from the DNVP to the *Deutsches Landvolk*, formed in 1928 to represent the interest of peasant smallholders. The *Deutsches Landvolk* served to radicalize the peasants further, and its high vote of 32·2 per cent in rural Middle Franconia demonstrated that the peasant voter there, normally a conservative creature, was capable of changing his political allegiance and presumably could do so a second time.[56]

56. *Deutsches Landvolk* was the shortened name of the Christian National Peasants' and Country Folk Party (CNBL). In the July 1932 Reichstag Election, the vote for this new party was in turn swallowed up by the NSDAP. This is seen in the case of the district of Rothenburg ob der Tauber. In 1928 the DNVP won a vote there of 78·6 per cent. In 1930

The NSDAP therefore won votes at the expense of the Nationalists in the towns and certain rural areas, and of the BBMB in the Catholic rural areas. This was a continuation of the pattern in the municipal elections the previous year with the additional factor of the collapse of the BBMB (except in Lower Bavaria, its old stronghold) and its replacement by the NSDAP as the spokesman of peasant radicalism.

The other new factor was the rise in voter participation, for the Nazi Party's greatest gains came from the new voters. The 1930 Election saw a large increase in voter participation from 75·6 per cent in 1928 to 82 per cent in 1930, which coincided with a drop in the votes for the splinter parties by one half (*135*). This suggested that people were less willing in a time of crisis to indulge in the luxury of voting for a party which had little influence and little chance of power. They found it more appealing to cast their votes for a party which seemed on the rise and gave the impression of dynamism and energy. It has been argued that an increase in the level of participation in a democratic election may reflect the breakdown of the democratic process just as political apathy may reflect a stable democratic system; and that non-voters are more likely than regular voters to oppose democratic values and favour strong leadership, because they tend to be disillusioned with the parliamentary system and with parliamentary parties.[57] The level of voter participation can depend on other factors, such as the form of voter registration; furthermore, voter participation in Weimar Germany was in any case high in all elections, local as well as national. The vote in Bavaria in the 1930 Election does nevertheless support the theory about voter participation, for the overwhelming majority of new voters seem to have supported the NSDAP.[58]

One surprising result in this election was the rise in support for the Catholic parties. In Bavaria, the BVP attracted 113,333 more voters than in

---

the DNVP vote dropped right down to 4·1 per cent, while the *Deutsches Landvolk* won 49·5 per cent of the vote and the NSDAP increased its share from 9·4 per cent in 1928 to 33·6 per cent. In July 1932, the NSDAP won the remainder of the former DNVP vote with 83 per cent of the poll in the district. The vote of the *Deutsches Landvolk* was now reduced to nil.

57. See S. M. Lipset, *Political Man*, p. 32.

58. The returns for Upper Bavaria show this clearly:

Gains:	NSDAP	101,551	Loss:	DNVP	29,153
	BVP	46,385		BBMB	19,077
	KPD	21,428			
	SPD	502			

Increase in voters: 125,482.

Source: Statistschses Jahrbuch für den Freistaat Bayern (1930), pp. 570–71.

1928.[59] Some were former supporters of the BBMB, but many others were new voters. Disillusionment with the political system apparently did not affect the electoral fortunes of the Bavarian People's Party. This phenomenon probably had less to do with policies and issues than with the fact that the BVP, with the support of the Roman Catholic Church behind it, offered a source of security and stability in the midst of political troubles.[60] Those former supporters of the BBMB who now voted for the Bavarian People's Party presumably did so for confessional reasons—judging by the comments of local police reports—because they saw no alternative to voting for a party which would uphold the interests of their Church. Their confessional ties proved stronger than the radical appeal of the NSDAP to their agricultural interests.

The rise in support for the Bavarian ruling party occurred in both town and country, but was more impressive in the latter. The BVP gained over 2,500 votes in the district of Erding and nearly 2,000 in the district of Donauwörth, not to mention its 6,000 new voters in the bishopric city of Augsburg. Although the NSDAP had made striking gains in popular support —more than any other party in any previous election in Bavaria—the result of the 1930 Election also emphasized that the Bavarian People's Party was the main obstacle there to the rise of the Nazis. In all nine districts in Southern Bavaria where the NSDAP won the second largest vote, the BVP was the majority party; and in the ten towns where the NSDAP became the second strongest party, the BVP came first in all but three cases. There was some justification for the claims of the Catholic press that the Bavarian People's Party was the only party capable of challenging the NSDAP.

The rise in Nazi support had some significant repercussions. Firstly, it gave a boost to party membership. A month after the election the Munich police reported:

Already in the weeks before the election, but more especially in the days following it, the party received an enormous increase in members; according to the latest report the 360 thousandth member was enrolled recently; this increase in members has also led to organizational measures by the party; almost all larger local branches have been sub-divided to make it easier to include these members and have then been combined in new districts, from which the *Gaue* are formed (*136*).

59. The BVP vote increased from 945,304 in 1928 to 1,058,637 in 1930.
60. See C. P. Loomis and J. A. Beegle, 'The Spread of German Nazism in Rural Areas' (*American Sociological Review*, 1946, pp. 724–34) on the importance of Catholicism as a factor resisting the NSDAP in rural areas.

Applications to join the NSDAP gained momentum from 1930. Membership had risen steadily since 1925 from 27,117 to 176,426 in 1929, but it increased in the year from the end of 1930 from 389,000 to 806,294 (*137*). The boom in membership necessitated the opening of new local branches. In the Upper Palatinate, an area where party organization had not been very strong, eleven branches were founded between the September election and the beginning of January 1931 (*138*).

Secondly, electoral success more than anything else gave the Nazi Party political respectability. The Nuremberg police noticed the more open commitment to support for the Nazis—such as the wearing of party badges in public—even among circles which for business and social reasons had previously maintained a reserved attitude towards the NSDAP (*139*). The regional administration of Middle Franconia quoted in evidence of the great impression made on the public by the election result the fact that in the district of Rothenburg

> politically mature people, who up to now have rejected the National Socialist programme and at the last election gave their vote to other right-wing parties, announce that they will even vote National Socialist at the next election in view of the present vacillating attitude of the Reich Government, in order to bring about the formation of a reliable right-wing government (*140*).

The most important individual example of the bandwagon effect produced by the rise in Nazi support was the mayor of Lindau, Ludwig Siebert. Lindau was a picturesque holiday resort situated on an island at the eastern end of Lake Constance. It was the only larger town in Southern Bavaria where the NSDAP became the strongest party in the 1930 Election (1,833 votes—22·1 per cent). Siebert had been mayor of Lindau since 1919 for the Bavarian People's Party, but in January 1931 he suddenly announced his decision to join the NSDAP. No doubt local political pressures resulting from the Nazi vote there helped to persuade him. He was not in fact a native of Lindau. Born in 1874 in Ludwigshafen in the Rhenish Palatinate, he later moved to Bavaria and became mayor of Rothenburg ob der Tauber from 1908 to 1919. With his Protestant background, unusual in a distinguished local dignitary of the Bavarian People's Party, one could possibly assume that he was not a fully integrated member of that party. A short balding man now in his middle fifties, Siebert seemed the archetypal bureaucrat. With his legal training and his mastery of financial matters he had made a name for himself as an efficient and painstaking administrator even to the extent of preserving the many splendid monuments in the city of Rothenburg, not to mention his extension and reorganization of the municipal area of Lindau.

The Nazis, conscious of the prestige implications of Siebert's open declaration of support for their party, paraded him around as a public speaker. Within a week or two Siebert was signed up to speak at many meetings around Bavaria, including one in the Hackerbräukeller in Munich. On 27 January he addressed a crowd of 1,750 in Lindau, which according to the local police was the largest number ever counted at a political meeting in the town (*141*). He was no rabble rouser and had no charisma but he nevertheless made an impression chiefly because of his change of political allegiance. According to the Munich police: 'The statements of the speaker were to the point; Siebert gave the impression of a quiet deliberate man, who informed his listeners that after careful reflection he had joined the NSDAP because on the basis of his observations he expected all the more help and salvation from this party' (*142*). It was not unusual at this time for mayors of smaller towns, especially those belonging to the DNVP, to announce their support for the NSDAP, but Siebert was by far the most interesting case because he later became Prime Minister of Bavaria after the Nazi 'seizure of power' in 1933.

The Reichstag Election of 1930 marked an important stage in the development of the NSDAP. It underlined the transformation of a former fringe party into a mass movement in terms of voting support, and confirmed the policy decisions and organizational changes of the previous two years. The Election showed that the political situation was sufficiently fluid—because of the economic crisis, the fragility of popular support for the Weimar Republic and the weaknesses of the party system—to allow an extremist party to become the second strongest party in the state. Moreover, electoral success had a significant effect on the further development of the NSDAP, because it provided a stimulus for important changes during the years which followed, including the institutionalization of the rural campaign, the greater emphasis on specialist propaganda and even the forlorn attempts to establish a party press. But the rise in Nazi voting strength also opened up new problems. The party organization had to accommodate the new members and retain the support of the new voters, but a problem of more significance for the future was relations between the Nazi Party and the Catholic Church.

Five

The NSDAP and Religion: the Problem of Roman Catholic Voters

The effect of the 1930 Reichstag Election on relations between the Roman Catholic Church and the Nazi Party showed the extent to which this election transformed the political scene. The Church, which had previously not viewed the NSDAP as a serious problem, had to face the fact that it was now the second largest party in Germany, and that many Catholics had voted for it in spite of the strengthened position of the Catholic parties. Equally the NSDAP, whose official stand on the question of religion had been deliberately vague and ambiguous, now found itself under pressure to reveal its true colours. Demands were voiced for a clarification of the NSDAP's emphasis on 'positive Christianity' in point 24 of the party programme, just as Hitler had 'explained' point 17 about land reform. The Nazi leaders were reluctant to do this because confession was still a divisive factor in politics, and a more precise definition of the party's policy here would have jeopardized its claim to represent the whole German people.

A study of the Nazi Party and Roman Catholics is useful in view of the importance of confession as a factor in German politics, and because the controversy over this question which followed the 1930 Election reveals much about the Nazi Party itself—its characteristics as a movement, the relevance of its ideology, the nature of its propaganda and its reaction to this controversial question. It is also important to determine what effect the controversy had on Catholic voters supporting the NSDAP. Bavaria is the best case for an examination of this question, because of its predominantly Catholic population, the fact that it was governed by a Catholic party and the importance attached by the Roman Catholic Church to the maintenance of Bavaria's position as a federal state within the Reich. The lower vote for the NSDAP in Catholic areas than in Protestant areas has resulted in a misconception of Catholic support for the Nazis. Confession could not be seen in isolation for it was related to other political, social and economic factors within a region. There was also the question of how far a Catholic region was strongly Catholic rather than nominally Catholic. The Catholic Church reacted in the way it did to the problem of National Socialism in the autumn of 1930 because of the large increase in support for the party among Catholics, but there was another possible reason, namely ideological. The 1930 Election coincided with the publication of Rosenberg's heathen views in his book *The Myth of the Twentieth Century*, which caused alarm in devout Catholic circles. But to what extent was the Church already influenced by earlier evidence of Nazi opinion about religion?

Relations between the Catholic Church and the Nazi Party from 1930 cannot be fully understood without reference to Nazi attitudes towards religion before the election of that year. The official position of the NSDAP on religion was expressed in point 24 of the programme of 1920:

We demand liberty for all religious denominations in the state, so far as they are not a danger to it and do not militate against the moral feelings of the German race. The party as such stands for positive Christianity, but does not commit itself on the matter of creed to any particular confession. It combats the Jewish-materialist spirit within us and without us, and is convinced that our nation can only achieve permanent health from within on the basis of the principle: *the common interest before self (1)*.

Point 24, with its implied demand that the interests of the state had priority over the interests of the Church, did not take on a sinister character in the eyes of Church leaders for some years, if only because there was no likelihood at this time of the Nazis coming to power.

The Nazi Party originated in the city of Munich, where its anti-Communist propaganda had found much sympathy even among devout supporters of the Catholic faith in the turbulent years after the First World War. In view of the Bavarian origins of the party, it was not surprising that many of its early leaders were Catholics, such as Streicher, Esser, Gregor Strasser and Hitler himself. This was also true of most local branch leaders in Southern Bavaria at the time the party was refounded in 1925, although it is doubtful from the limited evidence available that many devout Catholics took an active part in the NSDAP then. One notable exception was the Bavarian military hero, Franz Ritter von Epp, who earned the nickname of 'Mother-of-God General' in Nazi circles for his strong Catholic belief. Epp associated with conservative Catholic circles in Munich, but he appeared to show no religious qualms about his increasing involvement in the Nazi movement.[1]

1. See Epp's 'political confession', chapter 4, p. 82.

The confessional background of party leaders had a limited importance, as the prominent case of Dr Goebbels shows. Born in the Rhineland, Goebbels received a Catholic upbringing from his parents, both of whom were devout Catholics. He even joined the *Unitas Verband*, a Catholic students' organization at Bonn University (2). With his romantic turn of mind he was prone to a form of religious idealism. This did not in essence disappear after he lost his belief in the Catholic creed, for it helped to explain his attraction towards Hitler. One member of his staff later commented that Goebbels subjected himself blindly to Hitler's wishes 'as a monk does to his ecclesiastical superiors' (3). Goebbels joined the Nazi Party for a number of reasons—his search for a cause, his strong feeling of resentment, his radicalism—but his experience as a Catholic made him appreciate the importance of priests in social life and it also influenced his propaganda methods (4).

Hitler's attitude to religion was based partly on the view that nothing was to be gained from a direct attack on the Church, at least at this time. Hence his remark in *Mein Kampf*, written during his confinement in Landsberg prison, that:

> Anyone who believes that a religious reformation can be achieved through the agency of a political organization shows that he has no idea of the development of religious conceptions and doctrines of faith, and how these are given practical effect by the Church ... I hold that the foundation or overthrow of a religion has far greater consequences than the foundation or overthrow of a state, to say nothing of a party (5).

Hitler's caution was also influenced by the fact that the party was then still based in Bavaria and continued to depend on the goodwill of the Catholic Bavarian Government. For both these reasons he found Ludendorff's persistent diatribes against Catholics an embarrassment, although when challenged by Ludendorff he admitted: 'I entirely agree with His Excellency, but His Excellency can afford to announce to his opponents that he will strike them dead; but I need, for the building up of a great political movement, the Catholics of Bavaria just as the Protestants of Prussia; the rest can come later' (6). Hitler was also concerned that a dispute over religion, being a ideological matter, might cause divisions within the movement at a time when he least wanted this to happen.

Hitler knew there was a significant anti-clerical element in the party, which given encouragement could easily get out of hand. On more than one occasion this latent feeling came to the surface. In September 1925, a Jesuit priest called Fritz Pieper gave a sermon in Hof on the subject 'Nationalist or biblical God?' His remarks proved highly provocative to the local Nazis, who called a protest meeting where the resolution was passed: 'The Hof branch of the NSDAP, to which many members of the local Catholic Church community belong, registers the sharpest protest at the degradation of the pulpit to the level of a political speaker's platform' (7). The meeting was very well attended by party members and addressed by Karl Holz, the radical party leader from Nuremberg. In a speech sputtering vindictive abuse about the Church he attacked Pieper 'who from his statements is said to have preached against the swastika from the pulpit itself', and even worse was 'a Jesuit father, who took the opportunity to delivery a discourse on "Nationalist or biblical God" in the city parish church' (8).

The crudest attacks on the Church were reserved for the pages of *Der Stürmer*, which delighted in publishing scandalous and sometimes obscene stories and cartoons about the influence of 'cassocks' on their parishioners. Their 'misuse' of confessions to practise 'terror' and ask penitents about their political convictions was a theme which frequently appeared, often accompanied by lurid illustrations. Sometimes the propaganda of the *Stürmer* became too much to bear, and in November 1925 Catholic circles in Bamberg staged a protest meeting because of an article in the paper about 'The Archbishop as a wooer of advertisements and subscriptions' (an attack on the Catholic press in the city) (9). Streicher's paper attracted the anti-clerical supporters of the party. A Ferdinand Kohl from Nuremberg, who described himself as 'an old nationalist' (*alter Völkischer*), wrote to Streicher in August of the same year praising the *Stürmer* for its attacks on 'ultra-montanism'. Kohl could not understand the party's consorting with 'the black devils' earlier in the year[2] and commented: 'To the devil with it, those who recognize the false teachings and idolatry of the Catholic Church should have the courage to turn their backs on it' (10).

Such incidents were usually isolated, although Streicher's repeated criticism of priests in his public speeches and his deliberate use of scripture to illustrate his points became a source of irritation in the Catholic press. Hitler tolerated Streicher's attacks on the Church because of his usefulness in winning support for the party in Franconia. Other party leaders were more circumspect in their treatment of religion. Hans Schemm's more subtle approach to the question was more typical of Nazi propaganda then.

Schemm undoubtedly had an anti-clerical streak in him, not unusual among school-teachers with their traditional 'liberal' outlook. During the party's prohibition in 1924, he had been involved in a number of clashes

2. A reference to Hitler's negotiations with the Bavarian Government after his release from prison.

including one with Johann Leicht, the dean of Bamberg cathedral and leader of the BVP parliamentary group in the Reichstag, at a BVP meeting in Bayreuth during the spring elections of 1924 (*11*). By the late 1920s Schemm had developed a tactical line of argument, which he repeated in the many speeches he gave on the subject. At a meeting in Hof in April 1929, he began by reading out newspaper cuttings quoting speeches of left-wing politicians to exemplify 'the hostility towards religion of Social Democracy'. Schemm claimed that the Jews were behind this with their aim of uprooting religion, as part of their general attack on the 'moral life' of the nation and their promotion of free-thinking. He emphasized that 'love of the fatherland' was a 'moral factor' in the fight against 'Marxism' and was totally compatible with Christianity. Fortunately for Schemm the discussion speaker at the meeting was a Communist, who also happened to be a member of the committee of the Freethinkers' Association.[3] The latter was given little chance to present his case and was pelted with beer-mats from the floor. The Hof police, who were out in force in case of trouble, reported that this was one of the best attended Nazi meetings in the city so far, with people mainly from bourgeois circles and especially women. 'The statements of Schemm have made a very strong impression and have been effective in winning support for the party' (*12*). In a speech a few months later, Schemm presented National Socialism as the 'champion' of both confessions in contrast to the 'atheistic' Social Democrats (*13*).

The public attitude of the Nazis towards religion so far could be described as a mixture of patriotic appeals to Catholic Germans, the denial that the party was at all interested in any distinction between the confessions ('we are all Germans'), an emphasis on traditional values including religion, mere avoidance of the issue by concentrating on the 'danger' to religion from the Left, but accompanied by periodic outbursts of hostility.

It was a very defensive pose, which is suggested by the readiness of party speakers to reply to accusations and even suggestions that the NSDAP was hostile to religion. A speaker at a discussion evening in Berchtesgaden in 1929 reacted to such criticism by saying that the NSDAP was 'not a confessional party for it serves the universal Christian' (*14*). This sensitiveness to criticism was coupled with an awareness that confessional relations were a potentially explosive issue, especially in areas of mixed confession. The district of Lichtenfels in Upper Franconia with its population of one-third Protestant and two-thirds Catholic was a case in point. The appearance late in 1925 of a new Catholic newspaper, the *Lichtenfelser Neueste Nachrichten*,

3. The subject of the meeting was advertised as 'The fight against religion and Christianity —what do the Freethinkers want?'

which supported the Bavarian People's Party and spoke on behalf of the archbishopric in nearby Bamberg, caused a revival of bitter feelings even to the extent of affecting business relations between Catholics and Protestants (*15*). In Nördlingen, a largely Protestant town in a Catholic region, ill feeling was caused after the First World War when the BVP Government in Munich appointed Catholic civil servants there.[4]

The Nazis wanted to avoid a confrontation on religious matters and presented the party in the best possible light, at least as beyond reproach. Their reaction to Mussolini's conclusion of the Lateran Treaties with the Papacy in 1929, which settled the differences between the Italian state and the Vatican, showed this. Nazi propaganda used the Treaties to demonstrate that the Pope had recognized National Socialism (Fascism) and rejected liberalism (*16*).

The party line on religion may have satisfied a broad cross-section of the Bavarian public, but what about strong Catholic circles and the Church in particular? Incidents in the past had sometimes caused the Church authorities unease and even aroused the active opposition of local priests, like the one in Immenstadt (Allgäu) who carried on a pamphlet-war with local Nazi leaders and campaigned for the Bavarian People's Party (*17*). But one theme more than any other kept appearing in Nazi speeches, namely the Church's involvement in politics. This issue rankled in Nazi circles. 'Political Catholicism' became a term of abuse and covered all forms of involvement, from the active participation of priests in the Catholic parties to suggestions from the pulpit on election day that parishioners would be well advised to cast their votes for that party which best represented the interests of their confession.[5] Several Church leaders sensed an attitude of hostility behind this frequent complaint of the Nazis.

---

4. Until 1803, when Nördlingen as part of Swabia joined Bavaria, there were no Catholics in the town, a situation which had existed since the Reformation when Nördlingen was one of the first towns in Germany to turn Protestant. In 1826 a Catholic church was set up again in the town, but all mayors of Nördlingen have been Protestant and the Protestant tradition has been strong, although modified since the influx of (Catholic) refugees after the Second World War. (Conversation with Dr Gustav Wulz, director of Nördlingen town archives, July 1968.) Similar difficulties were experienced in the 1920s in Memmingen over the municipal foundations. Catholics had gradually formed part of the population since the early nineteenth century, and the Protestants, especially the patricians, did not wish to share the benefits of membership with the Catholics, and formed their own party, the *Treuhand*, to protect these privileges. The Catholics also had their own organization. (Interview with Dr Berndl, mayor of Memmingen, 1932–45 and 1952–66 in September 1968.)

5. Catholic priests in prominent political positions included Johann Leicht (leader of the BVP group in the Reichstag, 1920–33), Dr Georg Wohlmuth (leader of the BVP group in the Bavarian state parliament, 1924–33), K. Föhr (leader of the Centre Party group in the

The complex question of relations between the Catholic Church and the Nazi Party at this time cannot be explained without reference to the attitudes of the two most prominent leaders of Catholics in Bavaria during the period under study: Cardinal Michael von Faulhaber as Archbishop of Munich and Freising since 1917 was head of the Catholic Church in Bavaria, and Dr Heinrich Held as Prime Minister of Bavaria (1924–33) was the most distinguished Catholic politician in the state. Their attitudes were crucial in the formation of official opinion on the question of the Nazi movement.

Held's views are already known from the policy of his government on such matters as the release of Hitler from prison, the prohibition on Hitler's public speeches and the uniform ban of 1930, which suggested the outlook typical of a solid conservative that the NSDAP was a menace to public law and order and a possible political danger (see chapters 2, 3 and 4, pp. 35, 42 and 126 respectively). But did Held, a devout Catholic, also foster objections to the Nazis on religious grounds? Faulhaber represented the traditional Catholic view, which disliked the Nazi movement for its radicalism and its rowdy element; but at the same time as a staunch monarchist he harboured serious doubts about the republican political system of Weimar.

Both their attitudes had been influenced by events late in 1923. Faulhaber had preached a sermon criticizing the anti-semitic agitation then rife in Munich. His sermon coincided with the Putsch and so became politically explosive. The failure of the Putsch let loose a stream of abuse on him from its disappointed supporters, who were looking for scapegoats. Faulhaber was seen as the man behind Kahr, who had withdrawn his support for Hitler at the last moment, and became an object of hatred in Nazi circles. He was called 'the Jewish cardinal' and was reviled at a meeting of students at the university (*18*). Faulhaber's statement was welcomed in other quarters. Chancellor Stresemann praised him for drawing attention to moral values in public life at a time when they seemed to be in eclipse, and suggested that he might come to Berlin to discuss political matters. Faulhaber declined the invitation, saying it was the duty of the Church to participate in the moral revival of the people but expressing a reluctance to become involved directly in politics.

At the same time, Faulhaber received a letter from Dr Held, then leader of the BVP group in the state parliament, in which the latter declared his fears concerning the Nazi movement, which for him represented a 'falling-away from the Catholic faith and the Church, and also a studied attack on

---

Baden state parliament), Lauscher (leader of the Centre Party group in the Prussian state parliament) and most notably, Monsignor Ludwig Kaas, chairman of the Centre Party from 1928.

the state of Bavaria and the House of Wittelsbach'. The Nazi leaders, especially Ludendorff and Hitler ('the docile pupil of Wolf and Schönerer'),[6] attacked the Catholics for being 'anti-patriotic' and opponents of the Reich. Held revealed Catholic sensitivity about such accusations in his admission that Nazi propaganda with its 'patriotic phrases' was causing confusion among Catholics. Even priests were 'ensnared' by National Socialist ideas and let themselves be used as agitators. The danger was very great that the Catholic Bavarian people would be destroyed by 'political and religious cheats, charlatans and criminals'. The only escape from this danger lay in the hands of the Cardinal and the episcopacy (*19*). Two years earlier, Held had expressed the quandary facing patriotic-minded Catholics in his opening address as President of the German Catholic Assembly:

We German Catholics love our German Fatherland and our German people with all our heart, we consider the honour and the dignity of our nation something exalted and sacred, and are patriotic to the marrow of our bones; but we German Catholics repudiate the over-bearing, nation-destroying, hard-hearted nationalist spirit, which produces hostility and hatred and makes impossible all reconciliation and cooperative work among the peoples and nations (*20*).

Dr Held's statement contained several leitmotivs in the official Catholic attitude towards the NSDAP—an instinctive aversion to the political methods practised by the Nazis, the Church's reluctance to become involved in political controversy, the admission that National Socialism (especially its appeal to patriotic feelings) held a powerful attraction for many Catholics, and last but not least an uncertainty of how to deal with the whole problem. In addition, there was a lack of positive feeling for the Weimar Republic among conservative Catholic circles, as represented by Faulhaber.

In his Lent pastoral letter of 1920, Faulhaber had warned that 'no state constitution can overthrow the word of the gospel'. At the German Catholic Assembly in 1922, he made what was later considered a major attack on the legitimacy of the Weimar Republic:

Woe to the state which does not base its legal order and its legisla-tive activity on the Ten Commandments of God and which creates a

---

6. Georg Schönerer and Karl Hermann Wolf were Austrian politicians and leaders of the Pan-German Movement in Austria, which attacked the influence of the Catholic Church as well as being nationalist and anti-semitic. Schönerer's ideas influenced Hitler during his youth in Vienna.

constitution not in the name of God. The Revolution was perjury and high treason, and will remain tainted and branded with the mark of Cain. Even if it brings a few successes—a moral character is not valued according to successes, a misdeed cannot be made holy because of its successes (21).

Faulhaber was above all a monarchist, believing in the divine right of kings, and could not tolerate the idea of popular sovereignty, as inscribed in the Weimar Constitution. Faulhaber's reaction was typical of Catholic Church leaders at the time of the upheavals of 1918–19, concerned lest the revolutionary tendencies get out of hand and affect the position of the Church.[7] Faulhaber, perhaps surprised by the reaction to his remarks, later qualified his statement by saying that he had neither condemned the republican form of government nor advocated the overthrow of the Weimar Constitution, but had asserted that the Revolution was a sin. But he never overcame his basic antipathy towards parliamentary democracy, his strong dislike of all left-wing politicians and his objection to the coalitions between the Catholic Centre Party and the Social Democrats because in his eyes such compromises endangered Catholic principles. He even refused in 1925 to conduct a mourning service in his diocese for the dead President Ebert, a Social Democrat but hardly a radical socialist (22). For Faulhaber the political representatives of the Catholics outside Bavaria were suspect, for there was little essential difference between Socialism and Communism.

It was small wonder that less sophisticated Catholics, unversed in doctrinal matters, should have taken Faulhaber's statements amiss and failed to see the subtleties of his attitude. The element of doubt that remained was exploited by Nazi propagandists, ever on the lookout for a chance to undermine confidence in authority. Faulhaber's remark about 'perjury and high treason' was quoted on many occasions by party speakers in Catholic Bavaria. Johann Dauser, one of the party's regular speakers there, made the following remarks at a meeting in Ingolstadt in May 1928:

Cardinal Faulhaber once said that the consequences of the Revolution are perjury, lies and treason. We National Socialists want to fight against these consequences. In this fight we have the best example in our godly master. He did not go to a Pontius and beg for the cleansing of the Holy Place from the desecrators of the Temple. We also want to

7. The *Bayerischer Kurier* represented the views of the Catholic press then, when it warned on 13 November 1918: 'Above everything else we demand complete freedom for our religious confessions; otherwise we would rather die, rather suffer death.'

preserve our holy place on this earth from the desecrators. Two million people died for this holy place. The godly master gave us the lesson about the leaven. We must be the leaven and can only rise because the bourgeois parties have not done their duty in combating lies, perjury and treason. The godly master said further that the cowardly ones will not triumph but rather those who pursue an aim. We do not intend to be cowardly, we want to follow the banner boldly, which is like that on which the words were written: *In hoc signo vinces* (*23*).

The habit of Nazi propaganda of drawing such analogies often proved an embarrassment to the Church. Sometimes it was found necessary to issue a public statement dissociating the clergy from any support for the Nazi movement. In the summer of 1930, the deanery of Ingolstadt felt obliged to answer claims made at recent Nazi meetings that the clergy in the district were supporting the NSDAP:

We do not assume that anybody in Ingolstadt or the neighbourhood could give credence to this nonsensical talk, but for the sake of the matter and because in times of political conflict one must now and then patiently endure the most unbelievable things, we hereby declare finally and emphatically that a Catholic priest, no matter what his position, can never go along with a movement like that represented by National Socialism (*24*).

The Nazi Party was by then on the rise, so Church leaders had to be more discreet in their public statements. Cardinal Faulhaber had recently learned this the hard way, when he had preached a sermon in March 1930 against Bolshevism and its opposition to religion and Christianity. Faulhaber's comments were taken up by the Nationalist press, while the Bavarian leader of the Stahlhelm wrote to him thanking him and offering him his cooperation in a 'common front against Communism'. Faulhaber replied politely, thanking the Stahlhelm leader for his offer but pointing out the difference between the Stahlhelm and the Church. The Stahlhelm, the Archbishop wrote, used weapons and force while the Church wanted to abolish the same danger 'with legal methods and with spiritual and moral weapons'. His sermon could not therefore be taken for a call for a 'fighting front' (*25*). For the head of the Catholic Church in Bavaria to have made common cause with the Bavarian Stahlhelm at this time would have aroused considerable alarm, as the latter was known to be on close terms with the Nazis.

The Reichstag Election campaign was now in full swing, and helped to bring the impending ideological conflict between the two sides to a head. The Catholic press became more aggressive in its denunciations of National Socialism. The *Augsburger Postzeitung* urged Catholics to 'seize weapons' to defend the cross of Christ against the 'hostile swastika', and to tear 'the deceitful mask from the face' of National Socialism (*26*). The *Regensburger Anzeiger* published an article in June called 'National Socialism—a cultural-political danger', based on a speech made by Dr Georg Wohlmuth, provost of Eichstätt cathedral and leader of the BVP group in the Bavarian state parliament (*27*). This article argued that National Socialism had its origins 'in a movement hostile to Catholics, the All-German Movement in Austria of the eighties, which is known to be identical with the "Away from Rome" movement'. It provoked the local Nazis into holding a meeting on 11 June, when Franz Maierhofer, one of the party's list candidates for Lower Bavaria, made a defensive speech answering in detail every single charge made in the newspaper. The sense of the urgency felt by local clergy is shown by the leaflet distributed by Dr Erbacher, the priest in the village of Lengfurt near Würzburg, 'To all Catholic voters of the parish', at the beginning of September. This quoted a long statement from Bishop Schreiber of Berlin that the election was not just about economic and financial matters but also 'decisive questions of a cultural nature' for 'forces are at work aiming by means of legislation to break up marriage and the family and the moral and social order'. The new Reichstag will decide whether or not the process of 'de-Christianization' of the people would continue. Erbacher called on his 'worthy Catholic fellow-believers' to all cast their votes for the BVP on ballot paper no. 8 (*28*).

The Nazis were obviously afraid of jeopardizing their good prospects in the election by engaging in a major conflict with the Catholic Church over fundamental principles. At the same time, they were becoming increasingly frustrated with their apparent inability to break the hold of the Bavarian People's Party over the strongly Catholic electorate, which owed much to the active and moral support of the Church. In the village of Laimnau on Lake Constance, just across the Bavarian border in Württemberg, the local branch of the NSDAP sent a circular to its members in July:

As you know we National Socialists must always reckon in rural areas with the fact that the Catholic priest will use the influence of his position for propaganda in favour of the Centre Party, so that many a voter will vote for the 'most Christian' party to please the priest ... so long as Catholic priests, as we have experienced in a multitude of cases, give their views as convinced supporters of the Centre Party at political meetings in an objective manner there is no objection, for we National Socialists always respect an open and honest political opponent (29).

The circular described the problems with the Centre Party in the locality, and attacks made by the priest on National Socialism for being 'hostile to religion'. Dr Eisele, the priest, gave three sermons on successive Sundays in May about National Socialism, and according to the circular made threatening remarks like: 'No friendship is possible with these people' and 'I will not enter any more the inn where meetings of the NSDAP are held!' The local branch wrote in protest to the Bishop's office in Rottenburg am Neckar, claiming that the political activities of Eisele posed a problem of conscience for its members 'who are all Catholics' (30).

How much the political activities of priests influenced the voting in Bavaria is difficult to determine for want of satisfactory evidence, although one may assume they contributed more in reinforcing the support of strong Catholics for the BVP than in alienating voters from the NSDAP. The NSDAP did not provoke a public controversy over religion, and the outcry over the wearing of party uniforms in Regensburg cathedral in May 1930 was unlikely to lose the party much support. Those voters most likely to be influenced by talk about the Nazis' hostility to religion were devout Catholics, who in any case would have voted for the Bavarian People's Party.

The Catholic Church in Bavaria seemed taken aback by the large increase in Catholics voting for the NSDAP. The party had for the first time succeeded in penetrating the rural areas, thereby appearing to threaten the stability of community life which was so much dominated by the Church. The Nazi Party, having triumphed over the BBMB, had become a serious political rival to the Bavarian People's Party, which was stronger in the countryside than in the towns. A few days before election day Rupert Mayer, the Munich father, had written to Cardinal Faulhaber warning him not to underrate the impact of Nazi propaganda: 'It is incredible but nevertheless true that the Hitler swindle has laid hold of the widest, even Catholic, circles of the people; and not merely in the towns has the movement gained ground but to an enormous degree in the country' (31). Priests wrote to their bishops about the marked increase in support and sympathy for the Nazi movement. The priest in Holzkirchen, a village to the south of Munich, remarked that four-fifths of his believers were 'thinking National Socialist' (32). This may have been an exaggeration, but it did reveal the state of mind of some local clergy in the heated aftermath of the 1930 Election.

The reason for the rise in Catholic support for the NSDAP, in spite of the voting strength of the BVP, was that the latter monopolized the strong

Catholics but not the whole of the Catholic electorate.[8] The proportion of Catholics voting for the confessional parties had in fact declined since the end of the nineteenth century, especially in Bavaria. While the proportion of nominal Catholics voting for the Centre Party at the time of Bismarck's opposition to the Catholic Church in the 1870s had been more than 80 per cent, the figure now stood around 60 per cent and was highest among women and regular churchgoers.[9] This decline in support was very noticeable in Bavaria, surprising in view of the higher proportion of practising Catholics there than elsewhere in Germany (69 per cent as against 60 per cent elsewhere were Easter communicants in 1931). In 1924, the proportion of practising Catholics (rather than simply nominal Catholics) voting for the confessional party was only 56 per cent in Bavaria (for the BVP), compared with 76 per cent in the rest of Germany (for the Centre Party) (33). This tendency was very noticeable in Southern Bavaria, while the Catholic minority populations in Middle and Upper Franconia were more on the defensive, more conscious of their confessional interests and therefore more inclined to support the Catholic party.

This decline in support for the confessional parties among Catholics may be attributed to several factors: the protection of the interests of the Church had brought Catholics together at the time of Bismarck, but this need for unity was no longer so necessary once the Weimar Constitution guaranteed the rights of the Church and the Centre Party played a prominent role in Weimar governments;[10] in the easier atmosphere Catholics were more inclined to express their differing viewpoints over political, social and economic matters and to support other parties; and there seemed to be a

8. By 'strong Catholics' is meant practising Catholics, who attended church services regularly and whose connection with the Church was strong. Confessional behaviour is a safer criterion for estimating the likely effects of confession on politics, as problems of conscience are not easily measured by evidence. Seen in simple statistical terms, there were in Bavaria (according to the 1933 census) 5,370,719 Catholics out of a total population of 7,681,584, a proportion of 69·9 per cent. The number of Bavarians voting in the 1930 Election amounted to 3,776,904. One could assume for the sake of argument that the ratio of Catholics to Protestants was the same for the active electorate as for the total population, which would mean roughly 2,643,830 Catholics voting in 1930, although social factors such as the larger size of Catholic families would modify this calculation. All the same, it is a fair assumption in view of the size of the BVP vote in 1930 (1,058,637) that the BVP won the support of well under half of the Catholics participating in that election in Bavaria.
9. The figure for the 1870s refers to all Catholics as there was then only one confessional party (the BVP was not formed until 1918). The figure of 60 per cent is for 1932 (see Bracher, *Die Auflösung der Weimarer Republik*, p. 91).
10. For more than seven of its thirteen years' existence the Weimar Republic was governed by coalitions under Centre Party leaders: Fehrenbach (1920–21), Wirth (1921–22), Marx (1923–25 and 1926–28) and Brüning (1930–32), not to mention the numerous Centre Party ministers in the cabinets.

growing resentment at the dictates of priests, even among practising Catholics in Bavaria (*34*). This resentment gave an opening to the Nazis who sought to exploit it with their attack on 'political Catholicism'.

The election result only served to increase tension between the Nazis and the Catholic Church. In the case of the latter, previous suspicions and fears about National Socialism now seemed more real with the political success of the NSDAP. A month after the poll Dr Walter Krauss, the party leader in Eichstätt, described in a letter his relations with the Church in that very Catholic city.[11] Krauss was himself a Catholic but had developed a notorious hatred of the Church, which may have been connected with the various divorces he had experienced (*35*). Krauss, a doctor, joined the NSDAP as late as 1930 but he was very soon appointed district leader and in the election the party won a vote there of 17·9 per cent, which was high for a city as strongly Catholic as Eichstätt. His case was not necessarily representative, but his letter was typical of the virulent tone of Nazi correspondence when it came to the question of the Catholic Church's influence in politics. It also revealed something of developments at the local level following the electoral success of the Nazis.

Krauss claimed that 'the fury of the black masters'[12] was being vent on him, so that he had to choose between leaving the party or giving up his post as doctor at the monastery of St Walburg (*36*). He maintained that this experience had enabled him to find out much about what was going on 'behind the scenes' in the Bavarian People's Party: 'For a quarter of a year I know that efforts have been made to induce all the bishops to issue a declaration against National Socialism—at the present moment it seems that the conflict between National Socialism and the Bavarian People's Party is entering a decisive stage.' By his letter Krauss hoped to draw the attention of party headquarters to the need for an official statement by Hitler on point 24 of the NSDAP Programme and the question of a concordat, for in this way it would be possible to 'wrest a weapon out of the hands of our most dangerous opponent'. He pointed out that the situation was very confusing, all the more as very few Catholic priests, let alone ordinary Catholics, had any idea of their Church's law and the 'subtlety of Catholic dogmas' (*37*).

The basic reason for this persistent undercurrent of antagonism between the NSDAP and the Bavarian People's Party was that they were both

11. Eichstätt in Middle Franconia was the seat of an ancient bishopric founded in 741 by St Boniface. The population was almost totally Catholic, and not surprisingly the BVP had won a high vote there of nearly 60 per cent in 1930.
12. 'Black' was a popular term for 'clerical', and was often applied to the Catholic parties just as 'red' was to the Communists and 'brown' to the Nazis. It is used here as a term of abuse for the Catholic Church.

ideological parties more than other parties of the Weimar period, with the possible exception of the parties of the Left. This was particularly true of the BVP, which was far more conscious of the ideological than of any other aspect of the Nazi movement. In the same month as the election in 1930 Dr Alois Hundhammer, deputy General Secretary of the Bavarian Christian Peasants' Association, the associate organization of the BVP, published some articles in which he saw his party as a 'bulwark against National Socialism':

> The Bavarian People's Party is a pronouncedly ideological party. Its attitude to all programmatical questions is influenced decisively by the guiding principle of the positive belief in God, that is in the Christian, above all the Catholic, sense. From the very outset that brings it into a conflict with National Socialism, which ... in the essence of its nature and its activities is anti-Christian and neo-heathen in outlook. The speeches of its leaders and the attitude of its parliamentary groups show that sufficiently. In addition to these theoretical conflicts there is also in practical life an uninterrupted and openly bitter struggle. With the unbridled fanaticism of the Hitler supporters every campaign they fight is emotional and vehement. As a result, particularly rigorous positions of conflict are taken up in opposition to the Bavarian People's Party and conversely on the part of the Bavarian People's Party against National Socialism ... (*38*).

In Hundhammer's opinion only a party with an 'ideology' was capable of resisting the 'ideology of National Socialism'.

Ideological hostility was exacerbated by the new political rivalry between the two parties. It was significant that the Nazi reaction to the problem was a tactical avoidance of ideological controversy. On 30 October, Bouhler issued a memorandum from party headquarters warning the party press to beware of becoming embroiled in disputes with Catholic priests over religious matters because 'the Centre Party and the Bavarian People's Party have been attempting recently with all means to provoke the press of the NSDAP into making thoughtless statements, which can be used against the NSDAP in the next election campaign, surely not far away' (*39*).

It was not surprising that in the context of these developments the publication of Alfred Rosenberg's book *The Myth of the Twentieth Century* in October 1930 should have created alarm in Catholic circles. Rosenberg was the most prominent Nazi ideologist and editor of the party newspaper, the *Völkischer Beobachter*. His book was regarded by the Church as a direct attack on Christianity, and was quoted as evidence of 'real' Nazi intentions by those Catholics who had suspected National Socialism of being against religion. This ponderous book of some 700 pages, written in the most turgid prose imaginable, confirmed the worst fears of those who had felt all along that the NSDAP was a crypto-atheistic movement, because it emphasized the superiority of the Nordic race, advocated the abolition of the 'Jewish' Old Testament and expurgation of the New Testament, and proposed the creation of a German national church based on race and purity of blood rather than on dogma.

The *Bayerischer Kurier* immediately proclaimed that Rosenberg's book revealed 'the true views and intentions of the National Socialist Party' (*40*). During the whole of the autumn the Catholic *Augsburger Postzeitung* published frequent articles on National Socialism, a subject to which it had previously paid only sporadic attention. The first, on 7 October, was called 'The mask down—the "positive Christianity" of the National Socialist programme, an hypocrisy'. It maintained that some Nazis might be 'positive Christians', but this was not the case with the official line of the party. Like the following articles in the paper, it strongly abused Rosenberg's book which was 'full of the most dirty, common and base attacks against the Catholic Church' (*41*). Further articles in the series supplemented the criticism of Rosenberg with quotations from the *Völkischer Beobachter* to illustrate the point that the Catholic Church would enjoy no toleration in the Third Reich (*42*). Articles in the *Augsburger Postzeitung* later in October dwelt on the contrast between Christian ideals and Rosenberg's racial theories. One asserted that the crooked cross of the swastika and the cross of Christ were 'diametrically opposed' (*43*). Articles which appeared in November and December repeated the same argument that National Socialism was a pagan doctrine.

Hitler found the reaction to the publication of Rosenberg's book an embarrassment, particularly when the Catholic press kept saying there was nothing to distinguish his own views from those of the author of the *Myth*. It did not appear to matter to Catholic opinion that Rosenberg was not really a powerful figure in the NSDAP; the fact that he edited the party newspaper and remained in Hitler's entourage was sufficient evidence that he represented the views of the party on the question of religion. It was surprising in view of their previous caution that the Nazi leaders did not foresee the likely effect of the book's publication, although one reason was that they totally underestimated the impact it would make. Some precautions had been taken. The *Myth* was not published by the party publishers, the Franz Eher Verlag, but by another publishing firm in Munich, the Hoheneichen Verlag. The preface of the 1930 edition claimed in a dissembling way that the

NSDAP 'has important special tasks of its own, and must keep apart as an organization from all discussions of a religious and church–political nature'. Hitler appears not to have read it carefully, even after publication. He confessed later that 'like most *Gau* leaders, I have myself merely glanced cursorily at it; it is in any case written in much too abstruse a style, in my opinion' (*44*). Rosenberg had given Hitler the completed manuscript before publication, but the latter could not be bothered to vet it.[13]

The Nazi defence in the controversy over Rosenberg's book took two forms. Firstly, Hitler took great pains to emphasize that the *Myth* was Rosenberg's private work and did not represent official party policy. This was a difficult argument to defend because of Rosenberg's position in the party hierarchy, and because his views did have the sympathy of some elements in the party, especially anti-clerical Nazis. It seemed inconsistent with Hitler's treatment of the case of Dinter that Rosenberg did not suffer the same fate as other Nazi 'religious reformers' with expulsion from the party, particularly as Hitler expressed irritation with Rosenberg on several occasions over the book.[14] The reason was probably that Rosenberg, unlike Dinter and Ludendorff, did not persist in a crusade against Catholics, nor did he attempt to use his views to challenge Hitler's authority as leader. Rosenberg was considered a lightweight in leadership circles. Goering described the *Myth* briefly as 'junk'. Goebbels expressed his contempt in no more subtle terms when he referred to the book as 'philosophical belching', although on other occasions he did compliment Rosenberg for the 'industry and skill' with which he had 'joined the springs of our *Weltanschauung* into one mighty stream' (*45*).

If Rosenberg's book was an object of ridicule among some of his colleagues, it was taken more seriously in the lower ranks of the party. Rosenberg himself admitted that 'in Catholic regions doubts even arose in the ranks of the party' and continued: 'The situation was particularly difficult for some of the Catholic clergymen who were in accord with quite a few of the social demands of the party; this was especially true for the good old Abbot Schachleiter; he called the attention of several party functionaries to the fact that, in his opinion, I was endangering our entire movement' (*46*). Private work

13. According to Konrad Heiden, *Der Fuehrer*, p. 364; 'He gave Hitler the thick manuscript, for it contained some rather daring passages which Rosenberg, thinking of the party's reputation, did not want to publish without Hitler's approval. Hitler took the pages home and put them on his bed-table, where Rosenberg, when he called, saw them lying untouched. This went on for a year: then the author grew impatient and asked to have his manuscript back. Hitler gave it to him and said: "I feel sure that it's all right."'
14. Hjalmar Schacht, *My First Seventy-Six Years*, p. 358 quotes Hitler as saying: 'I have always told Rosenberg one does not attack petticoats and cassocks.'

or not, Rosenberg's *Myth* could not avoid becoming a source of disturbance both within the Nazi Party and outside it. It was, as the editors of Rosenberg's memoirs have put it, 'read primarily by National Socialist sub-ideologists in search of slogans of their own, and by opposition ideologists seeking weak points in the Nazi armour' (*47*). Hitler revealed the bitterness he felt over the Catholic reaction to the book when he remarked on the difficulty of selling the first edition:

It was only when the book was mentioned in a Pastoral Letter that the sales began to go up and the first ten thousand were sold; in short, the second edition was launched by Cardinal Faulhaber of Munich, who was maladroit enough to attack Rosenberg at a synod of bishops and to cite quotations from his book; the consequent placing of the book on the index, as a work of heresy on the party's part, merely gave an additional fillip to its sale; and when the Church had finally published all its commentaries in refutation of Rosenberg's ideas, the *Myth of the Twentieth Century* sold its two hundred thousandth copy (*48*).

The second form of Nazi defence was to answer point by point the accusations made by the Church. This method had been used before 1930, but Nazi speakers now made greater efforts to refute charges of 'religious hostility'. A major speech on the theme 'National Socialism and its position on religion and the Church' was made by Rudolf Buttmann, leader of the NSDAP group in the Bavarian state parliament, in the Thomasbräukeller in Munich on 11 December of that year.[15] Buttmann began by referring to the Bavarian Concordat of 1924 with the Vatican, which the NSDAP had opposed at the time. The party's stand on the Concordat had become a matter of frequent comment in the Catholic press. Buttmann replied that

15. Dr Buttmann, like most Bavarian Nazi leaders, was a strong opponent of 'political Catholicism'. His attitude derived from his national conservative views, his dislike of Bavarian particularism and his antipathy to what he called 'ultramontanism'. He was a Protestant (although not a practising one), was a native Bavarian born in Marktbreit near Würzburg in Lower Franconia in 1885 and was brought up in the Palatinate. After studying law at the universities of Munich, Berlin and Freiburg, he settled in Munich as a librarian, first with the State Library and then with the Bavarian parliament library. Before joining the NSDAP he was active in National Liberal youth groups and belonged to the DNVP, which he left because of his contempt for its 'parlour nationalism'. Buttmann was also a leading light in the German Philological Association, which protected the purity of the German language. His background helped to explain his dislike of 'political Catholicism', which he regarded as 'un-German' because of its ties with an external authority in Rome and because it was contrary to the idea of Reich unity. His feeling was reinforced by the association between 'political Catholicism' and Bavarian particularism in the form of the BVP. (Interview with his son, Günther Buttmann, September 1968.)

the NSDAP was not against a concordat as such, and referred approvingly to Mussolini's treaty with the Vatican. But he criticized the Bavarian Concordat for not recognizing the 'proper division' between the functions of the Church and those of the state. The state had the duty to maintain Christian ethics and should have the supervision of the confessional schools instead of the Church, but should not have to support the Church Establishment financially. In reply to charges that the Nazis were anti-Christian, Buttmann pointed out that in Thuringia the new Nazi Minister of the Interior, Dr Wilhelm Frick, had reintroduced morning prayers in the schools. Buttmann even contended that the NSDAP was more Christian than the Centre Party, because the latter had included Jews in its list of candidates for the last Reichstag Election. On Rosenberg's *Myth* he could only comment that some extracts from it had been taken out of context, that it contained some statements with which he could not agree and that it was the work of a Protestant and was not written for believing Catholics (*49*).

The principal result of the Rosenberg controversy was to increase pressure for an official statement on National Socialism by the episcopacy. The need for a clarification of the Catholic Church's position came under discussion during December 1930 in the light of increased electoral support among Catholics for the NSDAP (*50*). It was recognized that too long a delay in issuing a statement would look like tolerance of the NSDAP. In the absence of a pronouncement by Church leaders local priests often found themselves in a difficult position, particularly when numbers of their communicants were supporting the NSDAP or even taking an active part in it and yet had no intention of breaking with the Church. There were differences of opinion among the Bavarian bishops over such questions as the wearing of party uniforms at church services. Bishops Hauck of Bamberg, Ehrenfried of Würzburg and Buchberger of Regensburg argued strongly against allowing this, for as Bishop Ehrenfried pointed out such a practice would 'have a propaganda effect and induce the party to oblige its members to attend church in uniform' (*51*). Cardinal Faulhaber justified his more flexible attitude to the wearing of uniforms on the following grounds: 'My local priests have implored me to allow church attendance in uniform because the childlike pleasure in uniforms is so strong at present that they [the Catholic National Socialists] would prefer to forego a church wedding than forego their uniforms, although they have participated faithfully in church life up till now' (*52*).

A number of incidents earlier in the year had highlighted the confusion which could be caused by these problems. In May, formations of the SA had attended services in the cathedral of Regensburg, where the party was holding a *Gau* rally. Over 400 SA men attended high mass bringing with them their flags and banners. According to the police, they were 'drawn up in two columns in the right and left aisles of the cathedral; the heads of both columns were connected across the cathedral by a row of flags; between the flags and the lattice railings, which separate the choir and the high altar from the rest of the church, stood the public, which otherwise would fill the church as on Sundays' (*53*).

The event passed off without any disturbance, but it attracted national publicity and at once the question was raised if the Nazis had been granted permission to attend in uniform. Bishop Buchberger had not been present at the service as he was busy making confirmation visits, but it transpired that the NSDAP branch leader in Regensburg had in fact contacted the Bishop's office to enquire about the times of services and request that standing places be reserved in the cathedral (*54*). Confusion remained about what kind of permission was given by the Bishop's office and whether this included the wearing of uniforms. It is probable that the Nazis took advantage of the lenient attitude of the church authorities. The Bishop's office denied it had granted such permission, but this denial could not prevent the incident causing extreme embarrassment to the Church. The *Völkischer Beobachter* claimed that the carrying of party banners to church had followed an agreement with Bishop Buchberger, while the Social Democratic *Münchner Post* could not resist the caustic comment that 'the swastika, the old heathen symbol of sun worship, thus received the sanction of the Bishop' (*55*). Altogether, the State Ministry of the Interior summed up official displeasure over the affair in its report:

> Even in establishing the real facts of the case the behaviour of the Vicar-General does not seem fortunate. The Vicar-General does not appear to be clear about the political and cultural direction which the NSDAP is following, and what the 'permission' given to it for a closed formation in the cathedral means for the party, namely none other than support by the Church and recommendation of the party to the people. It would surely have been better if the Vicar-General had acted as the Protestant pastor's office did, by refusing the united participation of National Socialists at divine service (*56*).

A few months later, the Vicar-General of the diocese of Mainz took a stronger line. He replied, in answer to an enquiry by the local NSDAP branch, that Catholics could not become members of the NSDAP on the grounds that article 24 of the party programme was incompatible with

Catholic doctrine. This blunt declaration caused a sensation, especially after the Bishop of Mainz demonstrated his solidarity with his Vicar-General by refusing permission for the *Gau* leader of Hesse to lay wreaths at the graves of soldiers who had fallen in the War and were buried in Catholic cemeteries (*57*). The Nazis reacted sharply to this ruling. They published articles by anonymous 'Catholic priests' supporting their side of the case and letters from people who claimed they had left the Church in protest against the action taken by the Bishop of Mainz (*58*).

Opinions among the Bavarian bishops differed over the Mainz case. Many were critical of the absolute position taken, but all felt under increasing pressure to issue a statement of their own, especially after Cardinal Bertram of Breslau, chairman of the Fulda Bishops' Conference, indicated that he and other bishops were prepared to do so (*59*). Cardinal Faulhaber still hesitated, while some other Bavarian bishops expressed reservations about an official declaration. Archbishop Hauck of Bamberg was at first opposed to the idea, because he thought a premature statement might lead to a religious conflict and loss of members by the Church. Article 24 of the party programme was in any case 'too vague' to be used as evidence of the religious hostility of the NSDAP. As Hitler was very discreet about ideological questions, party speakers would find it easy to convince their supporters that the aims of the NSDAP were purely political. It would be better to wait until the Nazis were forced to declare their hand over a controversial 'cultural' issue like the new school law proposed by the Centre Party (*60*). Bishop Buchberger also felt concerned that a statement might put educated people on the spot, because they showed 'enthusiastic support' for National Socialism (*61*). At the same time, Cardinal Faulhaber made the revealing comment that the Mainz regulation had been right at the time, as the number of Nazis was then still small, while 'the number of supporters is now without doubt great' which meant that treatment of the problem had to be different (*62*). It was quite evident that the Church leaders felt themselves in a painfully difficult situation, and resented the fact that religion and politics had become so intermixed.

In February 1931, Cardinal Faulhaber finally took the initiative in calling a conference of the bishops at Freising. The statement they issued on 10 February was more comprehensive than that of Mainz, but also more flexible (*63*).

The statement opened with a denial that it was an attempt at electioneering, and affirmed that it was non-political and concerned only with the question of pastoral duties. National Socialism, it said, contained errors in its cultural–political programme which Catholic belief rejected because its leaders wanted to replace Christian belief by 'a new ideology'. Declining to condemn National Socialism outright, the statement protested that 'leading representatives of National Socialism' placed race higher than religion. The bishops therefore, as guardians of Christian belief and moral teaching, warned against National Socialism 'as long as and in so far as it proclaims cultural–political views which are not reconcilable with Catholic teaching'.

Catholic priests were prohibited from taking any part whatever in the Nazi movement, for they could not be unaware of those policies which were hostile to Christianity and the Church, such as the 'rejection of any concordat, the support for the undenominational school, the radicalism of their national-ist thinking and their opposition to the protection of embryonic life'. Furthermore, the declaration put a ban on the attendance at divine service of Nazi formations in uniform with flags 'since such parades in churches would make people think that the Church had come to terms with National Socialism'. An individual National Socialist could be admitted wearing his party badge, when this was not intended as a demonstration and did not disturb the church ceremony.

The question of a National Socialist receiving the sacraments and partici-pating in the Eucharist was to be decided on an individual basis, depending on whether the person concerned was a fellow-traveller, who did not approve of the religious and cultural–political aims of the movement, or whether he was an active member of the NSDAP. The bishops then de-clared:

Among the masses who voted National Socialist in the last election, there were without doubt a large number who only went along with the patriotic aims of National Socialism (for example, the revision of the Peace Treaty) or with the economic aims (for example, an improvement in the economic position of the working class, revalorization); while on the other hand they were not acquainted with the cultural–political opposition to Christianity and the Church, or at least did not want to involve themselves, and so lived personally in good faith (64).

In such cases, it was the responsibility of the father confessor to judge whether membership of the NSDAP constituted the next thing to sin or not. Equally, the decision on whether an individual National Socialist could receive Christian burial was left in the hands of the local priest, who would know best if the person concerned had taken part in church life, fulfilled his Easter duty and generally lived in peace with the Church. Finally, the Bavarian bishops warned that 'should National Socialism develop the methods of Bolshevism, then the existence of good faith can no longer be assumed'.

The declaration of the Bavarian bishops showed some perception of the problem facing the Church, but it was doubtful how far it clarified the issue. In view of the circumstances of the preceding months, the bishops had no real alternative to taking a moral stand against National Socialism. Yet their statement was a compromise, because it made an artificial distinction between the 'cultural' aims of the NSDAP and its purely political aims. This was an artificial distinction because even a statement on the 'cultural' programme of a political party was of some political importance. Some of the Bavarian bishops at least must have been aware of this. There were also certain obvious omissions in the declaration, such as the absence of any comment on the anti-democratic aims of the NSDAP and the party's anti-semitism (a question which surely concerned the moral and 'cultural' field as well as the 'political' one). The correspondence of the bishops before the Freising conference shows that they were afraid that an outright condemnation of the Nazi Party would have unfortunate consequences for themselves in the form of a crisis within the Church membership, reprisals by the Nazis and even the revival of the kind of political hostility towards the Catholic Church experienced under Bismarck. They attempted to rationalize their position, by arguing that the anti-religious statements of Nazi leaders of the second and third rank should not be taken literally because of the authoritarian nature of the party. Only remarks of its principal leaders should be taken seriously. Hitler had expressed himself very cautiously on religious matters, it was pointed out (65).

As a result of their flexible attitude, the Bavarian bishops left many important decisions with the local priests. It was not therefore surprising that inconsistencies continued to mark the behaviour of the Catholic Church towards the Nazi movement. The position was in fact made more difficult for the church-going Catholic who supported the NSDAP. There had been a certain blessing in the previous position of uncertainty. Now, as the *Regensburger Anzeiger* wrote: 'Many Catholics, who up to now have taken their Catholic attitude seriously and conscientiously but who nevertheless adhered to National Socialism, are faced with difficult conflicts of conscience through the judgement of our bishops' (66). Even some of the bishops had strong doubts about the impact of their statement on Catholics. Bishop Buchberger of Regensburg wrote to Cardinal Faulhaber that experience did not support the view that such declarations achieved much success. He had in mind the Austrian elections of the previous autumn, when the Christian Social Party had a disappointing result in spite of strong support from the Church. Moreover, a similar statement on socialism by the German Catholic Church in 1921 had had little effect on Catholic SPD voters (67). Buchberger seems to have been keenly aware of the political, economic and social circumstances which were favouring the growth of Nazism, and that the Church, with its preference for rendering unto God, could not entirely ignore Caesar's world. Writing later in 1931 to Cardinal Pacelli, Secretary of State at the Vatican, Buchberger remarked:

> In Bavaria the National Socialist danger is growing more and more. It has fruitful ground in the dreadful and almost unbearable distress, which is driving the widest circles to despair. With this despair it is a question of the irrational, simply of feelings and impulses, and for this National Socialism is suitably equipped. If it comes to power then the Bavarian Concordat is lost, all the more as there is no regard felt for the supernatural world when the most essential thing is absent in the natural world. And yet Communism, which proceeds from hatred of God to the radical destruction of the Christian religion and culture, is a much greater danger here (68).

On one point at least the bishops' declaration was very specific, namely the participation of priests in the Nazi movement. Catholic priests were in fact an extreme rarity in the party, of which two cases in Bavaria were noteworthy: Dr Philipp Haeuser and Abbot Albanus Schachleiter. Both were eccentric figures and were hardly representative of the Church, but their behaviour did create some embarrassment and, in the case of Haeuser, added to the urgency for the statement by the bishops. Haeuser was a rebel priest, who had published a book in 1923 called *Jew or Christ, or To Whom Belongs the Mastery of the World?*, in which he referred to the Jews as 'Germany's cross' who bore much of the blame for the defeat in the First World War and for the Revolution of 1918, and that the time had come to put them in their place (69). Haeuser achieved prominence in December 1930 when he delivered the sermon at the Christmas festival of the Augsburg Nazi Party. In his address, called a 'Christian message to the awakening Germany', he revealed his nationalist outlook and his attraction to the anti-Communist element in National Socialism: 'I have the right and the duty to preach the Word of God to my German friends, to those men who make great and bloody sacrifices weekly and almost daily in their fearless fight against Bolshevism' (70). Since Haeuser's speech received much publicity, the Bishop of Augsburg was obliged to make a public statement prohibiting Haeuser from speaking at future meetings of the NSDAP.

Catholic priests never played an influential part in the NSDAP in Southern Bavaria; they merely provided some useful publicity. The same was true of Abbot Schachleiter, one of the first Catholic priests to support Hitler openly. He came from a tradesman's family in Mainz, and had worked for twenty-eight years in the monastery of Emaus in Bohemia. Schachleiter became its abbot but was forced to leave during conflicts between Czechs and Germans at the time of the establishment of the new state of Czechoslovakia in 1918. He then came to Bavaria and took up a post at the All Saints' Church in Munich. Schachleiter had strong nationalist sympathies, resulting from his experience in Bohemia, which led him to early contacts with the Nazis. At first he held services for the SA and then in 1926 became a member of the NSDAP, a most unusual step for a Catholic priest at that time. The Nazis used him to demonstrate the universality of their appeal, so Schachleiter became a frequent showpiece at Nazi public occasions. Apart from his nationalism, he also showed a strong naïvety. He is supposed to have remarked once that 'one worry lies heavily on my heart, for if the Catholics do not cooperate with the NSDAP, there is a danger that National Socialism will become a purely Protestant movement' (71).

In addition to the feeling that the NSDAP was 'anti-Christian', the suspicion that it was Protestant in its sympathies also influenced some official Catholic attitudes towards the party. The *Bayerischer Kurier* voiced this in its comment on the results of the 1930 Election that support for the Nazis was by no means uniform throughout the country, and that the voting in Bavaria had 'a special character' for 'the specifically Bavarian electoral picture is not nearly so favourable for the National Socialists as elsewhere in the Reich' (72). The view that Bavaria had special qualities, above all its strong Catholicism, which enabled the state to resist National Socialism better than North Germany, was plausible in the light of the fact that the NSDAP's first electoral successes in Bavaria had been made at the cost of the DNVP, and that the party's vote was much higher in the Protestant areas.[16] It needed little reminder that the Nazis' chief hater of Catholics, General Ludendorff, had attracted the allegiance of Protestant priests,[17] or

16. The fact that the NSDAP's highest votes were mainly in the electoral districts of Prussia, which was a largely Protestant state, accounts for the preponderance of Protestants among the 107 deputies of the party elected to the Reichstag in 1930. The NSDAP parliamentary group consisted of seventy-five Protestants, twenty-seven Catholics, two dissidents and three without particulars. By comparison, all deputies of the BVP and the Centre Party were Catholics, while the large majority of DNVP deputies were Protestants (thirty-six out of forty-one) and the deputies of the KPD and SPD had a high proportion of dissidents. (*Augsburger Postzeitung*, 13 November 1930.)

17. For example, in April 1924 an organization called the Working Association of Racialist Priests was formed in Nuremberg under a Pastor Dorn for the purpose of uniting nationalist

that Protestant priests were sometimes active supporters of the Nazi Party. Speeches by Protestant priests at Nazi meetings on such subjects as 'National Socialism and Christianity', and services held by them at SA demonstrations were not an unusual event. A regular speaker at party meetings was Max Sauerteig, assistant priest in the Protestant church of St Johannis in Ansbach, who gave the address at the Christmas festival of the NSDAP branch in Würzburg in December 1928 (*73*). Sympathy among local priests was noticeable in certain Protestant towns in Franconia, where the NSDAP enjoyed wide support from the population. In Bayreuth, Protestant pastors tuned up to Martin Luther's famous hymn, 'A mighty fortress is our God' at a meeting where Hans Schemm had spoken; while the local branch of the Nazi women's organization, the *NS Frauenschaft*, was led by the wife of a Protestant priest (*74*).

The less hostile attitude of Protestant priests did facilitate the NSDAP's greater popular success in Protestant than in Catholic areas. In the summer of 1930 the authorities in Lower Franconia, a predominantly Catholic region, reported that 'in communities with a Catholic population the movement has so far no footing, on the other hand sympathies in communities with a Protestant population are somewhat greater' (*75*). Late in 1931, the same authorities quoted in a report on rising support for the NSDAP the case of the district of Kitzingen where 'the National Socialist movement is making unchecked progress in the Protestant communities of the district, while in the Catholic communities thanks to the influence of the Catholic clergy the movement is held back' (*76*). Protestant priests were often more lenient about Nazis taking part in church services during the course of weekend rallies, in spite of disciplinary measures taken by the Evangelical Church Council and a warning against National Socialism from Dr Veith, the Church's President (*77*). The general difference between the attitude of Protestant priests and Catholic priests towards the NSDAP could be attributed to the predominance of national conservative views among the former. This was shown clearly at a conference of Protestant theologians from Franconia at Steinach, near Rothenburg ob der Tauber, in January 1931. The main address on the subject 'The development of National Socialism, a question for theology and Church people' saw in the NSDAP the 'last bulwark against Bolshevism', applauded the principle of 'positive Christianity' and proclaimed that 'theology and the Church must concern itself about the inner motivation of the popular order newly proclaimed by National Socialism' (*78*).

and anti-semitic minded Protestant priests. This group emphasized its support for General Ludendorff.

Catholic leaders, who were suspicious of the intentions of the NSDAP, found an added provocation in the attempt by some Nazi leaders in Middle and Upper Franconia to exploit Protestant resentment against the Catholic influence in Bavarian politics. This sometimes coincided with irritation in the party over prohibitions by the Bavarian Government. After a meeting was banned in July 1931, Schemm commented: 'Never in the 121 years of its being part of Bavaria has the Franconian population had to put up with such incomprehensible behaviour; the suppression of the national will for freedom in Franconia, and especially in Bayreuth, is afflicting the soul of the Franconian people with a bitterness, which itself finds unpleasant' (79). Schemm was referring to new administrative regulations, which proposed to abolish the district office of Bayreuth and merge it with that of Ansbach (also a predominantly Protestant area) in the Catholic administrative district of Bamberg. Plans for the reduction in the number of district administrative units, as part of a policy for the simplification of regional government, had already aroused late in 1927 'a deep-seated animosity not just in Bayreuth but in wide circles of the Upper Franconian population, and was considered by the population as an open degradation of Franconia and above all as a punitive measure for the Protestant section of the population' (80).

It was not in the interests of the NSDAP to go too far in exploiting confessional antagonism. The Nazis were less dependent on the goodwill of the Bavarian Government than they had been after their party was refounded in 1925 because they now had strong areas of support outside Bavaria, but they realized that alienation of an important section of the public would have a detrimental effect on their electoral chances.

It is difficult to say how much the Rosenberg controversy and the declaration of Bavarian bishops really influenced the voting behaviour of Roman Catholics. Both received much publicity at the time, although press comment on the declaration (apart from the BVP papers) tended to be neutral (81). The controversy over the *Myth* was confined mainly to the elites of the Catholic Church and the Nazi Party, although Rosenberg's name became more of a household word than he deserved. The controversy was fought out largely in the press. A paper like the *Augsburger Postzeitung*, which concerned itself with the theological implications of National Socialism, appealed to an intellectual Catholic audience and had a restricted circulation. The dispute did not make much impact in the rural areas, where the Nazis were now concentrating their propaganda activities. Peasants were not in the habit of reading newspapers. Their political organizations, like the BBMB, did not make an issue out of the dispute, while the Bavarian People's Party was not in the habit of holding regular meetings in the country areas like the Nazis.

Peasants were in any case more interested in their livelihood and their land than in questions of religious doctrine. As far as their religion was concerned —for Catholic peasants were generally very religious—much depended on the readiness of local priests to take up the issue, like the one in Jachenau near the Walchensee who warned his congregation that, as the NSDAP was not recognized by the Bavarian episcopacy, those who attended a party meeting in the village would be damned (*82*).

It is useful to examine the behaviour of Nazi speakers and the opposition they met in a few strong Catholic areas during the time after the Rosenberg controversy and the bishops' declaration. The two neighbouring districts of Riedenburg and Parsberg in the Upper Palatinate, between Regensburg and Eichstätt, were totally Roman Catholic.[18] In both cases the question of the party's position on religion became a frequent topic at meetings from the autumn of 1930.

At a meeting in the village of Mindelstetten (district of Riedenburg) in February 1931, the NSDAP speaker informed his audience that the symbol of the swastika had existed 800 years before Christ, and went on to pontificate about the dangerous policies followed by the Popes in the Middle Ages (*83*). In November 1931, a speaker called Stubenrauch pointed out at a party meeting in Riedenburg that it was unimportant for the party whether people were Catholics and Protestants for 'they are all our fellow Germans', and they had the party to thank that they still had priests as the NSDAP 'is battling with Bolshevism to the end' (*84*). In an obvious attempt to stir up anti-semitic feeling at an NSDAP meeting for peasants in Riedenburg the speaker, who was mayor in Aipoln, remarked: 'In every party with the exception of that of the National Socialists there are Jews, especially in the Centre Party and in the BVP, which is the tail end of the Centre Party' (*85*). Many of these speeches were made on the assumption that religion must play an important part in rural community life, and that it was necessary to allay any possible fears about National Socialism. Other speeches were in response to direct attacks by the Bavarian People's Party and the Church. The speaker at a meeting in Mindelstetten in April 1932 attacked the behaviour of a local priest who, he claimed, had warned female voters not to support Hitler in the Presidential Election because if he were successful 'women over sixty years of age would have their heads cut off'. The only answer was for 'such priests, who spread base election lies of this kind, to be dealt with' (*86*).

In no case did the Rosenberg controversy appear to feature in Nazi

18. According to the 1933 census, the district of Riedenburg had a Catholic population of 99·4 per cent and Parsberg one of 99·2 per cent.

speeches, for it was clearly not in the interests of party speakers to raise the question if it had not disturbed people living in the area. This was also true of meetings held in the district of Parsberg during the same period. In March 1931 a speaker named Schikalla introduced his speech at Beratzhausen on the subject 'Can a Catholic be a National Socialist?' with the sarcastic question whether Christ was a registered member of the BVP or the Centre Party, as these two parties kept using his name. National Socialists could in all good conscience kneel down before the tabernacle 'for Christ does not ask which party one belongs to' (87). Many of the arguments put forward by Nazi speakers in the district were contained in a speech by one Engert at a village in the Parsberg area in December 1930:

> The swastika was taken up by Christianity. It is to be found in a church in Rome, in fact in a christening font. One can also see it in a church in Milan. It was adopted by Christianity centuries ago and not just today. It is a falsehood that we are enemies of Christ (Bravo!). Politics and religion cannot in any way be compared with each other. We say that religion is sacred for us (Quite right!). It will not be attacked by us. We stand on the basis of Christianity. Not only here, but also among the members of the movement, that I can assert (Bravo!). Religion belongs in the Church. Whenever we oppose the Bavarian People's Party and the Centre Party, then it is said we are treating Christianity abominably. When we attack the Centre Party, then it is said we are attacking Christianity. We ought not to put up with this reproach. It is exactly these parties which have the duty to tell the truth, and not to peddle around falsity. It is just those who preach the word of God, who should have the duty and obligation to tell the truth. Today we only have a phoney Christianity. We are the only right ones, because we tell the German people the truth (88).

Although the Rosenberg controversy did not have much popular impact, the controversy over the NSDAP's attitude towards religion did not really subside in 1931 and 1932. Relations between the Catholic authorities and the Nazi Party continued to be plagued by frustrations and attempts by each side to outmanoeuvre the other. The attitude of the bishops was basically hostile to National Socialism, although it did not appear so clear-cut in practice; the leaders of the Catholic party were hostile for the same reasons, but they were freer to indulge their hostility because they had the added incentive of political rivalry. There were several levels of Catholic opinion— the Bavarian episcopacy, the local priests and the Bavarian People's Party—

so the Nazis tried to take advantage of the confusion which sometimes followed. It is therefore worth summarizing the main arguments of Nazi propaganda in its attempt to deal with the question of the Catholic religion:

1. *The attempt to drive a wedge between Catholics and the Bavarian People's Party*

The NSDAP argued, contrary to the claims of the BVP, that the confessional party did not represent the best interests of Roman Catholics. The main point of argument was that the coalition between the SPD and the Catholic parties in the Reichstag was evidence of the latter's 'sell-out' of religion to 'atheistic Marxism'. Typical of this line was the NSDAP leaflet produced for the election to the Bavarian state parliament in April 1932, called *Save Church and Christianity*. This asked the question: 'Catholic Christians! Which is worth more to you? What the Bavarian People's Party says, or what the Vatican declares?' It quoted a statement supposed to have been made by Pope Pius XI that there was no such thing as a Catholic party, and produced the astounding piece of news that the BVP was intending to form a coalition with the SPD in the new parliament ('Social Democracy is the declared enemy of religion and the Church') (*89*). This attack on the BVP was combined with criticism of Catholic priests for their 'misuse' of religion for political purposes. For the July 1932 Reichstag Election *Gau* leader Adolf Wagner produced a party film called *Church and State*, in which he was seen introducing it with an inflammatory speech: 'Ultramontanism, represented by the BVP and the Centre Party in Bavaria, has from time immemorial done everything possible to thwart the great unification movement of Germany . . . in many places in Bavaria the church is no longer God's house and the priest no longer God's servant' (*90*).

2. *The claim that the NSDAP was only concerned with political questions*

This followed from the first argument. Party speakers were warned not to become involved in disputes over 'religious' matters, and were advised to concentrate on attacking 'political Catholicism'. An example of such an approach was Wagner's two election addresses, 'We want to remain Catholics!', for the 1932 election to the Bavarian state parliament. 'We Catholics in Germany and above all in Bavaria want in the peace of our conscience to fulfil our religious and church duties' (*91*). Not only did the

Nazis claim they were good Catholics; they also maintained they did not intend to harm the interests of the Church. All the party was doing was to advocate a change in the Bavarian Concordat, along the lines of Mussolini's treaty with the Vatican, whereby priests were forbidden to be active on behalf of political parties. The second election address did in fact briefly mention Rosenberg's book: 'The statements of Rosenberg or Reventlow[19] are not to be brought into this argument [with the BVP], for what they as Protestants think about the Catholic Church is left just as much to their discretion, as it is to us as Catholics to think what we like about the Protestant Church; it is a question here of a purely political matter to be settled between us Catholics' (92).

3. The avoidance of embarrassing issues

Party speakers either ignored or played down the Rosenberg controversy. Their reaction to the declaration by the Bavarian bishops in February 1931 on National Socialism was to forgo any attack on the episcopacy. Typical of this behaviour was the comment of the Nuremberg police early in March 1931: 'The speakers of the NSDAP place renewed and ostentatious emphasis on the "positive Christian" outlook of National Socialism and, considering the political character of the party, refuse to become involved in confessional arguments' (93).

4. The emphasis on the fact that Hitler was a Catholic

In Catholic areas it was not uncommon for Nazi propaganda to exploit the fact that Hitler belonged to the Catholic Church, assuming that most people would not be aware that he was not a practising Catholic. During an election campaign in Upper Franconia, a Nazi leaflet solicited as follows:

> When they say that Hitler is not sincere about his Catholic faith, they are liars because Hitler is a convinced, deeply believing and devout Catholic . . . to elect Hitler means to bow in humility and love before the Cross of Christ . . . Upper Franconian Catholic, when you do not want to burden your conscience, when divine commands are more important to you than party commands . . . then you elect Adolf Hitler (94).

19. Count Reventlow was a Nazi leader in North Germany who had been prominent in the German Nationalist Freedom Party (DVFP) in 1924.

5. *The emphasis on the danger of Communism*

The theme of Communism often appeared in speeches on religion. Communism was presented as a threat to Christianity and to traditional values like private property and the family. Hence the comment of Hans Schemm at a meeting in Bamberg, during November 1931, that the Catholic press had 'no reason to oppose the NSDAP for if the SA defence did not exist, Church-murdering Bolshevism would have swamped Germany long ago' (*95*). The NSDAP sometimes made use of Russian émigrés as speakers to spread terrifying stories about what was happening in Soviet Russia to the Church. A frequent speaker in Bavaria in the late 1920s was Gregor Bostunich on the subject, 'The bloody frenzy of Bolshevism'. It was often stressed that there was little essential difference between Social Democracy and Communism. The former was merely a weaker version of the latter.

6. *The appeal to patriotism and nationalist feelings*

The Nazis recognized that patriotic feelings were strong among the Catholic population. No less a Catholic paper than the *Augsburger Postzeitung* commented shortly before the Reichstag Election of July 1932 that:

> If National Socialism were patriotic, nationally minded in the Christian sense, then the German bishops would have had no cause to condemn this nationalism of National Socialism and characterize it as heresy; if the nationalism of the NSDAP were that love of nation and fatherland, as the religion of Christ teaches, then this national movement would be welcomed most joyfully and, seen politically, the Centre Party and the BVP would have from the beginning offered to make common cause' (*96*).

7. *The appeal to historical and religious anti-semitism*

Although Nazi anti-semitism was racialist, party speakers attempted to exploit Catholic feeling against the Jews based on historical reasons. An example of this approach was the speech by Karl Holz in Nuremberg in April 1927, which argued that Christ had been crucified by the Jews because he had called forth a new movement:

Just as the Jews did this 2,000 years ago, so they are trying to do the same again now; the National Socialist movement, which wishes to free the German people from the power of the Jews, is being fought by the Jews with all means; no means is shunned to get rid of the *Führer* of the NSDAP; but nothing will help them, for as Christ through the crucifixion called forth the great Christian movement, which spread over the whole world, so the National Socialist movement will also expand over the whole world, even when its leaders are removed (*97*).

8. *The use of spurious arguments and misrepresentations*

One feature of this kind of propaganda was the use of superficial analogies. At a meeting in Rothenburg in May 1928, Streicher indulged in his habit of alluding to scripture and compared the local authorities to Pilate because of their action in banning party meetings (*98*). This approach was typified by a party indoctrination course for peasants in Grafing, a village east of Munich, in January 1932. One speaker on 'National Socialism and religion' repeated the conventional arguments about Rosenberg's book being a personal work, Ludendorff's expulsion from the party for his attacks on the Catholic Church and Hitler's opposition to the involvement of religion in politics. He went on to claim that the swastika was not a pagan symbol, for there had once been on show in the National Museum at Munich a bishop's mitre ornamented with a swastika, and a communion bench in a church in Trier was marked with the same symbol. The speaker, who was not talking to a very sophisticated audience, finished by asserting that the Nazis should receive most credit for the fact that the movement of secularization had made less progress in Bavaria than in the rest of Germany (*99*). On other occasions, the party was not averse to spreading such wild rumours as: 'Hitler has personally been to see the Pope, presented him with his programme and changed some of its points at the request of the Pope, so that the Pope then sanctioned the programme and released Hitler in a friendly way with a greeting and a blessing' (*100*).

9. *The use of Catholic priests to demonstrate that good Catholics could be members of the NSDAP*

Renegade Catholic priests were few and far between, but they were paraded around Bavaria to demonstrate this point. As a poor substitute, rumours

178

were spread that many Catholic priests in a certain area were members of the NSDAP, but failing that attendance by groups of party members at church services was designed to have a similar propaganda effect.

These arguments put forward by Nazi propagandists helped to dispel some doubts among Catholics about the intentions of the NSDAP concerning religion. They were able to exploit the fact that Nazism was not such a black-and-white case as Communism, which was seen as nothing less than a direct threat to Catholicism. In contrast with the revolutionary image of the Communists, the Nazis' 'legal' approach to winning power went some way towards satisfying those Catholics who had a traditional aversion towards overthrowing the government by force. Nazi propaganda also emphasized similarities of outlook between traditional Catholicism and National Socialism, such as opposition to 'liberalism and materialism' as well as 'Marxism', the appeal to conservative values and the organic conception of the state.[20] The Nazis of course enjoyed the tactical advantage of not being in power (as the Communists were in the Soviet Union) and of not being forced to declare their hand. But there were bound to be limits to the success of any arguments in shaking the emotional and psychological ties of the Catholic Church, and hence attachment to the Bavarian People's Party. So if Nazi propaganda had little success in winning support from the Catholic party, the least it could do was to make the NSDAP appear harmless to Catholics.

The question of the Catholic religion was therefore a challenge to the party's control over its propagandists. The strength and influence of the anti-clerical element in the NSDAP is difficult to determine because the party did its best to disguise it, and because antipathy towards the Catholic Church was part and parcel of a general *völkisch* outlook which also deplored the influence of the Jews, the freemasons and freethinkers. Certain party leaders in Bavaria like Julius Streicher and Karl Holz of Nuremberg were quite clearly anti-clerical and made little secret of their views, while one detects a hostility towards the Church behind the smooth approach of *Gau* leader Schemm. Much anti-clerical feeling in the Nazi movement was channelled into the attack on 'political Catholicism', just as Rudolf Buttmann claimed at a meeting at Ebersberg in January 1931 that 'the Bavarian People's Party has absolutely no speakers apart from the priests, and if these were to remain in their churches the party would be finished (*101*). Anti-

20. One Catholic German historian has stressed similarities between Fascist ideology and Roman Catholic doctrine in the use of such terms as 'authority', 'trust in the leader' and 'peace and order', as well as ideas in the economic programme of the NSDAP and the organic view of the state. See Hans Müller, *Katholische Kirche und Nationalsozialismus.*

clerical outbursts continued to occur, as when a speaker at a meeting in Arbing, a village near Vilshofen, referred to Catholic priests as 'wolves in sheep's clothing, outwardly black and inwardly glaring red . . . they are notorious souteneurs of Russian Bolshevism' (*102*). A sensation was caused after Ludwig Hellebrand, a speaker at a Nazi meeting in Pforzen near Kaufbeuren, announced that the Bavarian Concordat had nothing whatever to do with religion—it was a clumsy 'piece of work' of Dr Held, a convert who had become a Catholic so he could marry the daughter of a devout family (*103*). At Windsbach, the Catholic priest had the windows of his house smashed by stones shortly after he had insulted Hitler at a public meeting and attacked the Nazis sharply on other occasions (*104*). But such incidents did not happen on a scale sufficient to cause alarm to the Catholic electorate.

Another aspect of this problem concerned the nature of the Nazi Party itself. The Church had underestimated the problems arising from the sharp rise in popular support for the Nazis, because the NSDAP was in some ways different from the other political parties of the time—in its professional organization of propaganda, its relatively wide popular appeal and the fact that it managed to exploit instinctive feelings in the German public to an unprecedented degree. In a more fundamental sense, the NSDAP presented a potential threat to Catholicism because of certain similarities between Nazi ideology and Roman Catholic doctrine.

National Socialists, like Catholics, had an all-embracing view of life with their quest for total power and their emphasis on the supremacy of politics over all other matters, which by implication involved a challenge to the position of religion and the Church in the state. One senses all along an admiration–envy attitude on the part of the Nazis towards the power of the Church. Hitler revealed this quite clearly in *Mein Kampf*, where he had much to say for the Church's power of mass psychology and for the force of religious fanaticism. The reason why the Catholic Church stood firmer than ever before was that in spite of the advancement of science 'it holds fast to its fixed and established dogmas, which alone can give to the whole system the character of a faith' (*105*). The Church reinforced its hold by the recruitment of clergy from the masses of the people, which explained 'the inexhaustible vigour which characterizes that ancient institution' (*106*). In another chapter, Hitler remarks on the influence of the 'mysterious artificial dimness of the Catholic churches', of the burning candles, the incense and the thurible on the freedom of the human will. Illustrating the point that he was not interested in the Catholic faith as such but in the techniques of mass persuasion, Hitler compared church services with political meetings which are held in the evening. The human will succumbs more easily then to the domination of a stronger will than during the morning and day, especially to 'the oratorical art of a man who has the compelling character of an apostle' (*107*).

The NSDAP had many characteristics of a religious movement—the role of the *Führer* as a kind of messiah (Hitler was attributed non-human qualities), the fanatical belief of many of Hitler's followers, the ritual of party occasions, the annual 'pilgrimage' to the Nuremberg rally, the role of symbolism and the emphasis on the relevance of ideology to life. The NSDAP even created its own martyrs, for whenever a party member lost his life in a street battle with political opponents, the incident would be headline news in the party press and the victim would be enshrined as a party hero. The most famous example of this treatment was Horst Wessel, an SA man who got himself killed in a personal brawl with a pimp in 1930 and lent his name to the famous party song.[21]

Goebbels showed admiration for the hierarchical structure and organization of the Catholic Church, and saw a model for the NSDAP in church festivals and processions (*108*). In fact, Hitler expressly drew a comparison between the Nazi movement and a religious movement in a speech he gave to representatives of the Party press at Party headquarters in Munich in June 1930. Hitler's speech was recorded by Albert Krebs, former party leader in Hamburg, in his diary:

> By its content and scope it was one of the most impressive speeches I have heard from Hitler; in it he developed a picture of the structure of the Catholic hierarchy and Church organization, which was clear in its outlines and bold in its strokes. Then, he presented to his listeners the inner spiritual forces, which had created the edifice of Catholicism and continued to hold it together, only this was indistinct and was distorted for propaganda reasons, which was certainly only noticed by very few. How far Hitler was rationally conscious of this distortion, which saw and recognized only the earthly power and authority not its spiritual origins and objectives, or whether this arose from the habit of all fanatics, only to see what they want in everything, was not possible to establish. Probably, both factors were influencing Hitler at the time and were so interweaved with each other, that with the greatest honesty it was not possible to distinguish between them. Apart from this, the aim

21. The Horst Wessel Song was originally a piece of political verse written by Wessel for Goebbels' paper in Berlin, *Der Angriff*. Goebbels made it into a Nazi anthem after Wessel's death. It was sung to a hymn-like tune.

of the speech was not concerned with the historical picture but with the political utilization of it. The NSDAP should be built on the model of the Catholic Church. On a broad basis of preachers and 'political clergymen' operating among the people, the leadership pyramid of the party should rise through the tiers of district leaders and *Gau* leaders to the senators and finally to its *Führer*-Pope. Hitler did not shun the comparison between *Gau* leaders and bishops and between future senators and cardinals, just as he unhesitatingly carried over the notions of authority, obedience and belief from the spiritual into the worldly field without intimating the change of notions. Apart from Count Reventlow, who whispered in my ear a scornful remark about His Eminence and Holiness Dr Josef Goebbels, most of the listeners seemed to be completely captivated by Hitler's exposition. They did not notice that these statements set the seal on the victory of the 'Fascist tendency' inside the party, and the final exclusion of all democratic elements and methods (*109*).

The similarities between the NSDAP and a religious movement were consciously cultivated by the Nazis as part of their mass appeal. The annual rallies of the NSDAP in Middle Franconia on the Hesselberg near Dinkelsbühl were a classic example of this. The Hesselberg, an old Teutonic fortification and the site of a mountain fair until the First World War, was used by Streicher for rallies each summer from 1928 for party members and peasants from all over Middle Franconia. The occasion was treated with the utmost solemnity with appropriate music played by an SA band from Nuremberg and 'mountain sermons' from Streicher. At the first rally there, Streicher got everybody present to kneel down on the hillside. Following his speech in which he said that 'dark clouds are hanging over Germany . . . but a man has arisen, who will succeed in the salvation of the people, Adolf Hitler', the peasants stood up to sing *Deutschland, Deutschland über alles*! At the 1930 rally Hitler himself put in an appearance for the crowd, estimated at several thousand.[22]

The question of religion in so far as it became involved with politics provides a useful case study of party propaganda in the context of developments after the 1930 Election. This was one area where the propaganda machine was not well-prepared, for there was not even a special department for religious questions at the Munich headquarters, as there was for agrarian

22. See the descriptive account of the Hesselberg rallies in *Das Bayernland*, May 1937. The Hesselberg also has Protestant associations. It is the site of annual services held by the Evangelical Church at Whitsun for people from Middle Franconia.

matters. Nazi policy towards the Church was not well formulated at this time, and consisted more often than not of a series of *ad hoc* reactions. The reason was that the Nazis were basically embarrassed by the whole issue, and preferred not to become too involved in it. Their approach to the subject was therefore tactical.

The Nazi movement presented the Church with more of a challenge than it was aware of at the time. Nazi propaganda was largely successful in forestalling an ideological conflict between the Catholic Church and the NSDAP, because skilful tactics played a considerable part in Nazi policy towards religion before 1933. Hitler is reported to have once said that 'when I have attained power the Catholic Church will have nothing to laugh about, but in order to attain power I cannot do without its help' (*110*). The more the NSDAP succeeded in attracting popular support, the more difficult became the position of the Catholic Church.

Six

The Mass Appeal of the Nazis: Party Organization and Propaganda (1930–32)

The Social Background of Party Members

Sociological studies of the Nazi movement have usually emphasized its lower middle-class character in terms of both membership and voting appeal; that it was basically an expression of the 'extremism of the centre', of the lower middle classes in revolt against their declining economic position since the First World War, their resentment at the outcome of that war for Germany and their dissatisfaction with parliamentary democracy.[1] The strong support for the Nazis among these classes must be related to social and economic developments in Weimar Germany such as the effects of industrialization on the 'small man'. The lower middle classes[2] had traditionally voted for the national conservative and liberal bourgeois parties, which had lost much of their electoral support to the NSDAP by 1930.

1. Harold Lasswell the political scientist, writing in 1933, saw the Nazi movement as basically 'a desperate reaction of the lower middle classes' against the threat of being 'overshadowed by the workers and the upper bourgeoisie, whose unions, cartels and parties took the centre of the stage—the psychological impoverishment of the lower middle class precipitated emotional insecurities within the personalities of its members, thus fertilising the ground for the various movements of mass protest through which the middle classes might revenge themselves' ('The Psychology of Hitlerism', *The Political Quarterly*, 1933, p. 374). S. M. Lipset ('Political Man' (1960), p. 149) commented: 'The ideal-typical Nazi voter in 1932 was a middle-class self-employed Protestant who lived either on a farm or in a small community, and who had previously voted for a centrist or regionalist political party strongly opposed to the power and influence of big business and big labour'. See also Hermann Glaser's *Spiesser-Ideologie, Von der Zerstörung des deutschen Geistes im 19. und 20. Jahrhundert* (1964) for an extensive description of the lower-middle class character of the Nazi outlook, and Erich Fromm's *Fear of Freedom*, chapter 6 on 'Psychology of Nazism'.

2. The term 'lower middle classes' refers to the German *Mittelstand* of self-employed businessmen, white-collar workers, shopkeepers and craftsmen. Civil servants are also included in this category, depending on their grade (see chapter 3, p. 70, footnote). The general term 'middle class' includes also higher civil servants as well as members of the 'liberal professions', such as doctors and lawyers, who received higher education.

Believing in the liberal ideas of the rights of property and of the individual, they found themselves pressed between the devil of the labour movement and the deep-blue sea of big capitalism. Industrialization meant for them not only a threat to their means of living, but also to their place in society. Being 'middle class' was more a way of life than simply participation in an economic group, so that the loss of secure employment involved a loss of face.[3]

Previous references to the social composition of party membership at the time the NSDAP was refounded in 1925 have shown that members came predominantly from these lower middle classes. Similarly, the occupational background of Nazi election candidates in the late 1920s—selected primarily for their speaking ability, although they did typify the social groups predominant at the leadership level—suggested little change in the class character of party activists.[4] But many questions remain unanswered in the light of the NSDAP's election success in 1930. How much did party leaders differ in their social background from the body of party members? If the NSDAP had achieved political respectability by 1930, how much did the social background of party members change after the NSDAP's success in the Reichstag Election? Did the bandwagon effect bringing a large increase in party membership therefore make certain social groups more willing to demonstrate their support for Hitler?

The problem is partly one of identification. Although comprehensive and detailed information on the background of party members is not available, there is sufficient evidence to make a study possible in the form of official party statistics, the personality files of the party, local membership lists and supplementary details from police reports.[5]

3. One contemporary observer from America commented on the excessive habit of addressing people by the titles of their occupations in Weimar Germany: 'The tendency to emphasize titles and other aspects of formal status even on what we would treat as "informal" occasions seems to indicate a difference from the predominant American pattern; with us, occupational status is to a relatively high degree segregated from the individual's "private life", while in Germany this seems to be considerably less the case; his special formal status as it were follows him everywhere he goes; in social life generally he is less significant as a person, as John Smith, than he is as the incumbent of a formal status, as an official, an officer, a physician, a professor or a worker.' (Talcott Parsons, 'Democracy and Social Structure in pre-Hitler Germany', *Journal of Legal and Political Sociology*, 1942, p. 103.)

4. For example, the twenty candidates of the NSDAP for the 1928 district elections in Southern Bavaria consisted of four craftsmen (a technician, a painter, a master baker and a wheelwright), two tradesmen (a butcher and a shopkeeper), six officials (a railway official, a teacher, a small-town civil servant, a judge, a mayor and a town councillor) and seven others (two veterinary surgeons, a doctor, a foreman, a farmer, a manager and an editor). *VB*, 21 April 1928 and 6/7 May 1928.)

5. The official party statistics, Reichsorganisationsleiter der NSDAP: *Parteistatistik*

Official statistics of the NSDAP conveniently provide information on party membership both up to 1930 and for the years 1930–33. Table 2, for party members in Bavaria, shows a high proportion of independent businessmen, workers and white-collar employees.

Between 1930 and 1933 the composition of party membership changed in several important respects, but there were some regional variations. In all cases, the three groups of white-collar employees, the self-employed and civil servants declined in their proportion of party membership. This may seem surprising in view of the fact that these groups had so far formed the backbone of membership. Their drop in the share of membership is due firstly to the great increase in working-class members from 1930 and secondly to the fact that, with the general rise in party membership, these groups did not increase at such a fast rate as workers because they were already well-represented in the party ranks. But the number of employees and the self-employed more than doubled and in some cases tripled in the NSDAP from 1930, while the rate of increase in membership among civil servants was slightly lower. The strong lower middle-class element among Bavarian party members is underlined by comparing it with the figures for the NSDAP in the whole of Germany. In all five *Gaue*, the proportion of civil servants was higher in Bavaria than in Germany both in 1930 and 1933. The same was true of the self-employed, except in Franconia in 1930 and Main Franconia in 1933. White-collar employees were in fact under-represented in the Bavarian party membership in most cases.

Two interesting factors need special attention—the high proportion of working-class members, and the low level of membership among peasants. The increase in the proportion of working-class members is all the more impressive when one considers that the total membership rose sharply for

(Munich, 1935), give the occupational background of party members according to the *Gaue*. Some of the *Gaue* had been renamed by 1935. In Bavaria they were called Munich–Upper Bavaria, Swabia, the Bavarian *Ostmark* (the area bordering Austria and Czechoslovakia: the Upper Palatinate, Lower Bavaria and Upper Franconia), Main Franconia (Lower Franconia–the Main basin) and Franconia (Middle Franconia). These statistics have the merit of providing a general idea of NSDAP members in each *Gau* but offer nothing on the variations in membership within each region, especially in relation to the character of particular towns or districts. To some extent this gap in information is filled by local police reports. German towns had efficient systems of registration, whereby all persons in a community were obliged to report their arrival, departure and change of address to the police. The questions asked were demanding, and the completed registration forms were little short of brief autobiographies. They contained such information as the person's occupation, date of birth and confession. The police used this information for reporting on political offenders. Their reports (such as the extensive ones on SA members when that organization was banned in 1932) give a detailed picture of party activists. The NSDAP personality files are to be found in the US Document Center, West Berlin.

Table 2   *Membership of the NSDAP in Bavaria before 1933**

	Workers %	Employees %	Self-employed %	Civil servants %	Peasants %	Others %
Munich–Upper Bavaria						
1930	19·0	21·7	25·0	13·0	2·3	19·0
1933	24·4	21·2	24·1	9·5	3·3	17·5
Swabia						
1930	27·8	16·6	24·2	11·7	12·2	7·5
1933	38·0	13·6	20·8	8·8	11·5	7·3
Bavarian Ostmark						
1930	29·1	20·0	23·0	13·6	5·1	9·2
1933	34·6	16·9	20·8	10·9	8·3	8·5
Main Franconia						
1930	20·5	22·5	19·7	16·3	8·5	12·5
1933	33·2	19·3	17·2	10·1	10·2	10·0
Franconia						
1930	28·4	21·6	18·7	12·5	5·7	13·1
1933	37·5	17·4	18·2	9·1	8·5	8·3
Germany						
1930	26·3	24·0	18·9	7·7	13·2	9·9
1933	31·5	21·1	17·6	6·7	12·6	10·5

Source: Parteistatistik (1935), pp. 146, 148.

The comparative figures for the population of Bavaria and Germany (1932) are:

	Bavaria %	Germany %
Workers	36·7	45·1
Self-employed	21·0	17·3
Employees and civil servants	13·0	16·5

The figures given for those in agriculture and forestry are 43·8 per cent (Bavaria) and 30·5 per cent (Germany).

Source: Statistisches Jahrbuch für das deutsche Reich (Berlin, 1932), p. 18.

* Party statistics are of course always questionable, especially as the Nazis sought to give the impression that they enjoyed strong support among all classes. While these statistics are generally confirmed by other evidence, the figure for workers in the NSDAP in Bavaria does seem unusually high and does not correspond to the impression gained from reading police reports and local membership lists. The problem must in part derive from the terminology. There is for instance a large proportion of 'others' in the party statistics. As far as this study is concerned, employees (*Angestellten*) refers to white-collar workers (for all classes after the 1930 Election. In Swabia, for instance, the number of working-class members rose from 586 to 2,834 during the period 1930–33, compared with the rise in total membership for the *Gau* from 2,112 to 6,880 (*1*). This is surprising because the Bavarian NSDAP made no special effort with 'socialist' propaganda, but it must be seen as chiefly a consequence of the Depression. During the period 1930–33 there was also a large increase in unemployed party members. In the Bavarian Ostmark, the number of total party members increased more than twofold during these years, while the number of unemployed members went up more than threefold (*2*). Since unemployment was highest in the cities and towns, one may assume that the large proportion of these unemployed party members were working-class who were looking for an outlet in party activities, especially as members of the SA. But, if workers provided a hard core of the grass-roots membership, very few of them rose to leadership positions in the NSDAP. It was unusual to find a local branch leader with a working-class background in Bavaria.

The small membership among peasants even during 1930–33 is curious, because it is totally out of proportion to the predominantly rural character of Bavarian society. In Swabia, where the Nazis increased their rural support more than elsewhere in Southern Bavaria in the elections of 1930–32, the number of peasant members rose from 257 to only 778 (*3*). It seemed that peasants were ready to vote for the NSDAP out of economic desperation or disillusionment with the Weimar Republic, but were unwilling to become active in the party. There were two reasons for this. Peasants were generally more interested in their land than in active politics, since economic interests accounted a great deal for their change in voting preferences. The influence of priests, who deplored their communicants becoming members of the NSDAP, was often strong in rural communities, especially in the Catholic areas.[6]

In spite of the influx of workers into the NSDAP from 1930, the party remained predominantly bourgeois in character. While workers accounted for a large share of the mass membership, the lower middle classes continued

---

example, technical, sales, managerial staff), although in some statistics (as with those for the population) employees and civil servants (*Beamten*) are grouped together. Civil servants covered the whole category from small-town officials to the high-grade civil servants working for the state government in Munich. They also included in Germany all school-teachers. The self-employed (*Selbständige*) meant independent businessmen like craftsmen, trades-men, shopkeepers and innkeepers, although in some groups of statistics they include members of the 'liberal professions' like doctors and lawyers.

6. Peasants in Bavaria took longer to win over to the NSDAP than in many other areas of Germany. See chapter 6, pp. 224–36.

to provide the main strength of the activist element.[7] Party propaganda gave furthermore special attention to the interests of these classes. The official party programme of 1920 had emphasized in point 16 that: 'We demand the creation and maintenance of a healthy middle class, immediate communalization of wholesale business premises and their lease at a cheap rate to small traders, and that extreme consideration shall be shown to all small purveyors to the state, district authorities and smaller localities.' Members were encouraged to patronize small businesses through the party sub-organization, the Fighting Association against Department Stores and Cooperative Societies (*Kampfgemeinschaft gegen Warenhaus und Konsumverein*).[8]

Several reasons for the success of the Nazi appeal to the self-employed were given by Anton Aigner, chairman of the General Trade Association in Munich, in his testimony, 'Why I became a National Socialist', in November 1931.[9] Aigner began by saying that like the majority of craftsmen he had taken no interest in politics before. The main duty of the bourgeois citizen had traditionally been peace and quiet (*Ruhe ist des Bürgers erste Pflicht*), but since the War things had changed. The lower middle class was now paying for its earlier political inactivity. It had become the 'whipping boy' of the 'present system' and bore the main brunt of the new taxes, because 'the Marxists, our enemies' held large majorities in the parliaments and the 'bourgeois' parties voted with them as they wanted to hold on to their

7. In the spring of 1932, following the ban on the SA and SS by the Brüning Government, the police made extensive lists of members of both organizations in each locality from whom they confiscated weapons, propaganda and other objects. (See HA 75/1556–7 and 87/1816.) Small businessmen, such as tradesmen, tailors, bakers, locksmiths, mechanics, carpenters and shoemakers, constituted a large part of these members. For instance, one list gives the names of 288 members of the SA and SS in fifteen places in Southern Bavaria. The following particular occupations were represented by more than ten people: workers (22), auxiliary workers (21), farmers' sons (20), tradesmen (19), locksmiths (13), carpenters (12), man-servants (11) and farmers (9). They accounted for 127 of the members. The remainder included a fair sprinkling of craftsmen and other occupations which came under the category of small businessmen. There were also several civil servants, small-town employees (especially those working for savings banks), electricians and railway employees.
8. The *Gau* departments of this organization drew up lists of shops and small firms, called 'Registers of German Tradesmen', available to party members at ten pfennigs a piece. One such list for Nuremberg, which boasted that 'only National Socialists are putting a real middle-class policy into practice', listed the names of twenty-five businesses, including a stationer, an optician, a grocery shop, a dairy, a seller of corsets (Anna Rossner, Schwabacher Strasse 5), a watchmaker and a shop which specialized in brushes, combs, candles and toiletries. Party members were required to show proof of their dedication to the bourgeois cause by signing special purchase coupons specially provided and stamped by the *Gau* office.
9. Aigner's statement was published in the *Mittelstands-Front* (28 November 1931), the *Gau* paper of Munich–Upper Bavaria for middle-class questions. Aigner was by trade a master locksmith, and became an NSDAP candidate for the Bavarian state election in 1932.

positions of power. The 'bourgeois' (*Mittelständler*) had become the 'victim of the false system', but 'thus far and no further':

> Now the fight must begin . . . Craftsmen, now we have our chance! If we miss this opportunity to join the German Freedom Movement, then we have lost everything. Look back at the last ten years again, and ask yourselves the question: What would have become of our middle class if we had had no Hitler, where would we be today? Social Democracy and Communism are the same in their basic ideas, and from time immemorial have been one in their suppression of the middle class. Only in the last few years has Adolf Hitler torn the mask from their face, and they are now beginning to waver.

Aigner continued that it was to the credit of craftsmen and tradesmen that they recognized this 'fearless fighter' as the 'saviour of the middle class'. In Hesse the Economic Party had already voted National Socialist, and for them there was no alternative. An end should be put to the dominance of the Bavarian People's Party in trade associations, for it used 'terror' as well as pressure to prevent the representation of those who dissented with it. Only the NSDAP really represented the interests of craftsmen, particularly as their former representatives had left them in the lurch. There should be no more divisions in the middle class, for everyone should now unite in the Hitler movement. Aigner's statement gave many of the reasons for the strong support which Hitler attracted among the lower middle classes in Bavaria: bitterness against the Weimar Republic, disillusionment with their own political representatives, strong anti-Communism and resentment at the dominant role of the Bavarian People's Party.[10]

If the lower middle classes provided the backbone of the activist element in general, the professional middle classes were more prominent at the leadership level. Doctors and lawyers were often found as branch or district leaders in Bavaria, to an extent out of proportion to their share of the total membership.[11] A prominent example of a lawyer as local party leader was Wilhelm Schwarz, branch leader and from 1927 district leader in Memmingen. Schwarz was born in Memmingen in 1902, joined the NSDAP in 1926 and

---

10. See chapter 6, pp. 238–39 for the anti-semitic appeal of the Nazis to the lower middle classes.

11. For example, in June 1931 there were twenty-five district leaders in the *Gau* of Munich-Upper Bavaria. The occupations of thirteen of them are identifiable, suggesting that most of them came from the professional middle class: two lawyers, two doctors, a dentist, two teachers, two civil servants, three businessmen and a tradesman (HA 90/1869).

set up legal practice in the town in April 1930. He was a gifted public speaker and was the leading light in the local party, as Dr Liebl was in Ingolstadt. In 1929, Schwarz became a town councillor, and the following year was elected an NSDAP deputy in the Reichstag. He also founded the local Nazi newspaper, the *Allgäuer Beobachter* (4).

A conspicuous role was also played by school-teachers in the Nazi Party, of which Julius Streicher and Hans Schemm were the most notable examples in Bavaria. School-teachers were well-suited to become party activists and ideologists, because of their gift of the gab and their tendency to be dogmatic. There were important ideological reasons why school-teachers should have been attracted by the NSDAP. The teaching profession was known for its strongly liberal, and therefore anticlerical, tradition, which showed during the Weimar period in resentment at the dominant position of the Bavarian People's Party. According to Wilhelm Hoegner, the Bavarian Social Democrat, the Concordat signed by Bavaria with the Vatican in 1924 continuing Church control over education was responsible for driving many elementary school-teachers into the arms of the Nazis, who had opposed the Concordat in the state parliament (5). By 1930, when the NSDAP had become the main political rival of the BVP, the left-wing press complained that teachers and civil servants, the 'descendants of the once proud Bavarian liberalism', now formed 'the main body of troops of the National Socialists' (6).

The political activities of school-teachers soon came under review by the Bavarian Government, following numerous complaints in the state parliament early in 1931 about the participation of school-teachers in the NSDAP and the effect of this on their pupils. The Minister of Education made a statement on 29 April based on reports from the regional authorities.[12] Goldenberger said that Lower Bavaria, the Upper Palatinate and the Palatinate had found little Nazi influence in the schools. The party's influence appeared stronger in Upper Bavaria, especially in the technical schools, but he concluded that Nazi propaganda in Bavaria had not yet 'seized hold of the pupils of elementary and technical schools to any considerable extent' (7). At the same time, Goldenberger was forced to acknowledge that elementary school-teachers were very active in the NSDAP:

12. These regional reports, based in turn on reports of each district, were a detailed compilation of the activities of elementary school-teachers in the NSDAP. The report from the Upper Palatinate, for instance, could find only isolated cases of school pupils joining the Hitler Youth. There were four definite cases where teachers had gone beyond the bounds of duty, including Franz Maierhofer, the *Gau* leader in the area. The report also mentioned eight other cases which were less clear-cut, such as one teacher from Fischbach who had been at variance with the local priest for years. (Report of Upper Palatinate Government, 10 April 1931, Staatsarchiv Amberg, Reg. v. Opf./14293.)

Concerning the participation of elementary school-teachers in the service of National Socialist propaganda, there has been a complaint that in various cases they have indulged in propaganda for the National Socialist movement to an unrestrained extent and that in many places have disturbed the peace of the local population. In this connection the Ministry requested reports from the regional governments. These reports show that in almost every district a not inconsiderable number of elementary teachers are active in the service of the National Socialist movement. The overwhelming majority of these teachers have kept within the bounds laid down for civil servants in general and those responsible for the education of youth in particular. To my regret, I must state that in almost every district there are cases, however, where elementary school-teachers have reached the limits of what is permissible in their activities for the National Socialist movement, and also where they have gone beyond those limits (8).

Education was a sensitive issue for a Catholic government, but there was another reason why this question was controversial. School-teachers were employees of the state, and therefore came into the same category as civil servants. Did their activity in the party violate their required loyalty to the state? This problem is best explained by looking at civil servants in general.

The Bavarian Government had so far placed no limitation on the political activities of civil servants, where the political parties concerned were loyal to the state. The position concerning the political activities of civil servants did vary from one state to another in Germany. Compared with the Prussian and Baden Governments, which took the view that civil servants should not belong to the NSDAP because it was 'revolutionary', the Bavarian Government was less stringent for it preferred to examine each case individually and simply warned its state employees to be cautious. The reason for its more flexible attitude was given in a memorandum of the Ministry of Finance in March 1931: 'This much seems in any case clear, that the question concerning the NSDAP is more doubtful than that of the KPD, for in contrast to the latter the former's hostile attitude to the state does not follow directly from the party programme, and the general attitude of the party authorities is not so clear-cut as that of the KPD' (9).

The Bavarian Government was probably influenced by its more instinctive dislike of Communism, but by the spring of 1931 the involvement of civil servants in the Nazi movement had become so great as to draw the attention of the Bavarian Cabinet. On 17 April a Cabinet session was held to discuss the subject. Franz Goldenberger, the Minister of Education, introduced the discussion by arguing that the previous open position taken by the government was no longer satisfactory, so that a government statement on the matter could not be avoided. It all depended on what view one took of the constitutionality of the NSDAP. The general opinion was that the matter should be dealt with by the disciplinary courts. Both Dr Stützel and Dr Held expressed their personal conviction that the NSDAP was in fact 'hostile to the state'. In the view of the latter, civil servants who took an active part in the party had unquestionably exceeded the bounds placed on their political activities (*10*).

It was surprising in these circumstances that so many civil servants did in fact join the party. Civil servants officially enjoyed a security of tenure, but they too were being affected by the Depression. A special levy had been imposed on people in public employment in 1930, as part of several strict measures to reduce spending and raise the income from taxation. The following year the Brüning Government cut the salaries of civil servants by as much as 23 per cent. This decision caused bitter feelings, for it led in Upper Franconia to further increases in party membership: 'People never cease flocking to the NSDAP; it is particularly encouraged by the commotion among civil servants occasioned by the reduction in salaries, which makes itself felt in mass recruitment for the National Socialists; in Bayreuth over 700 new members are said to have joined the party in the past weeks' (*11*).

The degree of the party's success in winning the support of civil servants did vary from area to area, according to the attitude of local authorities towards the political activities of their employees. In Neu-Ulm civil servants suffered dismissal if they joined the NSDAP, so that 'a large number of civil servants had to be content with being silent collaborators of the movement' (*12*). By contrast, the local branch in Starnberg outside Munich was virtually run by civil servants. Franz Buchner, the district leader, was a state official in the survey office, while the branch leader there was a Reich finance official. In October 1930 the district office of Starnberg reported with embarrassment that membership of the NSDAP was 'remarkably high' among younger civil servants and that employees of the local revenue office, the county court and the survey office had taken a lively part in Nazi election activities (*13*).

Political opportunism was a further reason for the increasing support among civil servants for the NSDAP. The Nazis took advantage of their rise in popular support to put pressure on civil servants. According to the authorities in Swabia 'civil servants above all are turning to the National Socialists in hordes, not a few because they hope to make a good business deal, particularly as the National Socialists drop hints that in their state only a registered member of the NSDAP can fill a post' (*14*). By the spring of 1932, the Minister of the Interior felt sufficiently alarmed about the matter to write to district offices. He quoted the case of a police official in Kronach who had been approached by a Nazi, himself a finance official. He had been invited to a discussion with other (Nazi) civil servants 'as the party will achieve power in the foreseeable future, and must know what kind of people are on its side and who is of a different inclination—the supporters of the party would then receive a post'. The official had been asked to act as contact man for the Nazis within the police force. Dr Stützel requested information on similar cases (*15*). The Ministry already knew of one other case, that of the finance office of South Munich, where

> the National Socialists were urging those who were friendly to put in writing that they will vote for Hitler. At the same time, the threat has been uttered that he who does not vote for Hitler will forfeit his position. In the finance office of South Munich, officials have even boasted they have their promotion inside the finance office for the Third Reich already in the bag, so that nothing can happen to them and their place is secured for all events. A vigorous agitation is being conducted there in spite of the prohibition on political agitation in official places (*16*).

The Nazis had found issues to exploit discontent among civil servants, but they had to take account of an understandable caution about joining the party. Their tactics varied. They took advantage of ignorance by claiming that there was no legal objection to civil servants working for the party, and invited (Nazi) civil servants to come along to meetings to support this claim. They also exaggerated the poor deal handed out to civil servants in the Weimar state. During 1931–32 special party meetings for civil servants (*Beamtenversammlungen*) became a common feature in and around Munich, and even in some provincial towns. A frequent speaker at these meetings was Leonhard Blank, head of the sub-department for civil service questions in the *Gau* office of Munich—Upper Bavaria. At one such meeting in Munich in January 1932, Blank asserted that no civil servant who was a member of the SA or SS need fear wearing the brown shirt in public. Those who declined to show their allegiance to the NSDAP were of no use and should keep away. It was up to all civil servants to join the party in changing the system, especially as their own professional associations had not properly represented their interests during the past thirteen years. Blank then made a long speech in which he discussed the effects of the government's emergency measures on middle and lower-grade civil servants (*17*). Blank had developed considerable expertise in the subject, and at another meeting even imported a law court official to confirm his opinion that no action would be taken against civil servants who participated in Nazi activities (*18*).

The case of civil servants does illustrate the kind of political and social pressures which could operate as a result of the NSDAP's rise to prominence. Civil servants formed a significant element in the party membership in Bavaria, although their official allegiance to the state forced them to take a less conspicuous part at the leadership level than members of other professional groups. Their position was confusing because of doubts about the NSDAP's 'legal' tactics in the pursuit of power.[13] Although the Bavarian Government's attitude of reserve and even hostility towards the NSDAP did not basically change, the government found itself in a state of perplexity over the party's growing popular support. Electoral success did give the NSDAP an aura of respectability, and facilitated its infiltration of different social groups. The party's support rose among all classes, but this most affected the character of its mass membership with the sharp rise in working-class members. Since peasants remained a small and usually passive element in the party, its activists came predominantly from the small-town bourgeoisie and the professional classes. The NSDAP still remained a largely middle-class movement in character and outlook.[14]

In view of the growth in mass support for the NSDAP from 1930, it is important at this stage to examine how the Nazis organized their appeal to different social groups in a wider context than that of civil servants.

13. For a discussion of Hitler's policy of 'legality' see chapter 6, pp. 255–59.
14. This view is reinforced by an examination of the voting patterns of the NSDAP during the Depression years. Peasant voting support for the NSDAP increased sharply with the party's penetration of rural areas. The class preference in party support in the towns is shown by the case of Nuremberg, where there was a dramatic contrast between the NSDAP vote in working-class districts and middle-class districts. Gartenstadt was a purely working-class area, in which support for the Nazis during 1928–32 rose from only 1·1 per cent to 7·7 per cent. St Johannis was basically working-class, although there were some civil servants and white-collar employees. The NSDAP vote was higher here than in Gartenstadt. But in the two middle-class residential districts of Stadtpark and Luitpoldhain, the NSDAP won an absolute majority in the July 1932 Election. In Luitpoldhain, populated chiefly by entrepreneurs, lawyers and doctors, the NSDAP vote rose from 15·9 per cent in 1928 to 51·2 per cent in 1932. (R. Gömmel and G. Haertel, *Arbeitslosigkeit und Wählerentscheidungen in Nürnberg von 1928 bis 1933*, mimeographed thesis, Stadtarchiv Nuremberg, pp. 36–42.)

NSDAP Specialist Organizations—the Party's Appeal to Youth

Although the NSDAP was a predominantly middle-class party in terms of both its membership and electorate, especially in Bavaria, it claimed to be a 'catch-all' party with its promise to create a 'People's Community' (*Volksgemeinschaft*), where traditional class barriers would be abolished and 'workers of the mind' and 'workers of the fist' would join together and work in harmony for the good of the German nation.[15] The impression that the Nazi movement appealed to all classes of the population, one strongly promoted by Nazi propaganda, attracted many supporters, particularly those who had little taste for party politics and were conscious of the class antagonisms aggravated by the economic situation. To these people the NSDAP appeared 'above party', a feeling encouraged by the seemingly 'non-political' nature of some of its propaganda, such as garden-party concerts, sports tournaments and even the performance of stage plays.

This impression of the broad appeal of the NSDAP was not without some foundation, for it attracted the support of a wider cross-section of the public than most other parties of the time. Interest parties rather than mass parties were the rule in Weimar politics. The SPD, the largest party in the Reichstag before the NSDAP assumed that position in 1932, was organized as a mass party but it appealed mainly to a working-class electorate with some middle-class support, especially among civil servants and intellectuals. The KPD was also a predominantly working-class party. The main exceptions to the rule were the Catholic parties—particularly the Centre Party with its support among Catholic workers in the industrial Ruhr—but their appeal across classes was confined within the limits of their confession.[16] Otherwise, middle-class support was divided between the various liberal and conservative bourgeois parties such as the Nationalist Party (DNVP), the People's Party (DVP) and the Democratic Party (DDP), as well as a number of agrarian and regional parties and splinter groups. It was from this third category of parties that the NSDAP won most of its vote in Bavaria. The NSDAP was therefore basically a 'catch-all' party for the middle classes, while at the same time winning some support from the working class. But the NSDAP did win the highest vote percentage nationally of any party in the Weimar period, with its 37 per cent in the Reichstag Election of July 1932.[17]

15. Hitler's first speech in Munich after his speaking ban in Bavaria was lifted in 1927 was devoted to this theme. See chapter 3, p. 74.
16. Only one-third of the German population was Catholic.
17. Strictly speaking, this was not absolutely true. The Social Democrats won 38 per cent of the vote in the 1919 elections to the National Assembly, called to decide on the Weimar

There were two important reasons for the relatively wide appeal of the NSDAP. Firstly, the flexibility and organization of its propaganda: the party claimed to appeal to all classes in general, but in practice appealed to many different interest groups at the same time. This kind of appeal was made possible through the elaborate development of specialist organizations. Secondly, much of the new support for the NSDAP in the elections of the early 1930s came from the young voters. The nature of the party's appeal to youth will be examined with special reference to such sub-organizations as the National Socialist German Students' League (NSDStB), the Hitler Youth and the National Socialist Schoolchildren's League. Members of the last two organizations were not themselves entitled to vote with the minimum voting age at twenty, but the Hitler Youth, whose membership was confined to the age group fourteen to eighteen, was involved in the party's propaganda efforts during election campaigns. The organization of these groups, particularly that for students, does illustrate how the NSDAP set about winning the support of the younger generation.

Even before the Reichstag Election of 1930, the party had been concerned about developing specialist propaganda instead of simply hammering away at a number of general themes designed to attract the discontented in the Weimar state. Konstantin Hierl, who became head of the second organization department at headquarters (for planning the future National Socialist state) in 1929, outlined his general scheme in a memorandum on 22 October 1929, called 'Intellectual preparations for the structure of the future National Socialist State':

Until now the emphasis of the NSDAP's political activities has been on exposing and attacking the ruling powers of the present state and present society, which are hostile to national interests and have a pernicious influence. This struggle must be continued in the future with greater force, utilising all legal means until political power in the state has been achieved. At the same time, intellectual preparations for the creation of the future National Socialist state must, considering the growth of the movement, gradually come into force. Once the rotten mask of the present state crumbles, then the foundations of the National Socialist state must be ready ... We must in all spheres of political and social life be clear what kind of new order we are going to put in place of

Constitution. This was before the final split in the Left, for the Communists did not take part in these elections. In the first Reichstag Election, held in 1920, the SPD vote dropped heavily. Otherwise, the highest vote of any party in the Weimar period, apart from that of the NSDAP, was the SPD's 29·8 per cent in 1928.

present conditions ... It is now a question of working out the consequences of our German nationalist outlook on life (*völkische Weltanschauung*) and conception of the National Socialist state for our basic
ideas in specialist fields, and in this way provide a firm basis and
definite practicable suggestions for the re-formation of the state (*19*).

Hierl followed this statement with a further memorandum asking *Gau*
leaders and leaders of large local branches to appoint 'specialists'' (*Fachar-
beiter*). He initiated one of the important new organizational developments
in the period between the Reichstag elections of 1930 and 1932—the proliferation of special offices at the *Gau* level. The *Gau* organization became more
elaborate, and resembled the model provided by party headquarters with
its system of sub-departments.

A good example in Bavaria of this development was the *Gau* of Munich–
Upper Bavaria, formed in November 1930 after the merger of the two *Gaue*
of Greater Munich and Upper Bavaria. The new *Gau* benefited from its
proximity to headquarters—its own office was also in Munich—and the fact
that it was based on the oldest organization in the party. The head of the
new *Gau* was Adolf Wagner, formerly *Gau* leader of Greater Munich.[18]

Wagner had been active in the party since 1923, first as a local branch
leader and from 1924 as a Nazi deputy in the Bavarian state parliament.
He was born in Algringen in Lorraine in 1890 as the son of a miner, and
studied mathematics and natural sciences at the University of Strasbourg,
then the science of mining at the Technical College in Aachen. Wagner
served on the Western Front during the First World War and was twice
wounded and gassed, losing most of his right leg. After the War, he became
the director of various mining companies in Bavaria and Austria for ten years.
Wagner was fanatically devoted to Hitler, even to the extent of aping the
Führer's mannerisms, like the raucous and shrill voice in public speeches
and the slapping of the knee in conversation (in his case the knee of the
left leg). He had earned a name for brutality and had a radical temperament.
He detested priests ('I can't stand priests; therefore I don't go to church'),

18. Fritz Reinhardt, the *Gau* leader of Upper Bavaria, was not given the new job. In fact
he resigned his post in the same month as Wagner's appointment, ostensibly on the grounds
that he already had enough commitments—he had recently taken over a second propaganda
department in party headquarters, as well as retaining his position as chief NSDAP representative on the Reichstag budgetary committee (see Hitler's statement in the *VB*,
7 November 1930). A major reason seems to have been a personality clash with Wagner (see
Reinhardt's letter to Hitler, 2 November 1930, in files of Reichsorganisationsleiter, Bundesarchiv Koblenz, NS 22/377). Reinhardt also complained to Gregor Strasser for deciding
to reorganize the *Gau* boundaries without consulting him (letter to Strasser, 24 October
1930, ibid.).

although he came from a Catholic family (20). Wagner was a suitable choice as leader of the new *Gau*, for with his desire to dominate others he proved a very energetic and effective propagandist. When he had taken over the *Gau* of Greater Munich the previous year, he had immediately gone round the city attending every discussion evening held by party members urging all of them to engage in 'unremitting dedication to the work of the election, and strong agitation to woo over political opponents' (21).

By June 1931 Wagner had built up the *Gau* of Munich–Upper Bavaria into departments as shown in Table 3 (see p. 200).

Local branches were required to duplicate many of the same offices, including even a women's representative and local chairman of the Fighting Association against Department Stores as well as the usual press secretary and agricultural specialist (22). In April, the *Gau* propaganda department had instituted a new filing system in order to 'maintain particulars for the cultivation of individual occupational groups, to provide statistics on *Gau* membership, and make possible more intensive activity and the drawing of party comrades into the individual sub-departments of our movement' (23).

This elaborate specialist organization seemed more impressive on paper than in reality, but there were valid reasons why they assumed a significant role in party propaganda. Firstly, the distinction between the two organization departments was in practice an artificial one. Those sub-departments under the second organization department, theoretically concerned with preparing the future Nazi state, were as much involved in propaganda against Weimar democracy as the ones in the first organization department. This distinction was not in fact made at the branch level, and even in the *Gau* offices all specialists were in common subordinate to the *Gau* leader.

Secondly, the blueprint outlined in *Gau* headquarters was by no means carried into effect by all local branches. Some branch leaders were simply lazy or incapable of putting into practice all the many organizational measures demanded by the *Gau*. Some of them were dismissed on the grounds of 'insufficient devotion to the *Führer*', but there was a limit to the number of such cases, if only for appearance's sake. Other branch leaders found there was no need to reproduce every office at the local level, depending on the nature of the community in which they were operating. Small branches in the countryside gave priority to agricultural specialists, while only in the larger towns was there any great proliferation of specialist groups. Rosenheim, a town of some 18,000 inhabitants with a relatively large working-class population, was a case in point. Soon after the 1930 Election a women's and girls' group was established, followed in 1931 by a local unit of the factory cells organization and a local unit of the motoring branch of the SA (24).

Table 3 *Organization of the Gau office of Munich–Upper Bavaria, 1931 (25)*

Department	Leader
Organization I ⎱	Adolf Wagner, deputy—
Organization II ⎰	Otto Nippold[19]
Propaganda	Nippold
Press	Karl Springer
Treasury	Hans Kuchenreuther

Organization Department I, with the following sub-departments:

1. Factory Cells and Trade Union Questions: Kurt Frey, with the special departments of:
(a) Civil Servant Questions: Leonhard Blank[20]
(b) Labour Law: Leonhard Blank

2. Middle-Class Questions: Georg Sturm
3. Questions concerning War Victims: Hans Dauser[21]

Organization Department II, with the following sub-departments:
1. Agrarian Policy: Artur Holzmann[22]
2. Financial and Economic Policy: Dr A. Pfaff
3. Cultural Policy: Professor Dr Gustav W. Freytag[23]
4. Social Policy: Kurt Frey[24]

Specialist for Municipal Questions: Lawyer Rudolf Schraut[25]
Specialist for Medical Questions: Dr Emil Ketterer
Specialist for Legal Protection and Legal Questions: Lawyer Dr W. Reiter and
 Lawyer Dr Philipp Hoffmann
Specialist for Youth Questions: Emil Klein
Specialist for National Socialist Self-Defence: Karl Springer
Specialist for Radio Questions: Matthäus Dötsch[26]
Working Association of National Socialist Women: Frau A. Kury
Investigation and Arbitration Committee: Lawyer Rudolf Schraut

---

19. Otto Nippold was a young man, not yet thirty, and one of the new generation of party activists. Born in 1902, he had become a member of the NS Students' League in Munich in 1928, joined the NSDAP in 1929 and was appointed a party speaker the same year. He gave up his legal training to become full-time business manager of the *Gau* in 1930.
20. Leonhard Blank, born 1876, was a former trade-union secretary living in Munich.
21. Hans Dauser, born 1877, had joined the party in 1921 and been a deputy in the Bavarian state parliament since 1928.
22. Artur Holzmann, born 1880, was a landowner. He joined the NSDAP in 1927, and became a district agricultural specialist.
23. Dr Freytag was a professor of medicine.
24. Kurt Frey, born 1902, was a political economist from Munich.
25. Rudolf Schraut, formerly branch leader in Pasing, was a Munich city councillor.
26. Matthäus Dötsch, born 1891, was a tradesman. He joined the NSDAP in 1929, became district leader in Dachau and was appointed *Gau* propaganda leader in 1932.

Thirdly, the creation of numerous party offices did, however, provide jobs for the many new members joining the NSDAP in the hope of benefiting from the party's rising fortunes. It was a question of patronage to siphon off possible disenchantment, once the immediate afterglow of electoral success wore off. One way of forestalling this was to give new members something to do. The sub-department of cultural questions illustrates this well. In April 1931, Professor Freytag was appointed head of the new department, officially known as the Department for Race and Culture. It was the *Gau* subdivision of the Fighting League for German Culture, a Nazi specialist organization led by Alfred Rosenberg, the purpose of which was to defend 'the values of the German character' and further 'the proper expression of German cultural life'. Freytag's first decision was to nominate eight district 'cultural wardens' (*Kulturwarte*) to encourage local branches to put on performances of a 'general cultural' nature such as film shows, lectures and theatre productions (*26*).[27] By September he had created numerous posts in his organization, which was based largely on the cities of Munich, Ingolstadt, Rosenheim and Landsberg. Freytag was assisted in his office by ten specialists (for racial questions, university matters, literature and the fine arts, etc.). 'Cultural district' number one included the city of Munich as well as surrounding towns. The Munich organization was further divided into four districts, each of which was once more subdivided into six or seven sections under separate 'cultural wardens' (*27*). These 'cultural wardens' included a high proportion of people from the artistic and academic professions, including several painters, a few art historians, a cabaret singer and a band leader.

Fourthly, specialist organizations were encouraged on the basis of the principle of 'something for everybody'. Almost every group was catered for except blind people, the deaf and dumb and the insane. Many of these organizations only had a propaganda value, and were not meant to collect together vast numbers of members or sympathizers. Propaganda among the war-disabled was an obvious example of this. The Nazis had long cultivated the image of the 'front soldier' in an attempt to win the support of that

27. In the autumn of 1931 the Fighting League for German Culture arranged for a tour of branches in Upper Franconia of the amateur players company of the *Gau Ostmark* (Frankfurt an der Oder). This company, which consisted mainly of teenagers and young people in their early twenties, offered a lively programme of political cabaret, patriotic music, folk songs and peasant melodies. The tour, which included a musical evening in Hof on 25 September and a garden concert with a dance in Nuremberg on 1 October, was such a success that groups of 'Franconian amateur players' were set up. The *Ostmark* group had been one of the first NSDAP companies to come into existence in 1930. Another was 'The Brownshirts', a group of amateur players in Berlin. (Report of Nuremberg-Fürth police, 18 September 1931, Staatsarchiv Nuremberg, Reg. v. Mfr. II/691.)

generation which had seen service in the First World War and returned to civilian life to become disillusioned. Politics was the continuation of war by other means. Hence, the use of military terminology in party orders, the emphasis on party ranks and uniforms and the 'campaign' against the 'enemy' in the 'struggle for power'. The *Gau* sub-department for the war-disabled organized special meetings for war victims (*Kriegsopferversammlungen*). In a memorandum of April 1932, the department announced that there were as many as two million war-wounded with relatives. An 'energetic attack' would bring success. Propaganda should emphasize that the war-disabled had been 'shamefully treated' by the Weimar system, and that 'we as the party of front-line fighters have the obligation to give our special attention to war casualties'. The next day the department urged local branches to select an 'overseer of war victims'. His job was to canvass support, and it would be better if he were a war victim himself (*28*).

Finally, the specialist organizations reflected the Nazi view that politics was not a part-time occupation but was total in its application to life. The multifarious collection of organizations provided a means of controlling the behaviour of party members outside conventional political events like election campaigns and public meetings. Severe restrictions were even placed on party members travelling abroad. In February 1932, the NSDAP organization leader for Munich–Upper Bavaria gave notice that:

> the bad habit of brownshirts travelling abroad, together with their taking advantage of the hospitality of organizations which are friendly with us (especially in Italy), has increased recently so much that the following instructions must be met: every party comrade, who gads about outside Germany without the express authority of party head-quarters, excludes himself automatically from the party according to clause 4 of the statutes (*29*).

Branch leaders and other officers who gave informal permission for such journeys would be called to account. The implication was that party members who were not reliably indoctrinated might be swayed by 'alien' influences when they were out of the country.[28]

How effective were these specialist organizations in terms of their contribution to Nazi propaganda, and their success in winning new members for the party? In view of the concentration now on rural propaganda, the most

28. The NSDAP had a Foreign Organization (AO), which had local branches abroad. One of the tasks of this organization was to control the movements and activities of party members outside Germany, and if necessary to confiscate their membership cards and order party members to return to Germany.

important of these organizations was the system of agricultural specialists.[29] The oldest sub-organization of the NSDAP was of course the SA, but it could not easily be classified with the specialist organizations because of its size of membership and the semi-autonomous role it claimed for itself. Tension between the political leadership and the SA had not been eliminated. It had come to a head again during the election campaign in 1930. Franz von Pfeffer had resigned shortly afterwards as chief SA leader, expressing dissatisfaction with the SA's role during the campaign. The real issue had been Pfeffer's demands for a more independent policy, which clashed with Hitler's wish to impose a tighter control over SA activities. Ernst Roehm was recalled to his former post during 1931, to reorganize the SA on more centralized and hierarchical lines similar to those of the German Army. Membership of the SA continued to expand enormously, reaching a total of 20,000 active SA men (with SS men) in Bavaria by July 1932, as well as 25,000 'reservists' (30). These changes did not make a great difference to its role in the party, for the SA continued to provide the backbone of propaganda activists.

Some of the smaller organizations had an extremely low membership. The factory cells organization (NSBO) never made much progress in Bavaria before the 'seizure of power'. Hitler had ambitiously introduced the idea of factory cells at the Nuremberg party rally in 1929 as being the means of 'not only influencing the workers in the direction of National Socialism, but to bind them organizationally to the party' on the model of the Fascist régime in Italy (31). But the NSBO suffered from the low priority it was given because the party was concentrating on winning over the middle classes, and did not wish to offend the latter by appearing to adopt 'Marxist' methods of agitation; its inability to break the monopoly of the left-wing parties over the trade unions; the lack of finance to run an extensive campaign; and the absence, in the case of Bavaria, of a large working class. Even in Munich, where one might have expected the organization to make some headway, it had little success. An NSBO unit was set up in the city early in 1931 and held its first public meeting in March, at which a mere hundred people put in an appearance (32).

The problem with the women's organizations in the party was similar, but for a different reason. Female members in the NSDAP were an extreme rarity, forming only a small fraction of the total membership.[30] Women played generally a small part in party politics in the Weimar period, and this

29. The system of agricultural specialists is discussed separately. See chapter 6, pp. 224–31.
30. In 1930 the total number of 'housewives' in the NSDAP in Bavaria was 1,065. This increased to only 2,800 by 1933, or roughly 4 per cent of the total membership. Women

tendency was magnified by the traditionalist attitude of the NSDAP on the role of women in society. Typical of the state of affairs governing female recruitment to the party was the fact that the local branch of the National Socialist Women's League (*NS Frauenbund*) founded in Holzkirchen near Munich in October 1931 consisted almost entirely of wives of local party members. The head of the group, which saw its main task as 'looking after the National Socialist unemployed twice weekly without cost', was one Frau Stitzinger, the wife of a local barber (*33*).

These specialist organizations did not involve any basic change in the totalitarian nature of the NSDAP. They were not based on any principle of representation for its own sake, but formed part of the attempt by Nazi propaganda to present the NSDAP as a movement which cut across classes and differed from other political parties, which appealed to sectional interests. But with certain important exceptions, such as the rural propaganda machine, the specialist organizations did not contribute much directly to the rise in party membership during 1930–32.

The specialist organizations amounted to a further elaboration of the 'leadership principle' at the horizontal level. Although the *Gau* of Munich–Upper Bavaria benefited from having an extremely efficient *Gau* leader and from its proximity to party headquarters, it was generally typical of the new pattern of sub-departments in other *Gaue* in Bavaria (*34*). The contribution of the specialist organizations to the development of the NSDAP as a mass movement should be further illustrated by looking at its various youth organizations.

Party youth organizations were nothing unusual in Germany, for they could be traced back to the German youth movements of the nineteenth century.[31] Several other parties in the Weimar Republic had their own youth branches: the Communists with their 'Red Youth Front' and 'Red Boy Pioneers'; the SPD with the 'Socialist Workers' Youth' and the 'Youth Banner'; and there was the Scharnhorst League, which was allied to the Nationalist Party. The difference with the Nazi youth organizations was that they were more obviously a political arm of the NSDAP, were more completely integrated into the party structure and were especially significant in view of the party's emphasis on winning the support of the young generation.

---

may well have been included under other occupations, but in view of their small role in most professions this was not likely to make much difference to the above estimate. In Bavaria at least, women were virtually unknown among party activists and certainly at the level of branch leader. (Figures from *Parteistatistik*, pp. 130–31.)

31. See Walter Laqueur, *Young Germany, a history of the German youth movement* (1962).

The role of the Nazi youth organizations must first be seen in relation to the age structure of the total membership of the NSDAP, which was by any standards extremely young, as Table 4 shows.

Table 4 *Membership of the NSDAP in Bavaria according to age groups*

	18–20 %	*21–30* %	*31–40* %	*41–50* %	*51–60* %	*61 and over* %
Munich–Upper Bavaria						
1930	0·3	24·1	28·6	20·0	17·1	9·9
1933	1·3	32·6	26·8	19·7	13·2	6·4
Swabia						
1930	0·3	28·4	33·2	19·9	12·4	5·8
1933	1·2	39·6	29·5	16·7	9·3	3·7
Bavarian Ostmark						
1930	0·4	31·5	33·9	19·1	9·5	5·6
1933	1·9	39·9	29·9	16·5	7·9	3·9
Main Franconia						
1930	0·7	31·2	34·6	19·0	9·8	4·7
1933	2·8	44·3	28·0	14·8	7·0	3·1
Franconia						
1930	0·0	36·2	27·2	16·8	12·1	7·7
1933	2·2	44·5	25·4	15·0	8·6	4·3

Source: Parteistatistik (1935), pp. 202, 204.

The predominance of the younger age groups is the most striking feature of the age structure of party membership. This became more marked with the rise in party membership during the early 1930s. Before 1930 the largest age group was thirty-one to forty, except in *Gau* 'Franconia'. During the period 1930–33, there was a small increase in the proportion of recruitment among the group eighteen to twenty, a large increase among those in their twenties and a proportionate drop among the older age groups in all cases. The increase in the proportion of party membership among the young generation is all the more impressive considering there was an over-all increase in the total number of party members. By 1933, the largest age group in every case was twenty-one to thirty. Party members under forty provided two-thirds, or more often almost three-quarters, of the total membership—in Main Franconia 75·1 per cent, the Bavarian Ostmark 71·7 per cent and Swabia 70·3 per cent. In Munich–Upper Bavaria, where party membership had a longer history, the under forties accounted for a lower proportion with 60·7 per cent.[32]

The young membership of the NSDAP, which contrasted dramatically with the age structure of the other political parties,[33] can be broadly explained by a variety of connected factors: the youthful and dynamic image cultivated by the party; the outlet it provided for political activism and youthful radicalism; the attention it gave to the emotional and 'idealistic' element in politics (for example, the youthful desire for hero figures); the promise of a more hopeful future, free from national humiliation and frustrating compromises with reality; and the fact that the party succeeded in channelling anti-Establishment feelings, strongly present in most young generations, which happily for the Nazis coincided with the increasing disillusionment with parliamentary democracy. How was this appeal to youth in fact organized? One must therefore examine the role of the youth organizations in training future party leaders, providing an extra source of propaganda activists and reinforcing the general impression of the Nazis' youthful dynamism.

The Hitler Youth (HJ) made little progress before 1930, although it had been founded as early as 1926. The first HJ group in Southern Bavaria was founded in Munich in November 1927, and by early 1929 groups had also started in Ingolstadt and Rosenheim. After the party rally in Nuremberg that year, the organization was extended with further groups in Augsburg, Memmingen, Traunstein and Starnberg. There were several reasons for these early difficulties: the lack of appreciation by party officials of the importance of a youth organization; the shortage of financial support; the hostility of local branch leaders to the establishment of local HJ groups; and the prohibitive attitude of school authorities.

After Adolf Wagner became *Gau* leader in the autumn of 1930, more attention was paid to the development of the Hitler Youth. The leader of

32. The official party statistics are confirmed by the evidence from police reports of membership of local branches. The young membership was especially noticeable in the SA, the most 'activist' of the sub-organizations. Lists of SA groups in Munich for 1932 show that by far the largest age group was twenty–twenty-nine; for example, the SA group in Munich–Laim had a membership of forty in September 1932, of which twenty-two were in their twenties (see extensive Munich SA lists in HA 73/1549). The same is true of party local branches in the rural areas; for example, the branch in Eggenfelden (Lower Bavaria) had a membership of forty-five in the spring of 1932, of which twenty-two were in their twenties (HA 75/1556).

33. For example, Richard Hunt (*German Social Democracy*, p. 106) concludes that the SPD membership was predominantly middle-aged. Over half its members were over forty, while by 1930 the group over sixty was larger than the group under twenty-five. The same was generally true of the liberal bourgeois parties. Only the KPD had a younger membership with 31·8 per cent of its members under thirty (1927 figure).

the HJ in the *Gau* was Emil Klein, a rather humourless-looking character, who had joined the SA as early as 1920. Born in Oldenburg in 1905, Klein was a tradesman by occupation and had become HJ leader in Munich in 1928, before taking over as leader in Southern Bavaria. He was assisted by his own staff of officials, including a business manager and treasurer, as well as sub-departments for propaganda, sport, education and travelling abroad (*35*).

The contribution of the Hitler Youth to the strictly political activities of the party appeared to be modest, especially in Bavaria where membership of the organization was lower than elsewhere in Germany. On the one hand, the HJ suffered from the problem of having to satisfy parents, especially in strong Catholic areas, that there were good reasons why their children should join; and, on the other hand, it had to establish the relevance of the HJ in the eyes of the *Gau* and branch leaders, who were only interested in it as a political organization and often despised its 'extra-mural' activities. At a meeting for members' parents in April 1930, Emil Klein maintained that the aim of the HJ was to 'train' youth in a love for their homeland by organizing excursions to see the beauties of the 'German' countryside, especially in the nearby Alps (*36*). Camping weekends, sports days and jamborees were a major activity of the HJ. But the tone of directives from the *Gau* office suggested that the Hitler Youth should get on with the serious business of helping the party to power.

The Hitler Youth did play a useful part in propaganda by distributing leaflets at street corners and in letter-boxes, sticking up posters on street-advertisement pillars and participating in processions. There was often a high degree of ideological commitment among teenagers who became members of the HJ, but also a tendency among those who joined more for 'kicks' to shirk their more irksome duties. Youthful enthusiasm and dedication to the cause was important, but the HJ did not have the resources to embark on an ambitious scale of activities. It was financially worse off than the SA, for, although it received an allowance from the *Gau*, it mainly had to finance itself.[34] Not much income could be expected from the contributions of its members, who were either school pupils or, more often, apprentices who earned little.[35]

34. Requests for assistance were frequently made by the HJ in the party press: for example, in January 1932 the HJ group in North Munich placed an advertisement in the *VB* for an office to be let at a moderate rent, an old writing table and a bookcase ('if possible without cost or very cheap'). A few months later, the press office expressed an urgent need for a type-writer and a writing desk with side-drawers that could be locked up (*VB*, 4 May 1932).

35. At the end of 1930, the HJ in Munich–Upper Bavaria consisted of the following: 16 per cent school pupils, 11 per cent in business and 'mental' occupations, 51 per cent craftsman-apprentices, 14 per cent industrial apprentices and 6 per cent agricultural apprentices. (Party history of the HJ in the *Gau* Munich–Upper Bavaria, 10 February 1931, HA 71/1542.)

Another difficulty facing the HJ, which helped to limit its membership, was the hostile attitude of school authorities, local priests and sometimes the police, who recognized the Hitler Youth for what it was; namely, a cadre for catching the young and training them as future National Socialists. As a fair number of boys under eighteen still went to school, the restrictions imposed by schools had a harmful effect on recruitment. Since bans were placed on school-children joining the HJ, public meetings for the young were held very infrequently and enlistment came mainly from personal canvassing among friends and acquaintances. In one instance, a member of the Hitler Youth in Munich wrote secretly to his HJ leader that he had to withdraw from the organization because his best friend had informed their teacher, who in turn had told the boy's parents. The father, a member of the BVP, had forbidden his son to take any further part in the Hitler Youth (*37*). Local Catholic priests, who were usually sensitive on the question of education, showed such antagonism towards the HJ in some rural areas that Hitler youths had to join local groups in other towns to disguise their activities (*38*).

Simila rproblems faced the National Socialist Schoolchildren's League (*NS Schülerbund*), founded at the end of 1929. Dr Adrian von Renteln, its national leader, showed an awareness of them in his directive of December 1929. He pointed out that schools could only ban participation in the NSS, but not the organization itself (only possible by a government order), and that it was sometimes necessary to use cover names. Such precautions need not be taken in certain states like Saxony, Thuringia and Mecklenburg, where the NSDAP parliamentary groups had an influence over the state governments. The main activity was ideological instruction. Groups should meet once a week, discuss extracts from Nazi literature and listen to a speech from a 'trained National Socialist'. When progress was made, discussion should become more sophisticated with the criticism of articles in the non-Nazi press. The most important method of recruitment was 'solicitation from mouth to mouth among school comrades', which must be systematically planned by NSS branch leaders. According to von Renteln, this kind of activity was more possible in the larger towns, where the organization was able to operate more openly and members could use relatives and friends at other schools to found groups (*39*).

The *Schülerbund* was a separate organization until its merger with the Hitler Youth in June 1932. It suffered from the same difficulties, all the more as it concentrated on school-children alone, while HJ members were more usually those who had just left school. It often had to act clandestinely even in the large towns. In the Catholic city of Würzburg, the police found out that the local group of the NSS was being run by a teacher from a secondary school, and that 'the young lads are being sworn to the strictest secrecy when they join, and their meeting place is changed each week' (*40*). Membership of the *Schülerbund* tended to be very sparse, and was based entirely on the cities. In September 1931, membership in Southern Bavaria was confined to Munich, Augsburg and Landshut, making a total of ninety-two. Small groups had been set up a few months later in a number of other provincial towns, but by December 1932 the total membership in Southern Bavaria was only 604, and of this two-thirds were considered 'passive' (*41*).

These two youth organizations were more important as cadres in preparation for the future Nazi state than as effective propaganda agencies, although the Hitler Youth did provide an activist element which operated in spite of adverse conditions. Both cases showed how seriously the Nazis took their appeal to youth, and the efforts they made to regiment young people before they were politically conscious. The difficulties they encountered arose from the fact that they were operating in a system which was still at least formally a parliamentary democracy, although one under increasing pressure. The Nazis' concept of 'total' politics brought them into conflict with the authorities. But they had one considerable advantage in their appeal to the young generation; namely, the latter's feeling of disillusionment and antagonism towards the Weimar political system. The Nuremberg police were already noticing late in 1930 that: 'It is especially among the younger generation—which proceeds less from a party political stand-point, and rather is led to join up with the NSDAP from emotional and oppositional motives—that the party is acquiring more and more numerous and resolute members, for whom the party means an ideological and fighting association, well beyond the scope of a parliamentary interest representative' (*42*).

The popular appeal of the Nazi party, with the strong emotional element in its propaganda and its role as the main opposition force to the Weimar Republic, was peculiarly suited to winning the support of the young generation. This was also evident from the success of that other party youth organization, the National Socialist German Students' League (NSDStB).

Student support for the NSDAP was extremely high for two reasons—social and traditional. Students in Germany, with their overwhelmingly middle-class background, came precisely from those classes which were predominant among party leaders, and to a lesser extent party members. They were therefore affected by the middle-class concern for social status, enhanced in their case by their belief they were an élite. Secondly, the conservative bent of students who were politically active derived from the importance of the student associations (*Burschenschaften*) and corporations, as well as the role of the universities as a hotbed of German nationalism in the nineteenth century. The right-wing ideological bias of these students was reinforced during the Weimar period because anti-Establishment attitudes involved opposition to the 'left-wing' ideals of the Republic.[36] Both reasons explained why students, who opted for political extremism, moved to the Right rather than the Left. Their support for the Communists was low. Since students were to a great degree ideologically motivated, it followed that they should have preferred the Nazis.

The case of students is also relevant to the question of young voters. German students usually began their studies around the age of twenty, and remained at university for four or five years, if not longer. They formed therefore a minority but an important vocal element among those in their twenties, who as already seen were the largest single group in the party from 1930. The NSDStB was the only one of the three party youth organizations under review whose members were entitled to vote. It is important to examine how the Nazis organized recruitment to the NSDStB, and won support among the student population at large.

The Nazi Students' League won a very high vote in annual student council elections, beginning with the academic year 1929–30. Its highest vote that year was recorded at the University of Erlangen, where it won an absolute majority with 51 per cent. Hitler saw Erlangen University as his 'student Coburg' (that is, stronghold), and the following year the NSDStB won an increased vote there of 76 per cent. The vote at the other Bavarian universities was much lower—40 per cent at Würzburg in 1930–31, and 33·3 per cent at Munich—but nevertheless well above the general vote for the party in those cities.

The difference in the size of the vote for the NSDStB had first of all a confessional reason, for the Catholic students' group was stronger at Munich and especially Würzburg than at Erlangen, where the student population was mainly Protestant. The Catholic corporations were, like their party equivalents, well-organized and enjoyed a stable vote.[37] The Nationalist,

36. Although the Weimar Republic was by no means a 'socialist' republic, its origins had been marked by 'socialist' uprisings and its chief sponsors were the Social Democrats. The Weimar Constitution did pay lip service to socialist ideals in spite of its many compromises, proclaimed the virtues of parliamentary democracy, emphasized the rights of citizens and provided for popular initiative as well as proportional representation. The formal political system of Weimar could be seen ideologically, rather than analytically, as 'left-wing'.

37. The vote for the NSDStB was generally much stronger at universities, where the large majority of students were Protestant. Erlangen was the most obvious example because it had a strong Protestant theological school. The NSDStB also won a high vote in 1930–31 at Jena (66·6 per cent) and Greifswald (60 per cent). The proportion of Catholic students

liberal and socialist groups were not so strictly political. They were therefore more vulnerable to attack from the Nazi students, who took advantage of the fact that the majority of students were politically indifferent. The Nazis now formed the hard core of activist students, and assumed an important position in university politics. Although the Catholic groups took an anti-Nazi line, they were not powerful enough by themselves to resist the advance of the Nazi students. In 1931 the NSDStB became the strongest group on the student council at Munich University with eleven seats, while the two Catholic groups between them won seven seats. At the Technical University in Munich, the Nazis did not win an absolute majority but they had the controlling influence. In July 1930 the student council there sent a message of solidarity to Dr Frick, the new Nazi Minister of the Interior in Thuringia, who had caused a public outrage by establishing a new chair for racial studies at the University of Jena in spite of strong opposition from the professors there. Representatives of the Catholic corporations in Munich supported this message (43).

The Nazi students achieved their dominant position because they had an effective organization, and put on a display of propaganda for student elections far superior to that of any of the other groups. They financed their propaganda through the high contributions which their members paid. Members of the NSDStB at Munich University, for instance, paid 12 Reichmarks a month in addition to their monthly party membership fee of 3 marks (44). For the student elections in the autumn of 1931, the Nazis arranged three mass meetings with *Gau* leader Schemm from Upper Franconia, Dr Frank (head of the legal department at party headquarters) and Hitler (45). Hitler addressed many student audiences in Munich during these years. He invariably adopted a more serious, reflective and 'academic' manner of speaking, quite different from the hysterical harangues at party rallies around the country.[38] Attendance at these meetings was usually very

---

at these universities was: Erlangen 27 per cent, Jena 4 per cent and Griefswald 13 per cent (*Augsburger Postzeitung*, 10 March 1931). Conversely, the NSDStB won only 19 per cent at Bonn University, where 57 per cent of the students were Catholic. The reason was that the Catholic corporations were the best-organized of the non-Nazi groups; for example, the Catholic Rhaetia Fraternity in Munich issued a declaration in support of the statement of the Bavarian bishops on National Socialism, February 1931, announcing that its membership was incompatible with membership of the NSDAP (James Donohoe, *Hitler's Conservative Opponents in Bavaria, 1930-45*, pp. 250-55).

38. Albert Speer relates in his memoirs his experience, as a young tutor at Berlin University, of hearing Hitler speak to a student audience there late in 1930. It was the first time he heard Hitler make a speech: 'Hitler entered and was tempestuously hailed by his numerous followers among the students. This enthusiasm in itself made a great impression upon me. But his appearance also surprised me. On posters and in caricatures I had seen him in

high. At one of Hitler's speeches late in 1928 there turned up a large contingent from the traditional corporations and duelling associations, like *Suevia, Frankonia* and *Saxo-Thuringia* (*46*). At another meeting of the NSDStB, in the Hofbräuhaus, a Catholic student had the courage to stand up after Hitler had aroused his large audience with a long speech and put the views of his corporation, saying that students should concentrate on working hard for their examinations instead of playing politics. He was immediately howled down with derisory laughter and pelted with beer mats (*47*).

Hitler would choose such subjects as the origins of the First World War, the problems of a people without 'living space' (*Volk ohne Raum*) and general questions of foreign policy. Nationalism was a predominant theme at Nazi student meetings.[39] The leader of the Nazi students at Erlangen was not merely toeing the party line when he remarked that 'the students get the impression more and more from present-day political life that it is not German' (*48*). This student nationalism was marked by a strong degree of romantic idealism, which appeared to affect Catholic students as much as others. The Catholic *Augsburger Postzeitung* admitted that:

> One cannot forget that more and more young Catholics are entering politics, who are completely unacquainted with the War and only think of the present and even reproach the older generation with leaving them with the liquidation of the War; they cannot get accustomed to the fact that a great people like the Germans should be so powerless ... This view is nourished wilfully by the National Socialists, and one hears in discussion with these young people the most impossible opinions ... We have today once again a total political romanticism of

---

military tunic, with shoulder straps, swastika armband, and hair flapping over his forehead. But here he was wearing a well-fitted blue suit and looking markedly respectable. Everything about him bore out the note of reasonable modesty. Later I learned that he had a great gift for adjusting—consciously or intuitively—to his surroundings. As the ovation went on for minutes he tried, as if slightly pained, to check it. Then, in a low voice, hesitantly and somewhat shyly, he began a kind of historical lecture rather than a speech. To me there was something engaging about it—all the more so since it ran counter to everything the propaganda of his opponents had led me to expect: a hysterical demagogue, a shrieking and gesticulating fanatic in uniform. He did not allow the bursts of applause to tempt him away from his sober tone.' (*Inside the Third Reich*, pp. 15–16.)

39. See the extensive police reports of meetings of the NSDStB in Munich, 1926–31 in HA 88/1839. Many of the themes at these meetings had a cultural and historical flavour about them as well as concentrating on nationalist and ideological matters; for example, there was a speech on 'Goethe' in 1926, and on 'Mussolini and the French Revolution' in 1927.

youth, which is no better than what it was in many circles before the War (*49*).

Connected with this romantic nationalism, which drew on traditional *völkisch* ideology, was a pronounced element of anti-semitism among students. At Erlangen University, the student council passed a motion in 1929 proposed by the NSDStB demanding that all universities introduce a *numerus clausus* excluding 'non-Germans' especially Jews from studying (*50*).

This nationalist and racialist attitude among students inevitably had its aggressive and intolerant side, and often found expression in violent behaviour. This sometimes took the form of defiance of the university authorities. In July 1930, a Nazi student at the Technical University in Munich collected protest signatures against the Young Plan. His action violated a prohibition by the Rector on political agitation among students, but the student council declared its support for the student against the new disciplinary measures and ordered new student elections (*51*). Nazi students often interrupted lectures with catcalls and booing, especially when they were given by professors who showed left-wing sympathies or even expressed support for the Weimar Republic. By the summer of 1931, this state of affairs had reached such a pitch that the SPD group in the state parliament made an appeal to the Minister of Education because:

> the University of Munich is once more nowadays the scene of wild National Socialist excesses, which can only be finally checked by the power of the police and the temporary cessation of all lectures. Through the terroristic behaviour of National Socialist students, academic freedom is being endangered and the overwhelming majority of students are hindered in their studies (*52*).

Earlier in the year there had been incidents in Erlangen, when Nazi students ran riot in the streets tearing down posters of political opponents, insulting members of left-wing parties and terrorizing people on the editorial staff of a local newspaper, which had criticized the Nazi Party (*53*).

Student radicalism obviously had its generational aspects, which took on a political significance for only the NSDAP seemed to offer a chance to break with the older generation of politicians and conventional party politics. Nazi students were not interested in discussion, as this represented the methods of compromise typical of parliamentary democracy; they joined the Nazi movement because it held out the promise of political action and a radical solution to the problems of society. The *Augsburger Postzeitung* commented in an article clearly inspired by a concern over the growing support among Catholic students for the Nazis:

> The National Socialist movement is still young. The activist spirit which prevails in it is easily suited to sweeping rebellious youth along with it. Here and there have occurred cases of students belonging to Catholic corporations, believing in their idealistic enthusiasm that their opportunity to apply their thirst for action lay with joining Hitler (*54*).

The most immediate problem confronting students in the early 1930s was economic. Politically conscious students were very ideologically motivated, but their desire for activism in the Nazi movement was intensified by the worsening prospects for them in society as a result of the Depression. The *Augsburger Postzeitung* complained that 'these young people fall only too easily for the insinuations of National Socialism, which promises everything possible and depicts the "Third Reich" in glowing colours' (*55*). The feeling of desperation at not being able to find employment suitable to their qualifications particularly affected 'work students' (that is, students who earned their living to finance their studies), who formed a high proportion of the total student population.[40] These poorer students, who came from less prosperous middle-class homes, were not favoured with good connections through the old-boy network of members of exclusive student corporations. The *Vossische Zeitung*, the Berlin liberal newspaper, had these students chiefly in mind when in reference to the demoralizing effects of the Depression it wrote on the student as 'a prey to Hitler':

> The overcrowding of the professions, the continual threat from different quarters of the introduction of the *numerus clausus*, the hopelessness of the most desperate efforts with the absence of the protective hand of a father or the protection of good 'connections'. Day after day, many students are weighed down by the impression that work is basically in vain and that finally there is only the endless knocking on closed doors. This is how thousands of young qualified students feel who come from simple or ruined families and who, in spite of their ability and hard work, face a precarious future and have no confidence in themselves or the world around them (*56*).

40. In 1922 'work students' constituted 42 per cent of students at universities, 62·5 per cent at the technical colleges, 88 per cent at the mining colleges, 64 per cent at the agricultural colleges and 68 per cent at the commercial colleges. (H. P. Bleuel and E. Klinnert, *Deutsche Studenten auf dem Weg ins Dritte Reich*, p. 80.)

Nazi students were not so typical of Nazi supporters in general, because they were recruited to the party primarily on the basis of ideological commitment than for reasons of social status or occupational interest. Nazi supporters in general were usually ideologically motivated to some extent—such as attachment to some facet of Nazi ideology, admiration for the *Führer* or opposition to the Weimar political system—but economic or social interests played a greater part in their support for the NSDAP. It was here that the Nazi specialist organizations assumed an importance. They were presented simultaneously as effective representatives of different interests, while at the same time the party claimed to be an integrative force in its aim of creating a new national community. This combined appeal of the Nazis found much response during the Depression years, when German society was under severe strain. It is therefore useful at this point to look at the problem of the Depression in a wider context.

Political Consequences of the Economic Depression

The expansion of popular support for the Nazi movement in the early 1930s has to be seen against the background of the economic crisis, which was the basic cause of the government's troubles during these years. Germany's economy was extremely vulnerable to any major shifts in the world economic situation because it was so dependent on foreign credits, especially from the United States. The collapse of the Wall Street stock exchange in the autumn of 1929 set in motion a train of events—with the sharp fall in foreign trade and the imposition of exchange and currency restrictions—the effects of which were quickly seen in Germany. There followed a steep rise in unemployment, already well above a comfortable level, especially in the cities where factories were dismissing workers by the hundreds.

The number of unemployed increased in Germany from 1,320,000 in September 1929 to three millions a year later, 4,350,000 in September 1931 and finally six millions in the early part of 1932. But the extent of the Depression could not be measured simply by official statistics, which were based only on the number of people out of work who had applied to the labour exchanges. The rise in unemployment imposed a crippling burden on social insurance, the extra cost of which had to be met from higher taxation. Many unemployed did not bother to apply for social benefits, and therefore were not registered because they had little hope of receiving anything. This attitude was particularly prevalent among the young, because a

natural preference for benefits was given to family men with large families.[41]
The plight of the farming population was marked not so much by a high
level of unemployment, as by a desperate concern over low prices for their
produce and the increase in taxation. Small businessmen and shopkeepers
took panic at their dwindling market. Finally, there was the atmosphere of
fear created by these developments especially among those who were in fact
still able to follow their occupation or profession, but were alarmed at the
social consequences of unemployment, both in terms of their own position
in society and the possible revolutionary effects of unemployment on such
a large scale. The Depression could be seen therefore as one gigantic crisis
of confidence. Its political consequences will now be examined.

The NSDAP was without doubt the main beneficiary of the Depression.
There was an obvious parallel between the rise in unemployment in 1930–32
and the rise in popular support for the party, but it would be misleading to
see these factors simply in terms of cause and effect. Bavaria had for example
a lower rate of unemployment than most other areas of Germany,[42] but the
lower vote for the NSDAP here than elsewhere could not be broadly attributed to this difference. Matters of political and social structure, such as the
existence in Bavaria of a well-established Catholic party, had to be taken
into account.

The initial rise in support for the NSDAP during the Bavarian municipal
elections of 1929, which coincided with the Young Plan referendum, had

41. The regulations covering application for social benefits were very strict. A person just
out of work had to wait for seven to twenty-one days after his application to allow for
details of his family status and the number of dependants entitled to benefits to be recorded.
The applicant had a legal claim to six weeks' unemployment relief, but further assistance
depended on the degree of hardship. After twenty weeks the unemployed person received
'depression relief'. The rates of this were no different from those of unemployment relief,
but the conditions for claiming it were much more limited. Certain occupations like agriculture and domestic services were excluded, and so were young people under the age of
twenty-one. Those who qualified for 'depression relief' enjoyed its benefits for thirty-eight
weeks—in other words, an unemployed person, who passed all the tests, received relief
for a total of fifty-eight weeks. After that, he had to fall back on public relief, which was
administered by the municipal authorities, and undergo a further means test as well as being
subject to liability for compensation. He then became one of the 'welfare unemployed'.
It is well to remember that all this time the recipient of relief was still expected to pay for
his own rent, heating, gas and light.

42. This was generally a result of the low level of industry in Bavaria. In February 1932
Bavaria had a rate of unemployment of 7·37 per cent, while the far more industrialized
state of Saxony had a rate of 14·45 per cent. Southern Bavaria had only two large cities
(*Grosstädte*) out of the total of fifty in Germany then. Unemployment in Munich and Augs-
burg was relatively low, for of the forty-eight other cities only eight had a smaller rate of
unemployment. The rate in Nuremberg, the main city in Franconia, was somewhat higher.
(See Cuno Horkenbach, *Das Deutsche Reich von 1918 bis heute* (1932), p. 506, and *Statistisches
Jahrbuch für das deutsche Reich* (1932), p. 303.)

occurred when nationalism was the prevailing theme, and the great Depression had not yet begun to make much impact in Germany. There were also strong variations in the incidence of unemployment, which did not really coincide with the variations in the vote for the NSDAP. During the Depression years the principal electoral gains of the party were made in the rural areas and the small towns, while the greatest concentrations of unemployment were in the large cities. By January 1933, half of the total of unemployed (still well over six millions) came from the large cities and towns with more than 50,000 inhabitants. Since the NSDAP had decided from 1928 to concentrate on winning support from the middle classes and the rural electorate in particular, it was to be expected that the unemployed, who came largely from the working class, would not be the principal source of new voters for the NSDAP.[43] The discontented working-class electorate generally transferred their support from the SPD to the Communists. One must look elsewhere to see how the Nazis benefited from the Depression.

Firstly, it is important to realize that the NSDAP had already developed the organizational framework of a mass movement by the time the Depression broke in Germany. What the Depression did was to facilitate enormously the expansion of its popular support. The NSDAP benefited from the Depression more than any other party partly because it had a propaganda machine far superior to those of its rivals. The Communists were also expected to gain from the crisis, but their appeal was mainly to the workers in the big cities. There was nothing comparable to the rural support for the Communist

43. Although the NSDAP did not make a special point of appealing directly to the working-class unemployed, unemployed members of the party were sometimes granted special conditions and benefited from the relief systems organized by the SA. In April 1931 *Gau* leader Adolf Wagner of Munich–Upper Bavaria decided that unemployed SA men were to be exempted from the general rule that members who did not pay their subscriptions should be expelled by local branches. Action could only be taken in consultation with the *Gau* office. (*Gau* directive, 7 April 1931, HA 9/191.) Among its various activities, the SA organized a winter aid programme (*SA Winterhilfe*), which provided for food collections and the opening of special kitchens. One enterprising SA leader called Friederichs even thought up the idea of a service to provide 'party cigarettes' at a cheap rate, because it was found that unemployed members were not prepared to forego the pleasures of the occasional smoke. Party members who obliged were informed that, in smoking these 'true National Socialist cigarettes', they were striking a blow in favour of the interests of the small business-man against those of the large cigarette firms. A whole assortment of enticing brands was offered including 'Drummer' at $3\frac{1}{3}$ pfennigs, 'Alarm' at 4, 'Storm' at 5 and 'New Front', the most expensive, at 6. The idea became official policy of the *Gau* of Munich–Upper Bavaria and was promoted under the slogan, 'We cigarette smokers can help the party.' (See *Gau* directives of 15 September 1931 and 17 September 1931 in HA 8/176.) The SA also provided their own homes, where members could spend a night if they had no accommodation, while some local branches even instituted collections to pay for SA uniforms. For many who were destitute the important thing about the SA uniform was not that it was 'brown', but that it was simply a shirt.

parties in France and Italy after the Second World War. The Nationalists (DNVP), the other main 'anti-Weimar' party, did not have the broad mass appeal of the Nazis. The DNVP had enjoyed strong support in Protestant rural areas in Bavaria, and it had a certain ideological affinity with the conservative Bavarian NSDAP. But it had paid a high price for its internal splits in the late 1920s and suffered from an élitist image, marring its appeal among the mass of peasant voters, who were distrustful of the backing it received from industrialists and landowners in Northern Germany. The referendum campaign against the Young Plan in 1929, when the Nazis and Nationalists had formed an alliance, had already demonstrated that the former had a clear advantage over the latter in the techniques of organization and propaganda. The Nationalists had provided the cash; the Nazis had used it to oil their propaganda machine. In 1929 the two parties had been complementary. But during the Depression years it was the organization rather than the cash which counted for more, although organization was not possible without cash for the party's financial difficulties did sometimes limit its activities.

The second principal reason for the NSDAP's success during the Depression was the nature of its appeal. The party's exploitation of the economic crisis was primarily political, as it used it to argue that the whole political system needed changing rather than simply the government in office at the time. The NSDAP was now in a stronger position than ever before to lambaste the governing parties, and claim the role of the main opposition force. The Depression severely affected loyalty to the state and sharpened class antagonism. It reinforced the tendency, especially among those who had an 'ideological' aversion to the Weimar Republic or were concerned about their social status, to opt for a party which offered 'a choice, not an echo' of what the traditional parties were saying. The Agrarian Programme, which formed the basis for their rural propaganda, was a classic example of the appeal of the Nazis. Although it proposed a number of remedies for specific economic grievances, its main content was psychological and political. It combined the promise of priority consideration in the Third Reich for those who worked on the land, based on a romanticized view of the peasant in society, with the argument that agriculture received nothing but neglect in the state of Weimar. It is useful therefore to look more closely at the ways in which Nazi propaganda exploited the Depression, and then to see how far these appeals were effective.

The following arguments were typical of Nazi propaganda, which sought to exploit political attitudes affected by the Depression:

1. The need for strong government to solve the crisis

Nazi speakers made little secret of the fact that the 'Third Reich' (the term was already often used in speeches) would bring fundamental changes in the structure of the state, including the abolition of the parliamentary system. In so doing, they were taking advantage of the lack of legitimacy of the Weimar Republic, for it was not accepted as the rightful form of political system by important sections of the Establishment and an increasing body of public opinion. In July 1931 Ludwig Siebert, the Nazi mayor of Lindau, made a long speech in Rothenburg ob der Tauber on the economic crisis. According to the local police:

> He showed ways in which the distress could be averted, and declared that if the NSDAP came to power today conditions would be changed in all essentials. First of all, the parliaments must disappear and in their place leaders who had a sense of duty would take over. Such men are not trained, they are born. History shows that the German people has never been able to survive without capable leaders. The National Socialists would install only responsible leaders, who would support wholeheartedly those measures which concern you. The National Socialists would not even shrink from a dictatorship, which we in any case ought to have in Germany today. As soon as they came to power, their first task would be to provide work and therefore bread for the many unemployed (57).

2. The claim that the government was ignoring the interests of the German people

This view was advanced to portray the evils and corruption of the Weimar political system ('the system of the November criminals'),[44] personified by the 'selfishness' of its leaders. It reflected the puritanical element in Fascism, the traditional belief of the authoritarian Right that the compromises of parliamentary government were a moral blemish on the nation, and that a thorough cleansing process was necessary to right these wrongs. A frequent line in Nazi speeches was that ministers and others in authority were taking advantage of their positions for personal gain, so 'cheating' the German

44. A reference to the leaders of the German Government, who signed the armistice in November 1918.

people. An example of this approach was *Gau* leader Wahl's speech to an audience in Krugzell in the Allgäu in January 1930:

> For ten years the Reich has followed a false economic policy, and has treated the agricultural population abominably. Hilferding,[45] the previous Finance Minister, is taking up the post of director of a firm with a yearly income of 60,000 marks and does not shy at pocketing his ministerial pension of 24,000 as well, instead of giving it to the Reich for assistance. These are the gentlemen who enslaved the people for generations through the Treaty of Versailles. Two Bavarian ministers would each have got 50,000 marks of state subsidy for furnishing a flat, but this was not sufficient. One of them claimed and received 53,000 marks, and the other a further 58,000 marks. In contrast, the poor victim of the inflation must beg for his monthly assistance of 25 marks. Just look at the work which these gentlemen do! All they do is to make promises before the elections, so they can safeguard their little posts and their little sums (*58*).

3. *The claim that National Socialism had more continuity with German traditions than Weimar democracy*

This was a continuation of the earlier argument that the Weimar Republic was not legitimate, that it was 'un-German': hence, the use of conservative 'patriotic' figures like Franz Ritter von Epp, and even members of the former royal house of Hohenzollern at Nazi meetings. During 1931–32 Prince August Wilhelm, the fourth son of the last Kaiser, appeared as a speaker for the Nazis in Southern Bavaria. On 1 May 1931, they staged a rally in Munich to rival the May Day demonstrations organized by the Social Democrats. Prince August Wilhelm began by taking the salute at a march past of the Munich SA and SS. In his speech he praised Hitler for making it possible for 'a Hohenzollern prince to fight in the company of workers', and ended by announcing that his father had written to him from exile in Holland that he should 'be proud that he now belonged to this great national movement of the people' (*59*). The following month, Prince August Wilhelm addressed a public meeting at Öttingen near Nördlingen. Streicher introduced him in a speech, suitably moderated for the occasion. The meeting closed with the playing of the traditional national anthem, and

45. Rudolf Hilferding, a Social Democrat, was Reich Minister of Finance in 1923 and 1928–29.

according to the police had 'the character not of a political but of a thoroughly patriotic demonstration' (60). Prince August Wilhelm was in fact a disappointing public speaker. Several districts reported that his Bavarian audiences could not understand him because of his 'North German dialect'. All the same, the point was made that Germany was suffering for having strayed from her traditional political course since the War.

4. The fear of Communism

The conventional argument was made that economic upheaval provides Communism with the ideal opportunity for exploiting discontent and coming to power. The social consequences for the middle classes of such a political change were emphasized. At a meeting in Forsting near Wasserburg, a party speaker claimed in November 1931 that the government's 'policy of fulfilment' towards the Western Powers was the sole cause of the economic troubles, and that 'if unemployment is not successfully removed, it must lead to Bolshevism, which means the deprivation of the individual's rights' (61). 'Bolshevism' often included all left-wing ideologies. At the beginning of 1931, the NSDAP organized an anti-Marxist propaganda action under the code name of 'Puss-in-Boots', which amounted to a full-scale attack on 'Red justice' and other abuses of the Social Democrats in power.

5. The promise of salvation

This took several forms. The impression was created through the use of new propaganda methods—such as 'personal propaganda' (that is, canvassing)—that the Nazi movement, unlike the Weimar state, cared for the fate of the ordinary man. Party members were expected to interest friends, relatives and work colleagues in the movement, and encourage them in the belief that the NSDAP offered the only chance of a break with the past. This technique was coupled with the habit of making wild promises about conditions in the future Third Reich. Streicher revealed to his audience at Eschenau near Nuremberg that Hitler had received a pledge from 'leading personalities' in England and Italy, who would bring an end to Germany's 'tribute payments' (under the Young Plan) once he came to power. Such extravagant statements, including the one that the Nazi state would assume responsibility for all debts accumulated during the Depression, were readily believed to the dismay of the police, who attributed this to the depressed and deperate mood of the population (*62*). Similarly, the speaker at a meeting in Würzburg said that the party was considering reducing ministers' salaries by 50 per cent in the Third Reich (*63*)!

6. Specific attacks on government policy

The Nazis were again able to take advantage of the fact they were not in positions of high authority and so not accountable. In the spring of 1931, the *Gau* of Swabia initiated a campaign to expose the 'failure of Brüning's promised action to reduce prices'.[46] The *Gau* propaganda leader announced that 'this colossal bankruptcy of the price-reduction action, which we have foreseen, must be exploited by us in our propaganda against the government —keep asking again and again, where is the promised reduction in prices?' (*64*).

The NSDAP sought to take advantage of general political disillusionment during the Depression, yet, as already seen, its appeal was most successful among the middle classes. The reasons for this were threefold: the NSDAP concentrated on exploiting discontent among the middle classes (for example, it made no special effort to win over the unemployed working class); the strong class consciousness of the middle classes *vis-à-vis* the working class; and the feeling of desperation among the middle classes, which expressed itself in resentment against the state.

Class divisions were very pronounced in Weimar Germany. They were reflected in the support for the various political parties, most of which appealed to a class or sectional interest. The NSDAP attempted to break this pattern by becoming a 'people's party'. It was quite successful in view of its relatively wide popular appeal, but it could not remain entirely unaffected by the nature of the party system in which it operated. Its success was influenced firstly by the strength or weakness of the rival parties, and secondly by the fact that its kind of appeal was more suited to winning the votes of the middle classes in the Depression.

The Depression influenced voting patterns to a considerable degree, because it affected not merely allegiance to traditional parties but to the state itself. It was more usual in Germany to express political discontent by voting for an extremist party than by abstaining. Voter participation rose

46. Brüning's policy of deflation was under severe attack at this time. While wages and salaries were being reduced, the cost of living fell less sharply, partly because of the decision to give preference to wheat-farmers in Eastern Germany by maintaining a high price level for their produce.

much in the elections during the Depression, chiefly to the benefit of the Nazis.

Official reports during this period continually emphasize the irrational nature of the support for the Nazi movement. The district office in Starnberg did not disguise its alarm in December 1931 at the support for the Nazis in wide circles:

> The NSDAP is now the reservoir for all currents of discontent and unsatisfied elements, hence its rise in votes. Those bourgeois elements, who uphold the state and have a conscious understanding of the problems and a feeling of responsibility, are losing influence. The mood is similar to that in the autumn days of 1918. Nobody trusts another and the Government much less still; possibilities for agitation are once again presented to those who think they know better and to false prophets. The intrusion of politics into everyday social and economic matters, even into conversations among intimate friends at their regular drinking sessions, produces a mood of excitement which tends to become explosive (65).

In Swabia, the middle classes were placing the blame for their misfortunes 'exclusively on the state with its unfavourable revalorization and taxation legislation ... these many dissatisfied members of the middle class are supplying a constant flow of supporters to the National Socialists, just as the dissatisfied unemployed workers do for the Communists' (66). Several months later, the same authorities remarked on the uncritical way in which people followed those who promised better times. 'It is small wonder that simple people do this when the intelligentsia in the country—doctors, veterinary surgeons, landowners, members of the nobility, retired army officers—not only increasingly join the movement but also appear as its leaders' (67). Similarly, the district of Bamberg in Upper Franconia showed concern that 'the population follows such leaders and expects alleviation from them, and does not ask about the fulfilment of such promises or the consequences for foreign policy ... the population feels instinctively without expressing it that they are on the verge of a violent upheaval in the situation, and expects salvation from the National Socialist movement' (68).

The NSDAP benefited more than any other party from the Depression of the early 1930s because of the superiority of its propaganda organization, its appeal across classes to a degree unprecedented in the short history of German parties at a time when social attitudes had become sharpened by economic distress, and the nature of its propaganda, which was very suited to exploiting the insecurity and discontent created by the economic crisis. But it did not succeed in attracting all classes equally, for its appeal was limited by political and social barriers. During the Depression the NSDAP developed as a mass movement especially for the middle classes, who for reasons of class tradition would not vote Communist. Most middle-class voters, who changed party allegiance during the Depression, turned to the Nazis because they wanted to reject the Weimar Republic without involving themselves in a proletarian revolution. Now, another section of the middle classes was supporting the party more and more—the peasantry. Since the peasantry formed the most important section of the Bavarian population, it is essential to examine the methods used by the Nazis to win its support.

The Rural Campaign

The most important single aspect of party organization and propaganda in Bavaria from 1930 was the institutionalization of the campaign to win the support of the rural electorate.

During 1930, the scene had been set for the Nazis' efforts to attract the peasantry with the publication of their Agrarian Programme, the crisis within the traditional agricultural-interest parties and organizations and the loss of votes in the Reichstag Election by the Bavarian Peasants' and Middle-Class League (BBMB) and the Nationalist Party (DNVP) in the rural districts of Southern Bavaria and Franconia respectively. But the Nazi Party's official announcement in March 1930 of its policy to win the rural vote had come too late for much organizational follow-up before the Reichstag Election in September, when the party had made significant but not impressive gains in the rural districts.

The rural campaign which followed accounted, together with the new voters, for most of the new electoral support of the NSDAP in the elections of 1932, but it did not proceed as smoothly as one would have expected with the Depression. The Nazis found that the peasants, especially in Catholic areas, were hard to win over with their native caution and suspicion of political newcomers. The rural campaign also involved new departures in political agitation, which created certain organizational difficulties.

On 21 August 1930, Walther Darré, head of the new special department at party headquarters called the Agrarian Political Office (*Agrarpolitischer Apparat*), initiated his system of party agricultural specialists. In a memorandum addressed to all *Gau* leaders, Darré emphasized that the campaign to win over the agricultural population should be 'enlarged by an organization, which covers German agriculture like a network' (69). The means of achieving this was the appointment of new officials at *Gau* and district level called agricultural specialists (*landwirtschaftliche Fachberater*), whose main task was to establish a system of local contacts among peasants in their areas of activity. The agricultural specialists were to act as 'the eyes and ears of party headquarters', and should regard all non-Nazi agricultural organizations as 'a fortress to be seized'. They should concentrate on creating a favourable attitude among the agricultural population towards National Socialism:

> Every specialist must consider himself a herald of National Socialism, to whom the very special and honourable task has been allotted of making the agricultural population conversant with the spirit of National Socialism in his area of political work, to saturate them so much with this spirit that through their voluntary submission to National Socialism they become the most trustworthy nucleus of troops among the followers of Adolf Hitler. For it is the peasant, the farmer and the agricultural worker who have always determined the decisive hours of history (70).

In short, the principal activity of the agricultural specialists was political education and infiltration rather than simply political agitation.

The first problem was to clarify the relationship of the agricultural specialists with the established structure of party organization. Darré pointed out that they were subordinate to the political leaders at both levels. The *Gau* specialist did not act as the superior of the district specialists in his area. Yet each specialist had direct access to the central office under Darré in order to facilitate the speedy coordination of rural propaganda, and should send his reports to Munich after receiving the countersignature of the *Gau* leader or district leader as the case may be. 'In this way the political leadership of the *Gau* remains firmly in the hands of the *Gau* leader, while party headquarters can be informed quickly by the districts about all local particulars without having to meet the requirements of laborious official channels' (71). Darré was tackling a difficult task. He was attempting to graft a new institution on to the already elaborate party bureaucracy, hoping at the same time to avoid the inconvenience of working through its complicated red tape. The new system involved some overlapping of responsibilities between the agricultural specialists, whose role became increasingly important, and regional and local propaganda leaders, who theoretically supervised all forms of agitation. Vested interests were inevitably affected by Darré's system, and the ensuing friction contributed to the difficulties and slow progress of rural propaganda in some areas.

Finally, Darré specified the qualifications for agricultural specialists: they must in all cases be farmers; they should have the complete confidence of local political leaders of the party, for it must be borne in mind that 'the main effort of the coming political struggle will lie to a considerable degree if not exclusively in the question of subsistence, and therefore the selection of the agricultural specialist is of the greatest importance especially for the *Gau* leader'; and they must wherever possible enjoy the respect of their professional colleagues, a factor to be taken into particular consideration with their appointment. Agricultural specialists should also have a good general education, so they could use their skill in writing to reply at once in the party press to attacks made by opponents (72).

The system of agricultural specialists marked a significant new stage in Nazi agitation, as it reflected the change of emphasis from urban to rural propaganda. The mass meeting remained the principal means of propaganda in the cities and provincial towns, but it was clearly a less profitable activity in the villages, which usually had only a few hundred inhabitants. Darré had the backing of party headquarters in his venture, but he was basically dependent on the cooperation of the *Gau* leaders, who were responsible for choosing the specialists in their areas. Many of the *Gau* leaders did not share Darré's overriding concern with the problem of agriculture, and acted too slowly for the latter's comfort. Darré was primarily an ideologist, who was too little aware of the administrative difficulties which arose during the course of the rural campaign. This campaign will now be examined from three points of view: the system of agricultural specialists in practice; the new techniques of rural propaganda; and the success of this propaganda in winning support for the NSDAP among the agricultural population.

The new rural propaganda machine was slow in developing in Bavaria compared with *Gaue* in other parts of the country. At the end of 1930, the Agrarian Political Office compiled an interim report on the progress made with agricultural specialists. The Bavarian *Gaue* did not feature among the fifteen most successful areas, which were in the Rhineland and areas of Northern and Eastern Germany. In Lower Bavaria the *Gau* specialist was very active, but party district leaders had been 'sluggish' in the selection of district agricultural specialists. The agrarian-political machine in Swabia was ready, but 'one hears nothing yet of the agrarian-political activities of the *Gau* specialist'. Little effort had been made in Munich–Upper Bavaria (73).

Pressure from headquarters was put on the less cooperative *Gaue*. Gregor

Strasser wrote in his capacity as party organization leader to the *Gau* office of Upper Franconia in Bayreuth, complaining that the *Gau* specialist was neglecting his duties and had failed to reply to requests from Darré for information. Strasser demanded his replacement by a more suitable person as *Gau* specialist, for 'seizing hold of the agricultural population is one of our most essential tasks during the coming months and if the *Gau* specialist does not fulfil expectations this can have a strongly inhibiting effect on the further development of the movement in the *Gau* concerned' (*74*). Early in 1931, the *Gau* of Munich–Upper Bavaria felt obliged to make some attempt to meet Darré's wishes. Nippold asked branch leaders in January for reports on the activities of the peasant movements in their areas, and a few weeks later instructed them to choose local agricultural specialists (*75*). The new emphasis on rural agitation is evident in *Gau* directives issued during 1931. Adolf Wagner issued a revised set of regulations in June for district and branch leaders, which urged the specialists to work hard at winning over the peasants as 'the most important representatives of the German future' (*76*).

Darré had his own reasons for this half-hearted cooperation of the political leaders of the party. In July 1931 he wrote a memorandum to Hierl, his superior at headquarters, claiming that district leaders and in some cases *Gau* leaders were not taking agricultural specialists seriously enough, so that the success of his operation varied from area to area (*77*). Specialists were powerless when not supported by the *Gau* leaders, who were the anchor men in the propaganda effort. When a *Gau* leader showed indifference to the need for rural agitation, 'the district leaders are not obliged to cooperate and then even the most able agricultural specialist cannot make progress'. Specialists were complaining about the lack of available propaganda material, for which Darré blamed *Gau* propaganda leaders who were responsible for its distribution. 'Party headquarters must without question intervene, and put pressure on the *Gau* offices.'

Darré also attributed his difficulties to the 'urban mentality' of the political leaders and their lack of adaptability because they employed propaganda methods 'tested and proved right in the struggle to win the towns' in rural areas, which caused more harm than good. The reason for the shortage of suitable rural speakers was the urban origins of the NSDAP:

This difficulty derives from the fact that the party grew up originally in the cities, and correspondingly its speakers were selected from urban points of view . . . These speakers either do not feel at home in the field of rural propaganda, or they do not even attempt it because they prefer to fight in the field of action to which they are accustomed, in which they are trained and the techniques of which they have mastered, than to trouble themselves with the very critical attitude of the peasant. Moreover, it is more easy to get thunderous applause at meetings in the cities (*78*).

Darré concluded that the experience of some *Gaue* showed that these difficulties could be overcome, when the *Gau* leaders were willing to look for suitable rural speakers and gave encouragement to the agricultural specialists. Darré's explanation of his difficulties was, however, one-sided, because the success of the rural campaign depended not only on the co-operation of the *Gau* leaders but also on the readiness of the peasants to follow the Nazis. In Bavaria there were certain social factors which inhibited this.

The institution of agricultural specialists throws interesting light on internal relations within the Nazi Party because of the conflicts of interest which resulted. The interests of Darré the ideologist coincided with those of party leaders at headquarters, who for strategic reasons had decided to give priority to rural propaganda. The regional and district party leaders, in the role of propagandists and administrators, saw the matter differently, although Darré was exaggerating their lack of interest.[47] *Gau* leaders were unwilling to win the disfavour of headquarters, and gave in to pressure whenever complaints were made. They did vary in their attitudes towards the rural campaign. Party leaders in Lower Bavaria like Franz Maierhofer, the *Gau* leader, and Otto Erbersdobler his deputy, were already aware of the need for agitation among the peasants because that region was so thoroughly rural. Hans Schemm was by contrast mainly concerned with winning the support of the bourgeoisie in the towns. Part of the difficulty was, as Darré realized, the different nature of rural propaganda.

47. A classic example of the clash of interest between Darré and political leaders of the NSDAP was the policy of the new Nazi government in the state of Oldenburg to introduce a slaughter tax, which was very unpopular with the peasants. The Nazi Prime Minister of Oldenburg was Carl Röver, the *Gau* leader of Weser–Ems, who formed his government after the party won an absolute majority of seats after the state election in May 1932. Röver's proposal caused alarm in the Agrarian Political Office, because the tax had been one of the main targets of Nazi rural propaganda. But the Röver Government was faced with considerable economic problems on entering office, and found itself compelled to take measures which contradicted his earlier attempts to please the peasantry. (For a discussion of the Nazi government in Oldenburg see Jeremy Noakes, *The Nazi Party in Lower Saxony*, 1921–33, chapter 12.) Before Röver introduced the slaughter tax, Darré wrote to him on 18 August 1932, that the party could not accept a change of face on this question, and pleaded with him to abandon the idea for otherwise it would do 'immense harm to the whole party organization'. (NSDAP organizational files, Bundesarchiv Koblenz, NS 22/360.)

Rural propaganda involved a new approach to political agitation. Many long-serving party propagandists had problems in adapting to its methods because this necessitated a change of attitude. The content of Nazi propaganda had so far been very negative with its condemnation of the Weimar political system, its attack on the Versailles Peace Treaty and its obsession with the influence of the Jews. The rural campaign, as already indicated by the Agrarian Programme, demanded a more positive approach with an emphasis on the benefits for the peasantry in the future Nazi state. The Nazis were therefore forced to be more specific about their policies. Rural propaganda provided little opportunity for party speakers who enjoyed the splendour and pomp of large public meetings, for the rule was 'personal' rather than mass propaganda, which meant harder work and more patient canvassing. Gustav Staebe, head of the press division in Darré's Agrarian Political Office, explained these points in his special guidelines for rural propaganda in June 1931. He said it was senseless simply to rave about disgraceful present circumstances, and advised that the peasants be provided with 'positive ideas about the National Socialist movement and its reconstruction policy'. It was most essential that the peasant, who was 'very proud of his occupation', should not be given offence through the 'disparaging criticism fashionable in large cities' (79).

Party directives on rural propaganda paid special attention to peasant susceptibilities, and the need for careful preparation. Staebe mentioned that the completion of membership forms and collections should not be carried out overtly at meetings, because this might offend the peasant's self-respect and sense of thrift. New methods should be considered such as talks illustrated by lantern slides, which had proved to be 'a splendid means of propaganda' (80). Many of the techniques of rural propaganda were summarized in an article by Hugo Fischer in the July 1931 issue of *Wille und Weg* (Will and Way), the monthly publication of Goebbels' Propaganda Department:

> The first meeting in a village must be prepared in such a way that it is well attended. The prerequisite is that the speaker is fairly well-informed about specifically rural questions. Then, it is most advisable to go to a neighbouring village some time after but to advertise the meeting in the first village there as well, then many people will certainly come across. After this, one holds a big German Evening in a central hall for a number of villages with the cooperation of the SA and the SA band . . . The German Evening, provided it is skilfully and grandiosely geared to producing a big public impact, primarily has the task of making the

audience enthusiastic for our cause, and secondly to raise the money necessary for the further build-up of propaganda. The preparation of the village meetings should best be carried out in the following way: most effectively through written personal invitations to every farmer or inhabitant. In the bigger villages by a circular, which is carried from farm to farm by party comrades. For the meeting itself, the money question has to be considered. We are such a poor movement that every pfennig counts. Therefore, it is necessary to hold collections during all discussion evenings as well as in the large mass meetings, if permitted by the police—either in the interval or at the end, even when an entrance fee has been taken at the beginning of the meeting. In this way, surprising amounts can sometimes be got out of a meeting, especially when plates and not caps are used, in which trouser buttons and small coins can disappear unseen (*81*).

A novel feature of these activities was the initiation of indoctrination courses for peasants. The purpose of the course was to turn peasants, who were already members of the party, into 'convinced fighters and propagandists'. By the beginning of 1932, courses had taken place in several localities in Southern Bavaria, including Günzburg, Markt Oberdorf and Grafing. A course would take the form of a public meeting in a tavern. The party programme was first explained to the peasants who were present, and certain 'misunderstandings' would be dealt with. The first speaker would stress that the NSDAP was a 'Christian party', and that it did not stand for the dispossession of land. A second speaker would talk about particular agricultural problems, and another would discuss the activities of the party in the parliaments to emphasize the special regard National Socialists held for the interests of the peasantry. The usual promises were offered that in the Nazi state no more foreign agricultural produce would be imported, and that the tax system would be altered. The course would end with a public meeting on a theme relating to agriculture (*82*).

These indoctrination courses and similar activities demanded an army of party speakers versed in rural propaganda. Darré lacked this at the beginning. Party speakers from Reinhardt's training school were at first transferred to rural areas, although not always with happy results. Speakers used to addressing town audiences sometimes unwittingly committed indiscretions. A great commotion was caused at a peasant meeting by a Nazi speaker in Upper Bavaria, who was tactless enough to remark that in the Third Reich the 'progressive' peasant who used artificial manure would remain on his farm, while farms which were uneconomic and in debt would be nationalized

(*83*). Such remarks confirmed deep suspicions among peasants about the Nazis, which other more skilful speakers found hard if not impossible to erase. Gustav Staebe had suggested in July 1931 setting up a tight network of party 'peasant speakers' (*Bauernredner*), as the party was suffering from a lack of speakers trained in agricultural questions (*84*). By 1932, a change was evident in the tone of Nazi propaganda in rural areas. The authorities in Lower Franconia noticed in February that Nazi speakers at their meetings in villages were avoiding 'the customary screaming diatribes and abusive language of earlier times', and were instead engaging in 'the most objective criticism of those very matters which are particularly felt to be displeasing by the agricultural population' (*85*).

Darré's concern for a more 'neutral' tone in rural propaganda was applied to his efforts to attract the agricultural population through a special press. In September 1931, the *Nationalsozialistische Landpost* started publication as a weekly Nazi paper for peasants. This appeared separately from all other party newspapers, as Darré emphasized in a private and confidential memorandum of 14 September (*86*). He said that he had received offers from a number of *Gau* offices to incorporate the *Landpost* as a supplement to their *Gau* newspapers. He made it clear that he spurned these offers, for he considered the system of *Gau* papers a 'cancerous sore for the movement' and a waste of valuable party funds. His paper would have nothing to do with them because they were so 'urban' in their style, for very few *Gau* papers had gained a footing in the rural areas. The *Landpost* would only lose its readership by merging with the *Gau* papers, because their blatant and provocative approach would alienate' the peasants and their tendency to incur official prohibitions would cause more permanent damage to circulation in the rural areas than in the towns. According to Darré, the 'special merit of the *Landpost* is a certain neutral tone, which does not make it easily vulnerable to the present fanaticism for prohibitions; in this way, it is possible to maintain contact with the rural population independently of the ban on political newspapers'. The principal motive of the *Landpost* was to give the peasant the feeling that he was in 'direct touch' with the national leadership of the NSDAP.[48]

48. The principal message of the *Landpost* was the good work the party was doing for the interests of the peasantry. A special number for the July 1932 Reichstag Election listed in detail the motions that the NSDAP groups had proposed in the Reichstag and the Bavarian state parliament, to demonstrate that 'we National Socialists are the strongest peasant party in the Reichstag' and that the party was keeping its word. This issue was well illustrated with photographs of Hitler shaking hands with peasants in traditional costume, and cartoons contrasting the simple life of the peasant with the wicked society in which he was living; for example, an honest-looking peasant casting out the 'old gang'

Darré's work must ultimately be judged by his success in winning the support of the peasantry for the Nazi movement. The rural campaign was generally successful in spite of the many organizational difficulties encountered, because of the peasants' increasing exasperation at their economic position and their disillusionment with the traditional peasant parties and associations.

The peasants found themselves crushed between lower prices for their produce and the growing burden of taxation. The peasants easily turned to political radicalism in their mood of desperation, since their occupation was not merely their livelihood but also their whole way of life. They were ready to accept any solution, so long as it offered some hope of relief from their situation. The district office in Traunstein summarized the political outlook of the peasantry as follows: 'The Peasants' League and the BVP will not help us out of our misery; we will therefore have a go with the National Socialists and see what they accomplish; we will then form a judgement whether we have acted correctly' (*87*). Although peasants in some areas were prepared to cast aside all inhibitions and even favour the Communists, their concern for property in their land and their god-fearing nature usually made them impervious to the extreme Left. The Nazis' anti-Communism was a distinct advantage, for the patriotic-minded peasants in Lower Bavaria were 'fearing for their property and looking for a dam against Communism, which in their view is opposed too weakly by the state' (*88*).

The peasants' bitterness towards the state followed its traditional course of hostility towards civil servants and the refusal to pay taxes. It is interesting to note the effects of Nazi propaganda on social behaviour among the peasants, for the promise of taxation alleviation made a great impression on them in their state of mind. The district office of Parsberg in the Upper Palatinate reported that the public mood was 'wretched', and that people were of the view that complete collapse could no longer be avoided. The opinion was common among peasants that if only the state did not have to pay out so much for its civil servants the position of agriculture would automatically improve. Whole villages were now under the influence of the Nazis in this district (*89*). The authorities in Upper Bavaria were uneasy

---

with a shovel; and an elderly and poor couple looking on while an obviously Jewish cattle-trader buys up their last cow, with the caption, 'Do you just look on? Call Hitler in! Vote for list number 2.' The Nazis had learnt a lesson about the need for more 'positive' propaganda, after their decision early in 1931 to boycott the Reichstag. According to the Upper Bavarian police, the flow of support to the NSDAP petered out because of the view among peasants that the party would have done more for their interests by remaining in the Reichstag, so preventing the influence which the left-wing parties were able to exert over the question of frozen meat. (HMB/Obb., 20 March 1931, GSA MA 102153.)

about the promises of Nazi speakers of freedom from taxation for two years, new protective tariffs, cheaper manures and the exclusion of Jews from the cattle-trading business, which were turning the heads of the peasants. Some peasants had been aroused to a pitch of intoxication at the prospect of the Nazis coming to power soon, and were withholding the payment of their taxes (*90*). Many peasants voted for Hitler in the Presidential Election of March 1932 in several districts of Middle Franconia, because speakers at Nazi meetings had continuously emphasized that the party would cancel all debts to Jewish cattle-traders (*91*).

Although the NSDAP benefited more than any other party from the mood of desperation, active support for it was not uniform among the peasantry. Younger peasants were more prone to favour the Nazis than their elders, because they were less conservative and found the radical message of the party attractive. They felt less attachment to traditional peasant organizations, as the district of Neustadt an der Aisch commented in February 1931: 'From the successes of the electoral propaganda of the National Socialists and the *Landbund* in the district, one gets the impression that agricultural youth will probably vote mostly for the National Socialists in the coming elections and that the older voters will as before cast their votes for the *Landbund*' (*92*). Younger sons of peasant households felt aggrieved for they were less likely than ever before to inherit anything from their fathers, who were more reluctant during the Depression to hand over or parcel out their land.

The peasantry were less tempted by the appeal of the Nazis in areas where the Bavarian People's Party was well-entrenched. In August 1931, party headquarters wrote to a local branch leader concerning the elections to agricultural councils in Catholic districts. The people in strong Catholic areas were 'a chapter by themselves'. It was essential that the representatives of the party's agricultural organization here should be 'respected Catholic farmers', who were 'old-established proprietors' (*93*). A party member from Brannenburg near Rosenheim wrote to the editorial office of the *Völkischer Beobachter* some weeks later that 'it is a hard piece of work winning over the Catholic peasants to our movement; no opportunity must be lost to enlighten them, for it is well known that the Christian leaders do the utmost to see that their sheep remain in the fold' (*94*).

The difficulties facing Nazi propaganda in these areas stemmed mainly from the opposition of the Catholic peasant organizations, above all the Bavarian Christian Peasants' Association (*Bayerischer Christlicher Bauern-verein*), the BVP affiliate. This often took a very aggressive line towards the NSDAP. An anti-Nazi leaflet of the *Bauernverein* distributed around

Pfaffenhofen made the following accusations: that the NSDAP was against private property, in favour of the expropriation of land 'for the common use' and against protective tariffs for the peasantry; that Nazi propaganda was partly responsible for the economic disorder because it undermined confidence in the established order; that the NSDAP advocated a unitary Germany which would destroy Bavaria, and was completely revolutionary and would lead to anarchy; and that the NSDAP was infected with 'Bolshevist ideas', financed by big capital, hostile to the Church and 'ideologically mistaken' (95). There was enough plausibility in some of these arguments for this propaganda to have some effect in checking sympathies for the Nazis. Certain peasant circles which were strongly Catholic saw little difference between the 'socialist' ideas in the NSDAP programme of 1920 and 'Bolshevism', as the *Bauernverein* was only too willing to remind them.

The *Bauernverein* was exceptional in that it alone managed to present a barrier to the growth of Nazi support. It owed this to the confessional factor, and the backing it enjoyed from the Bavarian People's Party. The other peasant organizations and parties were more vulnerable, in the words of one district in Lower Bavaria, to the need prevalent among peasants 'to join for want of anything better an active protection organization out of the fear of being left defenceless and unorganized in the midst of these serious times of crisis' (96).

The Bavarian Peasants' and Middle-Class League (BBMB), having lost much of its electoral support in the Reichstag Election of 1930, was automatically on the defensive and tried in vain to prevent its position from sliding further. Even in its stronghold of Lower Bavaria, the BBMB felt obliged to fight back desperately to stop the flow of its supporters to the Nazis so that a few months after the election 'the opposition between both these parties became prominent in the local press, and the fight was carried on with particular bitterness by the newspapers of the Peasants' League' (97). In Upper Bavaria, the situation had already got out of hand for influential peasant leaders were no longer able as before to alleviate the fears of their audiences. The feeling of indignation was running so high that long-established peasant associations were losing face through the criticism that they were inactive and ineffective (98).

The future of the BBMB seemed hopeless once its local leaders began to declare their open support for the Nazi Party. In February 1931 Baron von Weveld, a landowner and head of the BBMB branch in Neuburg an der Donau, joined the NSDAP and addressed a Nazi meeting for peasants on 'Why I became a National Socialist'. The meeting was very well attended, and the whole occasion was a great success for the Nazis (99). In December

234

Andreas Seitz, the BBMB leader in Mittenwald, announced his readiness to campaign for the Nazis in a letter published in the *Gau* newspaper: 'The representatives of agricultural interests have contributed more to the present chaos through splintering into many small organizations; it would be better if all these small peasant organizations united and joined the ranks of Adolf Hitler' (*100*). Several months later Fritz, one of the most radical BBMB speakers in Lower Bavaria, went over to the NSDAP, and soon afterwards BBMB leaders in the districts of Regen and Viechtach followed suit (*101*). The Nazis made considerable use of the prestige gained from these defections from the Peasants' League. In a pamphlet produced for the Reichstag Election in July 1932 they quoted statements from some of the twenty-seven BBMB leaders who had joined them, and urged all *Bauernbündler* (members of the Peasants' League) to 'vote this time for the peasants' and workers' leader Adolf Hitler, list 2' (*102*).

Support for the Nazis was also growing apace in the rural areas of Franconia. There the *Landbund*, the associate organization of the Nationalist Party (DNVP), which had not lost many supporters to the NSDAP before the 1930 election, now began to suffer from the divisions within the DNVP and the success of the new peasants' party, the *Deutsches Landvolk*, in winning votes from the Nationalists. Typical of the state of affairs by the spring of 1931 was a meeting of the *Landbund* at Wassertrüdingen near Dinkelsbühl, which drew a crowd of 2,000, mainly Nazis. Because of the size and hostility of the audience, the *Landbund* leader announced that the meeting would be held elsewhere, presumably in a smaller hall where not so many Nazis could turn up. The Nazis present then started shouting violently. Their speaker 'jumped excitedly on to a table or chair and shrieked in an incomprehensible manner', accusing the *Landbund* leader of 'cowardice, meanness and baseness'. The meeting had to be closed (*103*).

Although the *Landbund* had at its disposal a well-developed organization, based on the fact that many of its local leaders were the mayors of rural communities, this was not enough to resist infiltration by the Nazis. The *Landbund* remained curiously passive to competition fron the NSDAP, mainly because its leaders being supporters of the DNVP were more ideologically conditioned to favour the Nazis than was the case with the leaders of the BBMB in Southern Bavaria. By April 1932, the *Landbund* had virtually given up all resistance to the Nazis in Middle Franconia, its former stronghold, where it was 'losing more and more votes to the National Socialists, and has abandoned the field to them almost without a fight in its preparations for the Reich Presidential Election—its meetings nowadays are badly attended and half of the participants are usually National Socialists' (*104*).

The successes of the Nazi rural campaign owed much to favourable circumstances and the absence of strong political opposition. But the work of the Agrarian Political Office should not be underestimated. Darré faced the most difficult of political problems, that of changing other people's attitudes—indifference on the part of many political leaders of the NSDAP, and suspicion and cautiousness on the part of the peasantry. Darré's persistence and appreciation of peasant psychology gradually showed results. By 1932 his system of agricultural specialists, with its provision of specialist information and reports on the activities of all rival peasant organizations, had begun to pay off. Darré wrote to the organization department at headquarters in June 1932 that more advantage should be taken of the opportunity whereby the peasantry of Bavaria, particularly of traditional 'old Bavaria', was 'for the first time in history' deserting its fold. Now the 'historic moment' had come for the NSDAP to organize the Bavarian peasants. Plans were already going ahead for the building of National Socialist peasant cells in Southern Germany, along the same lines as the factory cells (*105*).

In September 1932, Darré initiated yet another organization called the 'National Socialist Peasantry' (*NS Bauernschaft*), the purpose of which was to establish a 'far-reaching control of the rural voting masses' (*106*). Because of the impoverishment of the agricultural population, it was not possible to do this by getting the peasant masses to join the party. Peasant membership of the NSDAP was still relatively low. The *NS Bauernschaft*, which came under the direction of the Agrarian Political Office, would prepare peasants for party membership when they were better off. Members of the *Bauernschaft* did not have to become members of the NSDAP, although posts in the organization were only held by party members. The new organization offered the peasants cheap legal advice and set up advisory boards for economic and tax problems.

The *NS Bauernschaft* pointed the way to the process of 'coordination' during the early months of the Nazi 'seizure of power'. The stampede of peasant voters to the NSDAP finally came in the Reichstag Election of July 1932, although this did not happen in the former BBMB stronghold of Lower Bavaria until the election of March 1933. These changes in the rural vote amounted to the greatest upheaval in the political loyalties of the peasantry up to that time.

Anti-Semitism

It has been seen that the Nazis used anti-semitic arguments to buttress their appeal to the peasantry, and that anti-semitism was present in the radicalism of Nazi students. But what part did anti-semitism generally play in the rise in popular support for the NSDAP during the early 1930s?

Racialism was a primary feature of Nazi ideology, so it is useful to examine how much this ideology motivated Nazi supporters. If the NSDAP was known for anything during its early years in Bavaria, it was its racialism or more specifically anti-semitism. The NSDAP had since changed from a fringe party into a national mass movement. Had the need to broaden its popular appeal compelled the party to soften its racialism?

Anti-semitism did not form specifically one of the major themes of party propaganda in the early 1930s, but it often provided a leitmotiv for the major propaganda themes since the NSDAP's appeal on economic and political issues was frequently couched in anti-semitic terms. The majority of Nazi voters in the elections of 1930–32 were probably little influenced directly by the racialist ideology of the NSDAP, as they were primarily voting for a change in circumstances. Anti-semitism was of course traditionally a largely middle-class phenomenon in Germany, and the Nazis were not slow to exploit this. But the influence of the party's racialism is difficult to quantify. Anti-semitism took many forms—including ideological, economic and religious—so it was not possible to make too fine a distinction between the ideology itself and the circumstances which gave it a wider acceptance among certain sections of the population. The problem can best be discussed by looking briefly at the party's anti-semitic activities in Bavaria then, and examining their impact in certain representative towns.

The aggressive and 'ideological' form of anti-semitism was more common among party leaders and activists than Nazi voters. Nazi speakers like Streicher, Münchmeyer, Holz as well as Hitler emphasized the Jewish question in their speeches. Hitler's overriding and consistent passion throughout his political career was his hatred of the Jews. It was characteristic to present an abstract view of the Jews, who were seen not as members of different occupations, classes or nationalities but as a single force. The stereotyped Jew was painted in the most extreme way by Streicher's paper in Nuremberg, *Der Stürmer*, especially in the caricatures of Philipp Rupprecht known under his pseudonym of 'Fips'. These caricatures exaggerated what anti-semites saw as the 'typical' features of the Jew with 'an immense expanse of body, crooked short legs, colossal flat feet and long hairy arms and hands which through a hunchbacked posture hangs forwards ... a thick head with bloated furrowed features grafted on, and protruding eyes, huge hanging ears and distended lips' (*107*). It was also usual to establish an automatic connection between Jews and 'Marxism' in such Nazi terminology as 'Jewish Bolshevism', irrespective of the support among Jews for the conservative parties and the fact that many of them were patriotic Germans. Anti-semitism was an attitude of mind among party leaders—a way of conforming to party ideology—but with varying degrees of conviction, for by no means all of them shared Streicher's total obsession with the problem.[49]

The party's anti-semitism expressed itself in other ways. Party meetings were frequently advertised with a ban on attendance by Jews, such as on the following street poster for a Streicher meeting in Nuremberg:

NSDAP MEETING   April 21 1932, in the Herkules Velodrom
STREICHER: 'The Jews are our Misfortune'

Fellow Germans of all classes and parties! Men and
women of Nuremberg come to our mass meeting!
Entrance 30 Pfg. Unemployed with identity card 10 Pfg.
Jews are not allowed in!

Music: The Heyland Band (*108*)

Anti-semitism was common in SA circles, and sometimes erupted in rowdyism. In May 1929 a meeting of the Jewish organization, the Central Association of German Subjects of the Jewish Faith, in Würzburg, was being addressed by Dr Wiener from Berlin and an SPD city councillor, when Nazis present interrupted with catcalls and caused such a disturbance that the police had to close the meeting (*109*). Late in 1931, the police reported several incidents in Leutershausen near Ansbach involving attacks on Jews. One cattle-dealer was molested by a Nazi, who 'beat him many times on the head and face with a steel-rod without any reason' (*110*).

The Nazis sought to exploit anti-semitic feeling when it was related to economic interest, especially concerning the lower-middle classes. Small

49. Streicher even built up a vast library of his own of anti-semitic and pornographic publications. Much Jewish literature was confiscated from Jewish homes, and was used along with the other publications in the library to document Streicher's articles in *Der Stürmer*. Disapproval of Streicher's activities by other party leaders could not be divorced from personal dislike, as with *Gau* leader Karl Wahl of Swabia: 'Streicher did what he wanted, he knew no restraints or consideration; he was an unpleasant contemporary; I have always genuinely attempted to get on with all people, even the most complicated . . . but with Streicher I did not succeed . . . His rabid anti-semitism was repugnant to me; Streicher's own rag *Der Stürmer* I never read, it was on my proscribed list' (. . . *es ist das deutsche Herz*, pp. 56–7).

businessmen, shopkeepers and craftsmen had reason to fear competition from the department stores, a large number of which were owned by Jews.[50] Hans Schemm exploited this issue in Bayreuth by attacking the department stores for being a 'weapon' of the 'Marxists' to destroy the German middle classes. Protest meetings were organized in the city whenever a new store was opened, as in February 1929 when Schemm criticized the supply of premises for new stores in a bitter speech on 'The attack by department-store Jews on Bayreuth' (*111*). Similarly, the Nazis appealed to the prejudices of hotel-keepers in Upper Bavaria. Rudolf Buttmann made a speech during the debate on the drop in tourism during 1926 in the Bavarian state parliament in July 1927, in which he described the adverse effect of the presence of Jews on the tourist trade in the Alpine spa of Bad Reichenhall. Quoting letters he had received from holiday-makers there, Buttmann argued that the root cause of the problem was not high prices or anti-semitic agitation, but the 'disturbing forms' which night life had taken there and other 'foreign' influences—such as the performance at the casino of a jazz band, which he deplored for its 'nigger music' and 'Hottentot music' (*112*).

In spite of the obsession of party leaders with the Jewish question, tactical considerations entered into the propagation of anti-semitism. In certain areas, where the social position and economic activity of Jews was not much in evidence, such propaganda might have alienated potential but cautious Nazi voters.[51] Anti-semitism was very much an attitude of mind, which often had its roots in social and economic causes, but its political importance depended on the prominence of Jews in community life and local traditions of anti-semitic feeling.

It is important to note that Jews preferred to live in cities and to concentrate on certain occupations. In 1910 half of the Jews in Bavaria were living

---

50. Jews were responsible for three-quarters of the business in department stores in Germany in the early 1930s, including large stores like Karstadt, Tietz and Wertheim. Department stores had begun to make an appearance in the late nineteenth century, but anti-semitism was already stronger among the trading lower-middle classes than among industrialists, workers or the aristocracy; for example, see P. G. J. Pulzer, *The Rise of Political Anti-Semitism in Germany and Austria*, p. 281, for membership by occupations of the anti-semitic Pan-German League in 1901.

51. W. S. Allen in his study of the rise of the Nazis in the town of Northeim in Lower Saxony where there was a very small Jewish population makes the point that if Nazi anti-semitism had any appeal there 'it was in a highly abstract form, as a remote theory unconnected with daily encounters with real Jews'. Local party leaders 'sensed this and in consequence anti-semitism was not pushed in propaganda except in a ritualistic way'. According to Allen, local inhabitants were 'drawn to anti-semitism because they were drawn to Nazism, not the other way round—many who voted Nazi simply ignored or rationalized the anti-semitism of the party, just as they ignored other unpleasant aspects of the Nazi movement'. (*The Nazi Seizure of Power*, p. 77.)

in the six cities of Bamberg, Augsburg, Würzburg, Fürth, Nuremberg and Munich (*113*). By 1933, there were nearly 42,000 Jews living in Bavaria, of which over 30,000 were settled in the cities and only 11,000 in the rural areas (*114*). This preference for urban life derived partly from the cosmopolitan background of Jews in general (who showed a high degree of mobility and migration), but more especially from the restricted outlets for their economic activity. Many professions were still in practice closed to them such as the civil service, so it was natural that Jews should have sought their livelihood in commercial occupations and the learned professions such as law, medicine, journalism and university teaching.[52]

The chief exception to this preference for urban-based occupations was, as already seen, the high proportion of Jewish cattle-traders. Jews had generally few possibilities in agriculture because of its conservative nature, so their only chance lay in becoming middlemen. Jewish cattle-dealers and creditors were particularly common in the country areas of Franconia, more so than in Southern Bavaria. In rural Franconia, where society was less integrated than in the solid Catholic areas of traditional Bavaria, Jewish creditors had found acceptance in certain aristocratic landowning circles and had been able to settle down to their business (*115*). Consequently, Jews seemed to play a more prominent part in rural life there than was suggested by their numbers, for they generally formed only a fraction (3 to 5 per cent) of the population in rural communities with the exception of a number of districts in Middle Franconia. The same was true of Jews in the cities. For economic, social and traditional reasons they were concentrated in the bourgeoisie and in certain occupations, which drew the attention of the racialist Right in politics in its campaign against the influence of 'foreign' elements in German society.

Since Nazi anti-semitic propaganda took into account the degree of social tensions concerning Jews, the effect of the party's anti-semitic appeal may be further explained with reference to three cities in Bavaria—Hof, Memmingen and Nuremberg.

Hof, a city with more than 40,000 inhabitants near the Bavarian border in Upper Franconia, had a small Jewish population of 0·2 per cent (1933 cen-

52. Pulzer offers another reason for the Jewish preference for these occupations, namely the fear of 'becoming submerged in a mass-organized Gentile world'. They were able to retain their independence although not always with economic benefit for 'shirt making or umbrella mending in a slum attic meant a low income and long hours, but it enabled the Jew to observe his religious festivals and dietary practices in peace, and to perpetuate voluntarily his own little ghetto'. The desire for 'being independent' was similarly satisfied in the liberal professions. (See *The Rise of Political Anti-Semitism in Germany and Austria*, p. 5.)

sus). Early in 1929, the district office of Hof compiled a report on the position of Jews there in answer to a complaint made by the Jewish Central Association following recent incidents (*116*). The Central Association claimed these incidents were the result of Nazi agitation. The report concluded that incidents over the previous months were 'possibly the consequence of National Socialist incitement against the Jews'. It mentioned the excitement caused by the opening of a department store by a Jew called Levy in the summer of 1928, which had been exploited by the Nazis 'with reinforced propaganda'.

In general, it was difficult to lay direct blame on local Nazis, because 'apart from the smashing of the windows of the synagogue it was only a matter of actions which amounted to insignificant disturbances of the public order'. There was no threat to the security of the twenty-five Jewish families living in the city, although there was a tendency in many circles to boycott Jewish shops. Social attitudes to well-educated Jews, including a doctor and a district-judge, were much more respectful. The report drew attention to a meeting of the Central Association, at which the local branch leader of the Bavarian People's Party had acted as discussion speaker and attacked Jewish influence to the applause of Nazis present. He maintained that in the past century the German character had been 'uncommonly damaged' by the Jews, who would not become Germans.[53] It could be assumed from these events that there was an undercurrent of anti-semitic feeling in the city, which related in part to business competition and could only have been to the benefit of the Nazis, even if they did not exploit it on every occasion. The district office of Hof was of the opinion that such attitudes were not easy to deal with, for 'police measures cannot be used to intervene in this respect' (*117*).

Anti-semitic feeling was often not easy to define, and need not have any overt connection with political preferences. It was often little in evidence especially in places with a minimal Jewish population, or where Jews were well integrated into society. Since more than 60 per cent of Bavaria's Jews lived in a number of towns in Franconia, it is interesting to take a provincial town in Catholic Southern Bavaria, where Jews were not so common. More than two-thirds of the Jews in Southern Bavaria were concentrated in the

53. Anti-semitism was not unknown in the other parties, including the Catholic parties. It was noticeable during the revolutionary upheavals after the First World War. The BVP had issued anti-semitic literature attacking Kurt Eisner, the head of the revolutionary régime in Munich, who was a Jew. One BVP pamphlet had claimed that the party 'values and honours every honest Jew . . . but what must be fought are the numerous atheistic elements of a certain international Jewry with predominantly Russian clothing'. (Quoted in Allan Mitchell, *Revolution in Bavaria, 1918–19*, p. 192.)

one city of Munich, while a few provincial towns like Memmingen in Swabia had one or two hundred Jewish inhabitants. Memmingen is an important example, because the NSDAP gained one of its highest votes here in the region in the Reichstag Election of July 1932 (36 per cent).

Memmingen had only 161 Jews according to the 1933 census out of a total population of more than 15,000, although it was one of the few towns where the Jews had their own synagogue. They consisted of some forty families, and were active particularly in the textile trade. Anti-semitism was not strong in the town during the Weimar period, although the influx of some Jewish immigrants after the War caused minor friction. The only public expression of anti-semitic feeling was in 1921 during the inflation, when wage-earners resented the progress made by dealers in merchandise. There were no further demonstrations of public feeling against the Jews until the Nazis organized the boycott of Jewish shops in the spring of 1933 (*118*). Apart from traces of opposition to certain Jewish firms, the Jewish families seemed reasonably accepted in Memmingen society. Many of them had a strong sense of local pride, and had fought in the German Army during the War (*119*). Although local Nazis occasionally indulged in attacks on the Jews, one may assume that anti-semitism had little to do with the strong support for the party in this town.

The discussion of anti-semitism in Bavaria can hardly conclude without mention of Nuremberg. Nuremberg saw the most virulent anti-semitic propaganda by the Nazis, because of the presence of Streicher who dominated the party there. The local Nazis were known for their anti-semitism, a reputation which owed much to Streicher's paper as well as to the high racialist content of speeches made by Nazi leaders in the city. Secondly, Nuremberg does illustrate the relationship between 'ideological' anti-semitism, of which Streicher was the foremost example, and the social and economic factors which encouraged such feelings among people at large. Nuremberg was not typical of Bavaria as a whole because of the size of its Jewish population, but it is only by looking at a city which had a relatively high proportion of Jews that one can finally answer the question to what extent the racialist ideology of the Nazis assisted the growth of their popular support during the early 1930s.

Nuremberg seemed to offer a microcosm of the role that Jews played in German urban society during the Weimar period. They were in all the typical professions—medical, legal, academic, journalistic as well as commercial. There were 7,502 Jews living in Nuremberg in 1933, accounting for 1·8 per cent of the total population of over 410,000. Jews formed a very high proportion of lawyers (97 out of 215) and doctors and dentists (140 out of

742) (*120*). A fair number of businesses and trades were also Jewish, including exports, private banks, clothiers, machine toolmakers, corn merchandise and department stores (*121*). Jews were not so numerous in the other named professions, but they were still prominent. They included the editors-in-chief of two newspapers—Dr Adolf Braun of the social *Fränkische Tagespost*, and E. E. Neumann of the independent *Nürnberger Zeitung*. Nuremberg did not offer the outlets in artistic life as did Berlin, where the highest number of Jews were concentrated in Germany, because it was not a cosmopolitan but a strongly bourgeois city. The city had once had an even larger Jewish community until pogroms in the Middle Ages had driven out large numbers of Jews, most of whom had settled in Fürth or in surrounding communities.

In spite of the important part played by Jews in Nuremberg's social and economic life, Streicher's propaganda bore little relation to reality. His charges about the preference given to Jews in the political life of the city were unfounded, for Dr Max Süssheim, the city councillor, and Freund, a junior mayor, were exceptional cases. Only six of the 3,000 civil servants employed by the city in 1925 were Jews (*122*). Anti-semitic propaganda in so far as it made an impression on the public was related more to economic competition among small businessmen and to the feeling of insecurity among the middle classes. Among the general public, only craftsmen and retailers used *Der Stürmer* to advertise their businesses (*123*). It was significant that of the city's newspapers only the *Fränkischer Kurier* failed to criticize the militant anti-semitism of Streicher. The *Fränkischer Kurier*, which was the paper most read by the middle classes there, usually reported sympathetically on the NSDAP, gave its activities generous coverage and even urged its readers to hoist swastika flags on their houses during the party rally there in 1929 (*124*). Both the Catholic *Bayerische Volkszeitung* and the left-wing press refused to have anything to do with the racialist agitation of the Nazis.

The electoral importance of Nazi anti-semitic propaganda was that it formed part of the party's effort to exploit the fears of the middle classes. Workers were not so influenced by anti-semitism, because there was no strong element of economic rivalry in their case. Their main political passion was class antagonism, which was directed against the capitalist middle classes in general rather than any particular ethnic group. The Jews usually belonged to the middle classes, which was often resented by middle-class circles. The exact degree of anti-semitic feeling is difficult to measure, because it was an attitude rather than an observable form of behaviour. It sometimes showed itself less harmfully in anti-Jewish jokes and generalized expressions of dislike, but there is no doubt that the social tensions created by the Depression helped to magnify this feeling.

The party's racialist ideology had a public impact in so far as it related to circumstances. Anti-semitism had received an impetus in Munich after the War, because it became linked with anti-Communism through the experience of the revolutionary left-wing régimes there in 1918–19. The broad mass of Nazi voters in the early 1930s were not conscious racialists, for they were motivated primarily by political and economic discontent. But in some areas the NSDAP's exploitation of discontent was reinforced by anti-semitic propaganda, depending on whether feeling against the Jews was based on a tradition there or was provoked by economic competition. Much depended on the public's consciousness of the party's racialism. Conscious anti-semites were more likely to be found among Nazi activists than Nazi voters. The possibility of the NSDAP alienating public support by the violence of its anti-semitism was diminished by the tactics of party propagandists, but more generally by the fact that the party's anti-semitism was at this time largely an abstraction, apart from physical attacks by individual Nazis on Jews. Although they had warnings in the racialist hatred of Nazi speakers, who made threats about the position of the Jews in the future Nazi state, the majority of voters did not seem to realize how seriously the Nazis meant to put their ideas into practice as part of their programme of social as well as political change.

The Party Press

The role of the party's propaganda in exploiting conditions during the economic crisis of the early 1930s has already been discussed, but chiefly with reference to mass agitation through public meetings and 'personal propaganda'. The NSDAP had an advantage over the other parties in this respect with the flexibility and versatility of its organization, but there was one field of propaganda where the Nazis did not excel and were definitely inferior to other political parties. That was the press. The Nazis made very little impact on the press before the 'seizure of power' in 1933, when their control of mass communications enabled them to turn the tables to their advantage.[54]

Apart from the *Völkischer Beobachter*, which had appeared since the early days of the party, there was not much of a party press before the 1930

54. By 1933, there were only 121 Nazi newspapers out of a total of 4,703 in Germany, roughly 2½ per cent. Their combined circulation amounted to over a million.

Election. Even then its progress was beset with innumerable and sometimes insurmountable difficulties. This may have reflected Hitler's own preference for the spoken over the written word, but the failure of the Nazi press was due to a variety of causes of which the subordination of press propaganda to mass agitation was only one. Nazi newspapers suffered from the rigid control and monopolistic attitude of the party central office, frequent prohibitions by the authorities, the long-established tradition of rival newspapers, the journalistic deficiencies of party propagandists and the lack of finance.

The press was merely an adjunct of mass propaganda for the Nazis rather than a different field of political activity which demanded special skills. Dr Goebbels, one of the few party leaders with a flair for popular journalism, pinpointed this problem:

> For us the press is propaganda by means of journalism ... It draws political consequences from its information, but does not leave it to the reader to form his own opinion. It exerts its influence in a determined and conscious fashion. A certain ideological direction should govern everything it thinks and feels (*125*).

Der Angriff (The Attack), which was Goebbels' personal newspaper with its leading articles signed 'Dr G.', first appeared in Berlin in July 1927 in response to a police ban on the party there (*126*). It provided Goebbels with an alternative outlet for his political views, while his public meetings were prohibited. By the end of 1928, there were two Nazi dailies, twenty-seven weeklies, one monthly and one fortnightly publication (*127*). Goebbels' paper had begun as a weekly, but it was converted to a daily from November 1930. This typified the way the Nazi press developed. Party newspapers generally started as weeklies in the late 1920s, and became dailies from 1930. This change reflected the need to take advantage of the political opportunities created by the party's success in the Reichstag Election of 1930.

The expansion of the Nazi press from 1930 did not bring any fundamental change in the party's management of its press policy. Headquarters sought to keep the press on a tight rein, as part of its overall policy of controlling all propaganda activities. Philipp Bouhler, who had sought as party business manager to promote the circulation of the *Völkischer Beobachter*, revealed the monopolistic approach of headquarters in 1926:

> If every private publisher in Germany, even one authorized to publish an official party paper, should seek to imitate or surpass a publication

established with great effort by the central party office, then soon we should have a dozen or two illustrated papers; and the *Illustrierter Beobachter*, which was begun in the first place as a support for our central party organ, would go to the wall (*128*).

Bouhler was writing to Gottfried Feder, who had plans for a rival illustrated paper to be produced by his own publishing house in Bamberg.

Aside from those published by the main party firm in Munich, the Eher Verlag, and the Strassers' firm the Kampfverlag in Berlin, a large proportion of party newspapers was the result of local efforts by individuals or party branches, such as the *Donaubote* in Ingolstadt. All of them had to receive either the status of official party organs (which allowed them to carry the swastika symbol on the front page), or simply official recognition by head-quarters. The regulations governing press policy, adopted at the party congress at Weimar in 1926, specified that the power of supervision and control of party organs was in the hands of the Propaganda Department in Munich, which could grant or withdraw permission to publish under the party's name. The conditions of official recognition included editorial sub-ordination to the party line, the publication of party announcements free of charge and the refusal of advertising from Jewish firms. All newspapers were subject to detailed scrutiny by the press section of the Propaganda Depart-ment, which demanded copies of every edition published (*129*).

The system of control was through local and regional press agents (*Presse-warte*), who were also often editors of *Gau* newspapers. This organization took a long time to establish itself. Even as late as June 1932, many district and branch leaders in Upper Bavaria had not yet appointed press agents (*130*). This could be explained partly by the lack of a strong interest in a party press at the grass roots, but also by the restrictionist attitude of the *Gau* leaders. They were taken to task for this in a long report on Nazi press policy compiled by the party's Press Office under Otto Dietrich in July 1932. Dietrich claimed that *Gau* leaders were using their authority too much in preventing the technical development of the party press:

It is deplorable that no scope is yet given to the principle of the free com-petition of all our party papers, because the realization of this principle had to give way to other important considerations in the initial stage of the development of our press system (*131*).

He referred to the numerous cases of suppression of smaller papers by *Gau* offices, including some which genuinely had the interests of the party at heart.[55] Sometimes there were good reasons for such action, but the *Gaue* should always take over any maverick 'Nazi' newspapers rather than 'smash them ruthlessly'. The Press Office would intervene, if fear of competition were the principal motive for suppression (*132*).

It was not surprising that most Nazi newspapers should have been no more than 'combat rags' (*Kampfblätter*). This had two adverse consequences. Their function as the mouthpiece of aggressive and provocative party propaganda often brought them into conflict with the authorities, but it also restricted their popular appeal. The frequency of prohibitions depended on a number of local factors such as the attitude of the town police towards the Nazis, the degree of radicalism of the newspaper editor and the strength of the NSDAP in the town in question. Strong support for the party could make local authorities more cautious about taking action. The number of prohibitions on Nazi newspapers was high compared with those on publications of other political parties. The usual reason given for official action was the danger to public security. The *Allgäuer Beobachter*, which began appearing in Memmingen soon after the 1930 Election, was banned in August 1931 because of an article which 'consciously pursues the aim of undermining the authority of the state and therefore endangers public security and order' (*133*). In Ingolstadt, the BVP authorities still felt powerful enough to issue four prohibitions on the *Donaubote* during the seven months from August 1931. In each case, they took exception to abusive and sarcastic articles about the government, including one entitled 'Who is still pumping up Brüning?' (*134*).

A certain kudos was attached to prohibitions by the more defiant editors, who took the view that a party newspaper had not 'made it' if it had not experienced a clash with the authorities. The *Neue Nationalzeitung*, the organ of *Gau* Swabia in Augsburg, could for instance boast of no less than six bans in the months June 1931 to March 1932, making a grand total of seven weeks without publication (*135*). This attitude made absolutely no business sense, for suspension of publication meant loss of income and often loss of regular readership. Many local Nazi newspapers ceased to appear because their failure to make progress was hampered by strict police measures. The local branch in Würzburg started its own newspaper early in 1931 called *Die Freiheit* (Freedom), but this lasted barely nine months. The

55. One such case which attracted much publicity was *Gau* leader Streicher's attempt to defeat Gottfried Feder's plans to buy up a publishing firm in Nuremberg called the Fränkischer Volksverlag. Although Feder's newspapers received official recognition from headquarters, Streicher saw this as an invasion of his domain and a challenge to his own paper *Der Stürmer*. Streicher took legal proceedings, but he failed to prevent Feder from carrying out his plans. (See Manfred Rühl, *Der Stürmer und sein Herausgeber*, pp. 189–91.)

paper suffered from feelings of reserve among branch members, who disliked the demands made on them for financial support, but also from the hostility of the *Gau* office of Lower Franconia there which issued a public statement repudiating the paper. What finally killed off *Die Freiheit* was the involvement of its editor in several libel actions, which brought heavy fines and further debts (*136*). Similarly, the *Deutsche Alpenwacht* (German Alpine Watch) ceased publication in April 1931 after only four months' appearance in Sonthofen, because of differences of opinion in the local branch and restrictions imposed by the police. Its editor, Manfred von Ribbentrop, was sentenced to several months in prison because of an offence under the Law for the Protection of Public Order (*137*).

These local efforts to open party newspapers would have been more successful if they had not faced strong competition from the long-established bourgeois press and the papers of the Social Democratic and Catholic parties. The Nazis excelled in mass agitation through public meetings, because such political activity was relatively new. Universal suffrage had only been introduced in Germany after the First World War. But the development of a party press had a much longer history, which stretched back into the nineteenth century to the revolution of 1848. Nazi papers found it difficult if not impossible to break the hold of the traditional press. Consequently, their circulation was low and usually based on a readership among party members. The *Völkischer Beobachter* was an exception because it could take advantage of its monopoly position. Its circulation figures rose from 26,715 to 126,672 during 1929–32 (*138*). But the *Neue Nationalzeitung* in Augsburg, which should have had an edge on local party papers because of its official status as *Gau* organ, managed to increase its circulation from 4,000 when it first appeared in February 1931 to only 9,500 by January 1933 (*139*).[56]

Various methods were used to encourage a rise in subscriptions among the party faithful. When the *Neue Nationalzeitung* began publication, the party office in Augsburg sent a circular to all members urging them not only to take copies themselves but also to persuade their friends and acquaintances to do so. Those who won five subscribers would receive free copies for a month, ten subscribers would mean two months' free reading and so on (*140*). To make the paper more attractive, the editor Baron von Zobel included a sports page and a section on local Augsburg news (*141*). Such pressure sometimes had a contrary effect on party members, who were satiated with demands to support the party press. The decision to turn a weekly into a daily was often determined less by the possibility of a wider readership than

56. Typically, the circulation of the paper rose quickly during the 'seizure of power', from 9,500 to 15,300 in the first six months after Hitler became Chancellor.

by prestige reasons. Such was the case with *Schaffendes Volk* (Creative People), the organ of the *Gau* of Lower Bavaria, which became a daily as late as October 1932. The *Gau* office was less subtle in applying pressure, for it demanded that all members order the paper or at least find a subscriber if they could not afford it themselves. Those who did not fulfil this 'duty' would be guilty of 'behaviour detrimental to the party and lack of interest', and would have to take the consequences (*142*). On a more general level, the party press suffered from the Depression, which had a dampening effect on circulation rates and street sales and made people less inclined to support a new newspaper except when they were already strongly committed to the NSDAP.

With their failure to build up an independent party press, the Nazis began to show more interest in influencing that section of the established press which showed sympathy with them. There was little hope of achieving this with the Catholic or left-wing papers, but the bourgeois press was more vulnerable because the parties which it supported (the DNVP, the German People's Party or the Economic Party) were losing their voters to the NSDAP. Otto Dietrich saw here an opening for party press policy. In his report of July 1932 he emphasized that 'numerous bourgeois newspapers are without a political master because of the collapse of the bourgeois parties' (*143*). He argued that the party needed time and money to build up a press of its own, but it had neither. The *Gau* leaders were aware of the restricted possibilities of finding a viable readership because of the bourgeois and Social Democratic papers, which had strong roots in 'tradition, local patriotism, the family, business life and in the control of power in the state'. The party was not in a position to provide eleven or twelve million Nazi voters with daily newspapers, which would in any case be a waste of energy when more could be achieved by other means. He maintained that it was better to have a bourgeois paper, which might have a circulation of 50,000, publish news about the NSDAP than try to set up an independent Nazi newspaper, which merely 'confirms 5,000 party supporters in their own outlook' (*144*).

Dietrich's solution was to strengthen the position of the *Gau* press agent, who should concentrate on gaining influence over the bourgeois press. The method of achieving this was by keeping himself well briefed on the situation of the press in his area, and to make direct contact with the bourgeois newspapers. This should take the form of a visit to the publisher to sound out his views on the Nazi Party. The press agent should emphasize the change in political allegiance of the newspaper's readers, and point out the likely change in power in the near future. Up to this point, the press agent should be 'friendly or at least objective' in his approach. If the publisher remained obdurate, he should then assume a tougher manner and threaten to organize a boycott of the newspaper. If the publisher readily complied, the press agent should propose a 'treaty of assurance'. This was a one-sided agreement, which obliged the newspaper concerned to give Nazi activities wide coverage in accordance with the party's new 'importance and size', to make use of the party information service and to sack any editors who resisted the new policy. Finally, Dietrich made a distinction between the city and the provincial press. *Gau* press agents would be advised to give their attention to the latter, because it was more amenable to Nazi pressure as a result of the party's greater electoral successes in the provinces (*145*).

Dietrich's policy of infiltration rather than direct competition with the bourgeois press had some success, for several well-established newspapers in Bavaria became more and more sympathetic towards the NSDAP in the year or two before the 'seizure of power'. The *Allgäuer Tagblatt* had appeared as an independent daily in Kempten since 1863, and had several subsidiary newspapers in the Allgäu region. The paper was forced to treat the party more favourably because of the combination of strong support for the NSDAP in the area and a drop in its advertising revenue because of the Depression, although it did not become an official organ of the Nazis until September 1933 (*146*). These older newspapers did not often become openly Nazi before Hitler became Chancellor, because they did not wish to alienate their more conservative readers through a radical break with tradition. Those which began to advocate support publicly for the NSDAP did so for opportunistic or ideological reasons. The *Oberbayerische Rundschau* had started publication in 1928 in an attempt to combat the influence of the Catholic press in the Ammersee region, but its circulation figures did not reach beyond a few hundred. Seeing that the NSDAP presented the most formidable challenge to the BVP, the paper sided with the Nazis as early as 1930 (*147*). The *Miesbacher Anzeiger*, by comparison, had established itself as an anti-semitic paper of some renown since its first appearance in 1874. It was now edited by Father Bernhard Stempfle, a member of the Hieronymite Order and notorious anti-semite who had assisted Hitler in the drafting of *Mein Kampf*. It was not therefore difficult for the *Miesbacher Anzeiger* to join the Nazi bandwagon, which it did in 1930.

There were two further reasons for the weakness of the Nazi newspapers before 1933, and the change of emphasis in Dietrich's press policy. Firstly, the party did not boast of much journalistic talent. Its newspaper editors and staff consisted almost entirely of party functionaries, who had little experience in the techniques of journalism. The development of the party press was determined exclusively by political considerations. This may be illustrated by the *Gau* press of Munich–Upper Bavaria. The main *Gau* organ, *Die Front* (The Front), started publication in September 1930 as a bi-monthly. It changed to becoming a weekly in 1931. In the same year several special editions made an appearance, such as the *Bauernfront* (Peasants' Front), *Die Arbeiter-Front* (The Workers' Front) and the *Mittelstandsfront* (Middle-Class Front). There was also *Die Jungfront*, edited by the leader of the *Gau* Hitler Youth, and a pictorial supplement called *Die Front im Bild* (*148*). These various editions had very little market justification, for they simply reflected *Gau* leader Wagner's attention to specialist propaganda. Each specialist organization had its own publication. The style of these papers was very uninspiring. In fact the sales of *Die Front* decreased sharply during the second half of 1932, only to rise again after the 'seizure of power'.

The NSDAP had only the bare minimum of organizational apparatus, because of the low priority given to the press in its propaganda. A party press agency (the *NS Partei-Korrespondenz*) was opened in January 1932, under the authority of Dietrich's Press Office, to feed Nazi newspapers with information and find ways of reducing production costs. The tasks of the agency did not extend to financial assistance, for, as Dietrich made clear, 'the Reich Press Office which does not itself have a business-like financial basis can only cooperate in an advisory and guiding capacity with the economic "rationalization" of the party press' (*149*).

The final reason for the difficulties of the party press before 1933 was financial. The financial state of Nazi newspapers was usually very precarious with their lack of capital, advertising revenue and regular subscribers. Their circulation consisted mainly of local branches in the area, which received bundles of copies from the *Gau* office. It was no wonder that the commercial failure of these efforts was often a matter of great concern to the *Gau* leaders. Karl Wahl gave this desperate picture of the attempt to maintain a daily *Gau* newspaper in Swabia:

Nothing can create greater security when a newspaper is founded than the availability of large capital . . . The heap of troubles on our shoulders was already much too great beforehand, but this heavy burden overwhelmed us completely. Reform after reform was carried out, new men with new formulas were tried, but it did not develop from its premature birth, became weaker and weaker and had a tough time . . . Our debts became greater and greater, and hope of saving the newspaper smaller and smaller. Bills became due for payment, were dishonoured and our furniture was mortgaged. On top of this, there were a number of prohibitions which brought losses. Whatever we tried, the terrible ghost of approaching catastrophe dogged our steps (*150*).

The press in the *Gau* of Munich–Upper Bavaria was hardly better off, for according to a later party report 'the 2,500 to 3,000 firm subscribers of *Die Front* and the small business in advertisements were not sufficient to provide the *Gau* paper with a stable economic basis' (*151*). The *Gau* simply did not have the money to provide the initial capital for newspapers nor to maintain or subsidize them. In September 1931, Nippold, the *Gau* business manager, wrote to branches announcing the introduction of a new monthly collection of 30 pfennigs per member as one way out of the dire financial straits in which the *Gau* found itself. According to this memorandum, the *Gau* of Munich–Upper Bavaria needed 3,000 marks a month for administrative expenses alone: 1,600 to pay the twenty employees in the *Gau* office; 1,050 for rent, telephone and stationery; 200 for propaganda, and 150 a month to pay off the debts still outstanding after the last Reichstag Election a year before. Nippold maintained that the *Gau* could just about make ends meet with the greatest of thrift, but this excluded all extra expenses such as the cost of mass rallies (*152*).

It was hardly surprising in these circumstances that few local branches with their even more limited funds were in a position to meet the costs of running a newspaper. Virtually all of their money was spent on other propaganda activities. Although the branches received propaganda material from Munich via the *Gau* offices, they had to meet the cost of hiring halls for the many public meetings they held. In some areas branches were run literally on a shoe string.[57] The *Allgäuer Beobachter* in Memmingen was typical of most Nazi newspapers with its history of crippling debt. It had to set up its own printing press, as no local printer was willing to cooperate. The printing press cost twice as much as the total amount of money collected from local party members to launch the newspaper (*153*). The financing of a newspaper was entirely the problem of the local or regional party organization.

57. For example, see the correspondence concerning the NSDAP branch in Kraiburg, a village on the Inn near Mühldorf (HA 8/176). The branch consisted of fifty members, most of whom refused to pay their membership fees, so that the branch leader, Rudolf Kraut, a dentist, was compelled to finance the party activities there largely out of his own pocket. Kraut's wife acted as press agent, and another relative was branch secretary. He could rely on the enthusiasm of an SA man, who with his dental assistant would deliver posters in the neighbouring villages but there was no money for newspaper advertisements and printed handouts. In the end, the *Gau* office for Upper Bavaria decided to close down the branch in 1932. Kraiburg was an extreme case, but it did illustrate the financial problems which the party could face in some places.

Behind all these difficulties lay the assumption that the press did not form an essential part of Nazi propaganda. The emphasis was on winning voters, and few voters were likely to be won over by reading a party newspaper. Nazi propaganda appealed to the emotions not to reason, and this was best achieved through the medium of a public meeting rather than the turgid prose of a party rag. Although the Nazis never liked to allow shortage of finance to inhibit their propaganda, public meetings and 'personal propaganda' were given a clear priority over the party press in the allocation of funds.[58]

The party press did perform a number of important minor functions. Since its readership was mainly party members, it did act as a channel of communication between them and the *Gau* offices, which used it to publish orders. But the Nazi press did not establish itself until after the 'seizure of power' in 1933. Hitler's appointment as Chancellor came as a great relief to the majority of its editors. During the months which followed, the mood of creditors and printers changed in favour of the Nazis and people made a point of subscribing to their newspapers. Most important of all, the Nazis' growing control over the power of the state allowed them to ban and put pressure on rival newspapers.

The Polarization of Politics

Although the Nazification of the political system began really with Hitler's acquisition of the Chancellorship in January 1933, the transition process from a parliamentary to a totalitarian system can be related to the disintegration of political authority in the Weimar Republic in the years before 1933. Chancellor Brüning's use of presidential decree in the absence of a parliamentary majority to carry out his policy from 1930 is often seen as a crucial stage in this development. It is useful in this context to draw some conclusions about the authority of the state in view of the new political situation created by the rise in popular support for the Nazi movement since 1930, and to look at this problem at the regional and local level.

58. The supreme example of where prestige overcame all financial scruples was the opening of new party headquarters in Munich in January 1931. The Nazis acquired an old mansion called the Barlow Palace in the fashionable Briennerstrasse in the centre of the city. They refurnished it and called it the Brown House, which provided a strong contrast to the previous headquarters in the Schellingstrasse. The building faced the Papal Nuncio's residence on the other side of the street. Kurt Ludecke's first impression on seeing the Brown House was that it might have been 'a cardinal's palace or a Jewish banker's luxurious residence' (*I Knew Hitler*, p. 390). It was obviously intended to give the impression of a shadow chancellery.

The attitude of the Bavarian Government towards the Nazis has already been examined in relation to the prohibition of the NSDAP after the Putsch, the ban on Hitler's public speeches during 1925–27 and the restrictions on the wearing of political uniforms in the summer of 1930. With the possible exception of the last case, these issues arose before the NSDAP had made its impact as a mass movement and before the Reichstag Election of 1930 had made the Nazi assumption of power a distinct possibility. The importance of this election for the further development of the NSDAP has been discussed, but what effects did the change in the balance of political forces with increasing support for political extremism have on the position of the state authorities in the early 1930s? If the NSDAP now appeared as the main opposition force to the Weimar Republic, what relevance did Hitler's 'policy of legality' now have in the light of the new political situation?

Judging by its past policy, the Held Government was motivated by an ideological antipathy towards the Nazis and a strict desire to maintain law and order. There was no reason to suppose any major change in its basic attitude over the years, for the same key ministers remained in the same cabinet posts. This does of course assume a continuity of attitude on the part of individual ministers. New political pressures arose during the early 1930s, but they made no dramatic difference to the government's basic attitude towards the Nazis before 1933. The government depended above all on the stability of the Bavarian People's Party and the moral support of the Catholic Church, but it had two weaknesses which became more serious with the political crisis at the end of the Weimar Republic. Its position was vulnerable from above and below. Owing to the greater centralism introduced by the Weimar Constitution, the Bavarian Government depended on full accord with the national government in Berlin in such vital matters as public security. If agreement between Munich and Berlin broke down, the Bavarian Government would find itself in an exposed position, as happened in the summer of 1932. Secondly, the government was vulnerable from below because its political base could still be weakened by the rise of a mass movement which attracted wide support among the population. It is this second factor which will now be discussed.

It does seem that the government's difficulties concerning the NSDAP derived more from its inability for constitutional and political reasons to deal with the problem than from its lack of perception of the danger which threatened. Bavarian official attitudes towards the party were characterized not so much by an underestimation of its importance as by a number of curious preconceptions. Shortly after the 1930 Election, the Reich Ministry of the Interior produced a lengthy report called *The Treasonable Activities of the NSDAP*. This was an extensive study of the party's organizations and aims, documented with numerous statements of Nazi leaders. The conclusion of the report suggested that its authors had few illusions about the intentions of the Nazis:

> The NSDAP is striving with all means at its disposal to bring about the violent overthrow of the German republic based on the Weimar Constitution. It is consciously carrying on the policy which led to the Hitler Putsch in 1923, but with other tactics. Drawing on its experiences from the failure of this Putsch, the party was induced to prepare a new revolution in methodical stages, the aim of which is the creation of a pure *völkisch* state organized dictatorially ... National Socialists only participate in the parliamentary system in so far as they intend to undermine the state and its power from within, in order to make easier their attack by weakening the inner power of resistance of the state (*154*).

If this view of Hitler's 'legality' approach as merely a tactical manoeuvre was representative of the authorities concerned with the maintenance of public security—and it appeared to be so with the Bavarian authorities— what prevented action being taken in accordance with this attitude?

The lack of a clear policy towards the NSDAP was caused partly by differences among the authorities about the measures to be taken, but also by a certain confusion about how the party posed a danger to the state. Dr Held and his Minister of the Interior, Dr Stützel, agreed that the NSDAP had revolutionary aims and was a menace to political peace, but they were inhibited by doubts about the advisability of taking drastic action.

These doubts emerge quite clearly from official correspondence at the end of 1931, when the 'legality' of the NSDAP was under discussion. In December, the Munich police submitted to the Bavarian Ministry of the Interior a report on the NSDAP and SA from the standpoint of a possible prosecution. Its conclusion was that proceedings against the party on a charge of treason were not likely to meet with success on the basis of the evidence available, and that adjournment of such a case would only result in loss of face by the authorities and reinforcement of Hitler's claim of 'legality'. On the other hand, the defence organizations of the party represented 'a great danger to order and security in the state'. This matter could only be settled by an emergency decree dissolving them (*155*). The Ministry of the Interior followed up with a memorandum, which remarked that in spite of the dangers emanating from the NSDAP:

Hitler has solemnly affirmed and publicly confirmed the legality of the party. Doubts based on evidence cannot be produced against the sincerity of his intention. So long as Hitler's leadership remains undisputed and he can maintain strict discipline in the party with his authority, then there is no cause to cherish fears about illegal behaviour and activities by the party. An internal political development, which results in the disintegration of the party because its aims are not fulfilled or attained, could lead to illegal actions (*156*).

This memorandum was accompanied by a circular from Stützel to local authorities, urging the police not to remain passive in the face of extreme statements by Nazi speakers as tolerance of this behaviour 'shatters the reputation of the state' (*157*).

A first reading of this attitude to the problem would suggest that the government was more concerned with checking excesses of the Nazis for the sake of maintaining public order than with the root of the problem, namely the potential political danger presented by the NSDAP. The authorities seemed to make a curious distinction between the political leadership of the party and its military wing and violent extremists, as if the two did not reflect the same problem of ambiguity created when a revolutionary party employed legal methods to achieve control of the state. Conflicts arose within the party between those who approved these methods for tactical reasons and those who despised them. The harmful effects of such conflicts were reduced by the nature of Hitler's leadership, but his ability to curb excesses in the party by using his authority did not thereby involve any change in his ambitions.

Restraints imposed by Hitler on his more radical followers did not mean they would not get out of hand on other occasions. Whenever the Ministry of the Interior passed new measures restricting party activities, the balance within the party was automatically tilted more towards the radical elements because the policy of 'legality' began to appear discredited. In July 1931, there were several incidents in Munich arising from infringements by Nazis of the restrictions on uniforms. The police then banned the posting of uniformed sentries in front of the Brown House. The Nazis defied this regulation repeatedly, so that the police were compelled to occupy the building on 4 July. A new order was issued prohibiting all party uniforms in public until 15 July. Party officials attempted to calm irate members, and an enormous banner was hung from a window of the Brown House calling on all 'party comrades' to preserve strict discipline during the crisis for the *Führer* would make a statement on the following day. But the action against the Brown

House let loose a feeling of extreme bitterness among Nazis in the city. There were further disorders. Officials of the Ministry of the Interior and Munich police headquarters received insulting telephone calls from persons 'who were obviously members of the Nazi organization', and were even threatened with murder (*158*). Defiance of the new order on uniforms took varied and sometimes strange forms. Nazis were seen attending garden concerts in Munich wearing civvies, but carrying the *Völkischer Beobachter* 'in a conspicuous manner over their hats or unfolded in front of them, whereby they greeted each other with loud calls of Heil and other gestures' (*159*). An extension of the general uniform ban later in the year provoked a strong dissatisfaction among the SA, especially those members who were unemployed and were hoping for 'a new existence through a revolution' (*160*).

It is legitimate at this point to ask about the Bavarian Government's view of Hitler's policy of 'legality'. The memorandum of the Ministry of the Interior late in 1931 seemed to be taking Hitler at his word, which was possible as the government had in the past shown a tendency to look at the question of the NSDAP from a legalistic point of view. But one wonders how far this attitude expressed a simple willingness to believe what Hitler said, or whether the government was rather making the best of a difficult situation—namely, the Nazis were winning wide public support, and the least that could be done was to encourage them to act within the law. Whatever the reason, this does reveal the lack of understanding by the Bavarian ministers of Hitler's mentality and the wide gulf between the outlook of both sides. Hitler and the Bavarian ministers were politicians of a completely different stamp. It does therefore seem that the latter in their attitude towards Hitler's 'legality' were expressing the hope that he would replace his 'crude' political methods with the methods of conventional politics. It is also conceivable that the government was influenced by the thought that the Bavarian judiciary had already shown leniency towards Hitler once before in 1924, and they could well do so again if a case were brought against the NSDAP. Furthermore, local authorities in Bavaria had often shown a greater concern over the threat from the Communists, which no doubt helped to reinforce the government's uncertainty about the problem of the NSDAP.[59]

This is where Hitler's skill in using 'legal' tactics proved so effective, for had the government developed a totally negative picture of the Nazis as they

59. For example, the district authorities in Upper Bavaria banned more meetings of the KPD than of the NSDAP (254 against 219) in the year from May 1931 to May 1932. A high proportion of the NSDAP meetings banned was in Munich. (See monthly reports for this period in Staatsarchiv für Oberbayern, Munich, RA 3790/16842.)

had of the Communists then skilful tactics would not have helped Hitler very much. The uncertainty of the leaders of the Bavarian People's Party in this sense reflected the similar uncertainty of the Catholic Church leaders towards the NSDAP. Hitler's policy of 'legality' contributed to the doubts of the Bavarian ministers about what action to take. His policy included the avoidance of provocation of the authorities and the use of deception. When President Hindenburg used his emergency powers to issue a decree against political disturbances in March 1931, Hitler sent an order to party members not to attempt any illegal action: 'In the interests of the whole movement I decree that: the entire party machine will at once be adapted to the provisions of the emergency decree, all efforts must be exerted to prevent any violation of these provisions, even the possibility of such a violation must be dealt with as soon as possible' (*161*). The presidential decree was aimed particularly at political meetings, and was used conscientiously by the police to stamp out political violence and even to refuse permission for meetings which might arouse public excitement. Consequently, the party called off many of its large meetings in the city of Munich. Different tactics were employed to evade the restrictions on meetings. Sometimes, the Nazis chose prominent personalities like Prince August Wilhelm of the House of Hohenzollern to come and speak, or they selected ridiculous subjects for their meetings. On one occasion, street posters in Nuremberg advertised a Streicher meeting with the unlikely topic of 'The Wolf and the Seven Kid Goats'. In other towns, the Nazis deliberately chose the same subjects as those of SPD meetings which were allowed to take place (*162*).

The question of the attitudes and policy of the Bavarian Government and Hitler's policy of 'legality' cannot, however, be divorced from the main reason why action against the Nazis became increasingly difficult during the early 1930s—the growing popular support for the NSDAP and the effects this had on the political atmosphere. Hitler had this point in mind when he wrote an open letter to Chancellor Brüning in December 1931, after the latter had criticized his 'legal' methods in a broadcast:

You refuse as a 'statesman' to admit that if we come to power legally, we could then break through legality. Herr Chancellor, the fundamental thesis of democracy runs: 'All power issues from the people.' The constitution lays down the way by which a conception, an idea, and therefore an organization, must gain from the people the legitimation for the realization of its aims. But in the last resort it is the people itself which determines its constitution. Herr Chancellor, if the German nation once empowers the National Socialist movement to introduce a constitution other than that which we have today, then you cannot stop it . . . When a constitution proves itself to be useless for its life, the nation does not die—the constitution is altered *(163)*.

From the beginning of 1931, the fortnightly reports of the district offices on the political situation began to emphasize changes in the mood of the public, in particular a sense of foreboding and a growing acceptance of a Nazi political victory. The district of Neuburg an der Donau compared the public mood to that a few months before the revolutionary upheavals of 1918 *(164)*. Economic distress heightened the feeling that something calamitous was going to happen. As the authorities in Swabia commented in June 1931, 'the view that in a few months economic and political collapse will come about is widely held; the radical parties are reaping advantage for National Socialists and Communists are convinced that their hour will come still this year' *(165)*. The district of Markt Oberdorf warned the government of the public fears about the future:

Wide circles of the population are very alarmed by the inflammatory speeches, made by leaders of the National Socialists and Social Democrats at public meetings in the large cities, threatening civil war. The Government should put an end to this dangerous game before it is too late *(166)*.

This trend towards political extremism only undermined the position of the government. The problem manifested itself in various ways. Firstly, the authorities became more and more concerned about the maintenance of law and order in the light of these developments. In September 1931, the mayor of Lichtenberg near Hof commented on the problems of police control in small communities: 'It is a well-known fact that the police in small localities have a tougher time in the performance of their duties than state officials, who have no personal, economic and social contact with the population' *(167)*. The fear that police forces were unable to cope with the numbers of Nazis was apparent during an incident near Garmisch in the spring of 1932. The NSDAP was planning a ceremony on the Zugspitze, Germany's highest mountain peak, to re-erect a plaque commemorating Leo Schlageter[60] which had been taken down during the building of the Alpine railway. The district office in Garmisch feared this would draw large crowds of people for it was seen as a 'patriotic demonstration', and there

---

60. Leo Schlageter was a German saboteur in the Ruhr during the occupation by the French in 1923. He was executed by the French, and later became a Nazi martyr.

was a rumour that Hitler would turn up to speak. The ceremony was prohibited under the official regulation that no political meetings were allowed in the open air until September. In a report on the affair, the office in Garmisch remarked that the meeting would pose a threat to security, which 'the local police, even with the addition of officers from other stations, was not in a position to meet' (*168*).

The limits to the authority of the police were revealed in an account from Upper Bavaria early in October 1931 of the implementation of the ban on political meetings. The question at issue was the long-term effect of such a measure in view of the radicalization of politics:

> The suppression of meetings brought visible relief to the police forces, but the question arises how long it is possible to continue this practice and what change can be brought about in the situation by proceeding to a more moderate state of affairs without loss of prestige. The district office in Traunstein reports that the National Socialists are utterly embittered about the bans imposed on meetings, and it must be feared that this fury will be released in a violent way when meetings are allowed to resume. It should be considered whether the radical prevention of official meetings doesn't further illegality, for it is widely rumoured that the National Socialists will seize power in the Reich in October or November (*169*).

The new ban on political meetings had been approved by the government, fully conscious of the weakness of its position. At a cabinet meeting on 9 July 1931, Dr Stützel had advocated stricter regulations on the grounds that Nazi excesses in recent months had strained the resources of the police, and the cost of mustering more police units was considerable (*170*). The Ministry of the Interior had therefore issued two new decrees prohibiting all display of party uniforms and all political meetings in the open air, demonstrations and propaganda marches.[61]

Secondly, the position of the government was undermined by the Nazi Party's control of power positions, especially at the local level. Sometimes, the party's influence was apparent in small ways not always directly related to its representation in municipal bodies. Early in 1932, Karl Ladenburger, chairman of the BVP in Ingolstadt, had written a timid letter to Dr Stützel about a forthcoming NSDAP meeting there with Münchmeyer as

61. These measures went further than the previous ban on political uniforms of June 1930, which had been limited to the wearing of uniforms by large numbers in processions and at open-air meetings, and had not applied to individuals. See above, chapter 4, pp. 126–27.

speaker. He did not know whether the district office had given permission for the meeting, but was afraid to enquire 'because of the spy system which this party maintains'. Many people who were not party members were always attracted 'when this gentleman speaks', for he was well known in the town for his provocative speeches. Ladenburger felt it his duty to call the minister's attention to this, and referred to the fact that the district of Memmingen had recently banned several of Münchmeyer's meetings (*171*).

The best example of the conflict which arose when the Nazis controlled a local authority was Coburg. Coburg had become a showpiece of the Nazis since their success in winning an absolute majority of seats in the town council election in 1929. A kind of local 'seizure of power' took place during the year or two which followed. The local Nazis revealed the methods they employed to gain control of local positions.

Although the NSDAP had a majority of seats on Coburg council, the two mayors (who were not Nazis) also had voting power, which meant that the Nazis were just short of an overall majority of votes (thirteen against fourteen). After several demands for the appointment of a third mayor, their leader Franz Schwede was finally elected in August 1930 following the decision of two DNVP councillors to support the Nazi motion (*172*). As a result of Schwede's appointment another Nazi councillor joined the council, giving the NSDAP overall control. The following April, the second mayor retired because of old age so that Schwede moved up to fill the vacancy, while a few months later Schwede reached the top post after gentle pressure had been put on the first mayor to go into retirement. The post of second mayor was occupied by a Nazi, and one of the DNVP councillors was made third mayor in return for his cooperation (*173*). There followed a 'coordination' of various local offices. The Nazis sacked the head of the school board and the director of the savings bank, and took over these positions themselves. Even the town theatre came under strong Nazi influence (*174*). In October, the Nazi majority on the council injected their own newspaper the *Coburger Nationalzeitung* with a new lease of life, by resolving to use it as the only publication for official announcements (*175*).

The developments in Coburg had a powerful effect in polarizing local politics, for the left-wing parties in particular resented these successes of the Nazis. Already in August 1931, the regional government of Upper Franconia reported with some alarm at what was happening there:

In Coburg the political situation has regrettably sharpened very much. At different times gatherings and brawls have disturbed public peace and order in Coburg—by Social Democrats, Communists and National

Socialists. Of course, every party makes out that it has been provoked by the other side. On the Social Democratic side, propaganda has been carried on for years against everything nationalist in Coburg. The *Coburger Volksblatt* especially has contributed to this. It is therefore understandable if the greatly strengthened nationalist movement in Coburg has gone over to the attack in a most bitter manner. Recently, the antagonism between National Socialists and Communists has been very evident (*176*).

The most controversial aspect of this state of affairs was the question of public security. As the report underlined, the police were in a difficult position. While the Left accused them of being the 'biased tool' of the Nazi majority in the town hall, they had to carry out the orders of the state which could bring them into conflict with the local authorities (*177*).

The contrary pressures operating on the police were illustrated by the ceremony in January 1931 celebrating the sixtieth anniversary of the founding of the German Reich by Bismarck. A dispute arose afterwards when the state authorities criticized the Coburg police for not taking action in carrying out the regulations of the uniform ban. Apparently, some Nazis had turned up in uniform and some in plainclothes, but the police claimed they had not seen any closed uniformed formations. There had in fact been a heavy snow-storm, so that many of the Nazis in plainclothes had put on party caps when the blizzard began. The district office of Coburg admitted the police had had a difficult job, for 'with the whole nature of the ceremony and the nationalist outlook of the Coburgers, the police forces were faced with cir-cumstances which were by no means simple'. Moreover, Schwede had had to act as 'official representative of the local police forces' in place of the first mayor, who was away on holiday, and the second mayor, who was ill. In this capacity, he had been responsible for issuing the police with instructions for the occasion (*178*).

The case of Coburg does illustrate some of the problems facing the government at a time when the authority of the state was being called increasingly into question. Parliamentary government was proving un-workable in Germany as a result of its failure to win a secure consensus of support, of the weaknesses of the political parties and the divisive effects of the Depression on society and the political system. The government did have official control over the security forces, but the changes in political circumstances imposed in practice limits on the use of these forces in the defence of the state. The leaders of the NSDAP had planned for a possible ban on the party during 1931, but all the time the government's political base was being eroded when wide sections of the public were attracted by the alternative solution offered by the NSDAP.

Electoral success was not sufficient by itself, for the Nazis not only claimed power in the state but also intended to change the character of the state. Hence, Hitler's distinction between political aims and political methods in his statement before the Supreme Court at Leipzig in September 1930: 'In this constitutional way, we shall try to gain decisive majorities in the legislative bodies so that the moment we succeed we can give the state the form that corresponds to our ideas' (*179*). The Nazis had decided to work within the political system (that is, 'legality'), but a consequence of that decision was that they should seek to infiltrate positions of power. This was evident from their use of those positions to further their cause, their attack on traditional political organizations and their attempt to involve different groups in the party through their specialist propaganda and the development of front organizations. The policy of 'legality' was designed to delude the authorities, but it was also used to make preparations for the future Nazi state.

By early 1932, the disintegration of authority in the Weimar state had advanced rapidly since the Reichstag Election of 1930. New elections would in turn mean an even greater increase in support for the NSDAP, and a further loss of face by the Weimar Republic.

Seven

The Year of Elections
(1932)

Although the year 1932 opened with dire prognostications about the political future of Germany, it did not bring the expected assumption of power by the Nazis in spite of their continued rise in mass support. As many as five major elections were fought as the year wore on, from which the NSDAP emerged as the strongest party in the country, but at the end of the year Hitler seemed almost as remote from office as he had done at its beginning. There were two reasons for this situation.

Firstly, electoral success had been central to Hitler's plans for the acquisition of power, but his party's failure to win an absolute majority necessitated a change in these plans. Hitler was now forced to consider a coalition government, but he insisted that it would have to be one dominated by the Nazis and led by himself as Chancellor. These conditions were not granted by the President, even after the NSDAP reached 37 per cent of the national vote in the Reichstag Election in July. If the Nazis doubled their vote of 1930, their electoral achievements during 1932 had also to be judged in terms of their own expectations. Although the presidential campaigns in the spring brought a great increase in support for the Nazis, Hitler's defeat by Hindenburg was regarded as a disappointment by many of his followers. In the later elections, signs began to appear that the NSDAP had exhausted its electoral support. Its propaganda machine was geared to intensive campaigning, but not to so many elections within the space of a few months as this involved an enormous drain on resources which the party did not possess. The momentum of the NSDAP started to slacken during the summer, so that disillusionment set in especially among the radical elements in the party. This crisis accelerated after the loss of votes in the November Reichstag Election, but significantly it did not involve a challenge to Hitler's authority as *Führer*.

Secondly, the acquisition of power by the Nazis now depended on agreement with the President and the conservative forces which surrounded him. An important shift had taken place in the location of political power with the effective replacement of parliamentary with 'presidential' government. Chancellor Brüning's use of presidential decree under article 48 of the

Constitution to carry out his policies since 1930 had become more than a temporary expedient. The Reich Government was no longer dependent on a majority in the Reichstag, and consequently the President assumed the key position in the political system. Brüning hoped to win for his experiment the approval of the moderate right-wing and middle-of-the-road parties, but his dismissal by the President at the end of May opened the possibilities for a new political solution. He was replaced by a government of the conservative Right, but like the Brüning experiment it suffered from two serious weaknesses—it was dependent on the cooperation of Hindenburg, who although a venerated public personality did not have the political acumen to deal with the prolonged political crisis, and it lacked the necessary basis of popular support. It was here that the mass appeal of the Nazi movement became important, for this persuaded conservative groups (such as Army leaders, industrialists and landowners) to consider a deal with Hitler, although Hindenburg's continued reluctance to offer the Nazis anything more than a subordinate position in a government provided a temporary obstacle to Hitler's acquisition of power.

Not all elections in 1932 had been expected at the beginning of the year. Hindenburg's seven-year term as President was due to end in the spring. The Bavarian state parliament like other state parliaments would have to be re-elected in April. But the two national elections in July and November followed in each case a premature dissolution of the Reichstag. It was not without some significance that the first of these contests should have been the election for the Presidency.

The Presidential Elections, March–April 1932

The election for Reich President, which took place in two ballots on 13 March and 10 April, turned virtually into a referendum on the Weimar Republic. This owed much to the propaganda of the Nazis, who presented the election as an opportunity to put 'an end' to the political system in existence since 1919. While avoiding abuse of Hindenburg as a person, they claimed he represented the parliamentary democracy they were aiming to destroy: 'He is the candidate of those November criminals who threw our people into a chasm . . . his name is inscribed on the Law for the Protection of the Republic, the revaluation laws, the Young Plan and the emergency decrees' (*1*).

Hindenburg was renominated for the Presidency by the parties in government, including the SPD and the Catholic parties. Leaders of the Bavarian

People's Party, whose support had been decisive in his first election in 1925, expressed strong reservations about the second candidature, because of doubts that he could offer sufficient protection for the Republic against the threat from the Nazis. Fritz Schäffer, the chairman of the BVP, suggested that Brüning should become the candidate of the moderate parties, but this plan failed because of the latter's sense of obligation to Hindenburg (2). The BVP like other supporters of Hindenburg eventually swallowed these doubts. The President, who at eighty-four had little taste left for active politics, therefore became the reluctant candidate of those who sought to defend the Republic against its enemies. One had the curious situation, where the Social Democratic *Münchner Post* advocated support for the staunch conservative figure and military hero along the following lines: 'This time it is more than just a party candidature, for the great decision in the election of Reich President lies between the united opponents of the Republic and those who in the interests of the working class adhere to the republican form of government' (3).

The Nazis outdid themselves in the intensity and thoroughness of their campaign, because the polarization in this election presented them with the role of the main opposition. In Upper Bavaria, the number of their meetings and the amount of their propaganda material—including posters, leaflets and adhesive labels—was 'gigantic' (4), while in Swabia the Nazis succeeded in covering the whole area 'down to the smallest villages with countless meetings, which were generally well attended' (5). The other parties were far less active, although Brüning went on a whirlwind tour of the country to drum up support for the President. The Hindenburg campaign was inhibited by the lack of real unity among the various parties which supported his re-election. Nevertheless, BVP supporters generally voted for the President for, as the *Bayerischer Kurier* pointed out, he offered 'security against civil war', although a few Catholic groups like the 'Election Committee of Catholic Action' in Bamberg refused to follow their party's line because Hindenburg was a Protestant (6).

A new tone of virulence was noticeable in this campaign. The Nazis used intimidation in many places against people who were working for the re-election of the President which had a dampening effect on their propaganda activities. The Hindenburg Election Committee complained of instances where Nazi terrorism was so prevalent that people were reluctant to show they favoured the President. This was especially noticeable in communities where the Nazis dominated local politics or held the position of mayor. People feared that 'Hindenburg will not take vengeance for a vote cast for Hitler, while Hitler will seek reprisals after the expected seizure of power for each vote in favour of Hindenburg' (7). In some localities, SA squads went round in lorries tearing down Hindenburg posters. The police had difficulty in tracing the offenders because the SA did not employ local members for the job, rather men who were unknown to the local authorities.

An illustration of the NSDAP campaign methods was the case of election rigging in the village of Dietramszell near Bad Tölz. Dietramszell had only a few hundred voters, but was well known as Hindenburg's summer hunting resort. In order to spite the President, the Nazis brought along some of their best speakers to this otherwise insignificant place and succeeded in beating Hindenburg by 228 votes to 157 in the first ballot, causing malicious jubilation in the party press. During the second campaign, a journalist from Munich went along to the village to do a 'story' on Hindenburg's popularity. He naïvely thought he might be able to tip the scales in his hero's favour by distributing to the needy of the village 400 marks on behalf of a 'Hindenburg friend'. Recipients had to sign receipts, some of which were unfortunately marked 'Hindenburg Charity'. This caused nothing but embarrassment to Hindenburg's supporters, as it gave the Nazis an excuse to accuse the President of trying to buy himself back to power. The *Völkischer Beobachter* published articles on three consecutive days about the incident in Dietramszell, including a picture of one of the receipts (8).

The arrogant behaviour of the Nazis was influenced by their belief that they were about to enjoy political power at the top. A victory for Hitler would not only have given him wide executive powers, but would also have had a powerful psychological effect on German politics at a time when the situation had become very fluid. Hindenburg's clear lead over Hitler in the first ballot on 13 March, which cancelled out any chance of a win for the latter in the run-off election four weeks later, produced a strong emotional setback for the Nazis. While Hindenburg just fell short of an overall majority with 49·6 per cent of the national vote, his lead over Hitler with 30·1 per cent was decisive. The difference between the votes for the two main candidates[1] was most pronounced in the Catholic areas of the country. In Lower Bavaria, for instance, Hindenburg won 69·9 per cent against Hitler's 22·2 per cent.

There were a number of reasons for the surprising outcome of the first ballot. The personal factor was important, as Hindenburg benefited from being the incumbent which in the case of the Presidency made an impression on the voters. Nazi propaganda against the Weimar 'system' did not rub off on Hindenburg as much as had been hoped, for Hindenburg symbolized

1. There were two other important candidates in the first ballot—Thälmann for the Communists, and Duesterberg for the Nationalists—but their vote was small compared with that for Hindenburg and Hitler.

stability to wide sections of the electorate.[2] The President also owed his high vote to the success of the different parties backing him in encouraging their voters to support Hindenburg despite the many handicaps facing their campaign. This was certainly true of the Bavarian People's Party.[3] The voting was therefore conducted along personal and party lines, but was above all dominated by the issue of the future of the political system. Such was the state of polarization that German politics had reached by 1932.

There were two possible criteria for judging the result of the Presidential Election—either in terms of expectations, in which case the Nazis lost on 13 March, or in terms of voting trends. Compared with the Reichstag Election of 1930, the vote for Hitler in March 1932 represented a great increase in popular support for the Nazis in the space of one-and-a-half years.[4] Hitler had won almost one-third of the national vote, but there were strong geographical variations in the voting. Hindenburg carried Lower Bavaria with a sweeping majority, although support for Hitler was high there in the flood areas of the Danube basin and in towns like Straubing, where civil servants felt aggrieved over a recent presidential decree reducing their salaries (9).

The main dividing line in the voting was confessional. This was apparent at different levels throughout the country. Hitler won the largest vote in only seven of the thirty-five electoral districts in Germany, which were all strong Protestant areas like Mecklenburg, Thuringia and Schleswig-Holstein. His support within Bavaria was again highest in Protestant rural areas with absolute majorities in eleven of the seventeen administrative districts of Middle Franconia. The confessional factor even operated at the lowest level. In Lower Franconia, a predominantly Catholic region, it was observed in the first ballot that 'communities with a Catholic population gave an overwhelming majority of votes for Hindenburg, and only in a few purely

2. In spite of Hindenburg's passive role during the election, the campaign in his favour succeeded in putting across the image of the father-figure to the voters. One poster featured the President as a rock-like figure towering over his rival candidates, who were either planning the execution of political opponents (like Hitler) or taking orders from Moscow (like Thälmann). Another poster urged voters to 'elect Hindenburg, elect the man, the leader of the people'. It drew a contrast between 'Fieldmarshal von Hindenburg' and 'privy councillor Hitler', pointing out that Kaiser Wilhelm I had led the German Reich up to his ninety-first birthday and 'according to Bismarck's testimony really did govern'.
3. The BVP campaigned vigorously for Hindenburg. In the Catholic city of Regensburg, the BVP held eleven meetings during the first election compared with nineteen of the NSDAP. The Social Democrats also held seven on behalf of the President. Hindenburg won 34,000 votes here and Hitler less than 10,000. (Report of Regensburg police, 15 March 1932, Staatsarchiv Amberg, Reg. v. Opf./14288.)
4. This was a valid comparison as the personal factor (support for the *Führer*) had played an important part in voting for the NSDAP in previous elections.

Protestant communities was the vote for Hitler greater' (*10*). This tendency became more marked there in the second ballot, when the increase in the vote for Hitler came chiefly from the Protestant communities (*11*). In the Upper Palatinate, which like Lower Bavaria was strongly for Hindenburg, the only area which gave a stronger vote to Hitler was the isolated Protestant district of Sulzbach (*12*).[5]

The confessional factor was more pronounced in voting for the Presidential Election than in parliamentary elections, but how did it relate to voting behaviour on personal and party lines? The latter can be explained simply as a result of the strong support for Hindenburg from the Bavarian People's Party. There was less inclination among strong Catholics to rebel against the decision of the BVP than there had been in 1925, because Hindenburg was no longer seen as the representative of conservative Prussian forces and had become identified with the *status quo*. The connection between the personal factor and confession was less clear, because Hindenburg was ironically a Protestant. It may have helped that Hindenburg's chief spokesman in the election campaign had been Dr Brüning, who was leader of the Catholic Centre Party, but the decisive point was that Hindenburg was recognized by the electorate as being a basically religious man rather than a Protestant. Hitler was by contrast seen in strong Catholic circles as a heretic. This view of the Presidential contest in confessional terms was argued by the BVP organ, the *Bayerischer Kurier*, which maintained that Hindenburg's Protestant background did not matter because of his 'historic personality and his conduct of office completely above parties'. Devout Catholics should have no inhibitions about supporting Hindenburg, for he was 'a believer and from his positive belief comes the recognition of the equality of political rights of the different confessions, the rejection of all confessional conflict and the national cooperation of the different confessions' (*13*). Hindenburg was seen by Catholics as a guarantee of their confessional rights. It was clear from this that the confessional factor was prominent in voting behaviour

5. The importance of the confessional factor is confirmed by examining a district like Nördlingen, where support for Hitler and Hindenburg was almost evenly divided—7,875 votes for Hindenburg and 7,505 for Hitler in the March election. The district consisted of eighty-five communities (fifty-four Protestant and thirty-one Catholic). Confession was an important factor in social integration, for each community with its few hundred inhabitants was entirely Catholic or entirely Protestant. This tendency to conform operated also in voting, for the Catholic communities voted heavily for Hindenburg just as they voted absolutely for the BVP in parliamentary elections. The same was true of the vote for Hitler in the Protestant communities, although some of the Protestant vote also went to Duesterberg, who won as much as 1,011 in the district. (Information from the *Nördlinger Zeitung*, 14 March 1932, and the register of inhabitants (*Einwohnerbuch*) for district of Nördlingen for 1926, pp. 95–198, in the Stadtarchiv Nördlingen.)

in the Presidential Election because it coincided with voting along personal and party lines.

Hindenburg won his absolute majority in the second ballot on 10 April. Voting tendencies were very little different from the first election, but even before the second ballot it was already evident that the Nazis would not achieve a short cut to political power by winning the highest office in the state. The pull of Hindenburg's image among the German public and traditional voting patterns were sufficiently strong to withstand their efficient propaganda machine.

The Ban on the SA and SS

After the first ballot for the Presidency in March, disclosures had been made of plans by the SA to seize power in the event of Hitler winning the vote. On 4 April, the Bavarian Government issued an official statement claiming that before election day 'both the leaders and the rank and file of the National Socialists were as firm as a rock in their conviction that Herr Hitler was bound to be elected, and that at midnight on 13 March he must seize the machinery of state in Bavaria' (*14*). These charges were similar to the ones made by Severing, the Prussian Minister of the Interior, against the NSDAP in Prussia. These revelations, which added considerable bitterness to the second presidential campaign, showed how strong were the expectations of a Hitler victory among party members, but they also underlined the impatience of the SA with the process of winning power through electoral success.

The Bavarian Prime Minister amplified these charges in a statement to the parliament four days later. He claimed that they were based on 'serious official material', and did not consist of rumours or spies' reports. The Bavarian Government had exercised 'great forbearance in the past', but the situation had now become intolerable because 'illegitimate pressure was being brought to bear especially on public officials, so that nobody dared any longer to do his duty'. Held concluded by saying that in publicizing these plans he had done his simple duty, which was 'to see that our officials should be rescued at all costs from the system of terrorism', which was being employed so that 'others should be able to seize power in our state' (*15*). Held's firm reaction reflected the abhorrence of the violent element in the Nazi Party among leading circles of the BVP, and their suspicions about Hitler's assertions that he did not intend to act outside the law. As the *Bayerischer Kurier* insisted, 'we have already expressed our conjecture several times that the National Socialists would not have remained legal in the event of an election victory on 13 March', and that they had plotted to 'seize the entire state machinery by force and fill all positions of control with Nazi party members' (*16*).

The government's evidence included detailed reports from district offices in Bavaria of the mobilization of the SA in the days before the election on 13 March. The size of the SA membership had expanded enormously during the previous months, so that these manoeuvres were taken with the utmost seriousness by local authorities. It was reported from Garmisch that speakers had made a habit of announcing that Hitler's victory was certain, which would produce jubilant shouts from the audience and cheers for 'The Reich President of 13 March'. The district of Altötting noted that Hitler's supporters were so certain of success that they were already allotting local offices among themselves weeks before the voting took place; while the district office in Freising commented that agitated mayors were ringing up about Nazi plans to occupy their own posts and those of town clerk, manager of the savings bank and officials in the post office (*17*).

Local authorities were well informed in advance about the Nazi plans. They were even able to quote the names of Nazis who would be appointed. Dr Karl Scharnagl, the Mayor of Munich, wrote to the Minister of the Interior on 29 March sending him a full report on the conspiracy by the Nazis in his electoral district. Some of the appointments would have brought an interesting change in the social background of local officials. According to Scharnagl, the mayor of Schleching was to be replaced by a master shoe-maker called Seegers while another party member called Dillis, a former engine-driver who ran a small coffee shop, was to take over as local magistrate (*18*). Numerous SA groups were reported as seen gathering during the last week of the election campaign carrying rucksacks and provided with food and clothes for a couple of days. The SA claimed it was preparing to stamp out an expected counterstrike from the Communists following a Nazi victory. SA groups were awaiting orders in the countryside outside Ingolstadt to march on the town and 'restore law and order against radical left-wing excesses'. The police confiscated a cache of arms from storm-troopers near Rosenheim, including one light machine-gun, three infantry rifles, 1,350 sticks of ammunition and eighty-four Very pistols (*19*).

The Munich police chief opposed the idea of banning such activities during future elections, because it was not possible to maintain guard over all taverns (the usual meeting-place of party members) without 'splitting up the police forces' (*20*). He viewed the problem in terms of public security, but ignored the political effects of these incidents. In the absence of clear public information at the time, rumours spread rapidly and were encouraged by over-confident statements from Nazi leaders. The official Bavarian news agency made much of the speech of the branch leader in Sprendlingen, who was reported as saying that 'by midnight tonight Hitler will have the Republic in the hollow of his hand; the Iron Front[6] will no doubt declare a general strike, but it will come too late for at two minutes past twelve all public offices, such as the town hall and the post office, will be occupied by our storm detachments' (21). During the evening of election day, rumours circulated that the SA and SS were according to the police intending to 'occupy all public buildings in Munich, especially the telephone and telegraph office, on the stroke of midnight' (22). In some places, Nazis made little secret of their intention of settling debts with political opponents. The SA leader in Immenreuth dropped the remark that after Hitler's election the priest in nearby Kemnath, a noted opponent of the NSDAP, would be 'stripped naked and flogged on the market square' (23). It was small wonder that these revelations about the plans of the Nazis helped to poison the political atmosphere in many localities.

Dr Held had calculated that the vote for Hitler in the run-off election could be harmed by giving publicity to the Nazi plans, but there was little sign of this judging by the result. Support for Hitler increased in most areas in the second ballot, except for the slight drop in Upper Bavaria which the authorities attributed partly to this cause for 'sensible elements felt alienated from this party because of the planned occupation of offices and posts' (24). Opponents of the Nazis exploited the whole affair. The socialist *Münchner Post*, always quick to produce evidence to damn the Nazis, was the first to air the rumours about the Nazi plot in public. Two days before the first ballot, the paper published an order from Roehm of 15 January giving marching orders to the SA complete with a map of the various routes to be taken, under the heading 'Ready for Civil War—the Marching Plan of the Nazis' (25).

The affair was largely an independent action of the SA under Roehm, backed by the spontaneous enthusiasm of Hitler's supporters during the election campaign. The political leaders of the party apparently had no direct hand in the plans, although their propaganda had miscalculated by committing itself so much to a Hitler victory. The immediate result of the exposure of these plans was that the Reich Government found sufficient reason to proclaim a ban on the SA and SS. The state governments, led by Prussia and Bavaria, had for some time been urging Groener, the Reich Minister of the

6. The Iron Front was a Social Democratic organization set up to defend the Republic. Its leaders included government ministers, trade union officials and officers of the Reichsbanner.

Interior, to take action against the military organizations of the NSDAP. Brüning now decided to make a move, and on 13 April the government issued a decree banning both organizations on the grounds that they were 'a source of constant disturbance for peaceful citizens' and constituted 'a private army whose very existence represents a state within a state'. The ban applied to all sub-organizations of the SA and SS, and involved the police in a gigantic task of confiscation of storm-troopers' uniforms, flags, tents and other equipment.

The government's decision confirmed the fears of Hitler that illegal action by the SA would provoke the authorities into taking such drastic measures. The public generally reacted to the news of the ban with relief because it promised a change from the prospect of increasing political violence and maybe civil warfare, but this feeling was not held by everybody. Right-wing circles were offended by the ban, because they saw it as discriminating against the NSDAP instead of applying to the military organizations of other parties. The view that the ban was an expression of 'black-red party domination' (that is, of the Catholic and Social Democratic parties) was even held among sections of the bourgeoisie which did not belong to the NSDAP (26). Although the action confiscating SA equipment was generally carried out smoothly, there were cases of hostility towards the state police. Sometimes, this ill feeling showed itself in a contemptuous attitude towards authority. In Bayreuth, the Nazis were well-prepared because they knew of the ban a day before it was announced. This allowed them to remove all compromising material overnight. When the police officers arrived to search SA headquarters the following day, they were received with unusual politeness and were willingly shown every room in the building. All the cupboards they searched were entirely empty (27).

The ban on the SA and SS was criticized in military circles, and was used by Brüning's opponents to bring about the fall of his government six weeks later. The ban was a necessary reaction to the threat from the Nazis, but the difficulties it aroused underlined the fact that it was introduced rather late in the day. The timing of its announcement was not very opportune. State elections were taking place in Bavaria and other states little over a week later, and the Nazis hoped to collect a sympathy vote.

The Bavarian State Election, 24 April 1932

In spite of the signs of electoral weariness among the voters, the Nazis were determined to exert themselves to the full in the elections to the Bavarian state parliament on 24 April. Their aim was to become the strongest party in the state in order to assume power or at least make government by the Bavarian People's Party unworkable. The Bavarian Government had long shown a particular severity towards the Nazis, who were now out for revenge. Their campaign was not restricted to Bavaria, for state elections were taking place on the same day in Prussia, Württemberg and Anhalt. Since four-fifths of the German electorate were once again going to the polls, these elections were almost the equivalent of a general election.

The Nazis had as usual planned their campaign long in advance. As early as June 1931, the *Gau* of Munich–Upper Bavaria held a meeting of district leaders at the Brown House to discuss preparations for the election. On 9 April 1932, Hermann Esser issued final propaganda instructions, which mapped out chronologically the course of the campaign (*28*). From 12 to 23 April, the party would increase the momentum of its agitation through a 'wave of meetings' to be addressed only by South German speakers, and would concentrate on the BVP strongholds of Upper and Lower Bavaria and Lower Franconia. Special slogans were devised for these meetings such as 'Black and Red are the Death of the Bavarians—Hitler is the Saviour' (*Schwarz und Rot macht die Bayern tot—Hitler ist der Retter*), or 'Away with the Black-Red Sinecure Coalition—Hitler will save Bavaria'. From 14 to 16 April, a special number of the *NS Landpost* would be distributed which would show a particular regard for 'Bavarian peasant peculiarities'. There would follow six further stages of the campaign, including the distribution of leaflets in letter-boxes in all towns, an appeal by Ritter von Epp to former soldiers of the Bavarian Army and on election eve a special number of the Bavarian edition of the *Völkischer Beobachter*. By way of summarizing its appeal, the propaganda directive concluded: 'The NSDAP is not only a good German party, it is above all a good Bavarian party; all top candidates on the party list are without exception native Bavarians; the headquarters of the party is not in Berlin, but in Munich.'

The NSDAP concentrated its attack on the Bavarian People's Party. The Nazis hoped to benefit from their publicity efforts in the two presidential campaigns, and to weaken the BVP by winning a high vote in the rural areas. Party speakers were required to emphasize that the NSDAP was in a stronger position to defend Bavarian interests at the national level, because it had 107 deputies in the Reichstag and would have as many as 200 after the next election, while the BVP had only nineteen deputies. Notwithstanding the prodigious efforts of the Nazis to retain the interest of the voters, the latter continued to show signs of boredom with politics. This was evident from the lower attendance at public meetings. The Swabian authorities recorded that the turnout was 'moderate', and that large crowds only appeared when Hitler or other well-known Nazi personalities spoke (29). On 16 and 17 April, Hitler addressed mass rallies in Augsburg, Donauwörth, Rosenheim, Traunstein and Miesbach. In Donauwörth 6,000 people were present, and at the other places the halls were overfilled. Some other Hitler meetings were banned by district authorities owing to the lack of adequate police forces.

A large increase in NSDAP representation in the state parliament was inevitable. The previous parliament, which had been elected in 1928 before the expansion of support for the NSDAP, hardly represented the new balance of political forces. The position of the parties in the new state parliament (compared with the 1928 parliament) was as is shown in Table 5.

Table 5   *Result of the Bavarian State Election, 24 April 1932*

	1928		1932	
	Seats	%	Seats	%
BVP	46	31·6	45	32·6
NSDAP	9	6·3	43	32·5
SPD	34	24·2	20	15·4
BBMB	17	11·5	9	6·5
KPD	5	3·9	8	6·6
DNVP	13	9·3	3	3·3

Source: Meinrad Hagmann, *Der Weg ins Verhängnis, Reichstags-wahlergebnisse 1919 bis 1933 besonders aus Bayern* (1946), pp. 28–9.

The result of the Bavarian election underlined the political landslide that had occurred during the past four years, for the NSDAP won almost five times the number of its seats in the previous parliament. The party's vote came very close to that of the BVP, but it had failed to break the latter's hold over its Catholic electorate. The gains of the NSDAP were made entirely at the expense of the remaining parties, for the BVP won 200,000 more votes than in 1928. The surprising stability of the BVP, already evident in the 1930 Reichstag Election, was very noticeable in strong Catholic cities like Würzburg, where its vote rose from 15,700 (1928) to 21,600. Even in Protestant cities like Nuremberg, it still registered a slight increase in support. Although the NSDAP vote in Catholic areas was not inconsiderable, its greatest increases were made in the Protestant regions of Middle Franconia (45·6 per cent) and Upper Franconia (44·2 per cent), where it was now by far the strongest party.

The election result further weakened the position of the Held Government. It had continued to govern as a minority 'business administration' since 1930, but its only chance now of acquiring a majority in the state parliament was through a coalition with either the Nazis or the Social Democrats. Dr Held made it explicitly clear immediately after the election that a pact with the former was completely out of the question. A coalition with the Social Democrats seemed more of a possibility, because there were precedents for an alliance between the moderate Left and a Catholic party. The Social Democrats might well have been interested in a coalition because of the collapse of their support in the Prussian state election, but this failed to materialize owing to the intransigent opposition of Dr Held, who adhered to the view of many in his party that there was a basic ideological cleavage between the two parties. This question caused serious divisions among BVP leaders, leading to strained relations between Held and Fritz Schäffer, the party chairman. Even Dr Georg Heim, a founder of the BVP, voiced the idea of some in the party that there should be a change in Prime Minister to facilitate such a coalition (*30*). But a BVP–SPD coalition would have enjoyed only a bare majority in the state parliament, and in the end Dr Held followed the advice of his close political friend Georg Wohlmuth to revert to the previous state of affairs.

The Held Government continued as a minority administration, but this hardly helped its position in the forthcoming constitutional crisis it had to face in the summer of 1932.

Conflict between Bavaria and the Central Government

Traditional antagonism between Munich and Berlin flared up in June 1932 over the decision of the new Papen Government to lift the ban on the SA and SS imposed by its predecessor in April. The revocation of the ban on 14 June was followed by many protests, but nowhere was opposition to the government's move stronger than in Bavaria, where the authorities believed this would lead to political violence on a scale greater than ever before. On the day the ban was lifted, one foreign correspondent wrote that 'in the South disturbances are feared from the reappearance of the Nazi uniform . . . the threat has been heard that if the Reich raises the ban on the Brown Army, Bavaria and possibly other states would reimpose it for their territory' (*31*).

Bavarian attitudes were bound to be affected by the absence of goodwill towards the new government in Munich political circles. The manner of Brüning's dismissal as Chancellor by the President at the end of May, following intrigues by military and landed interests, had aroused considerable ill feeling in Bavaria. Brüning was a Centre Party leader, and his replacement by Franz von Papen was not welcomed. Papen had been a Centre Party deputy, but he was seen now as a representative of the national conservative outlook because of his close connections with the land-owning class in Eastern Germany. The Hindenburg–Brüning team had been taken in Bavaria as a sign of stability in the leadership of the national government. The revival of confidence occasioned by Hindenburg's re-election as President in April was severely shaken.[7]

The Bavarian Government was prepared to take a firm stand over the issue consistent with its previous attitude to the wearing of political uniforms, but its scope for manoeuvre was limited by the fact that it could not act in open defiance of the President's decree lifting the ban on the two Nazi organizations. It attempted to find a constitutional loophole in its right to 'police the state' (*Landespolizeirecht*). On 16 June, the Held Government declared that its prohibition of July 1931 on all open-air meetings and processions, irrespective of whether those who took part in them wore uniform or not, remained in force in spite of the presidential decree. Support came from the government in Baden, which also kept its ban on party uniforms. Feeling in the South was all the more adamant because of disapproval of Papen's attitude of compromise towards the Nazis, such as his promise to lift the SA ban in return for Nazi toleration of his government in the Reichstag. Fritz Schäffer made a speech at a large BVP rally in Munich comparing the situation to 1923. He saw Hindenburg in the role of Gustav von Kahr, who had played the dangerous game of cooperation with the forces of the extreme Right. The Reich President had been re-elected to save Germany from a party dictatorship by Hitler, but he now seemed to have lost all sense of purpose (*32*).

The intransigence of the Bavarian Government released a storm of abuse from the Nazis. The *Völkischer Beobachter* warned Berlin not to tolerate any trouble from Bavarian 'separatists', and proclaimed that 'we cannot endure it when the unity of the Reich is destroyed in Bavaria'. The paper urged the

---

7. The reports of district authorities in Bavaria emphasized the feeling of depression among the public over the news of Brüning's dismissal. Feeling among official circles in Munich was so great that Dr Schätzel, the BVP Minister for Posts, was withdrawn from the Reich Government. Relations between Munich and Berlin were not improved by Papen's choice of Dr Gürtner as Reich Minister of Justice. Gürtner had been Bavarian Minister of Justice since 1922, but his relations with the BVP had become extremely strained. Erwein von Aretin, the Bavarian aristocrat, had an interview with Gürtner in Berlin shortly after the latter's appointment and commented: 'It was evident that Gürtner could not get over the ill feeling, which he had accumulated against Held and Schäffer during his ten years as minister in Bavaria.' (Aretin, *Krone und Ketten*, p. 375.)

Reich Government: 'One cannot negotiate with these gentlemen, they must be dealt with.' In a later editorial, Rosenberg even suggested that Berlin should despatch a Reich Commissioner to Bavaria with unrestricted powers and that the Bavarian Government should be put 'behind bars' (33). It was interesting to note the change in the public attitude of the NSDAP towards Bavarian federalism, for on earlier occasions the party had been careful to avoid offending the government in Munich. It now felt strong enough to defy the Bavarian authorities and take the side of the Reich.

There followed unpleasant scenes in the Bavarian state parliament on 17 June, when Nazi deputies appeared in their brownshirts in defiance of the ban of June 1930 on the wearing of party uniforms during sessions. When the president of the parliament ruled this out of order, the Nazis retorted with loud shouts and by singing the party song. He then proceeded to name the offending deputies but was interrupted by cheers for Hitler, the stamping of feet and shouts of 'Down with the Held Government'. There was general disorder, and the sitting had to be suspended. When it was later resumed, some of the Nazi deputies still appeared in uniform. The uproar started once again, so that the police had to be summoned to throw the Nazis out of the chamber. The NSDAP was suspended from the state parliament for twenty sittings. The Bavarian Cabinet met immediately after this incident and decided to issue a general ban on uniforms throughout Bavaria, to take effect at once and to remain in force until 30 September (34).

The new measure provoked a massive demonstration by Nazis in the streets of Munich on 19 June. Five thousand storm-troopers attempted to march to the residence of Dr Held, and wore full uniform in defiance of the ban. Although they were prevented by the police from reaching the Prime Minister's house, they succeeded in carrying out their organized demonstrations for nearly half an hour before reinforcements enabled the police to disperse the demonstrators. About 470 Nazis were arrested, but as the Munich correspondent of *The Times*, London, recorded:

A state of intense excitement and serious disquiet prevails in Munich in consequence of today's events. The strength and resources of the Brown Army have been demonstrated in a manner which Munich has not witnessed since the armed Hitler rising in 1923. The authorities have the situation completely in hand, but the difficulty of coping with so large a force of organized demonstrators is regarded as significant (35).

The fear of renewed political violence had been uppermost in the mind of the Bavarian Government. This was made clear in Dr Held's speech to the state parliament on 25 June, claiming that there had been less bloodshed in Bavaria than elsewhere in the country because of the measures taken by his government. But it was unlikely that Held would go to the limit in opposing the Reich Government. As the *Times* correspondent put it: 'A complete breach with the Reich would leave the Bavarian Government to face a resentful and excited Nazi force, estimated at about 70,000 with a police strength of fewer than half that number, whereas by giving way under protest the Bavarian Government could transfer to the Reich the responsibility for the preservation of order in Bavaria' (*36*). This is what happened. On 29 June, a new presidential decree restricted the ban by the states on uniforms and demonstrations to individual cases. The Held Government did not challenge this decree, and issued a statement on 1 July recognizing that the main responsibility for upholding law and order lay with the Reich.

The government's behaviour during the crisis had also been determined by its traditional strict adherence to constitutional law, but a more ominous lesson for the future was provided by the combination of pressure from the NSDAP in Bavaria on the one hand and from the Reich Government on the other. On 20 July, the worst Bavarian suspicions about the centralistic tendencies of the Papen Government were confirmed when the Chancellor deposed the Prussian Government and took over direct control of the largest state in Germany. The Bavarian Government applied to the Supreme Court in Leipzig against this decision, but political events were moving too fast. The new Reichstag election campaign was already in full swing, and there was every reason to expect a large increase in the national vote for the NSDAP.

The Reichstag Election, 31 July 1932

Brüning's replacement by von Papen served Hitler's purpose in another way, for the new Chancellor had promised the Nazis to call new elections to the Reichstag if they cooperated with his government. This he promptly did on 4 June. The election date was set for 31 July, as long as eight weeks ahead, but the Nazis had kept their propaganda machine well oiled since the elections of March and April.

A couple of weeks after the Bavarian state elections, *Gau* leader Adolf Wagner had sent instructions to branch leaders emphasizing that electoral success should not be taken as a reward for hard work, but as a propaganda triumph to be exploited. More people should be persuaded to join the party, for its rise in votes can only be made full use of when we cultivate our voting masses through the most intensive individual canvassing, so that they are always held securely in line. In this way, we can ultimately make an activist out of a voter. It is clear to me that the fatigue, which understandably sets in after an election, must give way as soon as possible to increased activity, for the National Socialist may know no fatigue (37).

Branches should give more attention to 'personal' propaganda. They should hold regular 'discussion evenings' for those who had recently voted for the NSDAP, sending them individual written invitations.

Once the election campaign started, the Nazis sought to vary their propaganda methods in an effort to check electoral weariness among the voters, which could harm the party as it depended much on the support of people who had not voted regularly, if at all, in previous elections. Goebbels had noted in his diary on 5 May that 'for the next few months the main burden of the work will rest on propaganda; our technique has to be worked out to the minutest particulars; only the most up-to-date and expert methods will help us to victory' (38). There had been signs that voters had become tired of attending endless party meetings during the campaigns in March and April. The NSDAP therefore decided to experiment with new devices in order to retain the interest of the electorate.

Goebbels elaborated his ideas in a special memorandum for the election (39). The Propaganda Department would as before organize an intensive programme of meetings. The *Gau* offices should make efficient use of party speakers by seeing to it that 'a good second speaker is in reserve, that the exact times of commencement are fixed and cars are ready for the use of speakers'. Speakers should be given every attention as making 'repeated speeches at mass meetings is extremely exhausting'. Goebbels then stressed the importance of new techniques in mass agitation. Hitler had made an impression with his use of an aeroplane to travel to meetings around the country during the second presidential campaign in April. The idea had been that of Goebbels, who had now come to an arrangement with the German Commercial Air Company to provide aeroplanes for the use of *Gaue*. The party should make better use of microphones and loudspeakers,[8] as well as sound films and gramophone records of speeches by prominent party leaders. The presidential campaigns had shown that street posters were no longer so effective. The *Gau* of Munich–Upper Bavaria now urged its propagandists to distribute their material 'not on the streets but in houses and places of business' (40).

8. Microphones and loudspeakers had come into general use at Nazi meetings during 1930.

The NSDAP faced a tactical problem in this campaign, for the recent change of government in Berlin to one with a more conservative image prevented the NSDAP from mounting a full offensive against it. Papen hoped to take some of the ideological wind out of the Nazis' sails, and force them into a position of participation in his plan to create a front of right-wing forces. Goebbels' answer to this problem was to emphasize that this election would be a 'reckoning' with the whole record of the Weimar Republic:

> The forthcoming Reichstag Election has the significance of a decisive battle . . . In this Reichstag Election the decision will not be made about the policy of the cabinet of von Papen, but about the actions of those governments and parties which are responsible for the November crimes of 1918 and which as the system from then until today have to carry the responsibility for the greatest historical collapse of the last centuries (*41*).

The change of emphasis in propaganda resulted in greater efforts to win the support of the workers in some places. The *Gau* office of Munich–Upper Bavaria, which saw the SPD as 'the last prop supporting the Bavarian People's Party', arranged for SA demonstrations in all places with a working-class population during the last week of the campaign in order to express the party's 'socialist purpose in life' (*42*). The Nazis wished to avoid being associated too much with the new 'reactionary' government in Berlin.

The SA took a major part in this campaign with frequent marches through the streets of towns to attract those people who were more inclined to stay at home than attend meetings. They felt particular annoyance when the Papen Government decided to ban all demonstrations on 18 July, after many violent and often bloody incidents during the previous weeks. The campaign did quieten down after this, but tension remained below the surface. Public enthusiasm for the Nazis was very evident. The party made particular efforts to attract young people who had become eligible to vote during the year. Specialist propaganda went one stage further with the selection of special party speakers to appeal to young voters (*Jungwählerredner*). A Hitler meeting in Bad Tölz on 6 July brought out a crowd of 5,000, in spite of one of those violent midsummer storms typical of this region near the Alps. Many people including tourists attending nearby spas came from the surrounding area, and waited patiently in the rain to hear the Nazi leader who arrived several hours late by train from Munich (*43*). On election eve, Hitler attracted a crowd at Kempten of nearly 18,000 people, including some from across the

Austrian border (*44*). That same evening, Hitler flew to Nuremberg to address a huge rally in the Stadium there.

The NSDAP became by far the largest party in Germany in the vote on 31 July, although it fell well short of an absolute majority. The party now had 230 seats in the Reichstag with 13,769,000 votes, representing 37·3 per cent of the total vote. The overall vote for the NSDAP in Bavaria was lower than the national average, but there were marked differences between its support in the three Bavarian electoral districts: Lower Bavaria 20·4 per cent, Upper Bavaria–Swabia 27·1 per cent and Franconia 39·9 per cent. Although these results confirmed to some extent previous voting trends, it is nevertheless worth looking at the sources of the rise in electoral support for the NSDAP in this election as it almost doubled that of 1930 (*45*).

1. *Rural Support*

The greatest rise in support for the party came from the rural voters. This is clear from the comparison with the 1930 results in Swabia and Middle Franconia which is shown in Table 6.

Table 6   *Rise in rural electoral support for the NSDAP, 1930–32*

	September 1930 %	*July 1932* %
Swabia		
Towns	15·9	27·8
Rural Districts	13·5	31·1
Middle Franconia		
Towns	24·4	39·0
Rural Districts	22·7	59·8

Source: Statistisches Jahrbuch für den Freistaat Bayern, 1930, pp. 570–79, and *Zeitschrift des Bayerischen Statistischen Landesamts*, 1932, pp. 458–65.

These votes reflected the concentration on rural propaganda since the 1930 Election, although the NSDAP was more successful in the predominantly Protestant area of Middle Franconia than in the predominantly Catholic area of Swabia. In both cases, the Nazis took many votes from the peasant parties. The BBMB lost half the vote it had retained in 1930, while the support of the *Deutsches Landvolk* went almost entirely to the NSDAP. In Middle Franconia, the vote of the *Deutsches Landvolk* fell from 32·2 per cent in 1930 to 0·1 per cent in 1932.

2. Confession

The sharp rise in Nazi support in Protestant rural areas is evident from the previous figures. The Bavarian People's Party, which had conducted a vigorous campaign, still continued to provide a strong confessional barrier to the advance of the NSDAP. The BVP gains in this election—its vote increased in Lower Bavaria from 38·4 per cent to 43·2 per cent, and in the Upper Palatinate from 49·1 per cent to 52·7 per cent—came mainly from the rural areas. The BVP won some support from the BBMB, in addition to the NSDAP. Although this result generally confirmed the reliability of BVP voters, there were signs that even the traditional support of this party was affected by economic circumstances. Some places in its stronghold of Lower Bavaria recorded that women voters had withdrawn their support from the BVP because of 'the increasingly deep and acute distress affecting the household budget' (46). Even the confessional barrier had its limits. While the NSDAP won a much higher vote in Protestant areas, its support among Catholic voters was nevertheless large. Among the nine rural districts in Swabia with above-average support for the NSDAP in that region (that is, over 31·1 per cent), five of these had Protestant populations of less than 5 per cent. Obviously, most of the 615,600 Nazi voters in the Catholic regions of Bavaria outside Middle and Upper Franconia were Roman Catholics.

3. New Voters

It is clear from an examination of the electoral returns, taking into account regional variations, that the majority of new voters supported the NSDAP. Almost 300,000 new voters in Bavaria participated in this election compared with 1930. This was very evident in South Bavaria. A study of the seven towns and ten rural districts in Upper Bavaria and Swabia, where the NSDAP became the strongest party in this election, shows that new voters were the primary source of the increase in support for the NSDAP although the party also won many votes from the BBMB. In Protestant Franconia, where the BVP was not a rival for the votes of the peasant party, the NSDAP benefited more equally from losses by the *Deutsches Landvolk* and the rise in voter participation. The example of Upper Franconia (rural districts) shows this clearly:

Main gains	NSDAP	81,000
	DNVP	7,000
	KPD	6,000
Main losses	*Deutsches Landvolk*	43,000
	SPD	9,000
Increase in votes		35,000

From these rough figures, one may assume that the SPD losses went largely to the Communists and that the DNVP owed its modest increase in the vote to former supporters of the *Deutsches Landvolk*, who were not sufficiently radical to vote this time for the NSDAP and chose instead to return to the DNVP. Consequently, the sharp rise in Nazi support came from both the new voters and supporters of the peasant party in 1930. The BVP also made small gains among the new voters in Catholic areas, but not enough to affect the upsurge of Nazi support among this section of the electorate.

4. *Local Factors*

A number of special factors determined local variations in the vote for the NSDAP. The party did well in the few towns with a relatively large working-class population like Ingolstadt and Bad Reichenhall, no doubt because of the emphasis on social issues in its campaign. The NSDAP also won a high vote among summer visitors to the spas of Upper Bavaria. There was a provision for people to vote outside their electoral districts, if they applied for a special voting certificate called a *Stimmschein*. In the July election, a large number of *Stimmscheine* were registered in districts like Garmisch, where 19,700 people were on the electoral register but 26,300 in fact voted. In border towns like Berchtesgaden, a high proportion of *Stimmscheine* were used by people taking a holiday in Austria, who had to cross over to German soil to vote. Local newspaper reports suggested that most people using *Stimmscheine* voted for the NSDAP. The reason was social for most people on vacation in Upper Bavaria, especially the visitors to spas (*Kurgäste*), came from well-to-do middle-class circles, including many businessmen and industrialists from Northern Germany.[9] Their strong support for the NSDAP

9. A large number of people in Berlin applied for *Stimmscheine* before the July election to vote in the Baltic coast resorts as well as Upper Bavaria and Baden. One report estimated

while on holiday during the July election is confirmed by the result of the November election in 1932, when they had all returned home. The Nazi vote in these summer resorts dropped dramatically together with the slump in the number of voters, quite out of proportion to the general decline in the party's support in this election.

This analysis of the results of the July 1932 Reichstag Election in Bavaria shows that the increase in the vote for the NSDAP was generally very large, but confessional, social and local factors modified the rate of increase in its electoral support. Confession was still the strongest factor determining voting support in Bavaria, as shown by the ability of the Bavarian People's Party to resist the expansion of the Nazi vote. In short, there was no major change in the NSDAP's voting patterns, except for its important breakthrough among rural voters. Otherwise, the party's main support still came from middle-class voters and especially new voters.

Crisis Within the Party

The Reichstag Election of 31 July did not bring the expected rewards of office for the Nazis, but ushered in a period of uncertainty in the party which lasted through the remaining months of 1932. The party's momentum, maintained during the elections in the first half of the year, depended now on the speedy acquisition of power. The Nazis had exhausted their energies and funds in the recent campaign. Hitler made it clear that he demanded nothing less than the Chancellorship together with a number of key positions in the government, but his claims as leader of the largest party were spurned by the President, who with his political confidant von Papen had no desire to see Hitler elevated to the top position. Matters were not made easier for Hitler by talk that the NSDAP had reached the zenith of its electoral support. It was not surprising that the SA, ever impatient with the methods of parlour politics, began to show a renewed restlessness over the extended process of winning power. Goebbels commented in his diary on 8 August: 'The air is full of presage . . . the whole party is ready to take over power; the SA downs

that 120,000 *Stimmscheine* were issued in Berlin, but applications were nearly all made in residential suburbs like Schöneberg and Wilmersdorf, where the NSDAP was strong. Accordingly, the NSDAP lost votes in these districts in July compared with the Prussian state elections in April, while on the island of Heligoland it suddenly found itself with 1,300 voters where it had previously had only a handful. (Report of the NSDAP Propaganda Department on the July 1932 election, undated, HA 15/289.)

tools every day to prepare for this; if things go well, everything will be all right; if they do not, it will be an awful setback' (47).

Goebbels' worst fears came true. Hitler's dilemma stemmed from the way in which politics was now dominated by camarillas, whose power depended not on a majority in the Reichstag but on the will of the President. It was almost like a medieval court, where the monarch was surrounded by different and sometimes rival groups of advisers to the exclusion of party politics. The President's appointment as Chancellor of Franz von Papen, a man who was neither leader of a party nor enjoyed wide confidence in the Reichstag, was itself a rebuff to the existence of political parties. Hitler, whose social background was so different from the landowning cliques surrounding the President, was not acceptable as a member of the magic circle. This was evident from Hitler's interview with Hindenburg in Berlin on 13 August, when the latter made it emphatically clear that he was not going to offer the Nazi leader the position he coveted. Hitler could become Vice-Chancellor under von Papen, but he would not consider this. Hitler's old aversion to coalitions reasserted itself. He was not going to accept a subordinate position under a political rival, although the outcome of the July election made it seem that Hitler's only chance of becoming Chancellor was through an alliance with one of the other parties. Having failed to win the favour of the President, he gave his approval to Strasser to initiate talks with leaders of the Centre Party towards the end of August. Together these two parties could form a majority in the Reichstag.

This turn of events put Hitler in an embarrassing tactical position. Firstly, he was in danger of losing the support of that section of the electorate which had voted for his party on the assumption that he would share responsibility in government and provide an effective solution to the many problems which faced the country. The authorities in Lower Bavaria were already observing a swing of public opinion away from the Nazis by the middle of August for this reason. People's eyes had been opened by Hitler's interview with Hindenburg to the fact that 'the National Socialists only claim exclusive power for themselves in the Reich, and are not prepared to share leadership for the fate of the German people in a legal way with other fellow countrymen' (48). Hindenburg's decided rejection of Hitler's demands on 13 August had won the approval of 'order-loving people'.

The possibility of a slump in Nazi support became more real as the autumn set in, causing nervousness among party leaders. On 12 October, the *Gau* office of Lower Franconia sent a report to Goebbels on the danger of losing votes among the middle classes. It blamed this alienation among the party's stock supporters on the clever propaganda of the Papen Government, which attacked the Nazis for conducting partisan politics. Party propaganda would have to take account of this development, and must show a readiness for positive cooperation (*49*). Such reports from the provinces had an effect on thinking in the Propaganda Department, which produced a long survey the following month based on evidence from the *Gaue* on the mood of the public towards the party (*50*). This survey deplored the fact that the party's middle-class supporters were less stable than those among the working class. The Nationalist press had exploited the divisions between the NSDAP and the conservative Papen Government, for 'the bourgeois citizen was strengthened in his view that Hitler should have joined the government of Herr von Papen on 13 August, and no election slogan was able to dissuade him from this opinion'.

In spite of its uncertain constitutional position, the Papen Government had succeeded in presenting an impressive image to those sections of the public which had been turning to the Nazis over the previous years. This was especially true of Protestant rural voters in Franconia. By mid-October, 'wide circles' of Protestant peasants in Middle Franconia had taken offence at the NSDAP's negotiations with the Centre Party. The Catholic parties had always been an object of hatred for them, and this feeling had been encouraged by the Nazis. The latter's change of stand was incomprehensible to them so that their confidence in the promises of Nazi speakers began to waver and the Papen Government won 'more and more ground with its agricultural programme' (*51*). The *Gau* office of Lower Franconia was forced to admit that 'the mood of our former voters among the agricultural population is turning against our movement to quite a great extent in many areas' (*52*).

The other problem facing Hitler after his failure to achieve office was the alienation of the radical elements in his own party. The SA in particular had been dissatisfied with Hitler's 'legal' tactics, but had been prepared to acquiesce in them so long as they produced results. These elements had reacted at first with delight at Hitler's intransigent attitude to the President, but when it became obvious that the *Führer* was failing to bend the will of his opponents their initial hopes turned sour. In Würzburg, where antagonism had grown up between the *Gau* leader Dr Hellmuth and the SA leader, the police expressed concern that 'they are publicly toying with the idea of returning to illegality' (*53*).

This friction between political leaders and the SA found an outlet in renewed innuendoes about Roehm's private life and carping criticism of SA drinking habits. It was claimed that the crude public behaviour of storm-troopers was losing the party support among respectable middle-class voters. On the SA side, the feeling was voiced that the Third Reich would not come about through 'the idle talk of political speakers and leaders' but through the 'fist of the SA'. One SA leader was reputed to have remarked that 'we will make a clean sweep of things after the 6 November' (the date of the new Reichstag Election), and that 'the elections have no value'. This deterioration in relations even affected the SA's role in propaganda after a while. According to Goebbels' Propaganda Department, a new spirit was pervading the SA which was 'no longer a political fighting instrument of the movement but an end in itself' (54).

Part of the trouble was financial. Intensive electoral activity of the party over recent months had drained its coffers to such an extent that little remedy could be found by November, when the Propaganda Department described the financial position as 'hopeless'. Local branches complained about their drop in income with the withdrawal of help from wealthy supporters and the adverse effect of economic distress on the payment of membership fees (55). Even before the July election, the *Gau* of Munich–Upper Bavaria had revealed that after the elections in the spring it had debts amounting to 90,000 marks, and that 50 per cent of its members were three months in arrears with their subscriptions (56). The party was forced to take severe measures to try and rectify the situation, even at the cost of further discontent among its members. An increase in membership fees caused tempers to flare especially among unemployed party members, and so did the fact that members now had to pay for their own uniforms. This brought a drop in the number of members, some of whom joined the Communists and others the Stahlhelm (57). Finance had long been a sore point with the SA. The dispute in Würzburg arose among other things from complaints by the SA leader that salaried party officials were 'swallowing up huge sums'. Streicher was singled out for much abuse because of his habit of demanding a high fee for speaking at public meetings (58).

The SA with its radical social outlook inevitably expressed disgust at Hitler's cavortings with the 'reactionary' Papen Government, referred to sarcastically as those 'fine people' or the 'palsied Excellencies with monocles'. Further consternation was caused by the contacts between Nazi leaders and the Centre Party. Unemployed SA men feared that their chances of relief from their state of misery had become more distant with the possibility of such a coalition in place of the Nazis assuming power alone (59). Even the Propaganda Department recognized that 'our propaganda directed against the Centre Party over the years has become the flesh and blood of our party comrades, and it will be impossible to a certain extent to convince them of the necessity of a coalition with the Centre Party' (60).

New elections to the Reichstag had meanwhile been announced as early as 12 September. The Nazis hardly felt confident about the forthcoming campaign in spite of their success with a no-confidence motion against the Papen Government carried by 513 votes to 32. They had to reckon with the possibility of a fall in electoral support for the first time during the Depression years. Behind their public display of bravado, party leaders felt desperate about the unending struggle for power. Four days after the new dissolution of the Reichstag, Goebbels noted in his diary: 'Now we are in for elections again! One sometimes feels this sort of thing is going on for ever ... our adversaries count on our losing morale and getting fagged out' (*61*). He viewed the elections with no less foreboding a month later: 'The organization has naturally become a bit on edge through these everlasting elections; it is as jaded as a battalion, which has been too long in the front trenches, and just as nervy' (*62*).

The Reichstag Election, 6 November 1932

Disillusionment affected not only the Nazis, for the public greeted the news of yet another general election with feelings of irritation over the inability of politicians to solve the economic crisis. The dissolution of the Reichstag on 12 September dispelled some of the hopes placed in the Papen Government, for people feared that the elections eight weeks later would merely whip up partisan passions and distract attention from the essential problems facing the country. In Upper Bavaria, the public had 'no understanding for the ever incessant political conflicts and is sick of them to the point of disgust' (*63*). The Catholic clergy in Augsburg sent an urgent message to the Reich Chancellor about the 'shocking and overwhelming distress' among families of the unemployed, invalids and those dependent on welfare schemes (*64*).

Public disenchantment with politics only added to the problems of the Nazis, who had previously managed to arouse electoral enthusiasm to their own benefit. The party was not in a position for financial reasons to fight a full-scale campaign this time. A meeting of local propaganda leaders in the *Gau* of Munich–Upper Bavaria was held in Munich on 15 October. Matthias Dötsch, head of the *Gau* propaganda department, said the first priority was to remove electoral weariness among the voters, but the need for economies meant care in the choice of propaganda methods (*65*).

The party was compelled to depend more than ever before on the individual enthusiasm of party workers, for the emphasis was on personal canvassing (*Kleinarbeit*) which was less costly. Street posters and leaflets were not generally available, because the cost was prohibitive. Party members were instead responsible for canvassing particular groups of people, and should write personal letters to known sympathizers with the party ('letter propaganda'). They should make a point of wearing their party badges. There should be 'no Nazi house without a Nazi flag', for 'everywhere our symbols must be seen on wooden fences'. The methods of soap-box oratory were even employed. Trained party speakers were sent out in plainclothes to stand in front of advertisement pillars and harangue passers-by. As to attacks on political opponents, party workers were warned to distinguish between the Reich President and Reich Chancellor. Von Papen was not popular in this part of the country, so whenever he appeared on the cinema screen all Nazis present had the duty to hiss and boo. But special care should be taken not to attack the President: 'The person of Hindenburg should whenever possible be treated with consideration, for in Southern Germany and especially in Bavaria Hindenburg has by virtue of his age and his former services many supporters who would take offence' (66).

As far as party meetings were concerned, the Nazis had little success in relieving the boredom of voters. Local branches reported on the low attendance at their meetings, which in turn meant a fall in income from entrance fees. Many meetings were cancelled because few people turned up. In country areas, peasants resented being distracted from the potato and turnip harvest by political propaganda and refused to come along to meetings. In Munich, the party only held meetings with its biggest names, but even a Hitler rally on election eve drew a crowd of only 9,000 so that many seats in the hall remained vacant (67).

The NSDAP's loss of votes on 6 November occurred uniformly throughout the country. Its decline in support was even evident from a comparison of the two 1932 Reichstag elections in individual districts. The rate of decline was marginally greater in the Protestant rural areas of Franconia than in Southern Bavaria. This reflected disillusionment with the NSDAP over its negotiations with the Centre Party. Some Catholic districts in Swabia like Günzburg, Krumbach and Wertingen did actually show a significant rise in Nazi votes against the general trend, possibly for the same reason. The overall decline in the NSDAP vote—in Lower Bavaria from 21·1 per cent to 19 per cent, and Middle Franconia from 47·7 per cent to 42·3 per cent—was not dramatic, but it was enough to represent a setback for a party which had continuously preached its irresistible rise in popular support. Other parties like the BVP and the SPD also suffered losses from the fall in voter participation. Only the Communists and the Nationalists made small gains, usually from disenchanted Nazi supporters. The main effect of the November election was therefore psychological, for it did not bring any radical changes in the voting support of the main parties. The position of the Bavarian People's Party seemed as steadfast as ever. In the sixty-eight districts of Southern Bavaria, it still had an absolute majority in twelve and a relative majority in forty-six.

The election result accelerated the crisis within the Nazi Party. Party leaders turned their attention inwards to search for scapegoats, and members began to desert the party. The Munich police commented on the state of the party at the end of 1932:

> Numerous resignations occur every day, dues arrive irregularly and expulsions because of arrears become more and more frequent. The party leadership has repudiated statements to this effect made in the opposition press in an official party denial, and has even threatened to issue a writ against the spreading of such reports ... All the sections of the party—the political organization, the SA and SS—give the impression of being run down. The view that the summit has been passed and favourable prospects possibly missed is commonly held among many National Socialists (*68*).

Rumblings of revolt against the party line grew louder among the SA with talk about the need for a 'revolutionary act'. According to the Munich police, 'one expects in the political circles of the party sweeping changes in leadership positions, mainly in the Organization Department but above all a basic change of attitude by the party' (*69*). Gregor Strasser's resignation as party organization leader on 8 December because of policy differences with Hitler must have confirmed the impression of many outsiders that the party's days were numbered. One further crisis now erupted in the party in Bavaria, but this did in fact illustrate the limited nature of the harm done to the NSDAP's importance as a political force.

The Stegmann Revolt

The Stegmann revolt, which followed soon after Strasser's resignation, arose from many of the usual sources of ill-feeling among the SA such as party finance, antagonism towards the political leadership and frustration with the apparent failure of Hitler's electoral strategy. It was led by Wilhelm Stegmann, leader of the SA in Franconia. He had been promoted to that post in the summer of 1932, after many years as party leader in the Rothenburg area. A young man in his early thirties, Stegmann had earned a reputation as a fanatical Nazi because of his radical views. According to the district authorities, who had long kept a wary eye on his activities, Stegmann was 'very temperamental' and 'easily lost all control of himself in the heat of battle' (*70*)

The crisis within the Franconian SA, which developed during the months of December and January, was an explosion of a long-felt dissatisfaction among its members, although the result of the November election provided the last straw. Even before the election, tension had appeared between the SA and the *Gau* office in Nuremberg over demands by the former for more financial support. The SA had run up heavy debts, but when these demands were not satisfied there were further resignations from its membership. In December, Stegmann began bringing out a weekly paper called *Der Nazi-Spiegel*, which proceeded to heap abuse on the 'Streicher clique'. The paper was a clear imitation of *Der Stürmer*, even to the extent of mimicking the latter's motto with the slogan 'The Party Bosses are our Misfortune'. *Der Nazi-Spiegel* revived the old charges of corruption and immorality which had long surrounded Streicher's name (*71*).

Stegmann's antics were extremely galling to Streicher's vanity. The conflict finally erupted when Stegmann removed a Streicher supporter from the leadership of the SA sub-group for Middle Franconia on 10 January. Stegmann followed his action with the statement that 'the entire SA of Middle Franconia stands united under my leadership hour by hour at the disposal of our Supreme SA Leader', and confirmed his allegiance to the *Führer* with the toast 'Onward march with Adolf Hitler' (*72*). Stegmann was shortly afterwards relieved of his command over the SA in Middle Franconia. Thereupon, Stegmann let loose some of his men to raid the SA headquarters in Nuremberg during the night and lay hands on any compromising material. A scuffle took place, and the police had to intervene. Stegmann now moved his own headquarters from Schillingsfürst to Nuremberg, and took up a position provocatively close to that of his rivals. The city police, fearing the worst, brought in reinforcements to patrol the 'no man's land' between the two camps (*73*).

At this point, Hitler felt sufficiently concerned about the affair to intervene in person. Hitler sent Stegmann a telegram confirming his dismissal as SA leader in Franconia, but the latter still refused to give way. He had strong support from the SA, for even in Nuremberg Streicher could count on only two SA groups which he bribed with a huge wage rise (*74*). The crisis finally turned when Stegmann met Hitler for an interview on 14 January. Hitler used a mixture of threats and appeals to loyalty to browbeat Stegmann into submission. After the interview, Stegmann made the following declaration:

Today, I was with my *Führer*. As I now realize that I was reprimanded by him for my behaviour with reason, I have of my own accord put my Reichstag seat at his disposal and promised him to do my duty as party comrade in loyalty and obedience (*75*).

Stegmann continued to complain that the party should become more revolutionary, but little more than two weeks later Hitler had become Chancellor of Germany. The Stegmann affair then fell into oblivion.

The revolt among the SA in Franconia was effectively solved before events at the national level changed Hitler's fortunes. Stegmann's decision to back down after his interview with Hitler came the day before the crucial election in the North German state of Lippe on 15 January, which demonstrated once again the party's vote-getting ability. It could not be claimed that Hitler's assumption of office quelled the revolt, although a continuation of the search for power as during the second half of 1932 would certainly have led to further crises in the party. Hitler had once more demonstrated on the critical eve of his appointment as Chancellor that his appeal as *Führer* worked even among his more insubordinate followers. Stegmann had never once questioned Hitler's authority as party leader, for he had emphatically proclaimed that his loyalty to Hitler remained untouched. Stegmann's dissatisfaction with the political leadership was directed against the person of Streicher.

The Stegmann revolt had shown like the Strasser affair that belief in the *Führer*, which was the linchpin of cohesion among the party membership, had not been adversely affected by the party's varying fortunes during 1932. Hitler's fears of a split in the party after Strasser's resignation had not come true because Strasser had chosen to make his decision a personal one, but also because Hitler had succeeded in reaffirming his control over the *Gau* leaders. As Otto Erbersdobler, *Gau* leader in Lower Bavaria, put it, Strasser had 'underestimated the magic of Hitler's personality', for 'differences and disagreements over the assessment of various questions and matters had in the end to be reconciled at the top'. Erbersdobler had reminded Strasser 'of what things were like when Hitler was in prison after the abortive Putsch . . . a picture of confusion', and 'Hitler alone built up the old NSDAP again, and uncompromisingly recommended all those groups to submit to him or go their own way' (*76*).

The difficulties which the NSDAP had met after the election in July had not yet begun to undermine seriously the party's infiltration of German political life. The party crisis during the autumn of 1932 had arisen more from disappointed expectations of power and old conflicts over policy than from any significant decline in the party's position. The NSDAP was still by far the largest party in the state, and for this reason was still an attractive ally for political schemers like von Papen. Moreover, these critical months for the NSDAP had not shown a corresponding revival of popular support for the Weimar Republic. The public had become even more satiated with party politics after the November election, and desired above all order and stability. This was a factor worth noting when examining the relative speed with which the Nazis established control over the country after Hitler became Chancellor.

Eight

The Nazi 'Seizure of Power' in Bavaria (1933)

Hitler Becomes Chancellor

On 30 January 1933, Hitler was appointed head of a coalition government which included two other Nazi ministers and various Nationalist and non-party conservative figures. Von Papen returned to government as Vice-Chancellor supposedly to act as a check on Hitler's ambitions for total power, after being ousted from the Chancellorship early in December by General von Schleicher. He had been the key figure in the negotiations preceding the formation of the new government. It seemed as if Hitler had compromised to win office, having overcome his known reluctance to enter coalitions.

The position was in reality more favourable to the Nazis than it seemed at first, for Hitler was not averse to coalitions if he were clearly the dominant partner. He had at last achieved his aim of the Chancellorship, even if that meant agreeing to an alliance with the forces which had supported the Papen Government. The position of the latter was weak compared with that of the new Chancellor, because they did not have the support of a strongly organized political base which Hitler enjoyed in the Nazi movement. Von Papen's abolition of the independent powers of the state of Prussia in July 1932 now assumed a greater significance, for it helped the Nazis immeasurably with their plans to centralize government in Germany. Although von Papen resumed his post as Reich Commissioner for Prussia, Goering became Prussian Minister of the Interior, giving him control over the security forces in the largest state in the Reich. There was finally the question of the Reich President. Hindenburg had appointed Hitler as Chancellor with reluctance, but his ability to resist Hitler's further tactics remained in doubt because of his advanced age. Hindenburg's attitude during the crucial weeks which followed appeared fatalistic, for a month later he signed away many of his powers to the new government. These powers included the right to intervene in any state in the Reich in the case of an emergency.

It was in this context that Bavaria assumed a special importance during the weeks after Hitler assumed the Chancellorship. Attention turned to the South German states because Prussia came effectively under the sway of the Nazis, especially after a presidential decree on 6 February confirmed the Reich Government's administration of Prussian affairs in spite of a decision by the Supreme Court the previous October invalidating the action by the Papen Government. Bavaria with the support of other states like Baden had shown the most opposition to the action against Prussia. Bavaria's opposition had been motivated by the fear that similar action could be taken against her own independence. The Held Government in Munich felt even more alarmed after 30 January, as the alliance between Hitler, Papen and Hugenberg meant a strong preference for a centralized state on the part of the new Reich Government. The Nationalist influence in the Cabinet also implied a lack of sympathy for Catholic interests.

The hopes set on Bavaria during these weeks were based less on a realistic assessment of the situation than on the reputation which Bavaria had earned for independent attitudes and hostility to the idea of a centralized state. The will to resist the threat of a Nazi takeover was demonstrated in official quarters in Munich, but it was inhibited by the Bavarian Government's vulnerability in the face of the strong powers acquired by the new Reich Government and the importance of the Nazi movement in Bavaria. The Reichstag Election on 5 March emphasized more the weaknesses than the strengths of the Bavarian People's Party, and made the NSDAP easily the strongest party in the state. Hitler had meanwhile isolated the President, and applied pressure on the Held Government in order to wear down its confidence. He secured the neutrality of the armed forces in Bavaria a few days later, and used manoeuvres by the impatient SA in Munich to achieve the final collapse of independent authority in Bavaria. The 'seizure of power' in Bavaria shows how thin the dividing line was between the Nazis' 'legal' methods and their willingness to resort to coercion and force to gain their ends.

The situation in the early months of 1933 was very different from that just under ten years before at the time of the Munich Putsch. Antagonism had arisen once more between Munich and Berlin, but in circumstances much more advantageous to the Nazis. Instead of exploiting Bavarian hostility to Berlin in order to seize power by force, Hitler had already gained control at the national level through constitutional methods. He was now leader of a national mass movement, instead of a fringe party concentrated in Bavaria. The position of the Bavarian Government was now much weaker. Support from the Army was not forthcoming as it had been in the autumn of 1923, nor could the police be counted on to deal this time with the large SA forces. It was small wonder that the Bavarian Government showed a brave determination to resist to the end, but proved indecisive in its confrontation with Hitler in his new and exalted capacity as German Chancellor.

The Attitude of the Bavarian Government

Hitler's appointment as Chancellor revived the feelings of expectation in party ranks that had been dashed by his failure to be elected President in the spring of 1932. The difference this time was that his replacement of General von Schleicher as head of the Reich Government occurred without the prolonged atmosphere of suspense and assumption of inevitable victory that had affected party activists the year before.

The news of Hitler's invitation to form a government in Berlin caused some surprise, and inevitably released the tensions that had accumulated within the party during the previous months. SA groups staged local torchlight processions and other demonstrations to celebrate the event. The authorities in Swabia observed that 'the joy among National Socialists over the success of their cause is very great', and that they were 'convinced that within a short time they will be in possession of total power' (1).

Threats that political debts would soon be settled were directed against the Left in these first weeks. A party speaker in Weiden attacked the Communists with the warning that in the Third Reich the greeting 'Heil Moscow' would be heard in three places only—in prison, in the express train back to Moscow and on the gallows (2). Communists in districts around Swabia responded to Hitler's appointment as Chancellor by distributing leaflets in factories, on the railways and among post-office employees (3). The Communists seemed to have few illusions about the turn of events, for by the middle of February they were making preparations for the illegal prosecution of their activities in case of a ban on their party. Their party functionaries were furnished with card indexes, so small as to resemble pocket calendars, in order that they could continue to identify their members and issue them with instructions (4).

The immediate reactions of the public to the Hitler Government were mixed, according to the district authorities. Apart from the contrary attitudes of Nazis and of supporters of the left-wing parties, people responded either with excitement or with scepticism to the formation of yet another government. Peasants in areas of Lower Bavaria showed an indifference to the Nazi festivities, so depressed were they about high taxes and the low prices for their produce. The change of government did not appear to signify any relief from their plight (5). Lower Bavaria was the region where the NSDAP had made the least impact on the peasantry, but a few weeks later district offices there were noting that peasant circles now welcomed Hitler's assumption of power. A swing of opinion in favour of the new government was reflected in the view among supporters of the BBMB that Hitler was the 'right man', and that the NSDAP should be given a chance to 'show what it can achieve in improving the economy' (6).

Gau leader Wagner's speech to party officials in Munich on 12 February revealed the new tone of aggressiveness in the party because 'we are the masters now'. The mood of the meeting was one of 'extraordinary jubilation'. Wagner began by remarking that Hitler's appointment as Chancellor was 'a turning-point in world history'. Hitler would not be checked by von Papen or any other coalition partner in his new task. The only problem to settle was the resistance of the Bavarian Government. While Hitler would meet 'relatively little opposition' in Northern Germany, the situation was 'more difficult in Bavaria, where the insidious Bavarian People's Party is still trying as before to drain away support from the National Socialists'. He said it was 'incredible' that it was still possible in Munich for people to insult 'the Reich Chancellor' in public without the police intervening. In future, the SA would help by taking action in such cases in the interests of 'order', so that people who inveighed against the state and the police would be shot. Hitler now had the power in his hands to 'bring a reluctant state to its senses' (7).

The Bavarian Government reacted at first with composure to the change of government in Berlin. The minutes of its three cabinet meetings during January give no indication of the impending political crisis, for they dealt with ordinary administrative and financial matters (8). The first session of the Held Cabinet after Hitler's appointment again gave no impression of urgency. On 1 February the ministers listened to a report from Schäffer on his discussions in Berlin of financial questions, including the possibility of introducing some measure of Bavarian autonomy in tax administration. The implications for Bavaria of the developments in national politics had begun to register by the next meeting on 7 February. Hitler had been in office a week, and the previous day the Reich President had set his seal of approval on the final abolition of the state government of Prussia. The case of Prussia had been a thorn in the flesh of the Bavarian Government ever since the coup by von Papen the previous July. Dr Held had written an anguished letter to Hindenburg three days before seeking reassurance. The latter had just replied that neither he nor the Reich Government was considering sending a Reich Commissioner to Bavaria (9).

Hindenburg's reply apparently calmed the fears of the Held Government, at least for the time being. It now concerned itself with the attitude it should take towards the new representatives of Prussia in the Reichsrat, the upper chamber of the parliament in Berlin. Dr Held continued to make a case for approaching the Supreme Court in Leipzig once more over the matter. The problem of Prussia and its consequences for other states arose again at the cabinet meeting on 11 February, but there appeared to be less immediate concern over the danger to Bavaria. The meeting on 20 February did not discuss the political situation at all (*10*).

Much of the Bavarian Government's attention throughout February was given to the question of constitutional reform. This was not so unrealistic as may at first appear. Since Hitler's first decision as Chancellor had been to call a new Reichstag Election in the first week of March, Dr Held and his ministers felt themselves under a different kind of pressure. They were still only a minority government, and it was very probable that the Nazis would make large gains in this election. Hitler's new prestige as Chancellor made that certain. In this case, the Nazis were bound to claim that the Held Government did not represent the new national will.

As soon as the new elections were announced, the executive committee of the BVP met in Munich on 4 February. Dr Held arrived to address the meeting on the party's draft proposals for a reform of the Bavarian constitution. Their purpose was to secure against the eventuality that 'a majority in the state parliament, which is not able to form a new government itself, might overthrow the present government and ruin its work' (*11*). The proposals included a strengthening of the position of Prime Minister through a 'constructive vote of no-confidence', whereby a motion of no-confidence could only be carried against the government if the parliament elected an alternative Prime Minister at the same time. There would also be greater provision for initiating a referendum in the event of the parliament refusing legislation by the government.

Discussions on these proposals continued through February, but the Bavarian Government's fears about attitudes in Berlin had meanwhile been revived. Schäffer travelled to Berlin to seek an audience with Hindenburg on 17 February. Schäffer repeated the arguments in Held's letter a fortnight before about the fateful decisions which lay in the President's hands, but the latter seemed distinctly irritated by the continued expression of concern by the Bavarians. Schäffer came away from the meeting with the impression that Hindenburg had fallen more under the influence of Hitler. He nevertheless made use of the President's further assurances about not sending a Reich Commissioner to Bavaria in public speeches he made soon afterwards in Würzburg and Forchheim (*12*).

Two days after his meeting with Hindenburg, Schäffer received alarming news about a meeting of SA leaders under Roehm in Berlin. According to the reports he was given, the meeting had come to the decision to impose a Reich Commissioner on the states outside Prussia on 6 March, the day after the Reichstag Election. This Reich Commissioner, who it was given to understand would be Roehm, would then appoint sub-commissioners for each of the individual states (*13*). The situation became even more tense a few days later when Wilhelm Frick, the Nazi Minister of the Interior in the Reich Government, made a highly provocative speech in Hamburg. He blatantly announced that force would be employed against states which refused to submit, and even outlined the programme for the political 'coordination'of all state governments along the lines of the Reich Government. Ending on a note of extreme sharpness, Frick warned the state governments south of the Main River[1] that they had failed to grasp 'the direction of the new times' and that the Hitler Government would intervene ruthlessly if the occasion arose (*14*).

Frick's speech caused jitters in Munich, coming as it did from an important minister in the new Hitler Government. Von Papen, who was head of the Nationalist list of candidates in Bavaria, sent a mollifying letter to Dr Held to try and undo some of the harm done by Frick's statement (*15*). This only added to the confusion in Munich over the real intentions of the Reich authorities. It was evident that there was a conflict in Berlin over the course of action to be taken over Bavaria. Suspicions of the Nazis' preference for using force were balanced by the President's assurance that he would not appoint a Reich Commissioner for Bavaria. Hindenburg continued to remain the crucial figure in the eyes of the Bavarian Government, although his ability to resist the pressures of the Nazis was regarded with diminishing confidence.

The President's decree on 28 February for the Protection of the People and the State came as a great blow to the hopes of the Bavarians. It followed the firing of the Reichstag, which the Nazis immediately attributed to the Communists. Hindenburg's decree, which had been drafted earlier the same day by the Cabinet under Hitler's direction, transferred important powers from the President to the Reich Government. The most relevant provision as far as Bavaria was concerned was that which empowered the government to assume full control in any state in so far as that state was not taking necessary measures to maintain public order. Von Papen had on behalf of Hinden-

---

1. The 'Main line', the boundary between North and South Germany provided by the river, assumed a special importance at this time because the southern states (like Baden, Württemberg and Bavaria) still retained their formal independence, while Prussia (which comprised most of North Germany) had already come under the control of the Nazis.

burg in fact raised the likelihood of objections by the South German states, but his reminder about the President's promise to Bavaria merely resulted in the re-wording of one sentence in the draft (*16*).

The crisis was now nearing its climax. Hindenburg's protective hand over Bavaria was now seen to be powerless. It was at this point that ruling circles in Munich considered a last desperate solution. Rumours had already been circulating in the Bavarian capital about the possibility of a monarchist restoration to forestall the Nazis. Fritz Schäffer, who was proving the most decisive of the BVP leaders, had a meeting with Crown Prince Rupprecht, head of the house of Wittelsbach, in the Leuchtenberg Palace in Munich. The Crown Prince said he would be ready to cooperate if the Bavarian Government gave him full backing. Schäffer agreed to propose the plan to the next ministerial meeting, but he failed to gain enthusiastic support (*17*). Dr Held procrastinated and expressed doubts about the practical usefulness of the plan. At a meeting with Baron von Stengel, a representative of the monarchists, on 20 February, Held had asked earnestly about financial backing and military support for a restoration attempt. Held's attitude of reserve hardened when his political mentor, Georg Wohlmuth, advised caution because of the drastic consequences which could ensue from over-hasty action. Even the willingness of the Bavarian Social Democrats to back the monarchy, expressed at a meeting he had with Wilhelm Hoegner, did not overcome Held's fatal hesitation (*18*).

It was in any case improbable that a Bavarian monarchist restoration would have had any success, apart from serving as a symbolic gesture of defiance. Held did not possess Schäffer's impetuous temperament, for his reaction to the plan had been based on a cool assessment of its likely outcome. Although the attitude of the military forces stationed in Bavaria was still unclear, the Nazis had sufficient power at their disposal to deal with a monarchist attempt if they decided that ruthless action was required. While it was a common assumption that the Wittelsbachs still enjoyed widespread sympathy in Bavaria, the monarchists were extremely weak as an organization for they were little more than an ineffectual political élite with no real mass support. Their political party, the Royal Party (*Königspartei*), had lasted less than two years after its inception in 1919 (*19*). The Bavarian Patriotic and Royalist League (*Bayerischer Heimat- und Königsbund*) had continued to encourage interest in the Wittelsbachs, but political circumstances had changed out of all recognition since their overthrow in 1918.

One day after the new presidential decree, Dr Held had an interview with Hitler in Berlin at the latter's request. The occasion was very painful for Held, now an ailing man of sixty-five, whose previous meetings with Hitler had taken place in totally different circumstances. Hitler obviously relished the fact that he was now in a superior position. Held's defiant stand of the week before, when he had declared that 'in keeping with the letter of the Constitution, I shall defend Bavarian independence at all costs, even in the face of force with which we may be confronted' (20), was no longer in evidence. Held was in no mood for trouble and behaved on the defensive. He assured Hitler that he would be received by the Bavarian Government with the same respect as any other Reich Chancellor. Hitler then got to the point of the meeting. He said that his intervention against some states such as Hamburg and Hesse had been necessary, as Social Democratic ministers controlled the police forces, but he was not thinking of acting against Bavaria. Hitler's remark seemed to alleviate some of the dread affecting Held, who asserted that his government had always taken care to act firmly against the Communists. He would not oppose the new Reich Government for the sake of opposition. Hitler brought up the question of the Bavarian monarchy, making it clear that any move in the direction of a restoration would lead to a 'serious catastrophe'. He indicated that the Army would be used in such an event. When Held emphasized that every government should be bound by Christian principles, Hitler assured him that his own government had Catholic interests at heart. Held departed for Munich feeling partially re-assured but also sobered. Hitler had achieved his intention of sapping the Bavarian Prime Minister's self-confidence (21).

This interview had taken place on Wednesday, 1 March. The Bavarian Minister of the Interior sent an order on the same day to police authorities for further action against Communists, as if to show the Reich Government that Bavaria was willing to cooperate (22). The Reichstag Election was only four days away. Hitler's assurances to Dr Held about Bavaria had undoubt-edly been made with an eye to the election, for any statement to the con-trary would certainly have been used by the BVP with some effect in the campaign now in its last week. Hitler knew that Bavarian voters could react sharply when their independence was threatened, for he was most concerned about the vote in the South. He calculated that a large rise in support for the NSDAP there would help solve his problems with Bavaria.

The Reichstag Election, 5 March 1933

The Nazis had several advantages in this election which they had not pre-viously enjoyed. Hitler was able to display his authority as Chancellor, and present himself at the head of a government of 'national awakening'. Since the NSDAP was now represented in the national government, the party could make full use of the state-controlled mass media which it had previously been denied. Major speeches by party leaders were relayed over the wireless, and loudspeakers were erected in public squares and at street corners.[2] Hitler's elevation to the Chancellorship removed furthermore the element of dissatisfaction among party activists, which had affected his campaign in November. The SA, which expected to reap rewards from his acquisition of national office, once more assumed its leading role in propaganda activities. Finally, the Nazis no longer suffered from their financial troubles as in 1932, for they had received plentiful funds from industrial circles for this campaign.

There was another aspect of the March election which distinguished it from earlier ones. It was conducted in a less free atmosphere, although violence and intimidation had already been evident in the campaigns of 1932. Instead of street clashes with political opponents, members of the SA had much greater scope to indulge their methods of terrorism, especially in Prussia where they had been appointed by Goering as auxiliary police. Social Democrats now took pains to avoid conflicts with the authorities, while the Communists were inhibited in their activities by the fear that their party would soon be prohibited.

There were initial signs that voters reacted to the dissolution of the Reichstag with the same feelings of aversion they had shown the previous autumn. Attendance at political meetings was once again low. But the mood of the electorate gradually changed with the realization that this election could be decisive. The Reich Government announced that it would not be the first of yet another series of elections, but the last election until the government had succeeded in solving the country's critical problems. NSDAP leaflets underlined Hitler's promise that he would solve the unemployment in four years if given a strong mandate:

Adolf Hitler has said, 'Within four years unemployment will be removed' . . . Six million people lie on the streets! What an Adolf Hitler promises, he keeps to! What an Adolf Hitler wishes to achieve, he will achieve it! His will led the NSDAP into government . . . Opponents were scornful, but his will overcame all opposition and he became Reich Chancellor . . . His will must once more conquer! Give Hitler four years' time for reconstruction (23).

2. Broadcasting was under government control, so it did not become generally available to the Nazis before 1933. Gottfried Feder, the party ideologist, had taken part in discussion programmes in 1930 and 1931, but the first Nazi leader to make a broadcast was Gregor Strasser in the summer of 1932.

Once the campaign was in full swing, Hitler's prestige and promise of effective action to deal with the economy appeared to produce a movement of opinion towards the NSDAP, especially in Catholic rural areas. Cardinal Faulhaber was amazed to hear that peasants in Lower Bavaria were often spending a couple of hours trekking to the nearest available radios to listen to what Hitler had to say to the peasants (24).

Hitler's implication that there would be no more elections for four years had an ominous ring about it. He made an ambiguous speech in Munich on 24 February, the same day as Frick's menacing speech in Hamburg. Hitler threw a sop to his audience by claiming (wrongly) that he was the first Bavarian to become Chancellor since Bismarck's time, but then remarked that he felt 'all the more responsible that the unity of Germany should not disintegrate under the Chancellorship of a Bavarian'. The German states should join together 'as rods in the bundle of rods of the Reich' (25). The Reichstag Fire three days later added a note of drama to the campaign, and it helped to dispel what feelings of indifference remained among the electorate. Even the moderate *Kaufbeurer Neueste Nachrichten* commented later that the Fire was 'a factor which turned the citizen, who was tired of elections, into a voter' (26). The reports of district authorities were by this time open to the suspicion of moving with the wind, but their observation that the Fire caused 'great alarm' among order-loving citizens and aroused anti-Communist feelings did correspond with the preconceived view of the Bavarian public towards the KPD (27).

The Nazis plugged the anti-Communist line even harder during the last week of the campaign. Party propaganda declared virtual war on the Left. Peasants were warned that their houses would be burnt down if the Communists and the Social Democrats came to power. Nazi speakers pointed to the Reichstag Fire as evidence that Germany would succumb to Communism if it were not for Hitler. Typical of the scare tactics used by the Nazis were the remarks of a speaker near Gerolzhofen on 2 March:

Adolf Hitler is fighting for and taking care of order. With Adolf Hitler we have no danger. Vote for Adolf Hitler, otherwise one doesn't know if there will be a Germany after 5 March. It is a divine gift that Adolf Hitler is in power. Without Hitler we would have Communism. They are trying to burn down villages and destroy everything. Fight and fight again so that Germany becomes free. The situation is serious, for Communism must not rise up. Adolf Hitler must win a majority, Adolf Hitler must make it. The people must help him to do so (28).

Although the Nazis attacked the Left viciously, their real competitor for votes was the Bavarian People's Party. Their emphasis on the danger from the Communists could be seen as an attempt to win over strong Catholic voters. The *Völkischer Beobachter* proclaimed on 1 March: 'Every Catholic vote for List 1, fight with us against the Red Flood.' The BVP, sensing that it might be fighting for its political life, remained by far the least passive of the other parties. In Lower Bavaria, where the BBMB already appeared to have accepted defeat, attendance at public meetings was sparse except at some held by the NSDAP and the BVP, including one with Dr Held. BVP speakers tried to check the drift towards the NSDAP by maintaining that the new Reich Government was a threat to the Catholic Church and to Bavarian independence. Hitler's coalition partner Hugenberg was seen as an 'outspoken enemy of Catholics', while Bavarian voters were reminded that Goering had banned Catholic newspapers in Prussia (*29*). One BVP speaker near Gerolzhofen even defied conventional opinion by making the obvious point that the chief beneficiaries of the Reichstag Fire must have caused it (*30*).

The most significant result of the election on 5 March was the breakthrough by the NSDAP among Bavarian voters, especially in Catholic rural areas. While the national vote for the party fell well short of the expected absolute majority (with 43·9 per cent), the party's vote in Bavaria rose from 30·5 per cent to 43·1 per cent. The NSDAP had become by far the largest party in the state. Goebbels wrote jubilantly in his diary: 'South Germany has especially taken the lead in the entire electoral success; that is all the more gratifying since it enables us to take radical measures against a policy of separatist federalism' (*31*). The immediate effect of the vote was that it destroyed remaining hopes that Bavaria might yet thwart Hitler's plans to establish full control over the country. The novelist Thomas Mann, who had visited Munich on a lecture tour during the height of the campaign, wrote from Switzerland:

We counted on Bavaria and hoped that the strength of the Catholic People's Party would prevent any violent change. Even the most knowledgeable experts could not have dreamt that the Bavarian elections would turn out as they did. The news fell upon us as an inexplicable disaster. Our confidence was utterly shattered (*32*).

Seen in terms of voting trends, the large rise in Nazi support came mainly from the new voters and not from losses by the Bavarian People's Party. The rise in voter participation was extraordinary in this election for as much as

88 per cent of the German electorate voted. The figure varied between electoral districts. Franconia had one of the highest national turnouts with 90 per cent, while in many localities in Southern Bavaria more than 95 per cent of the voters participated. The excitement and urgency of the campaign combined with pressure from the Nazis to push voting up to this high level. The new voters overwhelmingly supported the NSDAP. This is seen clearly in the case of the rural districts of Lower Bavaria, shown in Table 7, where the NSDAP vote rose the most compared with the result in November 1932 (from 18·5 per cent to 44·9 per cent).

Table 7   *Rise in NSDAP support among new voters, Reichstag Election, March 1933: Lower Bavaria (rural districts)*

Increase in voters		68,000
Losses in votes	BBMB	14,700
	KPD	8,600
	BVP	4,200
Gains in votes	NSDAP	97,900
	SPD	1,200
	DNVP	300

Source: Zeitschrift des Bayerischen Statistischen Landesamts (1933), pp. 92–3 and 322. Figures are to the nearest hundred.

The vote for the BVP showed that it still had at this late stage a stable bloc of voters, but it was unable to increase its electoral support. The BVP lost no more than 21,000 voters compared with the November result, but its constant share of around 30 per cent of the poll throughout the Weimar period now fell to 24·2 per cent with the rise in voter participation. The party suffered losses in the countryside, but partly compensated for these with a rise in support in the towns.

Although the BVP vote remained high in many areas, the result of the election in Bavaria was a moral triumph for the Nazis. Their successes in the Catholic rural districts were an important achievement, but one only finally accomplished with the weight of state authority behind them. The *Augsburger Postzeitung* admitted in a moment of resignation shortly afterwards that the BVP had failed after the November election to improve and extend its organization so as to attract new supporters. The BVP had now paid the price as its organization could not be compared with that of the Nazis, who had 'covered the whole country through their cell organization with a network of small herds of agitators' (*33*). The March election had served Hitler's purpose in further undermining the position of the Bavarian Government. The consequences were seen four days later in the events in Munich.

The Nazis Seize Control in Munich

Although the Bavarian Government realized that its days in office were probably numbered, it refused to give way to the Nazis without further resistance. Fritz Schäffer reputedly commented during the election night on 5 March: 'We can now be certain that the Good Friday has begun, but we must continue to believe that after the Good Friday an Easter will follow.' This did not prevent Schäffer from making a defiant statement the next day that the BVP was still 'the firmest and most reliable political force in Bavaria' (*34*).

During the following days, many other states ceded their independence one after another and acquiesced in the appointment of Reich Commissioners by Berlin—Bremen and Hesse on 6 March, followed by Baden, Württemberg and Saxony on 8 March. On 7 March, the Bavarian Cabinet met to discuss the situation. Dr Stützel reported on the events the previous night in other states, but said these were in accordance with Hitler's remarks to Dr Held in Berlin on 1 March (*35*). Hopes still persisted that Bavaria might be left alone in spite of all that had happened. Held once again sought the Reich President's assurance on 8 March that he would not send a Reich Commissioner to Bavaria, although he was hardly now in a position to prevent such an action.

Pressures from the NSDAP arose immediately after the election for a re-constitution of the Bavarian state parliament in order to reflect the new state of the parties. On 6 and 7 March, the *Völkischer Beobachter* demanded the replacement of the Held Government by a 'Hitler Government'. The Bavarian ministers still tried to save their skins in a last-minute effort to reshape the government. They informed the president of the state parliament on 7 March that they gave their full approval to Schäffer's initiative in this direction. The executive committee of the BVP met that same afternoon to discuss the plan and declare its support. The leaders of the other parliamentary groups were contacted, and four BVP representatives were nominated on 8 March to start negotiations (*36*). But the turn of events by this time had made these deliberations of little more than academic importance.

307

During the course of 8 March, rumours circulated through the Bavarian capital that the SA and SS were planning a coup. Stützel was notified that units of these organizations were going to march to the ministry buildings to force the government to resign. He tried at once to contact the Reich President but without success. The Reich Chancellor's office then replied that Hitler was 'unaware' of what was happening in Munich. During that night Adolf Wagner and Roehm, who had been awaiting events in Berlin, took the night express to Munich. They arrived on the morning of 9 March to find the city in a state of extreme excitement (*37*). The final stages of the takeover were now set in motion. Dr Held called a meeting with Stützel and Koch, the Munich police president, later in the morning in his office in the Ministry of External Affairs. They considered calling on the state police and even the military branch of the BVP at the Bayernwacht, but neither of these organizations had the forces to cope with the SA. Koch proposed reaching an understanding with the SA. At 12.45 Wagner, accompanied by Roehm and Himmler, arrived at the Ministry to demand Held's resignation. Wagner slapped his riding whip on the desk in front of the Prime Minister in a gesture of authority. Held refused to be cowed by Wagner's manner, and made no reply to the demand that Ritter von Epp should be appointed Reich Commissioner. He decided to call a Cabinet meeting at 2.30 (*38*).

The SA was now swarming along the streets of Munich without any opposition from the city police. Wilhelm Hoegner, the SPD leader, was walking past the editorial office of *Der Gerade Weg*, the strongly anti-Nazi Catholic weekly, when he noticed SA men wrecking the place. They were doing the same further along the street to the offices of the Social Democratic *Münchner Post*, where furniture was being thrown out of a fourth-floor window. Copies of the newspaper were being burnt on the street itself. Hoegner shouted to a policeman in the street whether he permitted this destruction of property, but the policeman replied that this street did not belong to his beat and that he would not get mixed up in the affair (*39*). Stefan Lorant, editor of the weekly *Münchner Illustrierte Presse*, was an eye-witness to the ransacking of the offices of the Catholic *Bayerischer Kurier* and other newspapers. He noticed that the police 'simply stood by in the street and looked on while the SA wrecked the offices', and then:

When the Nazis saw that the police took no measures against them, they swarmed into the streets. The swastika flag was once more hoisted over the Town Hall, this time for good. The crowd in the Marienplatz sang the national anthem. The SA occupied police headquarters. Captain Roehm carried out his plans to the letter (*40*).

The Bavarian Cabinet met that afternoon, but it could do little more than deplore what was happening. It persisted in rejecting the demands of the Nazi delegation, for one crucial question remained to be answered. What was the attitude of the 7th division of the Army in Bavaria? The commander of the division, General von Loeb, was conveniently absent from Munich on this day, so Held telephoned his chief-of-staff, Colonel Wäger. Wäger came to the Cabinet meeting, but was unable to provide the ministers with an immediate answer. Wäger went away to telephone the Reich Defence Ministry in Berlin, which told him that the crisis was 'an internal matter for Bavaria', and that the Army should 'stand at ease' and not intervene (*41*).

Wäger handed Dr Held a note with this reply when the latter was already seeing the Nazi delegation once more. Wagner, Roehm and Himmler were accompanied this time by Ritter von Epp. They repeated the demands made earlier in the day, but still failed to force the government's hand. The end finally came shortly before nine o'clock in the evening. The Bavarian Government was informed that the Reich Minister of the Interior had used the powers under article 2 of the presidential decree of 28 February to appoint Ritter von Epp Reich Commissioner with the power of authority in Bavaria. Epp arrived at the Ministry a quarter of an hour later to take over control (*42*).

During the night, some of the Bavarian ministers had a foretaste of the kind of treatment meted out to opponents of the régime. Stützel and Schäffer were dragged out of their beds by SA men and taken along to the Brown House. Stützel was not even allowed to dress, and had to go barefoot and in his nightshirt. His request to contact Epp was rejected by the SA men, who insulted him and beat him on the back of the head. He and Schäffer were later released when Hans Frank, head of legal affairs department at party head-quarters, appeared. The SA had apparently taken the law into their own hands. Both Stützel and Schäffer received an apology from Epp, and were fit enough to attend the last meeting of the Held Cabinet the following morning (*43*).

Dr Held arrived at his office to find that Hermann Esser, just appointed to a Commissary post, had taken over his anteroom. He was made to feel distinctly uncomfortable. The cabinet meeting which followed had to take place in the presence of Esser at the order of Epp. The ministers present related at length the events of the preceding day, but there was nothing more they could do. Dr Held had sent a telegram to Hindenburg expressing his bitter disappointment over the appointment of a Reich Commissioner. He was now a broken man, and left Munich for Switzerland on 15 March (*44*).

Wagner, Roehm and Epp had been the central figures in the drama of the past few days, but they had undoubtedly acted with Hitler's approval. Hitler had kept his distance in Berlin in case anything went wrong, so he could if need be put the blame on overhasty action by the SA. The SA had played an important part in both silencing opponents and giving the impression that the Nazi takeover was irresistible. The SA had needed little encouragement for they were determined to make their own revolution. There was at this stage no secure check on SA actions by the political leaders of the NSDAP, who in any case realized that the SA was doing the spade-work for them by dealing with opposition.

Hitler's hand was evident in the selection of ministers for the new Bavarian Government, which consisted of a balance between radical and conservative figures. Ritter von Epp, the Bavarian military hero, became Prime Minister. Ludwig Siebert, the mayor of Lindau, was also selected as a symbol of moderation in the post of Minister of Finance. For the sake of appearances Count Eugen von Quadt zu Wykradt und Isny, an insignificant BVP man, was given the position of Minister of Economics. Hans Frank, the party's legal expert, was appointed Minister of Justice. Rudolf Buttmann was an obvious choice as Minister of Education for his ability and interest in cultural affairs, but as a party conservative he was passed over for the more radical Hans Schemm. The other main appointment of a radical was Adolf Wagner as Minister of the Interior. Two other members of the government did not receive ministerial rank—Ernst Roehm and Hermann Esser became State Commissioners. Heinrich Himmler also took over as head of the Munich police, with Reinhard Heydrich as his assistant (45). This balance in the composition of the government was intended to soften the blow of the Nazi takeover among conservative circles in Bavaria.

The list of ministers was not completed until April, by which time Von Epp had been upgraded to Reich Governor for Bavaria. Ludwig Siebert replaced him as Prime Minister, so the formal position of head of government was kept in the hands of a conservative figure. Siebert failed, however, to provide strong leadership, and the balance between conservative and radical forces soon turned into a conflict.

The Process of 'Coordination'

The Nazi takeover in Munich on 9 March was followed by similar actions in other towns of Bavaria on the same day. They took place quietly in most places without any appearance of a revolution. In Ingolstadt, the mayor, Dr Listl, rang the commandant of the local garrison to be told that the troops were remaining neutral. He then telephoned the mayor of Munich, Dr Scharnagl, with whom he was well acquainted, to learn that the Nazis had already seized control in the city (*46*). The usual outward sign of the change in power was the hoisting of swastika flags on public buildings. In Traunstein, the SA occupied the town hall, the district office and the trade-union head-quarters in the evening and hoisted their flag on all of them. The mayor and the police chief showed resistance but they were overcome and arrested (*47*). The expression of conformity with the new régime went even further in some other towns, where Hitler was made an honorary citizen or public squares were named after him.

Organized resistance to the Nazis collapsed without much effort. In Upper Bavaria, the local authorities 'protested dutifully against the hoisting of the swastika flag but in view of the given situation offered no actual resistance' (*48*). The confidence of the other political parties had been so eroded during the last years of the Weimar Republic, as well as during the early months of 1933, that they had lost the will to fight. The Bavarian People's Party had previously shown the most determined opposition, but the shock of the election result on 5 March had not yet worn off. The Nazis' use of constitu-tional devices for their more important acts furthermore deprived their opponents of an opportunity to stage a more dramatic show of opposition in the face of naked force.

Other political parties were not disbanded for several months, but their importance had by then long since vanished. The Nazi Government in Bavaria now attempted to lay the foundations of the new political system, but the situation immediately after the takeover in Munich was one of confusion. The revolutionary urges of the SA, which had been pent up for so long, now burst out and threatened to get completely out of control. Only after many weeks did some degree of order begin to be established.

Since the state government was already securely in the hands of the NSDAP, it is important to see how this situation developed at the local level. The formation of the Siebert Government was followed by a 'co-ordination' of the state parliament, in which the other parties continued to be represented for the time being but with a reduced number of seats. The new state parliament appointed on 28 April included forty-eight Nazi deputies, thirty from the BVP, eighteen from the SPD, five Nationalists (now called the Fighting Front Black-White-Red) and three representatives of the BBMB. The process of 'coordination' (that is, Nazification of the political system) occurred less uniformly at the local level because so many actions at first were based on arbitrary initiative rather than calculated policy.

Similar methods of pressure were used to 'coordinate' town councils so that their composition also reflected the strength of the parties in the March election. The smoothness with which these changes were effected depended not least on the attitude of local Nazi leaders, some of whom held a grudge especially against the BVP while others were more ready to resist the demands of importunate party comrades who wanted jobs. The branch leader in Röthenbach near Nuremberg felt little charity towards the town authorities there. Röthenbach had an SPD mayor with two BVP deputy mayors, one of whom was a Catholic priest. The branch leader wrote to his *Gau* office on 18 March that the continuation of this arrangement had become 'unbearable' for the NSDAP as it represented 'a belittlement of the great things that have happened in the Reich since 30 January'. His impatience was provoked even further by the behaviour of the SPD mayor, who had been outspoken in his contempt for the Nazis. The branch leader warned of the need for a 'quick intervention' by the competent authorities (*49*).

One of the complaints in the case of Röthenbach had been that SA members had been passed over in the selection of occupants for a new housing estate. Such issues were a red rag to the SA, who now assumed they could take the law into their own hands and settle these issues by direct action. The 'coordination'of town councils was seen therefore not only as a struggle for positions but also as a means of carrying out social changes. This caused much friction in several areas, where older town councillors with a long service behind them were replaced by much younger men (*50*). Branch leaders sometimes took over as mayor themselves, although in other places the incumbent was allowed to keep his office at the price of his political independence.

Although cooperation between local police and the SA generally proceeded without too much friction, confusion was created when the SA and the district offices were sent contradictory instructions from Munich. As a result the chain of command between the SA leaders and SA members broke down. The district in Fürstenfeldbruck for instance complained that young SA men were behaving abruptly in their treatment of members of rival organizations (*51*). But such actions served the purpose of the party leadership for a while by adding to the atmosphere of fear necessary for the suppression of political opposition. The use of intimidation proved effective such as in Upper Bavaria, where early in March 'persons who only a short time ago were convinced monarchists, Chiemgau partisans and champions of Bavarian independence have now become centralists and work for Hitler's cause'. People who openly supported Bavarian independence were called 'traitors' (*52*).

The SA carried out frequent but often indiscriminate house searches to impress on people that they now had the upper hand. These raids were deliberately made during the night or early in the morning. The anti-clerical outlook of SA members showed itself on occasions, for there were several incidents involving Catholic priests. In Landau an der Isar, stormtroopers attempted to enter the house of a local father. Members of the Bayernwacht were sleeping in a side-room of the house for his protection. The priest was woken up by the noise outside, and got up to threaten the SA men with shooting. There followed an exchange of insults and further threats, but violence did not occur. When the priest related the incident in church the following Sunday, there was much excitement among the townsfolk (53). Stefan Lorant, who was arrested shortly after the takeover in Munich, described the chaos which could arise:

I was taken into the room. It was full of young men arguing excitedly. One or the other of them would dash into the next room and then come back. There was a senseless rushing to and fro. Apparently, the young men had no idea what they ought to be doing. It was easy to see by the look of them that they had not been attached to police headquarters very long. They were not yet used to their new jobs (54).

The need to create order asserted itself eventually in various ways, but this presented new problems. A conflict inevitably arose between the demands for spoils by party activists and the need to rely on experienced administrators. Although the second organization department at party headquarters under Hierl had claimed as its main purpose preparations for the period after the assumption of power, it had served primarily a propaganda function rather than as a means for training a body of administrators for the future Nazi state.

Some of the officials at party headquarters were aware of this problem early on. Karl Fiehler, head of the department for municipal affairs there, sent a memorandum to *Gau* leaders in February reminding them that in the selection of town councillors

only reasonable National Socialists of high quality should be nominated, taking into consideration that more value must be placed than up to now on the professional competence and sense of responsibility for work in the community ... the situation must be avoided, whereby people apply pressure because they want to use a council seat only for the purpose of re-adjusting their often disorderly business affairs (55).

313

Fiehler's words of advice were rarely heeded by the *Gau* leaders, who often encouraged a clean sweep of local offices or found they were not able to prevent such action taking place. District offices in Middle and Upper Franconia were complaining by the middle of April that 'young, ardent but also inexperienced mayors' were taking over in town halls, which was causing considerable difficulties in municipal administration (*56*). The matter took some time to adjust itself. Even by the end of July, the district offices in Upper Bavaria reported that:

The new occupants of these municipal offices are, as each day shows, largely not in a position to conduct the work of town-clerk and the registry office in a suitable way. The authorities in charge will therefore soon have a great deal of work to do in connection with the supervision of these offices. The head of the district office in Ingolstadt is considering holding an introductory course in municipal and registry-office management for the new mayors and town-clerks of his district (*57*).

On 7 April, the new Bavarian Cabinet discussed the problems arising from arbitrary action by SA members in their capacity as auxiliary police. Hans Frank, the Minister of Justice, announced that 5,000 people had been arrested in Bavaria by the end of March. He said the number would soon rise to six or seven thousand, and for this reason it was necessary to systematize the method of arrests. Frank said that official regulations were being interpreted liberally, and that grounds for arrest were often not sufficiently established. He therefore proposed a formal method of proceedings:

Arrests on the basis of simple denunciations and arbitrary arrests by subordinate organs must cease. The interrogation of those taken into custody must be completed at once. When the reasons for the arrest are not adequate, the person concerned must be set free. Normal proceedings must be introduced to regulate responsibility and offer those arrested certain securities and opportunities for complaint. The police commandant must procure exact information on all those arrested ... A committee should be set up to examine complaints and occupied by higher police officials and one or two judges from the administrative court after reference to the SA (*58*).

The following day, Ritter von Epp published an order in Hitler's name for an end to arbitrary actions. The work of state officials should no longer be interfered with, and unauthorized action by political leaders or individual members of the NSDAP must 'without fail be discontinued'. Only the Reich Commissioner had the power to appoint people with Commissary functions, so that all arbitrary appointments made by party leaders had to be revoked (*59*).

In spite of the Cabinet's approval of Frank's plan, party district leaders still found it possible to continue with unlimited arrests. A demonstration by stormtroopers was often sufficient cause for taking an opponent of the régime into custody. People simply disappeared, rumours started and sometimes these rumours became worse than the reality. This condition of semi-anarchy was prolonged in Bavaria by the fact that the government did not act as a united body in this matter. Epp, Frank and Siebert favoured the establishment of an orderly system as soon as possible. On the other side was Adolf Wagner, who saw himself as the 'strong man' of the government and resented the fact that he had not been chosen to head the government. Wagner hoped to make use of his association with Hitler, which had lasted since the former's early days as party leader in Bavaria, to build up a position of power for himself. Wagner's party connections contrasted with those of Siebert, who was not an 'old fighter' of the NSDAP, having joined it after the 1930 Reichstag Election (see chapter 4, p. 144). Siebert did not enjoy Hitler's special confidence and was despised by the *Gau* leaders as a 'simple party comrade'. His relative powerlessness was demonstrated when Wagner, Roehm and Himmler decided at the end of March to appoint 8,075 auxiliary policemen from the SA at much cost to the state without consulting Siebert although he was Finance Minister (*60*).

Wagner planned to use his position as Minister of the Interior to extend his authority over all security forces in Bavaria through an alliance with Roehm and Himmler. The common bond between all three was a radical outlook, which differed from the more conservative attitudes of Epp, Frank and Siebert. Wagner's scheme failed in the end because he lacked Hitler's unqualified support, but also because neither Roehm nor Himmler was willing in the long run to play the role of subordinate (*61*).

Roehm was somewhat blunt in making this clear, but Himmler preferred to consolidate and widen his control over the police forces in a less ostentatious manner. After becoming head of the Munich police, Himmler was appointed by Wagner as his political adviser in the Ministry of the Interior. Soon after, Himmler took over as head of the police in Nuremberg-Fürth but gave up this post and the one in Munich when Wagner made him Commandant of the Bavarian Political Police on 1 April. With Himmler's new appointment, the political police became a separate organization under the Ministry of the Interior instead of remaining under the authority of Munich police headquarters as in Weimar times (62). Himmler put its leading positions in the hands of SS men. The first concentration camp had already been set up late in March at Dachau, a small market-town ten miles outside Munich. Himmler arranged for its establishment in the grounds of a former gunpowder factory, and justified his decision with the argument that the existing prisons were already overfilled (63). Himmler's official career thus began in his native Bavaria, from where he rose to a position of power and notoriety in the Third Reich far greater than that of any of the ministers in the new Bavarian Government.[3]

The first political opponents of the régime to be arrested were usually Communists and Social Democrats, but it was not long before the Nazis used their new power to suppress Catholic political organizations. During the late spring, the arrests of leaders and members of the Bavarian People's Party increased and the BVP ceased to hold public meetings. Even closed meetings of the party did not take place after the end of May. In June, Himmler officially banned all meetings of political organizations other than those supporting the NSDAP. Church ceremonies were only allowed if they did not have a 'worldly character' (64). The leaders of the BVP finally decided to dissolve their party on 4 July.

The Concordat signed between the Vatican and the Reich Government on 20 July removed the Church's moral support from what remained of organized Catholic resistance to the Nazis. While the Concordat promised to recognize the Church's interests by re-affirming the right of freedom of worship, guaranteeing the legal status of the clergy and protecting the Catholic educational system; it also granted recognition to the new régime by the Vatican, thereby consolidating acceptance of it by Catholics in Germany,

---

3. Only Hans Frank achieved a position of importance outside Bavaria, when he became wartime Governor-General in Poland. He was executed at Nuremberg in 1946. Ritter von Epp remained an unimportant figure-head in Bavaria, was arrested by the Americans after the War and died in Munich in 1946. Siebert served as an unobtrusive Prime Minister in Bavaria until his death in 1942. Hans Schemm was killed in an air crash in 1935. Adolf Wagner established close cooperation for a time with Rudolf Hess, Hitler's Deputy. He became Bavarian Minister of Education after Schemm's death, and followed a policy hostile to the Catholic Church. He died in Munich in 1944 after a long illness. Among the other Bavarian NSDAP leaders, Buttmann became head of the Cultural Department in the Reich Ministry of the Interior, and took an important part in the negotiations for the Concordat with the Papacy in 1933. He retired to become director of the Bavarian State Library in 1935, and died in Munich in 1947. The two *Gau* leaders Julius Streicher and Karl Wahl remained essentially party leaders. Wahl was given the presidency of the administrative region of Swabia as a consolation prize. Streicher remained head of the party organization in Franconia, where he indulged his anti-semitic hatred. He was dismissed from his post as *Gau* leader shortly before the War after falling into disgrace, and was executed at Nuremberg in 1946.

and it satisfied Hitler's long-pursued aim of excluding the clergy from political activities.

The agreement with the Vatican reinforced the 'legality' of Hitler's new order in Germany because it had the force of international law. But the 'seizure of power' in Bavaria had demonstrated where 'legality' stopped and where force took over. A new Nazi concept of law emerged in time based on the will of the *Führer*, but meanwhile the Nazi Government gave a legal stamp to its political revolution. The one-party centralized state in Germany was formalized by the Law on the Re-formation of Parties in July 1933 and the Law for the Reconstruction of the Reich in January 1934. Bavaria was now reduced to the status of a mere province of the Third Reich.

Conclusion

The Nazi 'seizure of power' in 1933 brought a political revolution in Germany, but the relative ease and rapidity with which the Nazis secured control over the state can only be explained in the context of the enduring political crisis of the preceding years. The Weimar Republic had failed to establish its legitimacy making it vulnerable during a time of economic and political upheaval. The Depression of the early 1930s crystallized the weaknesses of its political structure and accelerated the disintegration of its authority. The NSDAP assumed at the same time the role of the main opposition force in the state and infiltrated many different levels of German political life. Although it acted generally within constitutional bounds, the NSDAP nevertheless managed to present itself not only as an alternative government but also as an alternative political system. This distinction became clouded towards the end of the Weimar period, when the Republic became less of a democracy in reality and moved towards an authoritarian régime.

The rise in popular support for the NSDAP within the space of a few years was still phenomenal in spite of all these conditions, for in 1928 it had counted as merely one of a number of small parties in terms of electoral support. The party's reputation at this time was based not on its success in attracting voters but on the dramatic event of the Munich Putsch and the notoriety of its leader as a mob orator. A study of the NSDAP in Bavaria offers many lessons on how the party achieved its success. These may be summarized under the general headings: the character of the NSDAP as a totalitarian movement; the nature and extent of its mass appeal; and the relationship between the NSDAP and the state.

Firstly, the party's rise in prominence in the early 1930s was made possible by the fact that it had already established an elaborate leadership structure and laid the organizational basis for its expansion as a mass movement. The NSDAP emerged from the period of its prohibition after the Putsch in a state of weakness owing to the divisions among its leaders and activists and its limited appeal to the public. Its principal strength then was the figure of Hitler, who had succeeded in surrounding himself with the myths associated with the Putsch by the right-wing opposition to the Weimar Republic. It was already apparent at this stage that Hitler's charismatic leadership was entirely separate from internal party disputes and conflicts over policies and tactics, a factor which remained constant throughout the years of the party's rise to power and proved crucial during the critical months which preceded Hitler's appointment as Chancellor.

The pull of Hitler's *Führer* appeal among his followers was especially strong in Bavaria, where his release from prison late in 1924 soon led to rival party groups dissolving their differences and submitting themselves without question to his control. Hitler encountered less difficulty in reasserting his authority in Bavaria than anywhere else in the country because his party had its strongest roots here, as it had certain 'Bavarian' associations which in fact made it less attractive among party circles in Northern Germany and because of the proximity of party headquarters which allowed Hitler to make greater use of direct contact with local party leaders there. But the memory of the Munich Putsch proved to be a double-edged sword. While it enhanced Hitler's image in the eyes of the extreme Right, it also dominated the view of Hitler held by the Bavarian authorities. Their decision to ban Hitler from making public speeches for two years shortly after the party was refounded neutralized the main asset enjoyed by the NSDAP.

The situation appeared stable when the ban on Hitler's speeches was lifted in 1927, but it was nevertheless evident that the NSDAP constituted a different kind of party from the others on the extreme Right of German politics, not to mention the moderate parties in the Weimar Republic. If the NSDAP was most akin ideologically to the Nationalist Party (DNVP), it had more in common in terms of party structure with the Communists (KPD) from whom it borrowed ideas on methods of organization and techniques of mass agitation. The NSDAP and the KPD were similar in their attention to new methods of propaganda, although the former used these more successfully in mobilizing wider sections of the electorate. Both parties would be classified as totalitarian, but the main difference between them was the prominence given to ideology by the Communists and the emphasis on the *Führer* figure in the case of the Nazis.

The '*Führer* principle', which had held the party together during the years of its eclipse in the mid 1920s, now became more elaborately systematized. The changes in organization during 1928–29 involved a rearrangement of departments at headquarters, alterations in the regional structure of the party to coordinate it with the electoral system, as well as a more methodical and centralized approach to party activities. These changes were prompted mainly by electoral disappointment in 1928 and the need to provide an outlet for the energies of the gradually increasing number of party activists. They were also the result of the decision to concentrate on winning electoral support, and were particularly significant in Bavaria where they paved the way for agitation among the peasantry. This re-orientation of party propaganda from the cities to the rural areas, dramatized by the publication of the NSDAP Agrarian Programme in March 1930, was the most important development during these years. It derived not so much from the failure to win support from the left-wing parties in the cities, which was more true of the party in industrial areas in Northern Germany, as from the fact that Bavaria was a largely agricultural state.

The continuous emphasis on propaganda activities and electoral success which followed created a momentum of its own among party activists. The image of activism which the party cultivated and its promise of a new kind of involvement in politics accounted for the increasing attraction felt by young people towards the NSDAP. A generational gap emerged between the totalitarian parties—for the KPD was also successful in winning the active support of young people—and the older traditional parties. This momentum furthermore reduced the possibilities of conflict within the party by providing a common focus of activity, although tension and differences were still apparent over adaptation to new techniques in rural propaganda, attempts to initiate a party press and in some cases over the development of specialist organizations. When the momentum lapsed, as during the second half of 1932, the consequences were seen in the rise in internal party tension. Such conflict arose also from Hitler's deliberate policy of 'divide and rule' as well as the existence in spite of the party's growing bureaucracy of a state of semi-anarchy with the overlapping of authority created by the proliferation of party offices. All these problems had no adverse effect on the central feature of the NSDAP, namely loyalty to the *Führer*, and in fact the accusation of insufficient loyalty to him was often used in internal party disputes. It was this characteristic together with the party's professional methods of organization and superior techniques of propaganda which distinguished it from conventional protest parties on the extreme Right.

Secondly, the NSDAP was distinguished by the unprecedented degree with which it attracted mass support. Its achievement could be attributed partly to its successful organization, but the answer must also lie in the nature of its popular appeal. There were two main sources of its electoral support: firstly, the liberal and conservative parties in the towns and the peasant parties in the countryside; and, secondly, the new voters. The NSDAP succeeded largely in attracting the support of the middle classes, although it endeavoured to present itself as an integrative force which claimed to represent different interests in society, a claim strengthened by the flexibility of its propaganda and its development of specialist organizations. The NSDAP came the closest there was in the Weimar period to a 'people's party' (*Volkspartei*) appealing across classes and interests, of which the CDU has provided a further example in postwar Germany.

This study has shown, however, that support for the NSDAP was not uniform and was influenced by the same factors which determined support for the other parties. The most important of these factors was confession. It is clear from the voting patterns of the NSDAP in Bavaria that support for the party was much higher among Protestants than among Catholics. The confessional factor was evident too at the local level of politics where Protestant and Catholic communities were neighbours in the same area and even cut across economic interests, for the NSDAP faced more problems in winning over the peasantry in Catholic areas than it did in the Protestant areas of rural Franconia. The reason for the importance of the confessional factor was firstly the existence of a strong Catholic party, and secondly the fact that in the case of Bavaria Catholic interests were allied with regional patriotism. There were certain similarities between the Bavarian People's Party and the NSDAP, for both managed to appeal across classes and both were essentially 'ideological' rather than interest parties, but the substructure of politics in the traditional region of 'Old Bavaria' was weighted in favour of the BVP. This party owed the stability of its vote until 1933 to the active and moral support of the Catholic associations and the Catholic Church as well as to its ability to project its own 'fundamental view of life' which offered a form of emotional security in a time of crisis.

The combination of regional loyalty and confessional attachment provided a strong barrier to the expansion of Nazi support, but even this had its limits. Bavarian society was not entirely homogeneous, for neither factor applied to Protestant Middle and Upper Franconia. The Nazis sought to exploit antagonism in these areas against the Catholic political establishment, for Bavarian particularism had never enjoyed much following here. Although the Nazis did not finally break the stranglehold of the BVP until they had acquired power at the national level, their support among Catholic voters was far from insignificant and caused concern among the Church hierarchy. The NSDAP generally won Catholic voters from parties other than the BVP. Since the latter did by no means monopolize the Catholic electorate, for it relied chiefly on the support of strong Catholics, it followed that the Nazis won support from that section of the Catholic population whose attachment to the Church was not so firm. Their ability to attract significant support among the Catholic electorate does demonstrate that the NSDAP was more successful than any other party of the time in bridging the confessional gap.

The NSDAP achieved this by exploiting the insecurity created by the Depression, skilful propaganda tactics which generally managed to avoid embarrassing confrontations on religious issues and the emphasis on such themes as anti-Communism. The Nazis were inevitably forced to take account of the conservative ethos of Bavarian politics. Although the NSDAP had in its early days in Munich promoted anti-capitalist views, some of which were incorporated in its programme of 1920, its lack of attention to radical social

Table 8   *Vote for the NSDAP in Bavaria, Reichstag Elections 1924–33*

	May 1924 %	Dec 1924 %	May 1928 %	Sept 1930 %	July 1932 %	Nov 1932 %	March 1933 %
Germany	6·5	3·0	2·6	18·3	37·3	33·1	43·9
Bavaria	16·0	5·1	6·4	17·9	32·9	30·5	43·1
Lower Bavaria	10·7	3·1	3·5	11·6	21·1	19·0	44·0
Upper Palatinate	9·8	2·9	3·6	12·4	19·7	17·9	34·0
Upper Bavaria	19·0	5·7	7·1	17·2	25·8	22·1	38·8
Swabia	12·9	2·8	4·3	14·3	29·8	29·7	45·5
Lower Franconia	10·1	3·3	3·7	12·3	23·7	22·6	33·9
Upper Franconia	24·5	9·3	10·8	23·9	44·4	41·3	48·7
Middle Franconia	24·8	9·0	9·1	23·8	47·7	42·3	51·6

Source: Statistisches Jahrbuch für den Freistaat Bayern, 1924, 1926, 1928 and 1930; Zeitschrift des Bayerischen Statistischen Landesamts, 1932 and 1933.

demands during the period after the Putsch could be explained by the predominance of Catholic and agrarian values in Bavarian society. There was no attempt in Bavaria to spread 'socialist' ideas in the party as occurred in Northern Germany during 1925 and 1926. The NSDAP was obliged to adapt to the environment in which it was operating, and for this reason appeared more conservative than in other regions of the country.

Thirdly, the NSDAP's rise to power has finally to be examined with reference to its relationship with the state. The case of Bavaria again throws interesting light on how such a totalitarian party operated in a parliamentary system like that of the Weimar Republic. Hitler had chosen the path of 'legality' out of necessity, but this did not exclude the violent element in the Nazi movement for it rather contained it. Hitler managed to siphon off the energies of the most revolutionary wing in the party, the SA, by using them as fuel for his electoral locomotive. Yet political violence was endemic in German politics then and helped to make a sham of Weimar democracy. It was evident not so much in the form of political assassinations, which had marked the early years of the Republic, as the way in which it intruded into everyday politics—through the existence of party military organizations, and the change in the political atmosphere with the growth of civil warfare during the last critical years of the Republic. Such a state of affairs seriously affected the authority of the Republic and brought about a polarization of politics, which could only benefit a party promising a new form of law and order.

Table 9   *The confessional structure of Bavaria*

	Roman Catholics %	Protestants %
Germany	32·4	64·1
Bavaria	69·9	28·7
Lower Bavaria	98·8	1·1
Upper Palatinate	92·2	7·5
Upper Bavaria	89·5	8·8
Swabia	86·1	13·2
Lower Franconia	80·6	18·0
Upper Franconia	39·7	59·7
Middle Franconia	28·5	68·7

Source: 1933 census figures from *Statistik des Deutschen Reiches*, vol. 451/3 (Berlin, 1936), pp. 56–9.

The NSDAP's attitude to Bavarian particularism was to some extent a barometer of its general attitude towards the state. Whereas previously the party had camouflaged its centralist tendencies and sought to take refuge in Bavarian hostility to the Reich, it showed less sympathy for Bavarian susceptibilities once it gained a wide popular following and was no longer dependent on the goodwill of the Bavarian Government. The Reichstag Election of 1930 was an important stage in this development, for electoral success blessed the Nazis with political respectability and made adherence to their cause not merely one of ideological conviction or hostility to the Republic but also one of political opportunism. The party's change of attitude to Bavarian particularism became clear during the summer of 1932, when the government in Munich found itself in conflict with the new Reich Chancellor over his decision to lift the ban on the SA. By this time, Bavaria had assumed a different role in the Weimar Republic. It was no longer the patron of right-wing extremism, as it had been in the early 1920s, and had become now a source of resistance to the growth of authoritarian tendencies in national politics.

Bavaria's importance as an individual state during the political crisis which enveloped Germany in the early 1930s was reduced, however, by the general disintegration of authority in the Weimar state and the dramatic rise in popular support for the NSDAP. The Bavarian Government proved incapable in the face of these developments to resist the Nazi 'seizure of power' and was further weakened by its adherence to the conventional rules of politics at a time when they were becoming less relevant. The NSDAP had succeeded in pervading German political life by working within the system, but at the same time it had not lost its essential revolutionary characteristics in the form of its radical energies, its aim to create a new political order and its promise to bring new social élites and a younger generation to the summit of politics.

Source References

1 Bavaria and the Weimar Republic

1. Axel Schnorbus, 'Wirtschaft und Gesellschaft in Bayern vor dem Ersten Weltkrieg (1890–1914)' in Karl Bosl (ed.), *Bayern im Umbruch, Die Revolution von 1918, ihre Voraussetzungen, ihr Verlauf und ihre Folgen* (1969), p. 113.
2. Wolfgang Zorn, *Kleine Wirtschafts- und Sozialgeschichte Bayerns 1806–1933* (1962), p. 43.
3. Ernst Deuerlein (ed.), *Der Hitler-Putsch, Bayerische Dokumente zum 9. November 1923* (1962), p. 14.
4. Heinrich Hillmayr, *München und die Revolution von 1918–19* in Karl Bosl, op. cit., pp. 474–6. See also the account of the revolutionary period in Bavaria by Allan Mitchell, *Revolution in Bavaria 1918–19, the Eisner Regime and the Soviet Republic* (1965).
5. See Anthony Nicholls, 'Hitler and the Bavarian Background to National Socialism' in Anthony Nicholls and Erich Matthias (ed.), *German Democracy and Triumph of Hitler* (1971), pp. 99–128.
6. Carl Landauer, 'The Bavarian Problem in the Weimar Republic, 1918–1923', part 1, in *Journal of Modern History*, June 1944, p. 103.
7. Quoted in Georg Franz-Willing, *Die Hitlerbewegung, Der Ursprung 1919 bis 1922* (1962), p 170.
8. ibid.

2 After the Munich Putsch: Ban on the Nazi Party in Bavaria (1923–25)

1. Wilhelm Hoegner, *Der schwierige Aussenseiter, Erinnerungen eines Abgeordneten, Emigranten und Ministerpräsidenten* (1959), p. 34.
2. Werner Maser, *Die Frühgeschichte der NSDAP, Hitlers Weg bis 1924* (1965), p. 462.
3. See Ernst Deuerlein (ed.), *Der Hitler-Putsch, Bayerische Dokumente zum 9. November 1923* (1962), pp. 665–79 for reactions of the foreign press.

4. Werner Maser, op. cit., p. 463.

5. Ernst Deuerlein, op. cit., pp. 485–6.

6. ibid., p. 576.

7. ibid., p. 561.

8. ibid., pp. 629–37.

9. ibid., p. 577.

10. ibid., p. 640.

11. ibid., pp. 587–8.

12. ibid., p. 639.

13. ibid., p. 693.

14. ibid., pp. 694–6.

15. H. H. Hofmann, *Der Hitlerputsch* (1961), p. 255.

16. Report of Reich envoy in Munich, 11 April 1924, AR K2138/K591762–3, Foreign Office Library, London.

17. Munich police report, 11 October 1924, GSA MA 101248.

18. Election results from *Statistisches Jahrbuch für den Freistaat Bayern* (1924), pp. 448–57.

19. Ingolstadt town council to Government of Upper Bavaria, 15 April 1924, Stadtarchiv Ingolstadt A III/23.

20. Ludwig Volk, *Der Bayerische Episkopat und der Nationalsozialismus 1930–34* (1966), p. 20.

21. State Ministry of the Interior to Government of Upper Franconia, 6 May 1924, BSA Amberg, Reg. v. Opf./Abg. 1949, 14279.

22. Allan Mitchell, *Revolution in Bavaria 1918–19, the Eisner Régime and the Soviet Republic* (1965), pp. 29–30.

23. Karl Schwend, *Bayern zwischen Monarchie und Diktatur* (1954), p. 274.

24. ibid., pp. 265–9.

25. Robin Lenman, 'Julius Streicher and the Origins of the NSDAP in Nuremberg 1918–1923', in A. Nicholls and E. Matthias (ed.), *German Democracy and the Triumph of Hitler* (1971), p. 135.

26. Manfred Rühl, *Der Stürmer und sein Herausgeber* (1960), p. 53.

27. ibid., pp. 39–40.

28. Letter from Walter Buch to Streicher, 11 November 1923, HA 17A/1731.

29. Report of Nuremberg-Fürth police, 22 July 1924, GSA MA 101236.

30. Report of Nuremberg-Fürth police, 2 August 1924, GSA MA 101236.

31. Werner Jochmann, *Nationalsozialismus und Revolution, Ursprung und Geschichte der NSDAP in Hamburg* (1963), p. 120.

32. ibid., pp. 125–6.

33. Kurt Ludecke, *I knew Hitler* (1938), p. 220.

34. ibid., pp. 217–18.
35. ibid., p. 218.
36. ibid., p. 217.
37. Letter from Pfarrkirchen to GVG Munich, 11 November 1924, files of NSDAP Treasurer NS 1/410, Bundesarchiv Koblenz.
38. Report of Reich envoy in Munich, 4 November 1924, AR K2138/K592057–64, Foreign Office Library, London.
39. Report of Nuremberg-Fürth police, 22 August 1924, GSA MA 101236.
40. ibid.
41. GVG branch Erkersreuth-Selb to Esser, 19 August 1924, files of NSDAP, Treasurer NS 1/410, Bundesarchiv Koblenz.
42. Völkischer Block branch Straubing to GVG Munich, 11 August 1924, NS 1/411, Bundesarchiv Koblenz.
43. Letter of GVG business manager to Emma Horn, Munich, 16 September 1924, NS 1/410, Bundesarchiv Koblenz.
44. Report of Ansbach police, 31 October 1924, BSA Nuremberg 250/II.
45. Report of Munich police, 15 November 1924, GSA MA 101248.
46. D. C. Watt, *Die Bayerischen Bemühungen um Ausweisung Hitlers 1924*, Vierteljahreshefte für Zeitgeschichte, July 1958, p. 272.
47. ibid., p. 273.
48. Report of Reich envoy to Munich, 26 September 1924, AR K2138/K592011–12, Foreign Office Library, London.
49. Letter from Fremdenverkehrsverein München und Bayerisches Hochland e.V. to State Ministry of the Interior, 2 August 1924, ASA, M. Inn., 73725.
50. *Garmisch-Partenkirchener Tagblatt*, 14 July 1924.
51. D. C. Watt, op. cit., p. 274.
52. e.g. Alan Bullock, *Hitler, a Study in Tyranny* (1964), p. 127.
53. Minutes of the Bavarian Cabinet, 18 December 1924, GSA MA 99519.
54. Report of Reich envoy in Munich, 20 December 1924, AR K2138/K592161–2, Foreign Office Library, London.
55. Karl Schwend, op. cit., p. 298.

3 The Years of Stagnation (1925–27)

1. Report of Nuremberg-Fürth police, 5 February 1925, GSA MA 101237/1.
2. Report of Berlin police, 20 December 1924, GSA MA 101248.

3. e.g. Jeremy Noakes, *The Nazi Party in Lower Saxony 1921–1933* (1971), pp. 65–8.
4. Werner Jochmann, *Nationalsozialismus und Revolution* (1963), pp. 133–4.
5. Kurt Ludecke, *I knew Hitler* (1938), p. 256.
6. Police report, 24 June 1925, HA 70/1515.
7. Adolf Hitler, *Mein Kampf*, trans. James Murphy (1939), p. 292.
8. Report of Munich police, 2 March 1925, BSA Obb., LA Berchtesgaden, AR 2184 b/1.
9. Order of the Munich police, 9 March 1925, HA 23A/1757.
10. Minutes of the Bavarian Cabinet, 9 March 1925, GSA MA 99519.
11. Report of the State Ministry of the Interior, 15 March 1925, HA 23A/1757.
12. HMB/Obb., 7 March 1925, GSA MA 102142.
13. HMB/Niedb., 19 January 1925, GSA MA 102142.
14. HMB/Schw., 23 June 1925, GSA MA 102142.
15. Report of the Nuremberg-Fürth police, 23 October 1925, GSA MA 101237/2.
16. *Augsburger Postzeitung*, 12 March 1925.
17. Völkischer Block, Munich, to local branches, 11 December 1924, HA 4/88.
18. HMB/Obb., 7 April 1925, GSA MA 102142.
19. Police report, 25 April 1925, HA 69/1509.
20. Andreas Werner, *SA und NSDAP: Wehrverband, Parteitruppe oder Revolutionsarmee?* (1964), pp. 314–16.
21. Report of Nuremberg-Fürth police, 2 March 1925, HA 85/1738.
22. Police report, 25 April 1925, GSA MA 101248.
23. Report of Munich police, 20 March 1925, HA 69/1509.
24. Report of Reich envoy in Munich, 23 September 1925, AR K2138/K592446, Foreign Office Library, London.
25. Report of Munich police, 21 July 1925, BSA Obb., LA Fürstenfeld-bruck 2/30.
26. Albert Krebs, *Tendenzen und Gestalten der NSDAP* (1959), pp. 197–8.
27. Kurt Ludecke, op. cit., p. 99.
28. Ernest K. Bramsted, *Goebbels and National Socialist Propaganda 1925–1945* (1965), p. 15.
29. Philipp Bouhler to local branch leaders, 25 May 1925, HA 69/1509.
30. Bouhler to branch leaders in Regensburg and Ingolstadt, 25 May 1925, ibid.
31. *VB*, 11 July and 24 July 1925.

32. Karl Wahl, ... *es ist das deutsche Herz, Erlebnisse und Erkenntnisse eines ehemaligen Gauleiters* (1954), p. 50.
33. Franz Buchner, *Kamerad! Halt aus! Aus der Geschichte des Kreises Starnberg der NSDAP* (1938), p. 19.
34. *VB*, 27 June 1925.
35. Rudolf Hess to local branches of the NSDAP, 21 September 1925, HA 9/185.
36. Report of Nuremberg-Fürth police, 3 December 1925, Streicher Nachlass/125, Bundesarchiv Koblenz.
37. Order of Nuremberg-Fürth police, 16 September 1925, BSA Nuremberg, Reg. v. Mfr., II/686.
38. Report of Nuremberg-Fürth police, 16 December 1925, GSA MA 101237/2.
39. Report of Nuremberg-Fürth police, 6 March 1926, ibid.
40. Wolfgang Schäfer, *Entwicklung und Struktur der Staatspartei des Dritten Reiches* (1956), pp. 11–12.
41. Memorandum of Bouhler, 20 March 1926, HA 25A/1762.
42. *VB*, 22 July 1926.
43. Letter from Hitler to Franz von Pfeffer, 1 November 1926, Schumacher Sammlung/403, Bundesarchiv Koblenz.
44. Statutes of the Storm Department of the NSDAP, ibid.
45. Report of Munich police, 1 April 1926, GSA MA 101250.
46. Report of Munich police, 15 July 1927, HA 25A/1762.
47. Report of Munich police, 1 April 1926, GSA MA 101250.
48. Report of Berlin police, 28 March 1927, HA 25A/1762.
49. HMB/Ofr., 3 November 1926, GSA MA 102155/3.
50. Report of Munich police, 28 April 1926, GSA MA 101250.
51. Report of Nuremberg-Fürth police, 5 February 1925, BSA Nuremberg, 344.
52. NSDAP branch Amberg to Streicher, 28 April 1926, Streicher Nachlass/124, Bundesarchiv Koblenz.
53. Report of Ansbach police, 8 October 1927, HA 5/134.
54. Report of Nuremberg-Fürth police, 20 June 1926, HA 84/1732.
55. BA Beilngries to Government of the Upper Palatinate, 26 January 1926, BSA Amberg, Reg. v. Opf./Abg. 1949/14180.
56. Report of Nuremberg-Fürth police, 31 March 1925, GSA MA 101237/1.
57. Report on the general party meeting, 30 July 1927, Munich, HA 3/81–2.
58. Report of Berlin police, 28 March 1927, HA 25A/1762.
59. Report of Munich police, 28 April 1926, GSA MA 101250.
60. Report of Munich police, 23 October 1925, HA 24A/1757.

61. Report of Munich police, 18 September 1925, BSA Obb. Munich, LA Fürstenfeldbruck 2/30.
62. NSDAP Propaganda Department to local branches of the NSDAP, 16 March 1925, Streicher Nachlass/81, Bundesarchiv Koblenz.
63. Police report, 4 May 1925, GSA MA 101248.
64. Oron J. Hale, *The Captive Press in the Third Reich* (1964), p. 39.
65. Report of Munich police, 4 May 1925, GSA MA 101248.
66. *VB*, 28 May 1925.
67. *VB*, 30 June 1925.
68. Report of Munich police, 15 November 1926, GSA MA 101250a.
69. Report of Munich police, 23 October 1925, HA 24A/1757.
70. Report of Munich police, 19 November 1925, GSA MA 101249.
71. Report of Munich police, 19 January 1928, HA 88/1838.
72. Report of Munich police, 26 October 1927, HA 27A/1772.
73. Report of Munich police, 9 November 1927, ibid.
74. Report of Munich police, 15 November 1927, HA 73/1552.
75. Karl Buchheim, *Geschichte der christlichen Parteien in Deutschland* (1953), p. 348.
76. Karl Schwend, *Bayern zwischen Monarchie und Diktatur* (1954), pp. 309–10.
77. BA Höchstadt an der Aisch to the Government of Upper Franconia, 30 April 1925, BSA Bamberg, Reg. v. Ofr., K3/1861.
78. BA Lichtenfels, 29 April 1925, and BA Kronach, 28 April 1925, to the Government of Upper Franconia, ibid.
79. Report of the Bavarian envoy to the Vatican, 9 November 1927, GSA 1009.
80. ibid., 30 October 1928, GSA 1009.
81. Karl Buchheim, op. cit., p. 351.
82. ibid., p. 365.
83. Adolf Hitler, *Mein Kampf*, pp. 468, 469.
84. *VB*, 4 March 1927 and 14 October 1927.
85. HMB/Niedb., 4 February 1929, GSA MA 102149.
86. BBMB Programme in HA 17A/1640.
87. HMB/Obb., 19 February 1926, and HMB/Niedb., 18 March 1926, GSA MA 102143.
88. HMB/Niedb., 4 November 1925, GSA MA 102142.
89. Party history of the NSDAP branch in St Johannis, Nuremberg, Streicher Nachlass/113, Bundesarchiv Koblenz.
90. Lewis Hertzmann, *DNVP: Right-wing opposition in the Weimar Republic* (1963), pp. 58–60.

91. Report of Munich police, 4 February 1927, HA 25A/1762.
92. Report of Berlin police, 28 March 1927, GSA MA 101251.
93. Report of Munich police, 21 March 1927, HA 25A/1762.
94. Order of party headquarters, 9 March 1927, HA 25A/1762.
95. Report of Munich police, 21 March 1927, HA 25A/1762.
96. Minutes of the Bavarian Cabinet, 20 April 1925, GSA MA 99519.
97. Government of Upper Bavaria to the State Ministry of the Interior, 6 July 1925, HA 18A/1745.
98. Dr Stützel to the regional governments, 9 December 1925, BSA Obb., Munich, RA 3804/16956.
99. Meeting of the State Committee on Public Finance, 16 March 1926, HA 25A/1762.
100. Statement by Dr Held to the Bavarian parliament, 15 December 1925, HA 24A/1757.
101. *Bayerischer Kurier*, 11 March 1927.
102. Report of the Government of Swabia, 7 February 1927, HA 25A/1762.
103. Report of the Reich envoy in Munich, 29 October 1927, AR K2138/ K593541-2, Foreign Office Library, London.

4   The Expansion of the Movement (1927–30)

1. *Der Angriff*, 30 April 1928.
2. Karl Wahl, . . . *es ist das deutsche Herz* (1954), pp. 53–4.
3. Report of Munich police, 19 June 1926, GSA MA 101250.
4. *VB*, 1 May 1928.
5. *Bayerischer Kurier*, 1 May 1928.
6. Report of Nuremberg-Fürth police, 23 May 1928, BSA Nuremberg, Reg. v. Mfr., II/688.
7. *VB*, 16 May 1928.
8. Report of Reich envoy in Munich, 18 May 1928, AR K2138/K594039– 40, Foreign Office Library, London.
9. *VB*, 31 May 1928.
10. NSDAP report on district elections in Upper Bavaria, 23 July 1928, HA 30/578.
11. *Münchener Katholische Kirchenzeitung*, 8 December 1929.
12. Memorandum of Heinrich Himmler on the municipal elections in Bavaria, 18 September 1929, Schumacher Sammlung FA 48/373, Bundesarchiv Koblenz.
13. HMB/Schw., 18 October 1929, GSA MA 102150.

14. HMB/Obb., 7 January 1930, GSA MA 102151.
15. Karl Fiehler, *Gemeindewahlen und Wirtschaftspartei*, in *VB*, 27 June 1929.
16. Fiehler to Hugo Engelhard, NSDAP branch leader in Bruckmühl, 3 October 1929, Hauptamt für Kommunalpolitik NS 25/297, Bundesarchiv Koblenz.
17. Report of Ingolstadt police, August 1929, HA 8/169.
18. Diary of Michael Neumayer, NSDAP branch leader in Traunstein, 12 July 1929, Schumacher Sammlung FA 48/206, Bundesarchiv Koblenz.
19. *Bayerischer Kurier*, 31 July 1929.
20. Results of the Bavarian municipal elections from the *Zeitschrift des Bayerischen Statistischen Landesamts* (1930), pp. 471–5.
21. HMB/Mfr., 7 January 1930, GSA MA 102154.
22. Order of Gregor Strasser, 9 January 1930, files of NSDAP Organization Leader NS22/348, Bundesarchiv Koblenz.
23. HMB/Obb., 20 January 1930, GSA MA 102151.
24. *VB*, 3 September 1928.
25. *VB*, 4 September 1928.
26. Report of Berlin police, 31 October 1928, HA 24A/1758.
27. Hitler's guidelines for the sub-organizations of the NSDAP, Schumacher Sammlung FA 48/374, Bundesarchiv Koblenz.
28. Franz Buchner, *Kamerad! Halt aus!* (1938), pp. 214–15.
29. Report of Berlin police, 31 October 1928, HA 24A/1758.
30. *VB*, 5 September 1928.
31. Karl Wahl, op. cit., p. 59.
32. Order of Fritz Reinhardt, 21 June 1928, HA 9/188.
33. Report of Munich police, 13 July 1928, HA 69/1509.
34. Order of Fritz Reinhardt, 8 June 1928, in Munich police report, 13 July 1928, HA 69/1509.
35. Order of Fritz Reinhardt, 28 July 1928, in Munich police report, 31 August 1928, HA 69/1509.
36. Memorandum of Heinrich Himmler, 6 May 1929, files of NSDAP Organization Leader, NS 22/1, Bundesarchiv Koblenz.
37. Order of Fritz Reinhardt no. 3, *Lehrgang zum nationalsozialistischen Sprecher*, June 1928, HA 69/1509.
38. Report of Munich police, 1 May 1930, HA 70/1529.
39. List of speakers for *Gau* Munich–Upper Bavaria, April 1931, HA 9/191.
40. Benedikt Lochmüller, *Hans Schemm* (1935), vol. 2, p. 107.

41. Report of Bayreuth police, 17 January 1929, ASA Munich, M. Inn. 73725.

42. Benedict Lochmüller, op. cit., p. 189.

43. Memorandum of *Gau* Upper Franconia to branch leaders, 4 February 1929, files of NSDAP Organization Leader NS 22/375, Bundesarchiv Koblenz.

44. Memorandum of *Gau* Upper Franconia to district leaders, 4 February 1929, ibid.

45. Memorandum of Karl Holz to district and branch leaders, *Gau* Middle Franconia, July 1929, Streicher Nachlass/102, Bundesarchiv Koblenz.

46. 'Meeting report' in HA 8/173.

47. Walter Grimm, business manager of *Gau* Upper Bavaria (Herrsching), to Weinbeer, NSDAP branch leader in Ottobrunn, 12 April 1930, HA 9/190.

48. 'Aus der Geschichte der Ortsgruppe Memmingen' by district leader Reiger, *Allgäuer Beobachter*, 16 February 1934.

49. Report of Augsburg police, no. 9, May 1930, HA 70/1516.

50. HMB/Schw., 5 July 1930, GSA MA 102152.

51. Report of Augsburg police, no. 9, May 1930, HA 70/1516.

52. HMB/Schw., 20 September 1929, GSA MA 102150.

53. Order of Fritz Reinhardt no. 10, *Deutsches Sommerfest*, 7 July 1928, HA 9/188.

54. ibid.

55. Benedict Lochmüller, op. cit., pp. 143–4.

56. ibid., pp. 144–5.

57. ibid., pp. 145–7.

58. Memorandum of *Gau* Upper Franconia to district leaders, 4 February 1929, files of NSDAP Organization Leader NS 22/375, Bundesarchiv Koblenz.

59. Benedict Lochmüller, op. cit., pp. 119–20.

60. ibid., p. 213.

61. Proposal of Knabe (Dresden), meeting on organizational questions, Nuremberg party rally 1927, HA 21/390.

62. Details on Dr Ludwig Liebl from 'Ein Doppeljubiläum für San.-Rat Dr Ludwig Liebl' in *Der Donaubote*, 13 November 1934.

63. HMB/Obb., 22 April 1930, GSA MA 102151.

64. *Der Donaubote*, 13 November 1934.

65. Report of Ingolstadt police, March 1928, HA 8/169.

66. Report of Ingolstadt police, 21 October 1927, HA 8/169.

67. Report of Munich police, 7 February 1930, HA 70/1510.
68. Report of Munich police, 22 May 1930, HA 70/1516.
69. HMB/Schw., 20 January 1928, GSA MA 102147.
70. Karl Wahl, op. cit., p. 61.
71. *Nördlinger Zeitung*, 2 February 1928.
72. ibid.
73. *Günz- und Mindelbote*, 14 February 1929.
74. Erwein von Aretin, *Krone und Ketten, Erinnerungen eines bayerischen Edelmannes* (1955), pp. 28–9.
75. Minutes of the Bavarian Cabinet, 29 April 1930, GSA MA 99523.
76. BA Traunstein to the Government of Upper Bavaria, 3 April 1928, BSA Obb., Munich, RA 3789/16837.
77. HMB/Schw., 8 November 1929, GSA MA 102150.
78. HMB/Niedb., 18 April 1930, GSA MA 102151.
79. HMB/Niedb., 18 September 1929, GSA MA 102150.
80. HMB/Niedb., 18 April 1930, GSA MA 102151.
81. HMB/Schw., 23 June 1930, GSA MA 102152.
82. *Die Entwicklung der nationalsozialistischen Bewegung des Kreises Neu-Ulm* (typed manuscript, probably 1934), HA 91/1881.
83. HMB/Niedb., 3 February 1930, GSA MA 102151.
84. HMB/Schw., 5 July 1930, GSA MA 102152.
85. Handbill of NSDAP branch Kulmbach, 31 May 1930, BSA Bamberg, K3/1967/4870.
86. e.g. HMB/Mfr., 20 February 1930, GSA MA 102154.
87. HMB/Ufr., 10 March 1930, GSA MA 102151.
88. Report of Nuremberg-Fürth police, 31 January 1929, GSA MA 101239/1.
89. Report of Nuremberg-Fürth police, 20 March 1930, GSA MA 101240/1.
90. Report of Munich police, 8 April 1930, HA 70/1512.
91. *Münchner Post*, 21 March 1930.
92. Order of Dr Stützel, State Minister of the Interior, on the maintenance of public security to local authorities, 5 June 1930, BSA Nuremberg, Reg. v. Mfr. II/689.
93. ibid.
94. *The Times*, London, 6 June 1930.
95. Report of Reich envoy in Munich, 12 June 1930, AR K2138/ K595102–3, Foreign Office Library, London.
96. Memorandum of the State Ministry of the Interior, 11 October 1929, HA 19A/1747.
97. HMB/Schw., 18 October 1929 and 20 December 1929, GSA MA 102150.

98. BA Lichentenfels to the State Ministry of the Interior, 1 October 1929, BSA Bamberg, K3/1967/4861.

99. ibid.

100. ibid.

101. HMB/Obb., 22 April 1930, GSA MA 102151.

102. BA Neustadt an der Aisch to State Ministry of the Interior, 13 May 1930, BSA Nuremberg, Reg. v. Mfr., II/689.

103. *Münchner Post*, 28 March 1930.

104. Oberammergau police station to BA Garmisch, 7 April 1930, HA 20A/1748.

105. BA Garmisch to the Government of Upper Bavaria, 30 May 1930, HA 20A/1748.

106. *Nördlinger Zeitung*, 7 June 1930.

107. HMB/Obb., 4 July 1930, GSA MA 102152.

108. Report of Reich envoy in Munich, 12 June 1930, AR K2138/K595102–3, Foreign Office Library, London.

109. *The Times*, London, 10 June 1930.

110. BA Coburg to Government of Upper Franconia, 15 July 1930, BSA Bamberg, Reg. v. Ofr., 1882.

111. BA Gunzenhausen to Government of Middle Franconia, 23 July 1930, BSA Nuremberg, Reg. v. Mfr. II/689.

112. HMB/Obb., 4 July 1930, GSA MA 102152.

113. Report of Munich police, 9 July 1930, HA 70/1510.

114. Memorandum of the State Ministry of the Interior, *Sicherung der Reichstagswahl*, 27 August 1930, HA 24A/1758.

115. ibid.

116. HMB/Ufr., 22 July 1930, GSA MA 102151.

117. Report of Württemberg state police, 7 May 1930, HA 58/1403.

118. Order of Fritz Reinhardt, *Gau* Upper Bavaria, 23 July 1930, HA 9/190.

119. ibid.

120. Dr Goebbels, Reich Propaganda Leader, *Ausserordentliches Rundschreiben der Reichspropagandaleitung zur Vorbereitung des Wahlkampfes zur Reichstagswahl am 14. September 1930*, Munich, 23 July 1930, Streicher Nachlass/24, Bundesarchiv Koblenz.

121. ibid.

122. NSDAP leaflet no. 5 for 1930 Election, Streicher Nachlass/24, Bundesarchiv Koblenz.

123. NSDAP leaflets nos. 14, 15, 16 and 19 for 1930 Election, ibid.

124. Goebbels' memorandum of 23 July 1930 (see above 120).

125. *VB*, 17/18 August 1930.

126. HMB/Obb., 19 August 1930, GSA MA 102152.

127. HMB/Schw., 5 September 1930, GSA MA 102152.

128. HMB/Obb., 3 September 1930, GSA MA 102152.

129. *Augsburger Postzeitung*, 9, 12 and 14 September 1930.

130. ibid., 10 and 14 September 1930.

131. Results of the 1930 Reichstag Election in Bavaria from *Statistisches Jahrbuch für den Freistaat Bayern* (1930), pp. 570–81.

132. HMB/Mfr., 19 September 1930, GSA MA 102154.

133. *Münchener Neueste Nachrichten*, 15 September 1930.

134. *Augsburger Postzeitung*, 17 September 1930.

135. K. D. Bracher, *Die Auflösung der Weimarer Republik* (1964), pp. 366–7.

136. Report of Munich police, 24 October 1930, HA 24A/1758.

137. Hans Volz, *Daten der Geschichte der NSDAP* (1937), p. 13.

138. Report of Munich police, March 1931, HA 24A/1759.

139. Report of Nuremberg-Fürth police, 8 October 1930, GSA MA 101240/2.

140. HMB/Mfr., 6 October 1930, GSA MA 102154.

141. HMB/Schw., 6 February 1931, GSA MA 102153.

142. Report of Munich police, 26 February 1931, GSA MA 101238.

5 The NSDAP and Religion: the Problem of Roman Catholic Voters

1. Kurt Ludecke, *I knew Hitler* (1938), p. 701.

2. E. K. Bramsted, *Goebbels and National Socialist Propaganda, 1925–45* (1965), p. 6.

3. Werner Stephan, *Joseph Goebbels, Dämon einer Diktatur* (1949), p. 25.

4. See E. K. Bramsted, op. cit., pp. 4–8.

5. Adolf Hitler, *Mein Kampf* (1939), p. 107.

6. Quoted in J. S. Conway, *The Nazi Persecution of the Churches* (1968), p. 5.

7. BA Hof to the State Ministry of the Interior, 26 September 1925, BSA Bamberg, Reg. v. Ofr. K3/4713, and BA Hof to the Government of Upper Franconia, 14 September 1925, BSA Bamberg, Reg. v. Ofr. K3/1862.

8. Report of Hof police inspector, 7 November 1925, HA 86/1742.

9. HMB/Ofr., 6 November 1925, GSA MA 102155/2.

10. Ferdinand Kohl to Streicher, Nuremberg, 5 August 1925, Streicher Nachlass/81, Bundesarchiv Koblenz.

11. Benedict Lochmüller, *Hans Schemm* (1935), p. 77.
12. Report of Hof police to the Government of Upper Franconia, 11 April 1929, BSA Nuremberg, P.D. Nürnberg-Fürth/378.
13. Report of Bayreuth city council, 15 July 1929, BSA Bamberg, Reg. v. Ofr. K3/1878.
14. Minute book of the NSDAP branch Berchtesgaden, 4 July 1929, HA 1A/217.
15. HMB/Ofr., 5 October 1925, GSA MA 102155/2.
16. See *VB*, 21, 22 and 28 February 1929.
17. Chronicle of the NSDAP branch in Immenstadt, HA 7/158.
18. Ludwig Volk, *Der Bayerische Episkopat und der Nationalsozialismus 1930–34* (1966), pp. 15–19.
19. Dr Held to Cardinal Faulhaber, 6 October 1923, quoted in Ludwig Volk, op. cit., p. 17.
20. Joseph Held, *Heinrich Held, Ein Leben für Bayern* (1958), p. 36.
21. Heinrich Lutz, *Demokratie in Zwielicht, Der Weg der deutschen Katholiken aus dem Kaiserreich in die Republik, 1914–25* (1963), p. 98.
22. See Ludwig Volk, 'Kardinal Faulhabers Stellung zur Weimarer Republik und zum nationalsozialistischen Staat' in *Stimmen der Zeit*, 1966, pp. 173–95, for a discussion of Faulhaber's political attitudes during this period.
23. Report of Ingolstadt police, 11 May 1928, HA 8/169.
24. *Augsburger Postzeitung*, 26 August 1930.
25. Report of the Reich envoy in Munich, 5 March 1930, AR K2138/K594996–7, Foreign Office Library, London.
26. *Augsburger Postzeitung*, 3 September 1930.
27. *Regensburger Anzeiger*, 8 June 1930.
28. Dr Erbacher, *An alle katholischen Wähler der Pfarrei Lengfurt*, 8 September 1930, Streicher Nachlass/24, Bundesarchiv Koblenz.
29. NSDAP pamphlet *Gotteshaus oder politisches Versammlungslokal?*, Manzell, 17 July 1930, Nachlass Streicher/81, Bundesarchiv Koblenz.
30. ibid.
31. Ludwig Volk, *Der Bayerische Episkopat*, p. 22.
32. ibid., p. 22.
33. ibid., p. 45.
34. ibid., p. 45.
35. E. N. Peterson, *The Limits of Hitler's Power* (1969), pp. 295–6.
36. Letter of Walter Krauss, Eichstätt, 19 October 1930, NSDAP organization files, NS 22/375, Bundesarchiv Koblenz.

37. ibid.

38. *C.V. Zeitung*, 26 and 5 September 1930.

39. Philipp Bouhler, memorandum 30 October 1930, Nachlass Streicher/81, Bundesarchiv Koblenz.

40. *Bayerischer Kurier*, 21 November 1930.

41. *Augsburger Postzeitung*, 7 October 1930.

42. ibid., 8, 11, 12 and 15 October 1930.

43. *Hakenkreuz gegen Christenkreuz*, ibid., 21 October 1930.

44. *Hitler's Table Talk, 1941–44* (1953), p. 422.

45. Quoted in 'The Story of Rosenberg's "Mythus"' in *The Wiener Library Bulletin*, vol. vii, no. 5-6 (1953).

46. *Memoirs of Alfred Rosenberg*, ed. by S. Lang and E. von Schenck, pp. 94–5.

47. ibid., p. 83.

48. *Hitler's Table Talk*, p. 422.

49. Report of Munich police, 12 December 1930, HA 88/1843, and *VB*, 13 December 1930.

50. See Ludwig Volk, *Der Bayerische Episkopat*, pp. 22–8.

51. ibid., p. 25.

52. ibid., pp. 25–6.

53. Report of police chief of Regensburg to the State Ministry of the Interior, 26 May 1930, HA 20A/1748.

54. Ludwig Volk, op. cit., p. 42.

55. *VB*, 22 May 1930 and *Münchner Post*, 31 May 1930.

56. Report of the State Ministry of the Interior, 30 May 1930, HA 20A/1748.

57. Guenter Lewy, *The Catholic Church and Nazi Germany* (1964), pp. 8–9.

58. *VB*, 17, 18 and 24 October 1931.

59. See Ludwig Volk, op. cit., pp. 22–4.

60. ibid., p. 25.

61. ibid., p. 25.

62. ibid., p. 30.

63. *Nationalsozialismus und Seelsorge, Pastorale Anweisung für den Klerus bestimmt*, Amtsblatt für die Erzdiözese München und Freising, 10 February 1931, Bavarian State Library, Munich.

64. ibid.

65. Ludwig Volk, op. cit., p. 37.

66. *Regensburger Anzeiger*, 12 April 1931.

67. Ludwig Volk, op. cit., p. 36.

68. ibid., p. 44.

69. Guenter Lewy, op. cit., p. 272.

70. Text of Haeuser's speech from BSA Obb., Munich, LA Pfaffenhofen 1/9.

71. Information on Schachleiter from the *VB*, 21 June 1937, personality files of the NSDAP in the Berlin Document Center and GSA MA 107279–81.

72. *Bayerischer Kurier*, 16 September 1930.

73. Report of the Nuremberg-Fürth police, 31 January 1929, GSA MA 101239/1.

74. *Fränkischer Kurier*, 18 April 1931 and 8 January 1932.

75. HMB/Ufr., 7 July 1930, GSA MA 102151.

76. HMB/Ufr., 4 December 1931, GSA MA 102151.

77. Report of Nuremberg-Fürth police, 6 March 1931, GSA MA 101241/1.

78. *Fränkischer Kurier*, 9 January 1931.

79. Benedict Lochmüller, op. cit., p. 267.

80. Report of Bayreuth city council to the Government of Upper Franconia, 6 December 1927, BSA Bamberg, Reg. v. Ofr./4863.

81. e.g. see HMB/Schw., 21 February 1931, GSA MA 102153 and report of Nuremberg-Fürth police, 6 March 1931, GSA MA 101241/1.

82. *Die Front*, 8 July 1931.

83. Mindelstetten police station to BA Riedenburg, 15 February 1931, BSA Amberg, BA Riedenburg/1773.

84. Riedenburg police to BA Riedenburg, 16 November 1931, ibid.

85. Riedenburg police to BA Riedenburg, 28 July 1932, ibid.

86. Mindelstetten police to BA Riedenburg, 23 April 1932, ibid.

87. Beratzhausen police to BA Parsberg, 23 March 1931, BSA Amberg, Reg. v. Opf/14189.

88. BA Parsberg to the Government of the Upper Palatinate, 30 December 1930, ibid.

89. *Rettet Kirche und Christentum*, NSDAP leaflet for the Bavarian State Election April 1932, Streicher Nachlass/109, Bundesarchiv Koblenz.

90. *Bayerischer Kurier*, 30 July 1932.

91. *Die Front*, 9 April 1932.

92. ibid., 23 April 1932.

93. Report of the Nuremberg-Fürth police, 6 March 1931, GSA MA 101241/1.

94. Quoted in Hans Müller (ed.), *Katholische Kirche und Nationalsozialismus* (1965), p. 39.

95. Report of Bamberg police to State Ministry of the Interior, 21 November 1931, BSA Bamberg, Reg. v. Ofr. K3/4983.

96. *Augsburger Postzeitung*, 3 June 1932.

97. Report of Nuremberg-Fürth police, 8 April 1927, HA 86/1743.
98. Rothenburg police to BA Rothenburg, 17 May 1928, BSA Nuremberg, Reg. v. Mfr. II/688.
99. HMB/Obb., 5 February 1932, GSA MA 102155.
100. *Fränkisches Volksblatt*, 20 February 1932.
101. HMB/Obb., 20 January 1931, GSA MA 102153.
102. BA Vilshofen to the Government of Lower Bavaria, 14 January 1932, ASA Munich, M. Inn./73719.
103. State Ministry of the Interior to the State Ministry of Justice, 29 December 1931, ASA Munich, M. Inn./73719.
104. Windsbach police to BA Ansbach, 18 March 1932, BSA Nuremberg, BA Ansbach/2205.
105. Adolf Hitler, *Mein Kampf*, p. 383.
106. ibid., p. 361.
107. ibid., p. 395.
108. See E. K. Bramsted, op. cit., pp. 7–8.
109. Albert Krebs, *Tendenzen und Gestalten der NSDAP* (1959), p. 138.
110. J. Nötges, *Nationalsozialismus und Katholizismus* (1931), p. 99.

6 The Mass Appeal of the Nazis: Party Organization and Propaganda (1930–32)

1. *Parteistatistik*, Reichsorganisationsleiter der NSDAP (1935), pp. 26–7, 86–7.
2. ibid., pp. 304–5.
3. ibid., pp. 112–17.
4. *Der grossdeutsche Reichstag 1938* (1938), p. 400.
5. Wilhelm Hoegner, *Der schwierige Aussenseiter* (1959), p. 41.
6. *Münchner Post*, 21 March 1930.
7. *Bayerischer Kurier*, 30 April 1931.
8. ibid.
9. Memorandum of the State Ministry of Finance to the other state ministeries, *Political Activity of Civil Servants*, 31 March 1931, GSA MA 102230.
10. Minutes of the Bavarian Cabinet, 17 April 1931, GSA MA 99523.
11. HMB/Ofr., 16 December 1931, GSA MA 102155/3.
12. Party history of the Neu-Ulm branch, undated, HA 91/1881.
13. HMB/Obb., 6 October 1930, GSA MA 102152.
14. HMB/Schw., 6 July 1931, GSA MA 102154.

15. Dr Stützel to district offices, 2 April 1932, BSA Bamberg, BA Pegnitz/ 566.

16. State Ministry of the Interior to the Finance Office of South Munich, 1 April 1932, HA 21A/1752.

17. Report of Munich police, 17 January 1932, HA 21A/1751.

18. Report of Munich police, 2 August 1931, HA 70/1514.

19. Hierl memorandum 22 October 1929, Organization Department II, Schumacher Sammlung/FA 48/375, Bundesarchiv Koblenz.

20. Material on Adolf Wagner from *Der grossdeutsche Reichstag 1938* (1938), pp. 439–40 and various reports in the Hauptarchiv, e.g. HA 70/1516 (report of March 1931).

21. Report of Munich police, 17 December 1929, HA 24A/1758.

22. From *Richtlinien für die Arbit der Bezirks- und Ortsgruppenleiter des Gaues München–Oberbayern*, 20 July 1931, HA 90/1869.

23. Memorandum of propaganda leader *Gau* Munich–Upper Bavaria, 20 April 1931, HA 9/191.

24. History of the Rosenheim branch of the NSDAP in the *Rosenheimer Tagblatt*, 10–11 August 1935.

25. From *Richtlinien für die Arbeit der Bezirks- und Ortsgruppenleiter des Gaues München–Oberbayern*, 20 July 1931, HA 90/1869.

26. Memorandum of Gustav Freytag, Department of Race and Culture, *Gau* Munich–Upper Bavaria, 27 April 1931, HA 9/191.

27. List of officials of the Department of Race and Culture, *Gau* Munich–Upper Bavaria, 1 September 1931, HA 9/191.

28. Memorandum of War Victims Department, *Gau* Munich–Upper Bavaria, 12 and 13 April 1932, HA 9/192.

29. Order of *Gau* Munich–Upper Bavaria to branch and district leaders, 12 February 1932, HA 8/176.

30. Figures announced at a conference of *Gau* leaders in Munich, July 1932, *Bayerischer Kurier*, 16 July 1932.

31. Hitler's manifesto on factory cells, 16 September 1929, HA 70/1510.

32. Report of Munich police, 20 April 1931, BSA Landshut, 168/5–30.

33. Report of Holzkirchen police, 22 October 1931, HA 74/1553.

34. e.g. see the files of the NSDAP Organization Leader, Bundesarchiv Koblenz, for the system of sub-departments for the *Gaue* of Swabia, April 1931 (NS 22/380); Upper Franconia, December 1930 (NS 22/374); and Lower Franconia, June 1931 (NS 22/381).

35. Report of *Gau* Munich–Upper Bavaria, undated but probably 1932, HA 71/1539.

36. Report of Munich police, 8 April 1930, HA 71/1540.

37. Letter from M. Heinloth to HJ leader Lohr, 4 November 1932, HA 71/1540.

38. *Vier Jahre Hitlerjugend im Gau München–Oberbayern* in *Die Front*, 3 September 1932.

39. *NS Schülerbund, Reichsleitung: Richtlinien für die Gründung und die Arbeit einer N.S. Schülerbundsortsgruppe*, December 1929, files of the NSDAP Organization Leader, NS 22/344, Bundesarchiv Koblenz.

40. HMB/Ufr., 5 May 1931, GSA MA 102151.

41. *Bestand des NS Schülerbundes 1930–31*, HA 18/344.

42. Report of Nuremberg-Fürth police, 18 December 1930, GSA MA 101240/2.

43. Report of Reich envoy in Munich, 19 July 1930, AR K2138/K595132–3, Foreign Office Library, London.

44. Report of Reich envoy in Munich, 10 July 1930, AR K2138/K595126–8, Foreign Office Library, London.

45. Report of Munich police, 29 December 1931, GSA MA 101238.

46. *VB*, 22 November 1928.

47. Report of Munich police, 22 November 1927, HA 34A/1796.

48. Wilhelm Hoegner, op. cit., p. 53.

49. *Augsburger Postzeitung*, 29 January 1931.

50. Report of Nuremberg-Fürth police, 9 April 1929, GSA MA 101239/1.

51. *Münchner Post*, 14 July 1930.

52. SPD parliamentary group, question no. 265 in Bavarian Landtag, 1 July 1931, GSA MA 100425.

53. See the report of the Mayor of Erlangen, 22 January 1931, BSA Nuremberg, Reg. v. Mfr. II/690, for a full description of these incidents.

54. *Augsburger Postzeitung*, 24 September 1930.

55. ibid., 29 January 1931.

56. *Vossische Zeitung*, 13 July 1930.

57. Report of Rothenburg police, 6 July 1931, BSA Nuremberg, Reg. v. Mfr. II/693.

58. HMB/Schw., 5 February 1930, GSA MA 102151.

59. Report of Munich police, 9 June 1931, HA 24A/1759.

60. Öttingen police report, 29 June 1931, BSA Neuburg a.d. Donau, BA Nördlingen/1315.

61. BA Wasserburg am Inn to the Government of Upper Bavaria, 30 November 1931, HA 21A/1751.

62. HMB/Mfr., 18 December 1931, GSA MA 102154.

63. HMB/Ufr., 4 April 1931, GSA MA 102151.

64. Memorandum of propaganda leader, *Gau* Swabia, 8 April 1931, Schumacher Sammlung/209, Bundesarchiv Koblenz.
65. BA Starnberg to the Government of Upper Bavaria, 8 December 1931, BSA Obb. Munich, RA 3804/16957.
66. HMB/Schw., 21 August 1931, GSA MA 102154.
67. HMB/Schw., 5 February 1932, GSA MA 102155.
68. HMB/Ofr., 2 December 1931, GSA MA 102155/3.
69. Agrarian Political Office memorandum to *Gau* leaders, 21 August 1930, files of NSDAP Organization leader NS 22/360, Bundesarchiv Koblenz.
70. Memorandum of Walther Darré, *The National Socialist Agricultural Specialists*, November 1930, ibid.
71. Memorandum of Darré, 21 August 1930 (see above 69).
72. ibid.
73. Memorandum of Darré, 9 January 1931, Schumacher Sammlung FA 48/214, Bundesarchiv Koblenz.
74. Gregor Strasser to Bayreuth, 31 December 1930, files of NSDAP Organization Leader NS 22/375, Bundesarchiv Koblenz.
75. Otto Nippold, business manager *Gau* Munich–Upper Bavaria, to district and branch leaders, 22 January 1931 and 5 March 1931, HA 9/191.
76. *Richtlinien für die Arbeit der Bezirks- und Ortsgruppenleiter des Gaues München–Oberbayern*, 20 June 1931, HA 90/1869.
77. Darré to Reich Organization Leader II, 23 July 1931, files of NSDAP Organization Leader NS 22/360, Bundesarchiv Koblenz.
78. ibid.
79. Report of Munich police, 9 June 1931, GSA MA 101238.
80. ibid.
81. From Munich police report, 2 August 1931, GSA MA 101238.
82. Report of Munich police, 22 February 1932, GSA MA 101239.
83. ibid.
84. *Wille und Weg*, July 1931, HA 87/1800.
85. HMB/Ufr., 2 February 1932, GSA MA 102151.
86. Darré confidential memorandum to the staff of party headquarters, 14 September 1931, files of NSDAP Organization Leader NS 22/360, Bundesarchiv Koblenz.
87. HMB/Obb., 19 November 1931, GSA MA 102155.
88. HMB/Niedb., 4 November 1931, BSA Landshut, 168/5–35, no. 88.
89. HMB/Opf., 4 December 1931, GSA MA 102144.
90. HMB/Obb., 21 December 1931, GSA MA 102155.

91. HMB/Mfr., 5 April 1932, GSA MA 102154.

92. HMB/Mfr., 4 February 1932, GSA MA 102154.

93. Party headquarters to Freiherr von Reibnitz, Maltschawe, 31 August 1931, files of NSDAP Organization Leader NS 22/360, Bundesarchiv Koblenz.

94. Letter from Brannenburg to *VB* office Munich, 30 October 1931, HA 49/1110.

95. Leaflet of *Bayerischer Christlicher Bauernverein*, BSA Obb. Munich, LA Pfaffenhofen 1/9.

96. HMB/Niedb., 18 February 1931, GSA MA 102153.

97. HMB/Niedb., 3 February 1931, BSA Landshut, 168/5–35, no. 88.

98. HMB/Obb., 20 October 1931, GSA MA 102154.

99. Report of Munich police, 26 February 1931, BSA Landshut, 168/5–30.

100. *Die Front*, 16 January 1932.

101. HMB/Niedb., 19 July 1932, GSA MA 102156.

102. *Bauernbündler! Heraus zum Protest!* NSDAP election pamphlet, BSA Amberg, BA Riedenburg/1773.

103. BA Dinkelsbühl to the Government of Middle Franconia, 24 March 1931, BSA Nuremberg, Reg. v. Mfr., II/690.

104. HMB/Mfr., 19 April 1932, GSA MA 102154.

105. Darré to NSDAP Organization Leader, 13 June 1932, HA 29/553.

106. *Die Nationalsozialistische Bauernschaft*, files of the NSDAP Organization Leader NS 22/360, Bundesarchiv Koblenz.

107. Manfred Rühl, *Der Stürmer und sein Herausgeber* (1960), p. 137.

108. NSDAP poster, 21 April 1932, BSA Nuremberg, Reg. v. Mfr. II/692.

109. Report of Nuremberg-Fürth police, 6 June 1929, GSA MA 101239/1.

110. State Ministry of the Interior to BA Ansbach, 14 December 1931, BSA Nuremberg, Reg. v. Mfr. II/691.

111. HMB/Ofr., 3 February 1929, GSA MA 102155/3.

112. Proceedings of the Bavarian State Parliament, 20 July 1927, Nachlass Buttmann.

113. Stefan Schwarz, *Die Juden in Bayern im Wandel der Zeiten* (1963), p. 302.

114. These figures and the following ones are from the 1933 census on the Jewish population published in the *Zeitschrift des Bayerischen Statistischen Landesamts* (1934).

115. See H. H. Hofmann, 'Ländliches Judentum in Franken' in *Tribüne: Zeitschrift zum Verständnis des Judentums* (1968), pp. 2890–904.

116. BA Hof to the Government of Upper Franconia, 23 January 1929, BSA Bamberg, K3 1967/4816.

117. ibid.

118. Dorothee Linn, *Das Schicksal der jüdischen Bevölkerung in Memmingen von 1933 bis 1945* (1962), pp. 6–8.

119. ibid., p. 13.

120. Arnd Müller, *Geschichte der Juden in Nürnberg 1146–1945* (1968), p. 203.

121. ibid., pp. 202–3 for the full list of Jewish businesses in Nuremberg.

122. ibid., p. 201.

123. Manfred Rühl, op. cit., pp. 160–1.

124. Arnd Müller, op. cit., p. 195.

125. Joseph Goebbels, *Kampf um Berlin* (1932), p. 188.

126. E. K. Bramsted, *Goebbels and National Socialist Propaganda 1925–1945* (1965), pp. 29–30.

127. Oron J. Hale, *The Captive Press in the Third Reich* (1964), pp. 40–1.

128. ibid., p. 40.

129. ibid., pp. 40–1.

130. Report of the *Gau* press agent, Munich–Upper Bavaria, 22 June 1932, HA 9/192.

131. Dr Otto Dietrich, Reich Press Office NSDAP, 27 July 1932, *Die Nationalsozialistische Pressepolitik und ihre Zukunftsentwicklung*, p. 3, files of NSDAP Organization Leader NS 22/4, Bundesarchiv Koblenz.

132. ibid., p. 3.

133. BA Memmingen report, 7 August 1931, HA 47/965.

134. Reports on *Der Donaubote* in HA 47/1005.

135. Reports on the *Neue Nationalzeitung* in HA 48/1065.

136. HMB/Ufr., 23 February 1931 and 18 December 1931, GSA MA 102151.

137. HMB/Schw., 6 March 1931 and 4 April 1931, GSA MA 102153.

138. Quoted in Z. A. B. Zeman, *Nazi Propaganda* (1964), p. 32.

139. Reports on the *Neue Nationalzeitung* in HA 48/1065.

140. NSDAP branch Augsburg to party members, 2 February 1931, Schumacher Sammlung/209, Bundesarchiv Koblenz.

141. Reports on the *Neue Nationalzeitung* in HA 48/1065.

142. Franz Maierhofer, *Gau* leader Lower Bavaria, to party leaders and members, 17 October 1932, NSDAP organization files NS 22/1, Bundesarchiv Koblenz.

143. Dietrich's report of 27 July 1932 (see 131 above).

144. ibid.

145. ibid.

146. See history of the *Allgäuer Tagblatt* in HA 47/966.

147. Report on the *Oberbayerische Rundschau* in HA 47/992.

148. See reports on *Die Front* in HA 49/1126.

149. Dietrich's report of 27 July 1932 (see 131 above).

150. Karl Wahl, . . . *es ist das deutsche Herz* (1954), pp. 66–7.

151. Report on *Die Front*, 18 March 1936, in HA 49/1126.

152. Otto Nippold, *Gau* business manager Munich–Upper Bavaria, to branch leaders, 4 September 1931, HA 9/191.

153. *Allgäuer Beobachter*, 16 February 1934.

154. Reich Ministry of the Interior, October 1930, *Das hochverräterische Unternehmen der NSDAP*, AR K2138/K646562–625, Foreign Office, London.

155. Report of Munich police to State Ministry of the Interior, 22 December 1931, HA 17/317.

156. Memorandum of the State Ministry of the Interior, undated, HA 90/1872.

157. Dr Stützel to district offices and police stations, 7 December 1931, HA 24A/1759.

158. Reports of *The Times*, London, 6 and 7 July 1931.

159. Report of Munich police, 2 August 1931, HA 70/1510.

160. Report of Munich police, 23 October 1931, HA 70/1510.

161. Hitler's order of 30 March 1931 in report of Nuremberg-Fürth police, 27 June 1931, GSA MA 101241/1.

162. Report of Nuremberg-Fürth police, 24 October 1931, GSA MA 101241/2.

163. Norman Baynes, *Hitler's Speeches* (1942), vol. 1, pp. 163–4.

164. HMB/Schw., 22 December 1930, GSA MA 102152.

165. HMB/Schw., 20 June 1931, GSA MA 102154.

166. HMB/Schw., 6 February 1931, GSA MA 102153.

167. Mayor of Lichtenberg to Naila, 24 September 1931, BSA Bamberg, BA Naila/1210.

168. Reports by BA Garmisch, 7, 10 and 11 May 1932, HA 21A/1753.

169. HMB/Obb., 7 October 1931, GSA MA 102154.

170. Minutes of the Bavarian Cabinet, 9 July 1931, GSA MA 99524.

171. Letter from Karl Ladenburger to Dr Stützel, 14 January 1932, HA 34A/1799

172. *Fränkischer Kurier*, 26 August 1930.

173. Franz Schwede-Coburg, *Kampf um Coburg* (1939), pp. 199, 204.

174. *Fränkische Tagespost*, 18 March 1931; *Fränkischer Kurier*, 6 June 1931.

175. *Fränkische Tagespost*, 16 October 1931.

176. HMB/Ofr., 4 August 1931, GSA MA 102155/3.

177. ibid.
178. Reports of BA Coburg to the Government of Upper Franconia, 24 January 1931 and 13 February 1931, BSA Bamberg, K3 1967/4829.
179. Nuremberg document 2512-PS.

7 The Year of Elections (1932)

1. NSDAP leaflet for the Presidential Election, BSA Bamberg K3/4966.
2. Karl Schwend, *Bayern zwischen Monarchie und Diktatur* (1954), pp. 418–19.
3. *Münchner Post*, 10 March 1932.
4. HMB/Obb., 21 March 1932, GSA MA 102155.
5. HMB/Schw., 5 March 1932, GSA MA 102155.
6. *Bayerischer Kurier*, 11 March 1932.
7. Report of Munich police, 24 March 1932, HA 87/1776.
8. Andreas Dorpalen, *Hindenburg and the Weimar Republic* (1964), p. 297 and *VB*, 10–11, 12 and 13 April 1932.
9. HMB/Niedb., 18 March 1932, GSA MA 102155.
10. HMB/Ufr., 18 March 1932, GSA MA 102151.
11. HMB/Ufr., 19 April 1932, GSA MA 102151.
12. HMB/Opf., 21 March 1932, GSA MA 102144.
13. *Bayerischer Kurier*, 1 April 1932.
14. Quoted in *The Times*, London, 5 April 1932.
15. ibid., 8 April 1932.
16. *Bayerischer Kurier*, 4 April 1932.
17. HMB/Obb., 21 March 1932, GSA MA 102155.
18. Dr Scharnagl to Dr Stützel, 29 March 1932, HA 29A/1776.
19. Report of Munich police to State Ministry of the Interior, 24 March 1932, HA 86/1776.
20. ibid.
21. *The Times*, London, 5 April 1932.
22. Report of Munich police, 24 March 1932, HA 86/1776.
23. HMB/Opf., 31 March 1932, GSA MA 102144.
24. HMB/Obb., 20 April 1932, GSA MA 102156.
25. *Münchner Post*, 11 March 1932.
26. e.g. see reports in HMB/Schw., 21 April 1932, HA 86/1776 and HMB/Mfr., 19 April 1932, GSA MA 102154.
27. Report of Bayreuth city council to the Bayreuth police inspector, 18 April 1932, BSA Bamberg, Reg. v. Ofr. K3/4959.

28. NSDAP Wahlpropagandaleitung Bayern, *Die Propaganda für die Bayernwahl*, 9 April 1932, HA 30/576.
29. HMB/Schw., 21 April 1932, HA 86/1776.
30. Karl Schwend, op. cit., pp. 423–4.
31. *The Times*, London, 15 June 1932.
32. Karl Schwend, op. cit., pp. 439–40.
33. ibid., pp. 443, 445.
34. *The Times*, London, 18 June 1932.
35. ibid., 20 June 1932.
36. ibid., 24 June 1932.
37. Wagner to branch and district leaders, *Gau* Munich–Upper Bavaria, 11 May 1932, HA 9/192.
38. Joseph Goebbels, *My Part in Germany's Fight* (1938), p. 76.
39. Joseph Goebbels, *Denkschrift der Reichspropagandaleitung zur Reichstagswahl 1932*, HA 15/289.
40. *Gau* Munich–Upper Bavaria, instructions for the Reichstag Election, 18 July 1932, HA 8/176.
41. See 39 above.
42. See 40 above.
43. BA Bad Tölz to the State Ministry of the Interior, 8 July 1932, HA 21A/1753.
44. HMB/Schw., 3 August 1932, GSA MA 102156.
45. Results of the July 1932 Reichstag Election from the *Zeitschrift des Bayerischen Statistischen Landesamts* (1932), pp. 458–69.
46. HMB/Niedb., 5 August 1932, GSA MA 102156.
47. Joseph Goebbels, *My Part in Germany's Fight*, p. 117.
48. HMB/Niedb., 18 August 1932, GSA MA 102156.
49. *Gau* office of Lower Franconia (Economic Department) to NSDAP Propaganda Leader Dr Goebbels, 12 October 1932, NSDAP organization files NS 22/381, Bundesarchiv Koblenz.
50. *Stimmungsbericht der Reichspropagandaleitung* for the period 6–15 November 1932, NSDAP organization files NS 22/1, Bundesarchiv Koblenz.
51. HMB/Mfr., 19 October 1932, GSA MA 102154.
52. See 49 above.
53. HMB/Ufr., 26 October 1932, GSA MA 102151.
54. See 50 above.
55. Confidential report of the NSDAP Propaganda Department on party activities, November 1932, NSDAP organization files NS 22/1, Bundesarchiv Koblenz.

56. Report of Munich police, 4 July 1932, HA 70/1516.
57. HMB/Ufr., 5 October 1932, GSA MA 102151.
58. HMB/Ufr., 20 October 1932, GSA MA 102151.
59. Report of Munich police, 8 September 1932, HA 24A/1759.
60. See 50 above.
61. Joseph Goebbels, *My Part in Germany's Fight*, p. 138.
62. ibid., p. 150.
63. HMB/Obb., 20 September 1932, GSA MA 102156.
64. HMB/Schw., 20 September 1932, GSA MA 102156.
65. Report of Munich police, 20 October 1932, HA 71/1529.
66. ibid.
67. Report of Munich police, 30 December 1932, HA 70/1511.
68. ibid.
69. Report of Munich police, 9 November 1932, HA 24A/1759.
70. HMB/Mfr., 4 November 1931, GSA MA 102154.
71. Manfred Rühl, *Der Stürmer und sein Herausgeber*, p. 192.
72. *Fränkische Tagespost*, 12 January 1933.
73. ibid., 11 and 12 January 1933.
74. ibid., 14 January 1933.
75. *Würzburger General-Anzeiger*, 16 January 1933.
76. Albrecht Tyrell (ed.), *Führer befiehl . . . Selbstzeugnisse aus der 'Kampf-zeit' der NSDAP, Dokumentation und Analyse* (1969), pp. 348–50.

8   The Nazi 'Seizure of Power' in Bavaria (1933)

1. HMB/Schw., 6 February 1933, GSA MA 106682.
2. HMB/Niedb., 3 February 1933, GSA MA 106672.
3. HMB/Schw., 6 February 1933, GSA MA 106682.
4. HMB/Niedb., 20 February 1933, GSA MA 106672.
5. HMB/Niedb., 3 February 1933, GSA MA 106672.
6. HMB/Niedb., 20 February 1933, GSA MA 106672.
7. Report of Munich police, 13 February 1933, HA 24A/1759.
8. Minutes of the Held Cabinet from January–March 1933 are in GSA Ministerratsprotokolle 99525. See also the summary of their contents by Ernst Deuerlein, 'Bayern im Frühjahr 1933' in *Unser Bayern, Heimatbeilage der Bayerischen Staatszeitung*, March 1953, pp. 23–4.
9. Karl Schwend, *Bayern zwischen Monarchie und Diktatur* (1954), p. 509.
10. See 8 above.
11. *Miesbacher Anzeiger*, 7 February 1933.

12. Karl Schwend, op. cit., p. 510.
13. Ludwig Volk, *Der Bayerische Episkopat und der Nationalsozialismus 1930–34* (1966), p. 56.
14. Karl Schwend, op. cit., pp. 510–11.
15. ibid., p. 511.
16. Andreas Dorpalen, *Hindenburg and the Weimar Republic* (1964), pp. 459–60.
17. Karl Schwend, op. cit., p. 522.
18. James Donohoe, *Hitler's Conservative Opponents in Bavaria 1930–1945* (1961), pp. 109, 111.
19. ibid., pp. 105 ff.
20. Interview of Dr Held with the *New York Times*, published on 22 February 1933, quoted in Donohoe, op. cit., pp. 110–11.
21. See Dr Held's account of his interview with Hitler at the meeting of the Bavarian Cabinet on 7 March, GSA 99525, and Karl Schwend, op. cit., pp. 524–5.
22. Dr Stützel to police authorities, 1 March 1933, BSA Würzburg, Schumacher Sammlung, Ochsenfurt/33.
23. NSDAP leaflet for March election, Streicher Nachlass/24, Bundesarchiv Koblenz.
24. Ludwig Volk, op. cit., p. 60.
25. Karl Schwend, op. cit., p. 511.
26. *Kaufbeurer Neueste Nachrichten*, 6 March 1933.
27. e.g. HMB/Niedb., 5 March 1933, GSA MA 106672, and HMB/Schw., 4 March 1933, GSA MA 106682.
28. Volkach police station to BA Gerolzhofen, 3 March 1933, BSA Würzburg, LA Gerolzhofen/1196.
29. See BVP propaganda for the March 1933 election in BSA Neuburg a.D. Donau, BA Nördlingen/1303a.
30. Altenschönbach police station to BA Gerolzhofen, 4 March 1933, BSA Würzburg, LA Gerolzhofen/1196.
31. Joseph Goebbels, *My Part in Germany's Fight* (1938), p. 226.
32. Letter by Thomas Mann of 13 March 1933, quoted by Harry Pross, 'On Thomas Mann's Political Career' in *Journal of Contemporary History*, April 1967, p. 75.
33. *Augsburger Postzeitung*, 8 March 1933.
34. Karl Schwend, 'Die Bayerische Volkspartei' in E. Matthias and R. Morsey (ed.), *Das Ende der Parteien, 1933* (1963), p. 487.
35. Minutes of the Bavarian Cabinet, 7 March 1933, GSA 99525.
36. Karl Schwend, *Die Bayerische Volkspartei*, p. 487.

37. Karl Schwend, *Bayern zwischen Monarchie und Diktatur*, p. 535.
38. ibid., pp. 536–7, and *Der 9. März 1933, Erinnerungen und Erkenntnisse* (1953), p. 7.
39. Wilhelm Hoegner, *Der schwierige Aussenseiter* (1959), p. 86.
40. Stefan Lorant, *I was Hitler's Prisoner* (1935), p. 30.
41. Karl Schwend, *Bayern zwischen Monarchie und Diktatur*, pp. 537–8.
42. *Der 9. März 1933*, pp. 7–8.
43. Ernst Deuerlein, *Bayern im Frühjahr 1933*, p. 24.
44. Karl Schwend, *Die Bayerische Volkspartei*, p. 489.
45. See Ludwig Volk, op. cit., pp. 63–5.
46. Interview with Dr Listl, former mayor of Ingolstadt, August 1968.
47. Diary of Michael Neumayer, NSDAP branch leader in Traunstein, Schumacher Sammlung FA 48/206, Bundesarchiv Koblenz.
48. HMB/Obb., 20 March 1933, GSA MA 106670.
49. NSDAP branch leader Röthenbach a.d. Pegnitz, 18 March 1933 to *Gau* office of Middle Franconia, Nuremberg, Streicher Nachlass/123, Bundesarchiv Koblenz.
50. HMB/Obb., 4 May 1933, GSA MA 106670.
51. HMB/Obb., 20 March 1933, GSA MA 106670.
52. HMB/Obb., 4 March 1933, GSA MA 106670.
53. HMB/Niedb., 20 March 1933, GSA MA 106672.
54. Stefan Lorant, op. cit., p. 38.
55. Karl Fiehler memorandum to *Gau* leaders, 14 February 1933, Hauptamt für Kommunalpolitik NS 25/75, Bundesarchiv Koblenz.
56. HMB/Ofr./Mfr., 20 April 1933, GSA MA 106677.
57. HMB/Obb., 5 August 1933, GSA MA 106670.
58. Helmut Witetschek, *Die kirchliche Lage in Bayern nach den Regierungspräsidentenberichten 1933–43, I Oberbayern* (1966), p. 4.
59. Order by Franz von Epp to Bavarian *Gau* leaders, 8 April 1933, Schumacher Sammlung/34, BSA Würzburg.
60. Peter Diehl-Thiele, *Partei und Staat im Dritten Reich* (1969), p. 86.
61. ibid., pp. 76–80.
62. Martin Broszat, 'The Concentration Camps 1933–45' in H. Krausnick et al., *Anatomy of the SS State* (1968), p. 404.
63. ibid., p. 405.
64. Heinrich Himmler to local authorities in Bavaria, 20 June 1933, Schumacher Sammlung 244 (vol. 1), Bundesarchiv Koblenz.

Bibliography

Note on Sources

The unpublished material used in this book was drawn mainly from the following archives: the *Hauptarchiv der NSDAP* collection (party archives), the Bavarian State Archives and the Federal Archives in Koblenz.

The *Hauptarchiv* was read in the Institute of Contemporary History, London, but the original material is available in the Federal Archives in Koblenz and the State Archives in Munich. The *Hauptarchiv* is a vast collection of party directives and memoranda, party correspondence, local party histories, official reports on party meetings and newspaper cuttings. This collection, which was organized after 1933, concentrates on the period of the NSDAP's rise to power and is especially useful for Bavaria as the Munich police and the Bavarian political police were the only regional authorities to hand over their files to the *Hauptarchiv*. The best documented of all the *Gaue* in this collection is that of Munich–Upper Bavaria.

Police records also constitute a large section of the material in the various State Archives in Bavaria. These contain furthermore government records and correspondence, the regular fortnightly reports of the regional governments on political activities in their areas as well as reports of local authorities. Much of this official material concentrates on the activities of the extremist parties, especially in the last years of the Weimar Republic. They are very informative, and the documentation is extensive especially for the period 1930–33. The lists below mention only those files quoted in the source references, although they constitute only a small part of those consulted.

The Federal Archives contain general files of the NSDAP, but some of them relate especially to the party in Bavaria. The most important collections were the organizational files of the NSDAP and the papers of Julius Streicher.

The documentary material on the NSDAP in Bavaria is therefore great in quantity in spite of much destruction during and after the War affecting part of the *Hauptarchiv*, the State Archives especially in Würzburg and many of the town archives I visited. Newspapers provided an additional source of information, although the reading of them has to be very selective. They were most useful for election campaigns and results and for relations between the Catholic Church and the NSDAP. Efforts to gain access to various church archives in Bavaria for the purpose of this study proved unavailing.

My attempts to arrange interviews with former leading members of the NSDAP in Bavaria were not successful, but I am grateful to the following for granting me interviews:

Dr Wilhelm Hoegner, Ministerpräsident a.D., Bayern
Dr Josef Listl, Oberbürgermeister a.D., Ingolstadt
Dr Heinrich Berndl, Alt-Oberbürgermeister, Memmingen.

Unpublished sources

1. *NSDAP Hauptarchiv (Hoover Institution Microfilm Collection)*, *Institute of Contemporary History, London*

3/81–2	Aufrufe zu Versammlungen, 1919–34
4/88	NS Freiheitsbewegung, 1925
5/134	Bayerische Ostmark
7/158	Schwaben
8/169, 173, 176	München–Oberbayern
9/185–92	München–Oberbayern
15/289	Reichstagswahl, 1932
17/317	Staatsminister des Innern über die SA.
18/344	NS Schülerbund, 1930–33
21/390	Reichsparteitag, 1927
29/553	Reichstagswahl, July 1932
30/576	Landtagswahlen in Bayern, 1932
30/578	Kreistagswahlen in Bayern, 1928
47/965–6, 992, 1005; 48/1065; 49/1110, 1126	NS Presse
58/1403	Berichte der Staatspolizei Württemberg, 1930
69/1509	NSDAP: Allgemeine Entwicklung und Bewegung, 1924–29
70/1510–11	NSDAP: Allgemeine Entwicklung, 1930–32
70/1512	NSDAP und Landwirtschaft, 1932
70/1514	NSDAP und Beamtenschaft
70/1515	NSDAP in Württemberg
70/1516	NSDAP Versammlungen, 1927–32

70/1529	NSDAP Propagandazellen und Wesen
71/1529	ibid.
71/1539	NSDAP Jungvolk
71/1540	NSDAP, Hitlerjugendbewegung München, 1930–32
73/1552	SA Versammlungen, 1925–33
74/1553	SA Verschiedenes
84/1732	Julius Streicher
85/1738	Polizeistelle Nordbayern
86/1742–3	Stadtrat Karl Holz
86/1776	NSDAP Pläne für den 13. März 1932
87/1776	ibid.
88/1838, 1843	NSDAP Versammlungen, München
90/1869, 1872	NSDAP Verschiedenes
91/1881	Stadtrat Neu-Ulm: Politische Polizei
1A/217	Ortsgruppe Berchtesgaden
17A/1731	Julius Streicher
18A/1745	NSDAP Einzelnes, 1925
19A/1747	ibid., 1929–30
20/1748	ibid., 1930
21A/1751, 1753	ibid., 1931–33
23A/1757	NSDAP Grundsätzliches, 1925
24A/1757	ibid.
24A/1758–9	NSDAP Allgemeines, 1928–33
25A/1762	Aufhebung der Redeverbote, 1927
27A/1772	SA, 1925–31
29A/1776	NSDAP Pläne für den 13. März 1932
34A/1796	NSDStB
34A/1799	Auftreten des früheren Pastors Münchmeyer in Versammlungen, 1929–32

2. Bavarian State Archives

(a) *Allgemeines Staatsarchiv, Munich*

71799	NS Sportbewegung 'Hitlerjugend', 1928–36
73438–631	Parteien und Verbände
73687/73689	Unruhen, politische Umtriebe, 1920–33
73707	Die Stellung der NSDAP zur Judenfrage, 1931–33
73718	Wahlversammlungen, 1930–32

73719	Redeverbote, 1922–35
73720	Versammlungsverbote, Bd. I, 1922–35
73721	Störung von Versammlungen, 1922–32
73725	Antisemitische Bewegung, 1924–35
73733	Bayerischer Bauern- und Mittelstandsbund
73734	Rechtsradikale Agitation in der Bauernschaft (Nazi-Bauern), 1928–32
120 6055 d 1,	Bayerisches Landwirtschaftsministerium
121 6055 e 1	

(b) *Geheimes Staatsarchiv, Munich*

999, 1003, 1009, 1014, 1024, 1027, 1031, 1038, 1041 Die Bayerische Gesandtschaft beim Päpstlichen Stuhl in Rom

MA 99519–25 Ministerratsprotokolle, 1924–33

MA 100425–6 Nationalsozialismus, 1922–32

MA 101236–42, 101248–51 Berichte der Polizeidirektionen München u. Nürnberg über radikale Bewegungen, 1924–32

MA 102142–57 Halbmonatsberichte der Regierungspräsidien von Oberbayern, Niederbayern, Schwaben, Mittelfranken, Oberfranken, Unterfranken, 1925–32

MA 102230 Parteipolitische Bestätigung der Beamten, Angestellten u. Arbeiter des Staates, 1920–32

MA 102434 Parteiangelegenheiten, Parteitage, Wahlen, 1930–32

MA 103304 Volksbegehren des radikalen Mittelstandes, 1932

MA 103325 Politische Bestätigung der Beamten, 1932

MA 103422 Stimmung der Bevölkerung, 1929

MA 106670, 106672, 106677, 106680, 106682 Halbmonatsberichte der Regierungspräsidien von Oberbayern, Niederbayern u. Oberpfalz, Schwaben, Mittelfranken, Oberfranken, Unterfranken, 1933

MA 107279–81 Akten vom Abt Schachleiter

(c) *Staatsarchiv Nuremberg*

Reg. v. Mfr. Abg. 1968 (Titel II):

250 Völkische Bewegung, 1924–26

684–96 Politische Polizei, 1924–32

P.D. Nürnberg–Fürth/340–57 Tätigkeitsberichte, 1923–34:

361–98 Lageberichte der Bezirksämter der Städte Nordbayerns, 1919–31

BA Ansbach/2205 Vollzug der Notverordnungen zur Bekämpfung politischer Ausschreitungen, 1932

(d) *Staatsarchiv Bamberg*

Reg. v. Ofr. (K3–Präs.)

1861–2   Halbmonatsberichte der Bezirksämter und Stadträte, 1925
1878–82 Halbmonatsberichte der Bez. Verw. Behörden, 1929–30

Reg. v. Ofr. (K3–Abg. 1967)

4816   Beschwerde des Zentralvereins deutscher Staatsbürger jüdischen
       Glaubens, Landesverband Bayern, 1929–32
4829   Anordnung zur Aufrechterhaltung der öffentl. Sicherheit, 1930
4861   Verbot des 'Bamberger Beobachter', 1932
4863   Die allgemeine Volksstimme, 1864–1931
4870   NS Bewegung, 1929–30
4959   Verordnung des Reichspräsidenten zur Sicherung der Staats-
       authorität, 1932
4983   Verordnung des Reichspräsidenten vom 28 März 1931 zur
       Bekämpfung politischer Ausschreitungen, 1931

BA Naila/1210   Bekämpfung politischer Ausschreitungen, 1931
BA Pegnitz/566 NSDAP, 1932

(e) *Staatsarchiv Amberg*

Reg. Abg. 1949

14180   Politischer Nachrichtendienst BA Beilngries, 1920–27
14189   Politischer Nachrichtendienst BA Parsberg, 1924–31
14279   NS Bewegung, 1923–28

BA Riedenburg/1773   Politische Versammlungen, NSDAP 1923–32

(f) *Staatsarchiv Würzburg*

Schumacher Sammlung/LA Ochsenfurt 33   1933
LA Gerolzhofen/1196   Politische Versammlungen, 1932–41

(g) *Staatsarchiv für Oberbayern, Munich*

RA 3789/16837   Der Bayerische und Oberbayerische Bauernbund, Bund
der Landwirte in Bayern, 1901–30
RA 3804/16956–7   Aufrechterhaltung der öffentlichen Sicherheit, 1919–32
AR 2184b/1   LA Berchtesgaden
LA Fürstenfeldbruck   2/30
LA Pfaffenhofen   1/9

(h) *Staatsarchiv, Landshut*

Reg. Abg. 1965

168/5–30   Sammlung der HC Berichte, 1924–32

168/5–35 No. 88 Sammlung der Halbmonatsberichte, 1929–33 des Reg.—
Präsidiums von Niederbayern
168/5–35 No. 89 Persönl. Mitteilungen des Reg. Präsidenten von Niederbayern, 1925–33

(i) *Staatsarchiv, Neuburg a.d. Donau*
BA Nördlingen/1303a Reichstagswahl, 1933
BA Nördlingen/1315 Politische Versammlungen, 1931

3. *Bundesarchiv, Koblenz*

FA 48 (vol. 3) Sammlung Schumacher, NSDAP Parteikorrespondenz,
1925–33
FA 48 (vol. 2) Gau Franken (Mainfranken)
NS 1 Akten des Reichsschatzmeisters der NSDAP
NS 22 Akten des Reichsorganisationsleiters der NSDAP
NS 25 Akten des Hauptamts für Kommunalpolitik
Nachlass Franz Ritter von Epp
Nachlass Streicher

4. *Foreign Office Library, London*

K 2134/K 588961–9838 Files of the Alte Reichskanzlei section on
Bavaria (photocopies), 1923–33
K 2138/K 591575–5296 Berichte des Vertreters der Reichsregierung in
München, Alte Reichskanzlei (photocopies), 1923–31
K 2138/K 646562–625 Alte Reichskanzlei file on NSDAP

5. *US Document Centre, West Berlin*

NSDAP Personality Files

6. *Nachlass Buttmann, Stockdorf*

7. Town Archives

The following town archives were visited:

Augsburg, Ingolstadt, Kaufbeuren, Memmingen, Munich, Nördlingen and Nuremberg

Published sources

1. Reference Works

Bayerisches Jahrbuch-Kalender, 1937 (Munich, 1937)

Das Deutsche Führerlexikon, 1934–35 (Berlin, 1934)

Einwohnerbuch für Nördlingen, Oettingen, Harburg, Wassertrüdingen, Wemding und für die Rieser Ortschaften (Nördlingen, 1926)

Der Grossdeutsche Reichstag, 1938 (Berlin, 1938)

Hagmann, Meinrad, *Der Weg ins Verhängnis, Reichstagswahlergebnisse 1919 bis 1933, besonders aus Bayern* (Munich, 1946)

Horkenbach, Cuno (ed), *Das Deutsche Reich von 1918 bis heute* (Berlin, 1932)

Milatz, Alfred, *Wähler und Wahlen in der Weimarer Republik* (Bonn, 1965)

Nationalsozialistisches Jahrbuch (Munich, 1927, 1928, 1933)

Reichsorganisationsleiter der NSDAP, *Parteistatistik*, vol. i (Munich, 1935)

Schwarz, Max, *MdR, Biographisches Handbuch der deutschen Reichstage* (Hanover, 1965)

Statistik des Deutschen Reiches (Berlin, 1936)

Statistisches Jahrbuch für den Freistaat Bayern (Munich, 1924, 1926, 1928, 1929, 1930 and 1934)

Statistisches Jahrbuch für das Deutsche Reich (Berlin, 1932)

Stockdorf, Erich, *5000 Köpfe, Wer war was im 3. Reich* (1967)

Volkszählung in Bayern, 1925 (Munich, 1927)

Volz, Hans, *Daten der Geschichte der NSDAP* (Berlin, 1937)

Zeitschrift des Bayerischen Statistischen Landesamtes (Munich, 1930, 1932, 1933 and 1934)

The above works are available in the Bayerisches Statistisches Landesamt, Munich, the Institut für Zeitgeschichte, Munich and the Institute of Contemporary History and Wiener Library, London.

359

2. Documentary Material, Memoirs and Contemporary Publications

Albert, Wilhelm, *Franz Ritter von Epp* (1934)

Amtsblatt für die Erzdiözese München und Freising (1931 and 1933)

Aretin, Erwein von, *Krone und Ketten, Erinnerungen eines bayerischen Edelmannes* (Munich, 1955)

Baynes, Norman H., *The Speeches of Adolf Hitler 1922–39*, vol. i (Oxford, 1942)

Buchner, Franz, *Kamerad! Halt aus! Aus der Geschichte des Kreises Starnberg der NSDAP* (Munich, 1938)

Buttmann, Rudolf, *Bayerische Politik, 1924–28* (Munich, 1928)

Der 9. März 1933, Erinnerungen und Erkenntnisse (Munich, 1953)

Deuerlein, Ernst (ed.), *Der Aufstieg der NSDAP, 1919–33 in Augenzeugenberichten* (Düsseldorf, 1968)

Deuerlein, Ernst (ed.), *Der Hitler-Putsch, Bayerische Dokumente zum 9 November 1923* (Stuttgart, 1962)

Dresler, Adolf and Maier-Hartmann, Fritz, *Dokumente der Zeitgeschichte (Dokumente der Sammlung Rehse aus der Kampfzeit)* (Munich, 1941)

Engelhard, Gildis, *Abt Schachleiter, der deutsche Kämpfer* (1941)

Frank Walter, *Franz Ritter von Epp* (Hamburg, 1934)

Fiehler, Karl, *Fünf Jahre nationalsozialistische Gemeindepolitik in München* (1929)

Fiehler, Karl, *Nationalsozialistische Gemeindepolitik* (Munich, 1933)

Goebbels, Joseph, *Kampf um Berlin* (Munich, 1932)

Goebbels, Joseph, *My Part in Germany's Fight* (London, 1938)

Haselmayr, Friedrich, *General von Epp als Kämpfer für das Dritte Reich* (1933)

Hitler, Adolf, *Mein Kampf*, translated by James Murphy (London, 1939)

Hitler's Table Talk, 1941–4 (London, 1953)

Hoegner, Wilhelm, *Der schwierige Aussenseiter, Erinnerungen eines Abgeordneten, Emigranten und Ministerpräsidenten* (Munich, 1959)

Jochmann, Werner, *Nationalsozialismus und Revolution, Ursprung und Geschichte der NSDAP in Hamburg* (Frankfurt, 1963)

Kanzler, Rudolf, *Bayerns Kampf gegen den Bolshewismus, Geschichte der bayerischen Einwohnerwehren* (Munich, 1931)

Krebs, Albert, *Tendenzen und Gestalten der NSDAP* (Stuttgart, 1959)

Krumbach, Josef (ed.), *Franz Ritter von Epp, ein Leben für Deutschland* (1939)

Lembeck, Bernd, *Hans Schemm* (Munich, 1936)

Linn, Dorothee, *Das Schicksal der jüdischen Bevölkerung in Memmingen, 1933–45* (mimeograph, Memmingen 1962)

Lochmüller, Benedict, *Hans Schemm, vol. 2 1920–1935* (Munich, 1935)

Lorant, Stefan, *I was Hitler's Prisoner* (London, 1935)

Ludecke, Kurt, *I knew Hitler* (London, 1938)

Memoirs of Alfred Rosenberg, ed. S. Lang and E. von Schenck (New York, 1949)

Nötges, J., *Nationalsozialismus und Katholizismus* (Cologne, 1931)

Preiss, Heinz, *Die Anfänge der völkischen Bewegung in Franken* (Erlangen, 1937)

Rosenberg, Alfred, *Der Mythus des 20. Jahrhunderts* (Munich, 1930)

Schwede-Coburg, Franz, *Kampf um Coburg* (Munich, 1939)

Tyrell, Albrecht (ed.), *Führer befiehl . . . Selbstzeugnisse aus der 'Kampfzeit' der NSDAP, Dokumentation und Analyse* (Düsseldorf, 1969)

Wahl, Karl, *. . . es ist das deutsche Herz, Erlebnisse und Erkenntnisse eines ehemaligen Gauleiters* (Augsburg, 1954)

Witetschek, Helmut, *Die Kirchliche Lage in Bayern nach den Regierungs-präsidentenberichten, 1933–43*, vol. i (Oberbayern) (Mainz, 1966)

Zöberlein, Hans, *München, die Stadt der Bewegung* (Munich, 1934)

3. Secondary Works

Allen, William S, *The Nazi Seizure of Power, the experience of a single German town*, 1930–5 (London, 1966)

Bennecke, Heinrich, *Hitler und die SA* (Munich, 1962)

Bleuel, H. P. and Klinnert, E., *Deutsche Studenten auf den Weg ins Dritte Reich* (Gütersloh, 1967)

Bosl, Karl (ed.), *Bayern im Umbruch, Die Revolution von 1918, ihre Voraussetzungen, ihr Verlauf und ihre Folgen* (Munich and Vienna, 1969)

Bracher, K. D., *Die Auflösung der Weimarer Republik* (Villingen, 1964)

Bracher, K. D., *The German Dictatorship* (London, 1971)

Bracher, K. D., Sauer, W., Schulz, G., *Die Nationalsozialistische Machtergreifung* (Cologne, 1962)

Bramsted, Ernest K., *Goebbels and National Socialist Propaganda, 1925–1945* (E. Lansing, Michigan, 1965)

Brandenburg, Hans-Christian, *Die Geschichte der HJ* (Cologne, 1968)

Broszat, Martin, 'The Concentration Camps, 1933–45' in Helmut Krausnick and others, *Anatomy of the SS State* (London, 1968)

Broszat, Martin, *Der Nationalsozialismus, Weltanschauung, Programm und Wirklichkeit* (Stuttgart, 1960)

Broszat, Martin, *Der Staat Hitlers* (Munich, 1969)

Buccheim, Karl, *Geschichte der christlichen Parteien in Deutschland* (Munich, 1953)

Bullock, Alan, *Hitler, a study in tyranny* (London, 1964)

Carsten, F. L., *The Reichswehr and Politics, 1918–33* (Oxford, 1966)

Carsten, F. L., *The Rise of Fascism* (London, 1967)

Conway, J. S., *The Nazi Persecution of the Churches* (London, 1968)

Deuerlein, Ernst, *Der Deutsche Katholizismus* (Osnabrück, 1963)

Diehl-Thiele, Peter, *Partei und Staat im Dritten Reich* (Munich, 1969)

Dittmann, Wilhelm, *Das Politische Deutschland vor Hitler* (New York, 1945)

Dittmar, William R., *The Government of the Free State of Bavaria* (1934)

Donohoe, James, *Hitler's Conservative Opponents in Bavaria, 1930–45* (Leiden, 1961)

Dorpalen, Andreas, *Hindenburg and the Weimar Republic* (Princeton, 1964)

Eyck, Erich, *A History of the Weimar Republic*, vol. ii (Cambridge, Mass, 1964)

Franz-Willing, Georg, *Die Hitlerbewegung, Der Ursprung, 1919–22* (Hamburg, 1962)

Geiger, Theodor, *Die Soziale Schichtung des Deutschen Volkes* (Stuttgart, 1932)

Goodspeed, D. J., *Ludendorff* (London, 1966)

Gordon, Harold J. jr., *Hitlerputsch 1923, Machtkampf in Bayern 1923–1924* (Frankfurt, 1971)

Grebing, Helga, *Der Nationalsozialismus, Ursprung und Wesen* (Munich, 1959)

Hale, Oron J., *The Captive Press in the Third Reich* (Princeton University Press, 1964)

Halperin, S. William, *Germany tried Democracy* (New York, 1965)

Heberle, Rudolf, *Landbevölkerung und Nationalsozialismus, eine soziologische Untersuchung der politischen Willensbildung in Schleswig-Holstein, 1918 bis 1932* (Stuttgart, 1963)

Heiber, Helmut, *Die Republik von Weimar* (Munich, 1966)

Heiden, Konrad, *Der Fuehrer, Hitler's Rise to Power* (London, 1944)

Heiden, Konrad, *Geschichte des Nationalsozialismus* (Berlin, 1932)

Held, Joseph, *Heinrich Held, ein Leben für Bayern* (Regensburg, 1958)

Hertzmann, Lewis, *DNVP, Right-Wing Opposition in the Weimar Republic 1918–24* (Lincoln, 1963)

Heuss, Theodor, *Hitlers Weg, eine Schrift aus dem Jahre 1932* (Tübingen, 1968)

Hofmann, Hanns Hubert, *Der Hitlerputsch* (Munich, 1961)

Holt, John B., *German Agricultural Policy, 1918–34* (Chapel Hill, 1936)

Klönne, Arno, *Hitlerjugend, die Jugend und ihre Organisationen im Dritten Reich* (Hanover, 1956)

Kühnl, Reinhard, *Die Nationalsozialistische Linke, 1925–30* (Meisenheim am Glan, 1966)

Laqueur, Walter Z., *Young Germany, a history of the German youth movement* (London, 1962)

Lerner, Daniel, *The Nazi Elite* (Stanford, 1951)

Lewy, Guenter, *The Catholic Church and Nazi Germany* (London, 1964)

Lipset, S. M., *Political Man* (London, 1960)

Lutz, Heinrich, *Demokratie in Zwielicht, Der Weg der deutschen Katholiken aus dem Kaiserreich in die Republik 1914–1925* (Munich, 1963)

Maser, Werner, *Die Frühgeschichte der NSDAP, Hitlers Weg bis 1924* (Frankfurt, 1965)

Mitchell, Allan, *Revolution in Bavaria, 1918–19, the Eisner Regime and the Soviet Republic* (Princeton, 1965)

Mosse, George L., *The Crisis of German Ideology, intellectual origins of the Third Reich* (London, 1966)

Müller, Arnd, *Geschichte der Juden in Nürnberg 1146–1945* (Nuremberg, 1968)

Müller, Hans (ed.), *Katholische Kirche und Nationalsozialismus* (Munich, 1965)

Natterer, Alois, *Der Bayerische Klerus in der Zeit dreier Revolutionen, 1918–1933–1945* (Munich, 1948)

Neuhäusler, Johann, *Kreuz und Hakenkreuz* (Munich, 1946)

Neumann, Franz, *Behemoth: the structure and practice of National Socialism* (London, 1942)

Neumann, Sigmund, *Die Parteien der Weimarer Republik* (Stuttgart, 1965)

Nicholls, A. J., *Weimar and the Rise of Hitler* (London, 1968)

Noakes, Jeremy, *The Nazi Party in Lower Saxony 1921–1933* (Oxford, 1971)

Nolte, Ernst, *Three Faces of Fascism* (London, 1965)

Nyomarkay, Joseph, *Charisma and Factionalism in the Nazi Party* (Minneapolis, 1967)

Orlow, Dietrich, *The History of the Nazi Party, vol. I 1919–1933* (Newton Abbot, 1971)

Peterson, Edward N., *The Limits of Hitler's Power* (Princeton, 1969)

Pulzer, P. G. J., *The Rise of Political Anti-Semitism in Germany and Austria* (London, 1964)

Sagerer, G. and Schuler, E., *Die Bayerische Landpolizei von 1919–35* (1954)

Schäfer, Wolfgang, *NSDAP, Entwicklung und Struktur der Staatspartei des Dritten Reiches* (Hanover, 1956)

Schlögl, Alois, *Bayerische Agrarpolitik* (1954)

Schoenbaum, David, *Hitler's Social Revolution, Class and Status in Nazi Germany, 1933–39* (London, 1967)

Schnabel, Franz, *Deutsche Geschichte im Neunzehnten Jahrhundert: Die Katholische Kirche in Deutschland* (Freiburg, 1965)

Schwarz, Stefan, *Die Juden in Bayern im Wandel der Zeiten* (Munich, 1963)

Schwend, Karl, 'Die Bayerische Volkspartei' in Erich Matthias and Rudolf Morsey (ed.), *Das Ende der Parteien, 1933* (Düsseldorf, 1963)

Schwend, Karl, *Bayern zwischen Monarchie und Diktatur* (Munich, 1954)

Stephan, Werner, *Joseph Goebbels, Dämon einer Diktatur* (Stuttgart, 1949)

Tormin, Walter, *Geschichte der deutschen Parteien seit 1848* (Stuttgart, 1967)

Turner, H. A., *Stresemann and the Politics of the Weimar Republic* (Princeton, 1965)

Volk, Ludwig, *Der Bayerische Episkopat und der Nationalsozialismus, 1930–34* (Mainz, 1966)

Wells, Roger H., *German Cities* (Princeton, 1932)

Woolf, S. J. (ed.), *European Fascism* (London, 1968)

Zeman, Z. A. B., *Nazi Propaganda* (Oxford, 1964)

Zorn, Wolfgang, *Kleine Wirtschafts- und Sozialgeschichte Bayerns 1806–1933* (Munich, 1962)

4. *Articles*

Angress, Werner T., 'The Political Role of the Peasantry in the Weimar Republic' in *Review of Politics*, 1959

Auerbach, Hellmuth, 'Zur Geschichte des Widerstandes gegen den National sozialismus in Bayern' in *Zeitschrift für Bayerische Landesgeschichte*, 1962

Böckenförde, E. W., 'Der Deutsche Katholizismus im Jahr 1933' in *Hochland*, 1961

Briefs, G. H., 'Limes Germanicus, Bridge and Frontier' in *Review of Politics*, 1939

Buchheim, Hans, 'Der Deutsche Katholizismus im Jahr 1933, eine Auseinandersetzung mit Ernst-Wolfgang Böckenförde' in *Hochland*, 1961

Deuerlein, Ernst, 'Bayern im Frühjahr 1933' in *Unser Bayern, Heimatbeilage der Bayerischen Staatszeitung*, March 1953

Doblin, E. M. and Pohly, C., 'The Social Composition of the Nazi Leadership' in *American Journal of Sociology*, 1945

Gerth, Hans, 'The Nazi Party, its leadership and composition' in *American Journal of Sociology*, 1940

Gollwitzer, Heinz, 'Bayern, 1918–33' in *Vierteljahreshefte für Zeitgeschichte*, 1955

Hellmuth, Wilhelm, 'Heute vor 30 Jahren in München' in *Münchner Merkur*, 9–10 March 1963

Hofmann, H. H., 'Ländliches Judentum in Franken' in *Tribüne : Zeitschrift zum Verständnis des Judentums*, 1968

Landauer, Carl, 'The Bavarian Problem in the Weimar Republic, 1918–23' in *Journal of Modern History*, 1944

Lenman, Robin, 'Julius Streicher and the Origins of the NSDAP in Nuremberg, 1918–1923' in Anthony Nicholls and Erich Matthias (ed.), *German Democracy and the Triumph of Hitler* (1971)

Loomis, C. P. and Beegle, J. A., 'The Spread of German Nazism in Rural Areas' in *American Sociological Review*, 1946

Nicholls, Anthony, 'Hitler and the Bavarian Background to National Socialism' in Anthony Nicholls and Erich Matthias (ed.), *German Democracy and the Triumph of Hitler* (1971)

Noakes, Jeremy, 'Conflict and Development in the NSDAP, 1924–27' in *Journal of Contemporary History*, October 1966

Parsons, Talcott, 'Democracy and Social Structure in pre-Hitler Germany' in *Journal of Legal and Political Sociology*, 1942

Pollock, James K., 'An Areal Study of the German Electorate, 1930–33' in *American Political Science Review*, 1944

Pross, Harry, 'On Thomas Mann's Political Career' in *Journal of Contemporary History*, April 1967

'The Story of Rosenberg's "Mythus"' in *The Wiener Library Bulletin*, vol. vii, no. 5–6, 1953

Stephan, Werner, 'Grenzen des nationalsozialistischen Vormarsches, eine Analyse der Wahlziffer seit der Reichstagswahl 1930' in *Zeitschrift für Politik*, 1931

Volk, Ludwig, 'Kardinal Faulhabers Stellung zur Weimarer Republik und zum NS Staat' in *Stimmen der Zeit*, 1966

Watt, D. C., 'Die Bayerischen Bemühungen um Ausweisung Hitlers 1924' in *Vierteljahreshefte für Zeitgeschichte*, July 1958

5. *Dissertations*

Gömmel, R. and Haertel, G., *Arbeitslosigkeit und Wählerentscheidungen in Nurnberg von 1928 bis 1933* (Seminarbeit, Nuremberg, 1968)

Hambrecht, Rainer, *Der Aufstieg der NSDAP in Franken von 1928 bis 1933* (Zulassungsarbeit, Würzburg, 1968)

Rühl, Manfred, *Der Stürmer und sein Herausgeber* (Diplomarbeit, Nuremberg, 1960)

Werner, Andreas, *SA und NSDAP, SA: 'Wehrverband', 'Parteitruppe' oder 'Revolutionsarmee'? Studien zur Geschichte der SA und der NSDAP, 1920–33* (diss., Erlangen-Nuremberg, 1964)

6. Press

The following newspapers were available in the Bayerische Staatsbibliothek, the Institut für Zeitgeschichte and the Stadtbibliothek (Monacensia), all in Munich; the Institute of Contemporary History, London, and the British Museum, London

Allgäuer Beobachter
Der Angriff
Augsburger Postzeitung
Bayerischer Kurier
Bayerische Staatszeitung
CV Zeitung
Der Donaubote
Fränkischer Kurier
Fränkische Tagespost
Fränkisches Volksblatt
Die Front
Garmisch-Partenkirchener Tagblatt
Günz- und Mindelbote
Kaufbeurer Neueste Nachrichten

Miesbacher Anzeiger
Münchener Katholische Kirchenzeitung
Münchner Merkur
Münchener Neueste Nachrichten
Münchner Post
Neue Nationalzeitung
Nördlinger Zeitung
Regensburger Anzeiger
Rosenheimer Tagblatt
Der Stürmer
The Times, London
Völkischer Beobachter
Vossische Zeitung
Würzburger General-Anzeiger

Index

Ebert, Friedrich (Reich President), 43, 154
Economic Party, 83, 86, 88, 136, 190, 249
Economics and Tax Review, 98
Ehrenfried, Bishop (of Würzburg), 164
Eichstätt, 72, 91, 156, 159 & n, 173
Eisele, Dr, 157
Eisner, Kurt, 6–7, 70, 241 n
Election Committee of Catholic Action (Bamberg), 266
elections, influence of regional differences on, 2–3; 1924 Bavarian State, 15–20, 21, 23, 111; conflict within Nazi movement over participation in, 22–3, 25, 26–8, 29–32, 78–9, 94; 1924 Nuremberg municipal, 32; 1925 Presidential, 43–4, 66–7, 75, 78; 1928 Bavarian State, 79, 80; and 1928 district council, 80, 84; 1929 Bavarian municipal, 85–91, 100, 142, 216–17; 1929 Thuringian State, 87, 91; 1920 Bavarian State, 112; 1930 district peasant council, 123; 1932 Bavarian State, 175, 196, 265, 273–6; effect of Depression on voting behaviour, 222–3; 1932 Presidential, 233, 235, 264, 265–70, 271; *see also* Reichstag Elections
Epp, Franz Ritter von, 69, 86, 110, 114, 220, 274, 308, 316 n; 1928 electoral campaign, 81–2; and 1930 electoral campaign, 138; appointed Reich Commissioner in Bavaria, 309; and Prime Minister, 310; upgraded to Reich Governor, 310; orders end to unauthorized actions of Nazis, 314–15
Erbacher, Dr, 156
Erbersdobler, Otto, 228, 293
Erlangen, 59, 114; Nazi students' movement in, 210 & n, 212, 213
Escherich, Georg, 7
Esser, Hermann, 62, 82, 86, 90, 147, 274; as leading member of GVG, 22, 25, 28 n, 29, 41, 45; N. German Nazi leaders' dislike of, 26, 48; expelled by national organization (NSFB), 30–1; his idolization of Hitler, 49; appointed Bavarian State Commissioner, 309, 310
Evangelical Church Council, 171

factory cells (Nazi) (NSBO), 199, 200, 203
Faulhaber, Cardinal, 19, 152, 153–5, 157, 163, 164, 166, 168, 304
Feder, Gottfried, 41, 246, 247 n, 303 n
federalism (regionalism; particularism), 65 & n, 67–9, 70, 72, 73, 82, 277–8, 305, 321, 323

Fehr, Dr Anton, 70, 120
Fiehler, Karl, 62, 85, 88, 313–14
Fighting Association against Department Stores and Cooperative Societies, 189, 199
Fighting Front, 123
Fighting Front Black–White–Red, 311
Fighting League, 10, 39 n
Fighting League for German Culture (NSDAP), 201 & n
finance (of NSDAP), 92, 99, 200; sources of, 59–62, 63, 92 n; 1968 directive on, 95, 96–7 & n; Reinhardt's directives to local leaders, 99; lack of funds for Hitler Youth, 206, 207; and for party press, 251–2; party crisis and, 288, 291, 292; financial resources in 1933 election, 303; *see also* membership; organization; propaganda
First World War, 1, 4, 6, 8, 11, 17 n, 23, 32 n, 34, 71, 74, 81 n, 86, 98, 147, 151, 169, 182, 184, 198, 202, 212, 248
Fischer, Hugo, 229–30
Fobke, Hermann, 26
Föhr, K., 151 n.
foreign travel, Nazi restrictions on party members, 202
France, 2, 218; occupation of Ruhr by, 9, 31
Franconia (Northern Bavaria), 19 n, 45, 49, 91; confessional structure of, 3, 323; craft industries in, 4; and agriculture, 5; separatism in, 13, 68; Streicher establishes Nazi party in, 23–4, 29; Nazi membership, 52, 186, 187, 205; strength of parties in, 64, 72–3, 83, 114–15, 116, 141; Nazi *Gau* and district organization in, 97, 100–3; and agricultural campaign, 122–3, 235; Protestants in, 171, 172; Jews in, 240–2; 1932 Reichstag Election results, 282, 283–4, 290; Stegmann Revolt, 291–3; 1933 election, 306; *see also* Lower, Middle, Upper Franconia
'Franconian amateur players', 201 n
Frank, Dr Hans, 45, 211, 310, 314, 315, 316 & n
Fränkische Tagespost, 243
Fränkischer Kurier, 243
Fränkisches Volksblatt, 65
Free Corps, 81 & n, 110
Free Peasants' Association, 71
Freethinkers' Association, 150
Freie Bürger (Free Citizens' party), 86
Freiheit, Die, 247–8

ciple, 319–20; *see also* finance; membership; propaganda
Öttingen, 117–18, 220–1

Pacelli, Cardinal, 169
Pan-German League, 8, 23
Papen, Franz von (Papen government), 288, 294; appointed Reich Chancellor (1932), 276–7, 285, 286; takes over direct control of Prussian state, 279, 295, 298; July 1932 Reichstag Elections, 279, 281; anti-Nazi propaganda of, 286–7; Nov. 1932 Reichstag Elections, 289, 290; downgraded to Vice-Chancellor (1933), 295, 300–1
Parsberg, 173, 174, 232
particularism *see* federalism
Passau, 121, 140 & n
Patriotic Alpine Club, 14
Peasants' League *see* Bavarian Peasants' and Middle Class League
peasantry *see* agriculture
Peasantry as the Life Source of the Nordic Race, The, (Darré), 124
peasants' councils, 117–18, 123
Pfaff, Dr A., 200
Pfaffenhofen, 47, 234
Pfeffer, Capt. Franz von, 54–5, 132, 203
Pichler, Dr von, 66
Pieper, Fritz, 148–9
Pius XI, Pope, 175
Pöhner, Ernst, 8, 17
political meetings, demonstrations, Bavarian government's ban on, 260, 277, 281; Nazi ban on, 316
press agents (Nazi), 246, 249–50; *see also* propaganda
press agency, *see NS Partei-Korrespondenz*
professional classes, 184 n, 190–1
propaganda and press (Nazi), 3, 12, 30, 50, 69, 197, 320, 321, 322; Bouhler's organization of local cells, 52–3; lack of wide appeal in mid-20s, 55–6; urban, 56–7, 71, 94; and rural, 57–9, 71, 73, 74, 94, 113, 114, 115, 117, 121, 124, 140, 172, 202–3, 204, 224–36, 282, 320; cost of, 59–60; speaking-ban on Hitler attacked, 73–4; electoral, 79, 80, 82, 84, 87, 88, 89–90, 91, 92, 134–8, 140, 264, 265, 266–7, 272, 274–5, 279–82, 289–90, 303–5; 1928–9 reorganization of, 95 & n, 96, 100, 103–8; training of Party speakers, 100–1, 121, 230; 'saturation' campaigns, 104; effect of uniform ban on, 131, 132;

religious, 149, 154–5, 157, 173–80; participation of school-teachers, 191–2; contribution of specialist organizations, 197, 199, 201–4; and youth, 204–5 *passim,* 281; economic Depression exploited by, 218–24; anti-semitic, 237–44; role of party press, 244–53; 1932 party crisis and, 286–7, 288; compared to KPD's, 319
Protection of the People and the State (Presidential decree, 1933), 300, 309
Protestants, 4, 5, 13, 18, 19 n, 24, 91, 97, 151 n, 173, 176, 182 n, 321; confessional structure of Bavaria, 3, 323; Hitler's attitude, 40; strength of political parties among, 72–3, 83; 1930 voting behaviour, 140; support for Nazis by, 170–1, 268–9, 275, 282, 283–4, 290; antagonism between Catholics and, 172; students, 210; peasants offended at Nazi talks with Centre Party, 287
Prussia, 3, 4, 7, 42, 44, 68, 126, 170 n, 192, 270, 272; 1932 State elections, 274, 285 n; abolition of state government, 279, 295, 296, 298, 299, 300 n; SA terrorism in, 303
Pulzer, P. G. J., 240 n
'Puss-in-Boots'(anti-Marxist propaganda), 221

Quadt zu Wykradt und Isny, Count Eugen von, 310

Race and Culture Department, 95 n, 200, 201
racialism, 19, 24, 101, 211, 213, 237; *see also* anti-semitism
Rauch, Hans, 19
Red Boy Pioneers, 204
Red Youth Front, 204
Regen, 115, 235
Regensburg, 57, 173, 268 n; SA wearing of uniforms in Cathedral, 157, 164–5
Regensburger Anzeiger, 65, 156, 168
Reger, Max, 112
regionalism *see* federalism
Registers of German Tradesmen, 189 n
Reich Commissioners, 295, 298, 299, 300, 307, 308, 309
Reichsbanner (SPD), 127, 128, 130
Reichstag Elections, May 1924: 18, 19 n, 109, 322; Dec. 1924: 28, 31–2, 36, 43, 64–5, 71, 73, 83, 112, 322; 1928: 45, 73, 78–84, 88, 90, 91, 92, 96–7, 108, 114,

116–17, 322; 1930: 104, 132, 133–45, 146, 155–7, 170, 197, 203, 245, 254, 275, 322; July 1932: 175, 177, 231 n, 236, 242, 264, 279–85, 322; Nov. 1932: 264, 285, 288–91, 292, 322; 1933: 296, 299, 300, 302–7, 322; *see also* elections

Reichstag Fire (1933), 300, 304

Reinhardt, Fritz, 98–100, 101, 113, 134–5, 198 n, 230

Reiter, Dr W., 200

'Religious Community of the Christian Spirit, 93

Renteln, Dr Adrian von, 208

reparations, war, 8, 9, 31, 84–5, 88

Revolution (1918: in Bavaria), 6–7, 17, 19, 70

Reventlow, Count, 26, 40, 176, 182

Rhine Palatinate, 97

Rhineland, 2, 3, 85, 226

Ribbentrop, Manfred von, 248

Riedenburg, 173

Riehl, Wilhelm, 124

Roehm, Ernst, 34, 39 n, 41, 54, 203, 272, 287, 300, 308, 309, 310, 315

Rosenberg, Alfred, 41, 147, 160–4, 172, 173–4, 176, 178, 201, 278

Rosenheim, 13, 45–6, 75, 115, 116, 199, 201, 206, 233, 271, 275

Rotfrontkämpferbund, 127 n

Röthenbach, 312

Rothenburg ob der Tauber, 141, 144, 171, 178, 219, 291

Röver, Carl, 228 n

Royal Party (*Königspartei*), 301

Ruckdeschel, Ludwig, 107

Ruhr, 9, 31 56, 196, 259 n

Rupprecht, Philipp ('Fips'), 237

Rupprecht, Crown Prince, 44, 66, 301

SA (*Sturmabteilung*), 74, 75, 89, 92, 103, 104–5, 106, 110, 113, 170, 181, 182, 188, 220, 255, 296, 297, 298, 322; Hitler's guidelines on role of, 39–40, 94; and 1926 statutes outlining functions, 54–5; crisis in Munich branch, 62–3; 1928 directive on, 95, 96; government ban on uniforms, 127, 131–2; insurance scheme, 127 n; increasing violence of, 128, 130; wearing of uniforms in Regensburg cathedral, 157, 164–5; Brüning government's ban on (1932), 189 n, 272–3; civil service members, 194; motoring branch, 199; semi-autonomous role, 203; youth membership, 206 n; benefits for unemployed

members, 217 n; anti-semitism among, 238; electioneering methods, 267, 281, 303; plans to seize power exposed, 270–2; von Papen revokes ban on, 276, 277, 323; dissatisfied with 'policy of legality', 285–8, 291; Stegmann Revolt, 291–3; Roehm meeting in Berlin, 300; Munich take-over, 308–10; and seizure of power in Bavaria, 310–13; arbitrary arrests made by, 314–15

Sauerteig, Max, 171

Save Church and Christianity, 175

Saxony, 16 n, 42, 44, 46, 52, 62, 77, 88, 92, 134, 208, 216 n, 307

Schachleiter, Abbot Albanus, 162, 169, 170

Schacht, Dr Hjalmar, 31

Schaffendes Volk (Creative People), 249

Schäffer, Fritz, 266, 277 & n, 298, 299–300, 301, 307, 309

Scharnagl, Dr Karl, 19, 271, 311

Scharnhorst League, 204

Schätzel, Dr, 277 n

Schellingstrasse, Nazi HQ (Munich), 46, 48, 49, 59, 253 n; *see also* Brown House

Schemm, Hans, 101–2, 106–8, 128–9, 149–50, 171, 172, 177, 179, 191, 211, 228, 239, 310, 316 n

Schiller, Friedrich, 89

Schlageter, Leo, 259 & n

Schleicher, General von, 295, 297

Schlittenbauer (BVP deputy), 120 n

Schmelzle, Dr Hans, 120

Schney incident (1929), 128–30

Schönerer, Georg, 153

schoolchildren *see* NS Schoolchildren's League

school-teachers (Nazi), 107, 191–2

Schraut, Rudolf, 200 & n

Schreiber, Bishop, 156

Schwabing NSDAP branch (Munich), 47 & n, 62, 85

Schwarz, Franz Xaver, 25, 48, 62, 96, 97 n

Schwarz, Wilhelm, 190–1

Schwede, Franz, 85–6, 261, 262

Schwend, Karl, 21

Schweyer, Hans, 21, 22

Second World War, 5, 218

Seidenschwang (SA leader), 62

Seipel, Dr Ignaz, 34

Seitz, Andreas, 235

Selb, 29, 90, 115

74 75 76 77 10 9 8 7 6 5 4 3 2 1